P9-DGS-144

OUTSIDERS AND OPENNESS

in the Presidential Nominating System

PITT SERIES IN POLICY
AND INSTITUTIONAL STUDIES

Bert A. Rockman, *Editor*

OUTSIDERS AND OPENNESS

in the Presidential Nominating System

ANDREW E. BUSCH

UNIVERSITY OF PITTSBURGH PRESS

Published by the University of Pittsburgh Press,
Pittsburgh, Pa. 15261

10 9 8 7 6 5 4 3 2 1

Library of Congress Cataloging-in-Publication Data

Busch, Andrew.
    Outsiders and openness in the presidential nominating
system / Andrew E. Busch.
        p.   cm.—(Pitt series in policy and institutional studies)
    Includes bibliographical references (p.   ) and index.
        ISBN 0-8229-3976-2 (cloth : acid-free paper). — ISBN
0-8229-5627-6 (pbk. : acid-free paper)
            1. Presidents—United States—Nomination—History.
    2. Presidents—United States—Nomination.   3. United
    States—Politics and government—1945–1989–   4. United
    States—Politics and government—1989–   I. Title. II. Series
    JK521.B87   1997
    324.6'3'0973—dc21   96-45916

A CIP catalog record for this book is available from the
British Library.

Portions of chapter 3 appeared as "In Defense of the 'Mixed'
System: The Goldwater Campaign and the Role of Popular
Movements in the Pre-Reform Nominating Process," *Polity*
(Summer 1992): 527–49.

CONTENTS

	Acknowledgments	vii
1	Openness, Stability, and the Presidential Nominating System	1
2	Movements in the Pure Convention System	28
3	The Conservative Movement and the Mixed System	33
4	The Triumph of the "New Politics"	81
5	Post-1972 Movements	108
6	The Rise of the Unconnected Outsiders	129
7	Outsiderism in the 1990s	152
8	Conclusion	168
	Notes	189
	Bibliography	223
	Index	243

Dedicated to my Mother and Father

ACKNOWLEDGMENTS

I would like to thank above all my adviser and friend James Ceaser, without whose input and direction this work would have been impossible. I would also like to thank Steven Finkel, Martha Derthick, and Norman Graebner, whose comments and suggestions were extremely valuable. I am indebted to Leon Epstein and several anonymous reviewers whose recommendations contributed to later stages of the manuscript. Finally, I would like to acknowledge the research assistance of James Meyer at the University of Denver and Jose Ceballos in the Office of the Secretary, Democratic National Committee.

I

Openness, Stability, and the Presidential Nominating System

W HEN THE DEMOCRATIC NATIONAL convention exploded in chaos in Chicago in August of 1968, the American political system was set on the road to what Byron Shafer called "the greatest systematic change in presidential nominating procedures in all of American history."[1] The post-1968 reforms were the most recent manifestation of an ongoing institutional conflict reaching back to the founding of the republic. Beginning with the Constitutional Convention, a central question in presidential selection has been how to manage the tension between the value of openness and that of stability.

By "openness" is meant a systemic capacity to accommodate, or even encourage, fundamental political change by allowing a role for popular forces, especially forces outside the dominant party structure. By "stability" is meant a systemic capacity to resist demagogues and frequent or extreme political swings. The two cardinal values are largely zero-sum in nature—in one sense, there are really only degrees of openness. The values, however, are more complex than is usually understood, which makes it possible not only to balance them by achieving a moderate level of openness but to actually blend them. Participants in the debate often see them as distinct, and almost always try to stake a claim to both. In practice, the effort to promote openness has meant increasing the scope of public participation and reducing influence by political "insiders." The effort to promote stability has included some form of "peer review" and the erection of institutional barriers designed to promote deliberation and impede movements or candidates considered "dangerous."[2]

If openness and stability have been at the center of the debate over presidential nomination, in practice the conflict between those values has played itself out most dramatically in numerous instances of attempted penetration of the parties by outside forces, especially forces promoting fundamental political change. Throughout American history, such forces have tested the capacity of the system to accommodate outside-driven change and to regulate and moderate that change. The ongoing importance of this question was demonstrated in 1992 and 1996, when the phenomenon of outsiderism reached a new zenith.

For our purposes, an "outsider" candidate can be defined as one who: (1) is outside the corridors of power, in the sense either of holding no office or of residing outside the "mainstream" or majority of his party, explicitly rejecting the party's leadership and dominant element; (2) serves as the spokesman or representative of a broader group (a political movement) outside the corridors of power; and/or (3) serves as the spokesman or representative of ideas, ideologies, or themes that challenge the dominant element in the party. In cases of third-party outsiders, these concepts can easily be transferred from a party framework to a framework of national politics. Thus, outsiders may define themselves ideologically, or by simple status, in the thematic "appeal of being 'not part of,' and thus not tainted by, the inside, the establishment, or the way things are done."[3] In either case, change in some form is a central promise of the outsider.

Altogether, political parties have been one of the key conduits for change in society, and presidential nominations have been a key conduit for and regulator of change within the parties. Ultimately, then, this study has to do with the capacity for change in America itself. Since the accommodation of forces seeking fundamental change is the essence of openness within the nominating system, the best way to test that openness is to study examples of these outsiders acting in a variety of institutional settings.

The Constitutional Convention

Attempts to find the proper balance between openness and stability in the presidential selection system were evident in the debates at the Constitutional

Convention. Some delegates, like James Wilson and Gouverneur Morris, endorsed the notion of direct popular election of the executive, arguing that "appointments made by numerous bodies are always worse than those made by single responsible individuals, or by the people themselves."[4] Others, like Charles Pinckney and George Mason, held that popular election would benefit demagogues and that "it would be as unnatural to refer the choice of a proper character for chief magistrate to the people, as it would, to refer a trial of colours to a blind man."[5] They generally preferred election by the national legislature.

The compromise of the electoral college sought to satisfy the concerns of both sides. Since the election was indirect, fears of demagoguery were softened; yet the selection was also taken out of the hands of Congress (except in unusual circumstances), so the people could play a greater role and the dilemma of the separation of powers was minimized. The electoral college was designed to operate in a nonpartisan environment, and the Framers assumed that nomination and election would be exercised simultaneously, by the electors.

When the convention's debate drew to a close, most of the elements of our current discourse were already identifiable. The theme of openness had been represented by the calls for popular election, accentuated by fears of cabal and corruption in the relatively narrow and secretive confines of the legislature and by desires to render the executive independent of that legislature. The theme of stability could be seen in the fear of demagogues and organized special interests and in the importance given to peer review by those who supported legislative selection. Promotion of candidates of high quality was claimed by both sides. While the presidency was not conceived by the Founders as an explicit instrument for popularly driven change, presidential reeligibility and frequent elections provided a mechanism for change.[6]

Soon after the adoption of the Constitution, the nature of the electoral system changed tremendously, due to the extraconstitutional development of political parties, which rendered impractical the simultaneous nomination and election of the president in the electoral college. For the most part, the issues of popular participation and the management of change were transferred to the nomination of presidential candidates by the political parties and the entry of new parties. Since the rise of the parties, the presidential nomination has been "one of the most decisive choices in the nation's politics."[7] Virtually every question faced by the Constitutional Convention in devising an election system would be faced in the nominating process.

The Congressional Caucus

Party structures first developed within Congress, so it is not surprising that the first system of party nomination was the congressional caucus, in which legislative members of each party met to endorse a candidate. This practice was mirrored in similar procedures at the state legislative level for state offices. By 1800, both parties in Congress and both parties in most states (Federalists and Republicans) made their executive nominations by means of the legislative caucus.[8]

However, by the election of 1824, the Federalist Party had vanished; thus, the Republican caucus nomination was equivalent to election. An arrangement that had worked reasonably well to impose party discipline within the context of a two-party system failed when party competition was replaced by personalism.[9] The caucus in 1824 had to choose among five candidates (John Quincy Adams, John Calhoun, Henry Clay, William Crawford, and Andrew Jackson), and chose Crawford in a meeting that less than half the congressmen attended. The other candidates refused to accept the legitimacy of this procedure—calling it "King Caucus"—and each ran independently, splitting the vote enough to force the election into the House for the second (and thus far last) time in the nation's history. No party used the congressional caucus after 1824.

The system had drawn its strength from its claims of securing peer review and thus, presumably, good candidates and a check on popular passions. The principle of separation of powers was clearly violated, however, and the president was made dependent upon Congress, a problem magnified by the collapse of two-party competition.[10] Thus, a danger existed of undue influence by the legislative branch over the executive, and more generally of corruption or factional cabal in a small, closed group. Lack of grounding in the "great body of the people" also cost the system legitimacy; "the people discovered that they had no voice in the nomination, and thereafter the system was doomed."[11]

The Pure Convention System

After a brief experiment with nomination by state legislatures in 1828, the convention system was the next method of presidential nomination used in the United States. Some historians trace the roots of the convention system back to 1788–1792, when Pennsylvania held statewide assemblies for the purpose of nominating candidates for state office.[12] However, the national convention was not used by a major party—the Jacksonian Democrats—until 1832, months after the Anti-Masonic Party used it for the first time on a national scale.

The convention system was promoted on grounds of openness and democratization, and was made possible (and perhaps necessary) by the organizational growth of the party from the bottom up. The convention took the power of nomination out of the hands of a few legislators, who often did not represent all elements of the party, and put those nominations in the hands of grassroots party workers.[13] At the same time, there is evidence that Andrew Jackson favored the convention of 1832 largely because he believed it was necessary to enforce central party discipline and secure his choice for vice president (Martin Van Buren).[14] It was thus at once an answer to the "unrepresentativeness" and closed nature of the congressional caucus and a means to reestablish the stability and mediating influence of two-party competition.[15]

Over the next three decades, conventions, which originated simply as mass meetings, developed fully into representative assemblies.[16] The system was characterized by "party-activist control of nominations and platforms through the convention," and was built at least nominally on a foundation of local party meetings, or "primaries" (what we would today call "caucuses").[17] These primaries, combined with party committees and nominating conventions, constituted the three essential organs of the political party.[18] Technically, all party power flowed from the primaries.

In reality, the party committees played the pivotal role in the system, because they generally had the capacity to dominate the primaries. The local committee chairman was usually the chairman of the primary meeting, and the committee generally put forward a prearranged slate of candidates, who usually won. The parties were free to permit or restrict participation at their discretion. The committee sometimes excluded between three-quarters and four-fifths of party voters from the official party "lists." The committees' control of the lists enabled them "to have practically whatever primary they desire[d]."[19] If procedural control and control of the lists were not sufficient, force and fraud were often employed.[20]

Committees above the local level (e.g., county) had even greater power in the system, with the capacity to dismiss or refuse to recognize local committees and sometimes to directly appoint convention delegates. These higher committees held effective control over the nominating conventions. Thus, through control of the primaries and the convention, a party organization could ensure its own maintenance and dominate candidate selection. Control was aided by the adept use of patronage.[21] This process led ultimately to the national nominating convention, where state and local organization leaders dominated their delegations and undertook a combination of deliberation and bargaining, with the emphasis heavily on bargaining.

Factions had the power to maintain themselves once they achieved dominance, but they still had to achieve that dominance at some earlier point under less favorable conditions. Furthermore, rural areas were less easily controlled than urban areas, primarily because neighbors knew one another and the "lists" were not deemed necessary. Party leaders were often sensitive to trends in public opinion, and convention bargaining clearly accommodated the "pluralist" tradition.[22]

Nevertheless, the system revolved around the party committees in reality and the primaries only in name. Just as the average party voter had little influence over the selection of delegates, so too could candidates themselves generally exert only minimal influence over the delegate selection process. The party organization truly sat in the middle, an intermediary between candidate and voter.

Criticism of the convention system grew enormously in the last third of the nineteenth century, focusing on accusations that the local and state meetings were "undemocratic exercises in the unrestrained use of power."[23] This criticism was intertwined with general accusations of party corruption and unresponsiveness. As a result, between 1890 and 1920 most states adopted legal codes regulating the state parties' internal affairs.[24] These externally imposed reforms came in three waves.

First, states began minimal (and often optional) regulation of local primaries.[25] Second, with the government takeover of ballots and elections as a result of the adoption of the Australian ballot in the 1890s came a much stronger effort to regulate the parties' nomination procedures.[26] These remedies, like the features they were meant to counteract, were unevenly spread. The South, in particular, tended to leave the most power in the hands of the party organizations.[27] These regulations were often unenforced, but, as a scholar noted in 1897, "the honest enforcement of such laws has accomplished much."[28]

The third wave overlapped with the second, and constituted the drive for the direct primary, a device reformers hoped would entirely remove the power of nomination from the party organization. By 1899, two-thirds of the states had laws making the direct primary optional, and by 1900 some states began making it mandatory for state or local offices. In 1904, Florida held the first direct primary for the selection of delegates to a national convention. In 1910,

Oregon became the first state to pass a law for national convention delegate selection that included a presidential preference vote.

This drive toward primaries was a fundamental part of the progressive movement's efforts to "democratize" the nominating system, end the rule of the bosses, and energize the electorate. While some progressives, like Robert La Follette, thought the direct primary would ultimately strengthen parties by purifying them, others, like George Norris, thought it would hurt the parties, but approved of it for precisely that reason.[29] Woodrow Wilson thought it would open the route to decisive presidential leadership, introducing a systemic bias for change by removing the intermediary role of the party structure.[30]

By 1912, the direct primary bandwagon was clearly in the ascendant, having largely triumphed at the state and local level and in fourteen states at the presidential level. In 1912, the Progressive ("Bull Moose") Party endorsed a nationwide presidential primary, a proposal supported unsuccessfully by President Woodrow Wilson in 1913. The direct primary drive reached its peak in 1916, when twenty-three states choosing 65 percent of the delegates held direct primaries. By 1920, the figure had fallen to twenty-one states choosing 55 percent of the delegates, and in 1924 the extent of primaries fell to approximately one-third of the states and one-third to two-fifths of the delegates, a level at which it remained for forty-four years.[31]

The pure convention system, created as a result of popular pressures for greater openness and participation, was thus destroyed by the same impulse. The mechanisms that had once been seen as an avenue of greater openness—control of presidential nominations by local parties—were ultimately seen as unacceptable barriers.

The Mixed System

The "mixed" system stabilized by 1924, when it became clear that no purely primary-based "outside" strategy could succeed.[32] That system was not the result of design but of an equilibrium reached between the old system and the unsuccessful drive for a complete transformation. Most states continued to choose delegates without a primary, usually by state or local (usually congressional district) conventions, but sometimes by closed conventions or even appointment by a party central committee—the means used in the pure convention system prior to the advent of primaries. Furthermore, the plebiscitary impact of the primaries was diluted. Most primary laws permitted delegate discretion at the convention; many other primaries were mere preference surveys entirely divorced from actual delegate selection, which remained in the hands of the party.

Party organizations in primary states also circumvented the intent of the primary through "favorite son" candidacies, usually incumbent governors where possible. Write-in candidacies were an important part of the system and occurred with great frequency through 1968. Candidates were able to pick which primaries to enter depending on their strategic needs. Thus, only a few of the approximately sixteen primaries—those that were contested by all or most of the viable candidates—actually carried major strategic significance. As a result of the predominance of caucus/convention procedures, the generally unbound nature of primary delegates, and the lack of guaranteed head-on competition, candidates were not always sure of translating primary success into nomination.[33] Altogether, "despite the widespread use of primaries, party leaders retained control of presidential nominations."[34] It should be noted that the presidential nominating process was thus something of an anomaly in mid-twentieth-century America, since most lower-level nominations were already decided by direct primary.

This is not to say that the presidential primaries were unimportant. They were directly or indirectly tied to at least one-third of the convention's delegates. While it soon became clear that a campaign based entirely on an "outside" primary strategy was not feasible, candidates could also seldom avoid primaries entirely. It was unwise to concede such a large bloc of potential delegates, and the party professionals who exerted influence over the vast majority of delegates came to expect entrance—and success—in at least a few primaries as a demonstration of broader appeal and vote-getting ability. This expectation was shared in large measure by the party's rank and file, as a demonstration less of electability than of legitimacy. Starting in 1948, particular primaries such as New Hampshire and Wisconsin began to influence convention outcomes.[35]

Although the "mixed" system developed on an ad hoc basis as a response to divergent forces in American politics, its supporters have seen it as a successful modification and refinement of the old convention system. The mixed system, in this view, had the virtue of combining a high level of party leadership involvement and "peer review" with enough popular influence to guarantee broad candidate appeal and democratic legitimacy; it reduced the "corrupt" stranglehold of the bosses while avoiding the instability and potential extremism of a fully plebiscitary system; it upheld the principle of strong parties and maintained the discretion and flexibility of the convention, without making the nomination completely dependent on the "smoke-filled room."[36] The system continued to promote moderation by imposing rigorous party hurdles for access by outside forces, but "permitted it when powerful and persistent forces in the nation called for new and different approaches."[37] In sum, public opinion could "exert substantial influence, without being given full control over decisions that can best be made by the parties in their corporate capacities."[38]

The Reforms

The identification of legitimacy with victory in the primaries was so advanced by the twilight of the "mixed" system that Hubert H. Humphrey's nomination by the Democratic Party in 1968 was seriously called into question when he conducted an "insider" strategy that deliberately avoided all contested primaries. Amid the convulsions racking the nation, insurgent campaigns were run by Eugene McCarthy and Robert Kennedy, allied with the anti–Vietnam War movement. Party regulars, however, remained loyal to President Lyndon Johnson and his heir Humphrey, and they used their predominant influence in the mixed system to secure Humphrey's nomination. This outcome led to charges by critics that the mixed system was an oligarchic system, not significantly different from its pure convention predecessor. "Reform" Democrats began an assault on the nominating process.

Before the Democratic national convention in Chicago, an ad hoc commission chaired by Iowa governor Harold Hughes released a report assailing the nomination process. The commission was "ostensibly neutral," but had in fact been organized by the McCarthy campaign as a response to perceived unfairness in the Connecticut delegate selection process.[39] The commission's report claimed that important elements of the nominating system lacked "fidelity to basic democratic principles."[40]

Two weeks later, the convention voted to ban the unit rule, establish a commission to study the nominating process, and require that future delegate selection be opened to public participation and held within the calendar year of the convention. Few delegates seemed to understand the implications of any of these issues, except perhaps the unit rule.[41] Shortly after the 1968 election, two commissions were established by the Democratic National Committee to fulfill the "mandate" of the convention. The decisive organization was the Commission on Delegate Selection and Party Structure, or McGovern-Fraser Commission (after its two chairmen, Senator George McGovern of South Dakota and Congressman Donald Fraser of Minnesota). Both commissions were named by the newly appointed DNC chairman, liberal senator Fred Harris, who "planned to install the growing 'reform wing' of the party within these commissions."[42] Although many commission members had supported Humphrey in 1968, the membership as a whole was characterized by "a consistent if unfocused sympathy for reform in the abstract, along with a willingness to be instructed in what the details of that abstract concept implied."[43] In any event, the dominant influence was exerted by the proreform leadership, staff, and ten-member executive committee.[44]

The McGovern Commission held seventeen regional hearings, where it heard numerous complaints of heavy-handed state party control and "unfair" procedures.[45] By the summer of 1969, "participation" had become "the crucial standard for party democracy."[46] The report issued in April 1970 maintained that unfair procedures were reducing the access of party members, limiting their influence, or both. Problems included "procedural irregularities," such as use of the unit rule, proxy voting that facilitated control by party leaders, closed methods of delegate slate making, and irregular and arbitrary selection of alternates; intentional or unintentional discrimination against blacks, women, and young people; and structural irregularities such as "untimely" (early) delegate selection, use of ex officio delegates, committee appointment of delegates, apportionment rules within states that underrepresented urban areas, and insufficient representation of "minority views" and dissent.[47]

One-third of delegates had been chosen prior to McCarthy's announcement in November 1967. A Missouri precinct leader allegedly overwhelmed McCarthy caucus voters with 492 proxies. The unit rule, plurality elections, and delegate selection procedures in which delegates ran independently of candidate preference led to delegate totals largely disconnected from popular vote totals.[48] In short, according to the reformers, the old system was still too reliant on the party leadership and still insufficiently permeable by popular forces. In the words of William Crotty, the system used in 1968 had been "arcane . . . indefensible . . . an unpleasant mix of unresponsive, outdated, and arbitrary practices . . . biased and repressive."[49]

In response, the commission outlawed or severely restricted these practices in order to increase party "openness." The commission report, *Mandate for Reform*, proclaimed:

> Since its inception, our Party has been an open party—open to new ideas and new people. . . .
> We believe that popular participation is more than a proud heritage

of our party, more even than a first principle. We believe that popular control of the Democratic Party is necessary for its survival.

If we are not an open party; if we do not represent the demands of change, then the danger is not that people will go to the Republican Party; it is that there will no longer be a way for people committed to orderly change to fulfill their needs and desires within our traditional political system. It is that they will turn to third and fourth party politics or the anti-politics of the street.[50]

The commission's eighteen guidelines had the effect of banning two of the five long-standing methods of delegate selection—delegate primaries, in which delegates ran unattached to any candidate, and party caucuses, where party leaders alone met to choose delegates. They limited a third method, appointment by party committees, to no more than 10 percent of a state's delegation. The only forms of delegate selection remaining were the candidate preference primary and the open caucus. These rules thus eliminated methods that had been used to choose 60 percent of the delegates to the 1968 Democratic convention.[51]

Additionally, the commission came within one vote of requiring proportional representation. Instead, the commission required that at least 75 percent of delegates from caucus/convention states be selected from units no larger than congressional districts; it urged primary states to adopt proportional representation in 1972 and urged the 1972 convention to require it thereafter.[52]

The guidelines also required publicized meetings and rules, and prohibited proxy voting, ex officio delegates, and selection processes prior to the calendar year of the convention. Finally, they established complex delegate slate-making procedures ensuring that the regular party held no advantage. Primaries would become more plebiscitary, establishing a direct connection between votes and delegates, while caucuses would resemble primaries much more closely.[53] In short, "the official party had been *erased* from what was still nominally the party's nomination process."[54] The mixed system was dead, killed by claims that it was not open enough to popular movements and that the reforms would better provide that openness.

Once the precedent was established, centralized rule making became a quadrennial rite for the Democratic Party. In 1974, the New Delegate Selection Commission (or Mikulski Commission, after chair Barbara Mikulski) mandated proportional representation in the caucus states for all candidates receiving over 10 percent of the vote (the DNC later increased the threshold to 15 percent). For the first time, caucus participants would have to declare a presidential preference. The candidate emphasis was accentuated by a revision of the slate-making rules that gave to the candidates the slate-making power that had been removed from the party organizations in 1972.

In primary states, winner-take-all systems were banned, and preference was given to proportional representation at either the statewide or congressional district levels, though so-called loophole plurality primaries were allowed, in which at least 75 percent of the delegates were chosen at the congressional district level or lower. The Mikulski Commission also banned open primaries, thus implementing another suggestion of the McGovern-Fraser Commission. The commission moved away from a few of the original reforms, but the overall effect of the Mikulski Commission was a consolidation and extension of those reforms.[55]

The reforms coincided with a sharp increase in the number of primaries. From sixteen Republican and seventeen Democratic primaries in 1968 choosing approximately one-third of the delegates, the total jumped to twenty-two Republican and twenty-three Democratic primaries choosing over one-half of the delegates four years later. By 1980, three-fifths to two-thirds of the states held primaries, and both parties chose over 70 percent of their convention delegates in this manner. While many reformers hold that they did not intend to promote primaries at the expense of caucus/convention systems,[56] and some even argue that the increase in primaries occurred independently of the reforms,[57] there are many reasons to believe that the reforms were instrumental in driving this trend.

First, the reforms made dominant a plebiscitary ethos that could best be satisfied by a primary election. In the words of Donald Fraser, "the rhetoric of many reformers at first identified the presidential primary as a means of assuring greater participation without the arbitrary constraints imposed by state party leaders."[58] Second, numerous state leaders feared the complexity of the new caucus rules, and believed that a switch to primaries would reduce the specter of a credentials challenge.[59] As McGovern himself said: "This quantum leap in primary contests was part of a reform tide that has swept the Democratic Party since 1968. In part it was a response to our commission guidelines. By adopting primary systems, state parties could most easily comply with the guidelines without having to revamp their internal organization."[60]

Third, the uncertainties introduced by the new rules made it appear prudent to many party leaders to separate state party business from the presidential nominating process, which could best be accomplished by holding a presidential primary.[61] In a related vein, some believed that the reformed caucuses were more liable to takeover by ideological forces than were primaries.[62] In any case, a vast expansion in the number of primaries became part of the reform system. This trend was consistent with the earlier reform impulse of the progressives.

Finally, in the wake of revelations regarding questionable fund-raising practices in the 1972 presidential election, Congress enacted the 1974 Federal Election Campaign Act Amendments. No candidate for federal office could receive individual contributions in excess of one thousand dollars, or contributions from any party or independent committee in excess of five thousand dollars, per election. In an attempt to curtail the importance of "big money" and to encourage grassroots participation, Congress permitted candidates for presidential nomination to receive federal matching funds for every individual contribution of two hundred and fifty dollars or less once they raised at least five thousand dollars that way in each of twenty states. At the same time, both national and state-by-state spending limits applied to any candidate receiving federal funds.

The Reform System

In the words of Edward Banfield, "The 'reforms' of the late 1960s and early 1970s were the culmination of more than a century of efforts to bring party politics into correspondence with the democratic ideal."[63] The reform system that resulted exuded an ethos, or general set of characteristics, as well as specific elements corresponding to those characteristics.

The "ethos" had three parts, most of which can be traced back to the progressives:[64] first, an emphasis on participation, including hostility toward notions of representative decision making; second, hostility toward the party organization and a preference for a candidate-centered (or plebiscitary) system; and third, a predisposition in favor of change. The specific elements of the reform system were: first, the dominance of presidential primaries over caucus/convention processes; second, greater independence of caucus/convention procedures from the influence of the regular party and a divorcing of party business from presidential selection caucuses; third, a direct connection of primary votes to delegates, preferably through proportional representation; fourth, a lack of delegate discretion, enhanced by same-year selection; and fifth, federal campaign finance reform.

Additionally, the closed primary became a "reform" tenet, even though it would seem to operate in the opposite direction and even though the progressives had favored open primaries.[65] The systemic components of each of the three major nominating systems can be seen in table 1.1.

While it is possible to identify the prototype of the reform system, some elements have been more consistently applied than others since 1968, and there are differences between the parties. The influence of primaries grew from 1968 to 1976 and has remained basically steady thereafter with only marginal shifts, such as in 1984, when more than half the states held caucuses. This development has applied equally to both parties (see table 1.2).

Reforms removing party influence from the caucuses affected the Democratic Party especially, since they were a result of the McGovern-Fraser Commission and not subject to state law. The secondary effects of the reforms on caucuses have likewise been felt primarily by the Democrats, who have, for example, divorced party business from presidential caucuses to a much greater degree than the Republicans. The Republicans approved similar rule "suggestions" at their 1972 convention, but these have remained largely unenforced, and on balance GOP caucuses are significantly less reformed.[66] Republican rules still permit state parties to limit caucuses to party officials; Arizona and Montana, for example, limit participation in first-round caucuses to precinct committee members.[67]

Proportional representation (PR) has affected both parties, though the effect has been much greater on the Democratic side. For years, California

Table 1-1. Nomination System Components and Characteristics

	Convention	*Mixed*	*Reform*
Caucuses	all states unregulated	most states regulated	few states regulated
Primaries	no states	few states	most states
Open or Closed primaries	n/a	mixture	closed
Plurality or Proportional delegate allocation rules	plurality	plurality	proportional
Plebiscitary ethos	nonexistent	moderate	high
Finance regulation	none	low level	high level

was the only Republican winner-take-all state, but others have now rejoined it, and Republicans still use plurality rules at lower levels more often than do the Democrats. In caucus states, the Democrats alone have been affected by centrally imposed PR; although some GOP caucuses have become increasingly proportional in actual operation, most still operate on a plurality basis.[68] Similarly, the Republican bias in favor of winners is reinforced by a rule, absent in the Democratic Party, that candidates cannot be placed into nomination at the national convention unless they have won a majority of delegates in five or more states.

Furthermore, the application of proportional representation has differed within the Democratic Party from year to year; thresholds have been raised and lowered, bonus delegates and loophole primaries allowed and disallowed. The Democrats hewed closely to proportional representation in 1976 and 1980, shifted away from it in 1984 and 1988 when they permitted loophole primaries and bonus primaries (in which winners of each congressional district receive the first delegate and the rest are distributed proportionally), and reimposed strict proportional representation in 1992.

Lack of delegate discretion has generally been evident in both parties to an increasing degree since 1972, to the extent that there has been no outcome left in doubt prior to the convention since the Republican nomination campaign of 1976. If the Republicans have maintained marginally greater discretion, it has been in caucus states.[69] The introduction of "superdelegates" rep-

Table 1-2. Primaries 1968–1996

	Democratic Primaries (N)	Delegates (%)	Republican Primaries (N)	Delegates (%)
1968	17	38	16	34
1972	23	61	22	53
1976	29	73	28	68
1980	31	71	34	76
1984	25	54	30[a]	66
1988	39	67	39	77
1992	39	79	38	80
1996	34	63	43	85

Sources: For 1968–1992, adapted from Stephen J. Wayne, The Road to the White House 1996 (New York: St. Martin's Press, 1996), p. 11; for 1996, adapted from Rhodes Cook, "GOP's Rules Favor Dole If He Doesn't Stumble," CQ Weekly Report, January 27, 1996, pp. 230–31; and "1996 Democratic National Convention—First Step and Delegate/Alternate Allocation Information," Democratic National Committee Office of Party Affairs and Delegate Selection.
[a]Five of these Republican primaries in 1984 were later canceled.

resenting 15–20 percent of Democratic convention delegates since 1984 has been a deliberate reassertion of party influence, and as such has been a clear step away from the reform model. The superdelegates have restored a substantial percentage of Democratic leaders and officeholders to delegate status after the low point of 1972–1980, with the result that the gap between the parties has narrowed considerably. Democratic attempts to restrict open primaries were generally unsuccessful, and were abandoned after 1984.

Thus, while there is substantial truth to Nelson Polsby's observation that "in many respects, the Republican Party remains unreformed,"[70] it is also true that in many important respects—like the balance of primaries and caucuses, the degree of delegate discretion, finance law, and to a lesser extent proportional representation in primaries—the party has been carried along, albeit largely against its wishes, into the reform system.[71] This consistency has been much less pronounced regarding rules such as national committee membership, delegate apportionment, and race and sex quotas, in which the Republicans have largely refused to emulate their partisan rivals. Nevertheless, state legislative control of election law—and Democratic control of most state legislatures—has produced considerable interparty consistency on the essence of the nominating system, and on Democratic terms.

Scholarly analysis of the new nominating system has broken down largely along lines of openness and stability; "Where defenders of the convention and mixed systems have spoken of imposing restraints on new movements, proponents of direct democracy have spoken of stimulating them."[72] To Polsby, "there is a necessary tradeoff between the satisfaction of urgent needs for the representation of current feelings and the maintenance of the stability of the party organization,"[73] but the tradeoff has gone too far against stability. This dominant criticism of the reforms takes several forms.

First, it is argued that the removal of the party organization from the process has severely damaged the ability of parties to serve as moderating intermediary institutions. The barriers to popular passions have been torn down, and extremism encouraged. Peer review has been drastically curtailed, negatively affecting not only the ability of the organization to restrict demagogues but the parties' ability to choose qualified candidates. Dominance of primaries, and thus of factional rather than consensual campaigns, combines with lack of peer review to ultimately harm the cause of effective government as well. Deliberation has been removed from the convention and from most processes leading to the convention.

Additionally, the media became a key actor, rather than simply an observer, in the process, and the increase of "participation" has been illusory:

primary participants are unrepresentative of party voters; participation in primaries is not qualitatively equivalent to participation in caucuses; invalid outcomes result because no second choices can be expressed in primaries; and the later primaries are often held after the nomination has already been secured by one of the candidates.[74] In short, the reforms did produce greater openness, though not as much as their supporters have claimed, and at the cost of stability and of presidential and government quality.

Defenders of the reforms argue that they have indeed made the system more open. McGovern held that his nomination was "all the more precious in that it is the gift of the most open political process in our national history."[75] To Crotty, the 1972 reforms produced openness both in the sense of procedural fairness to outsiders and in the sense of promoting a substantive and fundamental change through issue choices:

> Reform opened the presidential nominating process and involved more groups in party decision-making. It gave the primary voter and caucus participant a direct and decisive voice in presidential nominations. Power has been transferred from a select group of party and interest group leaders gathered in convention to a more representative cross-section of the party's grassroots membership. It has allowed for meaningful choices among candidate issue positions.[76]

Furthermore, reformers have denied the accusations of their opponents that primaries are not representative (they say that caucuses are even less so), that the reforms removed the party from the system (they maintain that the number of party officials at the Democratic national convention increased substantially after 1972), and that the lack of peer review is dangerous (they point out that peer review produced Franklin Pierce and Warren Harding).[77] In short, defenders of the reforms agree with many critics that the reforms produced the openness that had been promised. They hold, however, that this is good.

There is a third school of thought on the reforms. Some scholars believe that the reforms were simply not very important in producing the current system. In this view, historical trends, most notably party decline and modern communications technology, not only preceded but actually produced the reforms, and many of the consequences associated with them.[78] This judgment is largely analytical, and entails no defense of either of the central values of openness or stability. It is clearly true that the reforms were not the sole cause of the change in the nature of the nominating system; party decline was already far advanced. It is important to keep that decline in mind as an explanatory variable. Outsiders do not act in a vacuum; their success is dependent not only on their own strength and their ability to operate within existing rules, but also on the strength of the party they seek to overthrow.

Nevertheless, the vast growth of primaries after half a century of stability was surely triggered by something, and the reforms make more sense than any other explanation. This growth in primaries clearly drove other factors, such as campaign length and cost, and media influence. The candidate-centered nature of the race and delegate binding had grown prior to 1968 but was accelerated by party rules regarding slate making and proportional representation in caucuses. It seems indisputable that the regular party had less influence, for better or worse, after the reforms than before, with many fewer delegates chosen by caucus, and many mechanisms for even caucus control stripped from the regulars. The party decline school provides an important reminder that rules cannot be fully separated from broader social trends, but the thesis is almost certainly overdrawn.

Openness and Outsiders: The Key Questions

This outline of the ongoing debate over openness in presidential nominations raises three broad sets of questions, which will serve as the focus of this study.

First, taken as a whole, how has each of the three historical systems—convention, mixed, and reform—managed the tension between openness and stability?

Second, what effects on openness and stability do individual components of presidential nominating systems have? Each system can be viewed as a set of different components. These components include: the method of delegate selection, such as state and local caucuses and conventions or primaries; types of primaries, such as open or closed and proportional or plurality; the existence or lack of a plebiscitary ethos and several specific candidate-centered mechanisms affecting delegate discretion; and the existence or lack of provisions regulating campaign finance. It is important to be able to examine these components individually. For instance, the reform system has seen constant adjustment and considerable interparty variation. As a result, it makes sense to think of the reform system as consisting of certain reform components that can be combined in the abstract even if they have all seldom coexisted in practice. Thus, I shall rely both on empirical observation and on logical extrapolation from the properties of each component. A consideration of possible future systems is also made easier if past systems can be disaggregated in this manner.

Third and finally, what can be learned about the nature of openness and stability in presidential nominating systems? For instance, is party "openness" an undifferentiated property, or does it contain numerous and potentially conflicting dimensions? It is also important to ask, "Openness to what?" How do different systems or combinations of components open the parties to different types of forces? Perhaps we can determine to what degree and in what manner openness and stability can be not merely balanced but blended. This last set of questions is the most abstract and ambitious, and the most important for the consideration of future systems.

The only way to answer these questions and to understand what this debate means in practice is to study situations in which the parties were put to the test by popular forces seeking entry. How did the nominating system respond? How permeable was it, and in what ways did that permeability show itself? How was stability enforced? In short, what happened to the outsiders?

Political Movements and the Presidential Nominating System

It seems natural to begin a discussion of outsiders by thinking of political movements. Throughout American history, political movements have arisen with the goal of shaping society through political action. Political parties have been a natural target of movements, which often seek either to infiltrate or capture existing parties or to form their own parties.

Since presidential nominations are so crucial in defining the character of parties, those nominations have been key conduits for movement influence on parties: "All reformers have accorded a prominent place to the presidential selection process, viewing it as one of the best points of entrée in the system for new initiatives."[79] It stands to reason that the institutional evolution of the parties generally and of the presidential nominating process specifically has affected the ways in which movements operate—and the degree to which they succeed.

Furthermore, one of the most salient features of movements is that they are mobilized almost exclusively on behalf of a program of change, and the systemic capacity for change has long been a key element of the concept of "openness" as defined by its advocates. Many progressives supported the direct primary not only because it would provide citizen participation but also because it would free the candidate from the grip of the "bosses" and provide greater opportunities for bold policy initiatives.[80] Likewise, the reformers of 1972 hoped that their reforms would produce a bias for change: "Most [reformers] wanted to change national policy and all wanted to change the national leadership. . . . Reform of the party's nominating process became the vehicle through which the eventual policy and leadership changes the reformers held to be important could be realized."[81]

Finally, movements have consistently engaged in two-way interaction with the nominating system. Not only have they been affected by the system, they have themselves been crucial in both of the major transformations of the nominating system this century. The progressives created the first primaries and with them the mixed system, and Eugene McCarthy's movement campaign was the catalyst for the post-1968 reforms. As a result, movement efforts should serve as excellent tests for the openness of a given nominating system. The ability of political movements to operate (and, if sufficiently strong, to succeed) within a nominating system can be taken as a sign of openness.

Sociological literature characteristically defines a movement as "a conscious, collective organized attempt to bring about or resist change in the social order by noninstitutionalized means."[82] Thus, the concept of change is central to the definition of movements; movements are often simultaneously the agents and the products of change, threatening the existence of old cleavages in society by raising new issues (or old issues in a new way).[83] A movement is thus built around a fairly coherent view of the world—an ideology—which consists of values, ideas, beliefs, moral standards, and perceptions of interest.[84]

Furthermore, organization is an important component of movements. Movements are "organized" in the sense that they undertake deliberate cooperative efforts, and in the sense that one or more organizations are often constituent parts of the movement, but they are not synonymous with any particular single organization.[85] Indeed, movements "are often characterized by a host of competing-cooperating organizations."[86] In combination, "the scope of the movement's support is, actually or potentially, large," and the movement, despite its variegated nature, will often maintain at least a rough hierarchy and division of labor.[87]

Within the American context, then, a political movement is a loose association of citizens who mobilize to bring about substantial change, based on at least a rough ideology, through political organization and action. This politicization is often the final stage in a social movement's growth, after initially "forming" through the creation of autonomous institutions, large-scale recruitment of members, and education of those members.[88] Such movements often consist of a hard core of "relatively small numbers of faithful adherents," surrounded by an informal coalition of organizations and intellectual centers. Thus, more discrete and narrowly based organizations aimed at affecting a particular issue through political action (e.g., civil rights, nuclear arms race, abortion laws) can also be part of a broader political movement.

The movement coalition can also include some "securely institutionalized" sympathetic groups on the "inside" of the system, whose support may be a prerequisite for success.[89] This latter group will most often consist of disaffected members ("insurgents") from within one or both of the major parties. While not all insurgencies are part of a broader popular movement (some are instead a strictly internal revolt), movements will almost always seek to establish ties with insurgencies. In much the same way, although many movements will seek an outlet in third parties, not all third parties represent movements. Political movements in America do not represent a majority, at least when they begin and fight their most important battles; they are sustained by a small hard core, but are fairly broad-based.[90] While loose, they are well formed enough to be given a name (e.g., populism, conservatism, the new politics). While volatile, they also have some degree of staying power.

Political movements enter the electoral process either by forming a new or third party—which is difficult, due to the nonproportional nature of the American electoral system—or by trying to capture one of the two major existing parties so as to turn it into an instrument of the movement. The latter aim can be attempted best through the short-term effort to win the presidential nomination for a spokesman of the movement. The fortunes of the movement can thus be intertwined with an individual candidate; in this way, the nominating process becomes the key link between movement and government. However, genuine movements have substance beyond, and independent of, the individuals who serve as their standard-bearers. They must be distinguished from phenomena that are solely candidate-centered and that have no purpose or staying power beyond the immediate campaign.

In sum, a movement has the following characteristics: first, it has an actually or potentially broad base of support, but is less than a majority and is driven by a relatively small and committed hard core; second, it is organized, generally through an informal coalition of groups, and is an identifiable entity to outside observers, but is less institutionalized than a political party; third, it is motivated by at least a rough ideology; fourth, it attempts to promote change based upon its ideology through political action; fifth, while not a permanent fixture in the polity, since it arises in response to particular conditions or problems, it nevertheless has staying power beyond a single election; sixth, it exists independently of any single individual personality.

In American political history since the Civil War, there are a number of political phenomena that fit this definition and that are well suited to study in relation to the presidential nominating system. These include the populist movement, the prohibition movement, the progressive movement, the conservative movement, the new politics movement, the rainbow coalition, and the Christian right. These movements will serve as the subjects of case studies meant to test the level of openness of different forms of the nominating system.

Some movement characteristics are absolute values: for instance, popular forces either are or are not less than a majority, and either do or do not seek change through political means. However, some aspects of movements also exist along a continuum, such as comprehensiveness of ideology, degree of organization, breadth of base, staying power, and independence from an individual personality. An assessment of relative strength can be made only partially in abstract terms divorced from actual success or failure, since there are numerous characteristics—such as a broad base and organizational capacity—that are best revealed in political combat. Thus, any attempt to rank movements in terms of strength is necessarily somewhat tautological. Nevertheless, at least a rough ranking of movements can be made. It should especially be possible to reach conclusions about relative strength when studying movements across multiple elections; it is clear that the 1972 version of the new politics was stronger than the 1968 version, and that the 1988 version of the rainbow coalition was stronger than the 1984 version. By studying the entire range of electoral movements—the strong and the weak, the successful and the failed—we will be able to see a variety of outcomes under a variety of circumstances, and will gain greater insight into the question of whether different nominating systems (or components of systems) benefit different types of movements.

Unconnected Outsiders

It is apparent, however, that movements are not the only type of outsiders. There are many candidates in the mixed system and reform system who call themselves outsiders, and who virtually everyone would agree are outsiders, but who do not fit the definition of a movement. They are not supported by a preexisting organized political force that has substance beyond their own candidacy. Rather, they are personalist and, for lack of a better term, "unconnected" outsiders.

To define these unconnected outsiders, one must think back to the definition of a movement. While movements have several features, there are per-

haps three that truly capture the essence of a movement and that are empirically testable. The first is organization beyond the candidate: does the phenomenon possess a substance that is distinct from the campaign? The second
is staying power: how long has the phenomenon been observed before the
campaign? The third feature is a shorthand way of measuring the first two as
well as other important movement characteristics, such as ideology. It is decep-
tively simple, capturing a great deal of information in a straightforward manner: does the political phenomenon in question have a name? Precisely
because they have distinct organizational structures, staying power, and ideologies, movements have names, either self-affixed or affixed by others, that
describe their worldview and ascribe to them independent substance. When
we can think of nothing better to call a political phenomenon than the name
of the candidate, this is an indication that it is a personalist phenomenon without rootedness or independent substance; if, for instance, we can think of no
better name for a phenomenon than the "Wallace movement" or the "Perot
movement," it is not really a movement.

When examining the clearest examples of outsiders in the convention,
mixed, and reform systems, the differences between movement candidates and
unconnected outsiders become apparent. The populists, prohibitionists, progressives, conservatives, members of the new politics movement, of the rainbow coalition, and of the Christian right constituted movements and the candidates they supported were movement candidates; on the other hand, Estes
Kefauver, George Wallace, Jimmy Carter, Gary Hart, Paul Tsongas, Jerry
Brown, David Duke, Pat Buchanan (at least in 1992), Steve Forbes, and H.
Ross Perot were unconnected outsiders (see table 1.3). Just as not all movements are created equal, neither are all unconnected outsiders. Some are more
extreme in their outsiderism than others. Some are so lacking in the qualities
of a movement that no one even tries to name them, while others (the Wallace
and Perot candidacies) seem to occupy an awkward position in which they
share virtually none of the defining characteristics of a movement but attempt
to fashion a pseudomovement in their own image. This accounts for the labels
attached to them, which ascribe to them the name "movement" in such a personalist fashion as to nullify the very meaning of movement. Many rely on
soft, virtually content-free personality appeals; some rely on hard, divisive
issue appeals; a few rely on detailed policy proposals.

All, however, run explicitly as outsiders; indeed, often to a much greater
extent than movement candidates, they cultivate a reputation as outsiders and
mavericks. Furthermore, like movement candidates, they usually attempt to tie
themselves to some concept of change, though this appeal is often less ideo-

Table 1-3. Outsiders, 1865–1992

Candidate	Independent Organization	Prior Staying Power	Name of Phenomenon
Multiple 1872–c.1900	yes	c. 20 years	Prohibitionist Movement
Multiple 1892–c.1900	yes	3–25 years	Populist Movement
Multiple 1904–1924	yes	c. 10 years	Progressive Movement
Estes Kefauver 1952–1956	no	0	
Barry Goldwater 1964	yes	c. 10 years	Conservative Movement
George Wallace 1964–1976	no	0	Wallace Movement
Eugene McCarthy 1968	yes	0.5–6 years	New Politics
George McGovern 1972	yes	4.5–10 years	New Politics
Jimmy Carter 1976	no	0	
Ronald Reagan 1976	yes	c. 22 years	Conservative Movement
Gary Hart 1984	no	0	
Jesse Jackson 1984–1988	yes	0.7–25 years	Rainbow Coalition
Pat Robertson 1988	yes	c. 10 years	Christian Right
David Duke 1992	no	0	

Table 1-3. Continued

Candidate	Independent Organization	Prior Staying Power	Name of Phenomenon
Jerry Brown 1992	no	0	
Paul Tsongas 1992	no	0	
Ross Perot 1992	no	0	Perot phenomenon Perot movement
Pat Buchanan 1992	no	0	
Pat Buchanan 1996	yes	c. 18 years	Christian right
Steve Forbes	no	0	

Notes: "Independent organization" refers to a freestanding organizational structure independent of the candidate. Prior staying power is calculated as the time prior to candidacy (or in a series of candidacies, prior to the first candidacy) that the political phenomenon in question had been active. Variations are due to differences among varying strands of the movement. The prohibitionist movement is dated from earliest state activity; the populist movement from establishment of the Grange (25 years before the first candidacy) or first People's Party activity in Kansas (3 years); the progressive movement from the rise of first progressive mayors; the conservative movement from establishment of the *National Review;* both new politics candidacies from establishment of Dump Johnson organization (0.5 years for McCarthy, 4.5 years for McGovern) or SDS Port Huron Statement (6 years for McCarthy, 10 for McGovern); the rainbow coalition from black candidate organizational meeting (.7 years) or civil rights movement (25 years); the Christian right from establishment of Moral Majority. Some of these datings are somewhat arbitrary, but are meant to serve as reasonable guideposts. The prohibition, populist, and progressive movements all had numerous standard-bearers during the years listed, and because of the primacy of the movement (and often a third party), candidate names are relatively unimportant. The 1996 Buchanan campaign is listed as a movement campaign because it was dependent on substantial local elements of the Christian right organization which backed him, but it should be noted that the movement was divided and Buchanan seldom received a majority of Christian right voter support.

logical than personal or thematic. They tend to rely more heavily on personal charisma and on what the Founders called the "popular arts" and their modern manifestations, such as the media, often through direct appeals to popular alienation.

Whatever imprecisions may exist in definition, and whatever variations may exist among types, the candidates identified above as unconnected outsiders are a different breed from movement candidates. As this study progresses, it will become clear that important differences also exist in the way they are treated by varying mechanisms of the nominating process. Just as implications abound in the possible distinction between strong and weak movements, important normative questions are raised by the distinction between movements and unconnected outsiders. If not all outsiders are the same, what complexities are added to the consideration of openness? If different systems prove to advantage one type of outsider at the expense of the other, is one inherently preferable, and on what grounds?

Conclusion

These case studies cannot provide definitive answers to the questions we are asking; there are a limited number of cases, and each case occurs in its own peculiar historical circumstances. Furthermore, the nominating system is not the only factor in nomination campaigns. As the party decline school correctly notes, social factors independent of the nominating rules, such as the media and overall party strength, have a great impact. Other factors that might affect outcomes (aside from random events and the strength of the candidate) include: rules such as delegate apportionment formulae, which can take numerous forms within the same system; the strength and unity of the outsider's opposition; whether the opponent was an incumbent president or not; and more generally, whether the party targeted for takeover was the majority or minority party. Finally, the openness of the nominating system cannot be viewed in isolation from the openness of the electoral system as a whole. These factors will be acknowledged as far as possible. To the degree that the rules are a factor, one can only speculate about outcomes under alternative rules, since strategies would presumably change as well.

Nevertheless, "rules are never politically neutral," and, unlike the broader social and political context, they are within our capacity to directly adjust.[91] As John Aldrich points out, "The institution of party nominations—the rules, laws, procedures, and norms that describe how presidential hopefuls become party nominees—plays a major role in structuring the politics of nominations and, consequently, in the behavior of candidates and the outcome of their campaigns."[92] Furthermore, if patterns can be seen across such widely varied circumstances in both parties, conclusions can be drawn with some degree of confidence. These case studies can provide important information and can offer important possibilities.

Above all, this study of outsiders will draw two broad conclusions. First, openness (and its mirror, stability) has a variety of dimensions. There is a difference between openness of initial access (the ability of outsiders to compete), openness to short-term success (the ability of outsiders to win a nomination), and openness to long-term success (the ability of outsiders to consolidate long-term control of the party). These dimensions of openness are potentially conflicting; some nominating mechanisms that promote openness of access, for example, can actually make winning the nomination or consolidating a hold over the party more difficult, and vice versa.

Second, it is clear that a single component of nominating systems can treat different types of outsiders differently. For example, where organized movements seem to thrive on caucuses, the "unconnected outsiders" would benefit from their elimination. Stronger movements and weaker movements are not always treated the same by a given mechanism. Sometimes strong outsiders of both types are treated one way, and weak outsiders of both types another.

This complex understanding of openness leads to a more complex understanding of the varying systems. The convention system, pilloried for its smoke-filled rooms, was closed to initial infiltration but ultimately provided an avenue for openness to very strong movements if those movements could prove their strength and staying power at the polls as a third party. The mixed system, scarcely less excoriated in 1968 for being too closed, was closed to the unconnected and to weaker movements, but was also open—both in the short and long term—to strong movements like the one that Barry Goldwater rode to victory in the Republican Party in 1964. And the reform system, both praised and condemned for its alleged openness, has turned the mixed system on its head, opening the floodgates to the unconnected and encouraging weak movements, while making it more difficult for stronger movements either to win or to gain long-term party control from their victory.

This complexity means that one can no longer simply be for or against openness. Outsiderism may always be with us, but we have the institutional means to channel it in a variety of directions. The institutional choices we make, either deliberately or accidentally, determine which dimensions of openness are promoted and which are hindered, which sorts of forces are encouraged and which are restrained.

2

Movements in the
Pure Convention System

THE PURE CONVENTION SYSTEM DOMINATED
American presidential politics from the Jacksonian era until the introduction of presidential preference primaries in 1912. In this chapter I
examine the ways in which the system maintained stability and permitted a measure of openness. In short, the convention system provided more
openness than is often recognized but much less than the system that followed
it.

The ethos and structure of the convention system discouraged open candidacies prior to the national convention; thus, it is very difficult to identify
an "unconnected outsider" in this time period. From the end of the Civil War
until the advent of the "mixed" nominating system, four major political movements competed for power: the populist and union movements, which in
many ways grew up side by side; the prohibition movement; and the progressive movement. They offer a study of the convention system put to the test of
popular revolt.

Despite their differences, they formed certain consistent patterns. Each of
these movements had to operate within a nominating system controlled by
party regulars through conventions, until the progressives succeeded in fundamentally transforming the system itself. When the major parties first

brushed away their challenges, the broader electoral system provided opportunities. The convention system proved difficult to enter directly but much
easier to influence indirectly if a movement could prove its strength. This
requirement of strength enforced a degree of stability, since groups had to
attain a broad base of support and exhibit staying power. Furthermore, one of
the chief routes to movement influence was through third-party "fusion" with
a major party—an arrangement in which the two parties would form unified
candidate slates and/or platforms.[1] A certain amount of stability was thus
introduced, since fusion was more often a compromise than a full-scale
takeover. Furthermore, since the smaller of the two major parties was both
more organizationally vulnerable and more in need of fusion allies, it tended
to be more open to this sort of influence. As a result, the majority—and hence
generally governing—party was more heavily insulated from the destabilizing
effects of movements.

When primaries were adopted in the name of openness, some of these
mechanisms of stability were lost. We will consider whether over time an
equivalent degree of openness was won, and what balance between openness
and stability resulted. Because local and state conventions led directly to the
national convention, and primaries at local levels share many of the properties
of presidential preference primaries, we shall examine local movement efforts
to help illuminate the national situation.

The Populists

The populist movement serves as an excellent example of the pattern of
openness found in the pure convention system. A grassroots movement arises
and initially attempts to infiltrate the major parties, but the failure of these
attempts due to regular control of the process leads to the creation of a third
party. The third party attempts to supplement its strength through fusion,
while the major parties seek to blunt the challenge by taking away the salient
issues (and sometimes by perpetrating electoral fraud). Finally, the third party
disintegrates due to a combination of internal factionalism and opportunities
to gain greater influence through other means. Movements are faced with a
series of choices and calculations that have to be adeptly negotiated.

There were two basic points of entry for movements in the convention
system: the first was through attempted infiltration of the major party through
normal processes, and the second was the attempt to influence a major party
by becoming a minor party. The populists, enjoying a strong grassroots base,

made a serious attempt at infiltration but were rebuffed. Only then was the third-party route taken, which ultimately led to substantial populist influence in the Democratic Party.

The populist movement was by far the strongest movement active entirely within the period dominated by the convention system; indeed, Lawrence Goodwyn calls it the "largest democratic mass movement in American history."[2] It was truly a bottom-up movement, built around deep-seated popular grievances. The Populist Party at the peak of its power in 1896 was the culmination of a movement that had already spawned numerous organizations and minor parties over a period of three decades. Populism was as much a culture as a political force, a "democratic culture" characterized by "massive parades . . . huge summer encampments . . . far-flung lecturing system . . . rituals . . . trade committees and warehouses."[3] This movement was driven primarily by the wrenching changes in American social and economic life following the Civil War. Farmers, who represented the core of the populist movement, faced the economic effects of overproduction and currency deflation, including intermittent but massive waves of foreclosures, and perceived exploitation by monopolies and by the railroads on which they depended. The rural population largely blamed their troubles not on a "world-wide economic network controlled by an impersonal price and market system that they hardly understood," but on lenders, railroads, and trusts (in short, the "Eastern money power").[4] At the same time, urbanization and industrialization resulted in the rise of an industrial working class that was faced with unpleasant living and working conditions as well as the vagaries of an unregulated business cycle. The union movement arose out of these circumstances.

The first sign of serious agricultural discontent came in 1867 with the formation of the "Patrons of Husbandry" organization (the "Grange"), a secret society modeled after the Masons and Oddfellows. The Grange reached its peak in the early 1870s after the organization declared itself in favor of railroad regulation and the creation of farmers' cooperatives to eliminate economic middlemen. The farmers' movement, which was originally nonpolitical, moved into electoral politics in 1873 in Illinois, where the movement was especially strong. The Grange served as the organizational basis for a third party that went by the names of the "Anti-Monopoly Party" and the "Reform Party."

After some successes in 1873–1874, largely obtained through local fusion arrangements with Democrats, by 1876 the "Granger phase of the farmers' revolt had burned itself out."[5] The Grange quickly melted into the National Independent Party (or "Greenback" Party), which advocated paper money.

By 1878, the Greenbackers appeared to be in a position to offer a serious presidential challenge in 1880.

At virtually the same time that the Grange movement was reaching its peak, the National Labor Reform Party was formed in 1870. While it fared poorly in 1872, labor activity was on the upsurge by 1877; railroad strikes rocked the country and inflamed the labor situation, and in 1878 the Knights of Labor organized on a national scale.[6]

The Greenbackers and the Labor Reform Party began informal cooperation in several states in 1877, and were "really two branches of the same party."[7] In February 1878, they made the union official, formally merging into the "National" (or "Greenback-Labor") Party. By this time, there were nearly four thousand Greenback clubs nationwide, plus widely distributed party newspapers and tracts. The national economy was still in depression, and 1878 proved to be the high point of the Greenbackers. With minimal fusion, they won over 1 million votes in the congressional elections and elected fourteen congressmen. However, prosperity returned, the party was unable to reconcile the interests of western agriculture and eastern labor, and candidates were increasingly "lured down the path of fusion." That may have provided influence when the party was on its way up, but it led to its submersion as the party slipped.[8] By 1882, the Greenback-Labor Party held only one House seat, and the party largely disintegrated.

The Greenback-Labor Party was then followed in rapid succession by the Anti-Monopoly Party, formed in 1884 in fusion with the remainder of the Greenbackers, and the Union Labor Party of 1887, based on the Knights of Labor. To these parties might be added a collection of nonparty organizations, including the "Nationalist Clubs" started in 1888 in Boston advocating nationalization of industry, and the "National Bimetallic League," which started in 1889 and advocated currency inflation through greater use of silver specie. None of the new parties had substantial success in the 1880s, though in many ways the foundation had been laid for future endeavors. The anti-railroad, Granger, and Greenback efforts were "all phases of one large movement," and each new wave expanded on the ideas of the previous wave.[9] The problems that had led to agricultural and labor discontent had not been fundamentally alleviated, but from 1880 on, neither major party seemed prepared to address those problems at the presidential level. Major party unresponsiveness both fueled the discontent and left a space in the electoral system for other forces to fill.

In 1892, this train of third parties converged with a second phenomenon: the incredible growth of the Farmers' Alliances, which (like the Grange) started as nonpolitical local associations. With its roots in Texas groups dating back to 1875, the Alliance had a northern and southern branch. In the South, a Farmers' State Alliance had been formed in Texas by 1880, and by 1889 had merged with other groups to form the "National Farmers' and Laborers' Union." In addition, a "Colored Farmers' National Alliance" was started in 1886. In the North, the "National Farmers' Alliance" was formed in 1880. By the early 1890s, the Southern Alliance claimed 3 million members, the Northern Alliance 2 million.[10]

Like the Grange, the Alliances established cooperatives; and like the Grange, the Alliances found they did not work economically (though they did have important social and cultural effects that helped to energize subsequent political activity). With this discovery, and with an again worsening economic situation, the Alliances turned to politics. While the failure of the cooperatives made the venture into politics necessary, the cooperative attempt made it possible, by serving as the basis for the development of an autonomous "movement culture."[11] In 1889, the Northern and Southern Alliances met together for the first time, along with the Colored Alliance and the Knights of Labor. There was no merger yet, but a joint statement of principles was issued, which later became the basis of the People's Party platform.

While agreeing on principles and on the need to become politically active, the Northern and Southern Alliances diverged on the question of tactics. The Northern Alliance called for a third party, and in 1889 the People's Party first appeared in local elections in Kansas, with great success. The next year the Kansas People's Party ran a statewide campaign, electing ninety of one hundred and twenty-five legislators; sixty-two of the ninety had been Republicans. This pattern was repeated elsewhere in the upper Midwest. Indeed, throughout the Northwest, Alliancemen were overwhelmingly Republican, and were generally more inclined toward a third party than toward fusion with the Democrats.[12]

The Southern Alliance, conversely, preferred to work through the Democratic Party, since "anything that might threaten the political solidarity of the whites was regarded with grave suspicion."[13] This strategy was initially very successful. After the 1890 elections, the Alliance controlled eight southern legislatures, forty-four congressmen, and the governorships of South Carolina, Tennessee, Texas, and Georgia, all under the label of the Democratic Party. In Georgia, for example, six of ten congressmen were "defeated for renomination at the primaries by the influence of the Farmers' Alliance."[14] As the *Atlanta Constitution* put it, "The Farmers' Alliance *is* the Democratic Party."[15] Given this sort of success, and the risks of third-party action, the

Southern Alliance was hesitant to venture into the realm of a third party. Unlike previous manifestations of the movement, it had been able to use the established mechanisms of party nomination to secure its own ends on a large scale.

Within two years this situation had changed. The party regulars changed their rhetoric while redoubling their efforts; southern Democratic parties shifted toward free silver and populism, undercutting the Alliancemen. Furthermore, officials who won with Alliance help had a disappointing record on issues of importance to the Alliance. In particular, the Democrats rejected the "subtreasury" plan that was central to Alliance demands.[16]

Southern Democratic regulars also vigorously exercised the organizational prerogatives they continued to hold. For instance, in Texas, the Democratic Party attempted to preempt an Alliance takeover in 1890 by nominating James Stephen Hogg for governor on a platform of railroad regulation. This succeeded until farmers became frustrated with Hogg's apparent waffling on the railroad issue. At that point, the Democratic state committee declared that the Alliance was engaged in the political promotion of the "subtreasury" plan, which was in contradiction with the Democratic platform; hence the Alliance was a "party," and Alliance members would not be permitted to participate in Democratic Party meetings or primaries. The Texas People's Party was formed immediately with the Alliance as its organizational nucleus, and later merged with Democratic insurgents who had held on longer in the hope of still working within the party.[17]

In North Carolina, where the Alliance made great strides in 1890, the nomination of Grover Cleveland by the Democratic national convention in 1892 caused numerous Democratic Alliance voters to desire to vote for the Populist national ticket and Democratic local ticket. The North Carolina Democratic Party insisted that no such ticket splitting would be permitted, thus driving Alliancemen who would have preferred to remain Democrats into the state's Populist Party.[18]

This pattern was repeated across the South, as Democratic regulars reestablished control. Furthermore, the creation of the third party split the movement's strength, since many Alliancemen (and a few Alliance officeholders, such as Governor Ben Tillman of South Carolina) refused to leave their traditional party. The ability of the regulars to drive the Alliance out of the party even when outnumbered depended heavily on the adept manipulation of party rules within the states, such as the requirements for party participation established in Texas and North Carolina. It was this sort of manipulation that the state legislation discussed in chapter 1 later sought to end.

In the Midwest and West, the Alliance encountered a similar situation. The Alliance took over the Iowa GOP in 1887, and in Minnesota succeeded in getting the two parties to bid against each other for Alliance support.[19] Nevertheless, in most places, party control of nominations stifled reformers from achieving a permanent foothold. While farm discontent initially brought a certain amount of sympathy and responsiveness from regulars, this turned to hostility when farmer activism became more than a perfunctory phenomenon.[20] This response to the Alliance was identical to the response to earlier phases of the movement, like the Greenbackers in Iowa. In addition, members of the Northern Alliance were more willing than their southern brethren to break the taboos of party loyalty by forming a third party.

Finally, at a conference held in St. Louis in February 1892, the Alliances and twenty other organizations proclaimed a national People's Party. This marked a new stage in the agrarian revolt, as well as the end of southern efforts to take over the Democratic Party from within. While some pro-Alliance Democrats kept their offices, most "were either silenced or eventually driven into the Populist party."[21]

The formation of the Populist Party represented the convergence of the series of third parties with the vast agricultural organizations seen in the Alliance systems. The Populist platform drew primarily from these earlier groups, and the Populists basically absorbed the Alliance, using it as a base for organization. The Alliance itself collapsed as an independent entity within a short time. The Populists retained, however, a large lecture system and a national reform press consisting of some one thousand journals. The populist movement would occupy the stage for the better part of the next decade. Indeed, after the Populist Party's first presidential election, the Populists— like the Greenbackers in 1878—believed they were poised to become one of the major parties.

The Populist national convention of July 1892 nominated James Weaver of Iowa, who had carried the banner for the Greenback Party in 1880. Weaver won 8.4 percent of the popular vote and twenty-two electoral votes, the first minor party candidate to win an electoral vote since the Civil War. The Populists also won gubernatorial races in Kansas, Colorado, and North Dakota. Although the socialist tendencies of the Populists were limited to government ownership of railroads and telegraphs, they were "decimating" the socialist parties in the North and West; socialist votes fell from 147,000 in 1888 to 21,000 in 1892.[22] The presidential election, however, was won by Democrat Grover Cleveland, who returned to the presidency after a one-term hiatus.

Weeks after Cleveland took office, the United States plunged into the worst depression it had yet known. As the economy continued to worsen, the currency issue became the central political issue of the 1890s. Cleveland was firmly in favor of an undiluted gold currency system. As a result, he not only refused to expand the money supply but actually secured repeal of the Sherman Silver Purchase Act of 1890, which had permitted a limited degree of bimetallism. Ultimately, "the silver question divided the country as had nothing else since the Civil War."[23] This was so partly because Cleveland himself made no effort to compromise with dissidents within the Democratic Party, either on the silver issue or on other issues such as tariff reform. By 1894, unemployment was estimated to be 20 percent, Coxey's Army had marched on Washington, the Pullman strike had been broken up with federal troops, and Cleveland had vetoed the Bland Bill mandating silver coinage. The deteriorating situation produced two winners in 1894: the Republican Party, which made the largest gain in congressional seats in American history, and the Populists, who seized the silver issue and increased their vote by 42 percent (though they actually won fewer races than in 1892). In North Carolina, for example, the Populists formed fusion tickets with the Republicans, winning both houses of the legislature. They also won numerous county offices in Alabama, and 44.5 percent of the vote in Georgia.[24]

The elections of 1894 resulted in a parallel process. First, a debate ensued within the Populist Party over whether to downplay the rest of their reform agenda and emphasize the silver issue, a question ultimately answered in the affirmative. At the same time, silver sentiment accelerated within the Democratic Party in reaction to the defeats of 1894 and Cleveland's obstinacy:

> Many Democratic leaders in the south and west, where the party was far stronger than it was in the east, read a solemn warning in the election results. . . . With room in a two-party system for only one conservative party, the Democratic left-wingers felt that the Populists would soon displace the Democrats unless the latter quickly changed their ways.[25]

The Populists had thus begun a process of pulling the Democrats in their direction and causing turmoil in both major parties. The "permeation" of Democratic policy by Populist ideas, which had begun in the South, advanced steadily nationwide, starting with Democratic congressional approval of the income tax even before the electoral disaster of 1894. By March 1895, large portions of the Democratic congressional contingent, including William Jennings Bryan, "took the warpath" against Cleveland and issued a manifesto calling for free coinage of silver at a 16:1 ratio. In June 1895, silver forces held a nationwide convention in Memphis that was nominally nonpartisan but 90 percent Democratic in attendance, the primary objective of which was "to lure the Populists and western silver men of all varieties into the Democratic Party."[26] Subsequently, a conference was held in Washington, D.C., to construct an organizational framework to achieve that objective; the Bimetallic Democratic National Committee was formed, "each member of which was assigned to the task of organizing the silver forces of his state by establishing bimetallic Democratic clubs in every county and election precinct."[27]

After the Washington conference, "the silver crusade spread like wildfire."[28] Silver Democrats not only formed their own clubs, but worked with outside organizations like the National Bimetallic Union, the American Bimetallic League, and the National Silver Committee. The Bimetallic Democratic National Committee "established reliable organizations in each of the states west of the Alleghenies and south of Maryland."[29] In the meantime, local and state conventions were held early in many western and southern states, providing early commitments of state parties to the "silver at 16:1" program. At the beginning of 1896, the silver Democrats were poised to compete at the national convention; by April 1896, 60 percent of congressional Democrats could be counted as prosilver.[30] In short, "the popular revolt which had created the People's Party in 1892 had now penetrated the ranks of the Democratic Party."[31] However, its radicalism was diluted; silver, while inflationary, was still less radical than the subtreasuries, whose advocates envisioned an overhaul of the banking system and an irredeemable currency.

The Populists misjudged the strength of the Democratic silver insurgency, and scheduled their 1896 convention after the conventions of both major parties in the expectation that both would nominate gold candidates. The Populists would then be in a position to rally all silver forces under their own banner. The Republicans followed the formula, nominating William McKinley and producing a bolt from the silver Republicans. However, the Democratic silver forces, having already prevailed in thirty of forty-five state conventions, controlled their national convention from the beginning. A platform was approved giving unqualified support to free silver at 16:1, attacking strike-breaking labor injunctions and the 1895 *Pollock* Supreme Court decision ruling the income tax unconstitutional, and favoring labor arbitration, stricter railroad regulation, antitrust legislation, and tax-free state banks. While not going as far as the Populist stand on many issues (rejecting, for example, subtreasuries and government control of the railroads), the Democratic platform "was still more radical than any presented to the people by a major party within the memory of any but the oldest living men."[32]

William Jennings Bryan, whom some saw as a "Populist in all but name," was then nominated for the presidency.[33] Bryan had participated in the formation of a silver Democrat organization in Nebraska as early as 1893, had helped spearhead the congressional revolt against Cleveland in 1895, and had subsequently traveled around the country on behalf of silver forces. By 1896, he had made a strong name for himself, especially among those in the farm belt who were most sympathetic to the Populist appeal. He was therefore already in a good position to take the nomination when he delivered his famous "Cross of Gold" speech on behalf of the platform's prosilver plank.

The Populists were thus faced with a dilemma: instead of being in a position to unify silver sentiment of all parties under their banner, they ran the risk of splitting the silver vote and electing McKinley. The silver Republicans, facing a similar situation, had quickly endorsed Bryan, putting added pressure on the Populists to do the same. In the end, and without Bryan's permission, the Populist national convention voted for fusion with the Democrats and gave Bryan their own nomination. To retain some semblance of independence, they voted to run their own vice presidential candidate, Georgia radical Tom Watson.[34] The task of making fusion arrangements to accommodate two vice presidential candidates proved exceedingly difficult.

In the meantime, the gold Democrats bolted and formed their own party, with the intention of drawing Democratic votes away from Bryan so that McKinley would win, but with the effect of leaving the party machinery in the hands of the Bryanites.[35] Thus, the Populists had succeeded in drawing the bulk of the Democratic Party toward their position, as well as sorting out the parties on gold-silver lines. A philosophical realignment had occurred, in ways generally satisfying to the Populists. As Roscoe Martin writes in his study of Texas Populism, the Populist Party "forced the Democratic Party to the drastic step of accepting its cardinal demand and nominating Bryan on a free silver platform. Thus it virtually recast that party, causing it to renounce the leadership of Cleveland and become, in effect, a new party whose nature is revealed by the appellation, 'the Popocratic party.' "[36]

The effect of the fusion arrangement with the Democrats was not so salutary from an organizational perspective, however. The Democrats were usually the "senior partners" in fusion arrangements regarding electors, congressional seats, and other state and local offices; especially in the West, "so many Populists had supported Democratic candidates that the machinery of the Populist party had suffered too much to be repaired." Here, many Populists after 1896 simply drifted into the Democratic Party.[37] In the South, the animosity between the Populists and Democratic regulars was too great to be overcome, and the Populists ultimately fused not with the local Democrats but with the local Republicans, producing the anomalous situation of supporting the Democratic presidential nominee and Republican local candidates. Here, the Populists broke down, as southern whites became hostile to the Populist-Republican alliance, largely because the fusion arrangement had resulted in the election of a number of black Republicans. These former Populists returned to the Democratic Party, where they were once again taken under the wing of the Bourbon regulars; a few, like Thomas Watson of Georgia, ultimately attained positions of influence within the party, though usually at the cost of jettisoning some of their populist principles.[38] The rest stayed with the GOP and let the Populist Party collapse. What remained of the Populist Party after 1896 was consistently beset by bitter factionalism over the fusion strategy. Thus, the populist movement at once saw the pinnacle of its success, with the nomination of an ally and the adoption of a sympathetic platform by a major party, and the collapse of its organizational embodiment.

After Bryan's general election defeat in 1896, the Populist Party rapidly fell into ineffectiveness. Prosperity returned, the money supply increased due to the discovery of new gold fields, and the Spanish-American War distracted the nation and introduced the new issue of imperialism. Bryan, however, was renominated twice by the Democratic Party in the next three elections, each time with a more strongly reformist platform. Although Bryan was not fully a populist, and the populists themselves diverged from the progressives in certain important respects (most notably their agrarian orientation), Bryan (and by extension the populist movement) "was in some measure responsible for the successes of the progressive movement."[39]

The populist recourse to the third party was clearly a response to the difficulty of wresting power away from entrenched party regulars in the convention system. In the words of John Hicks, at first, "individual Alliancemen were to exert their utmost influence in the party to which they happened to belong to have candidates nominated and platforms adopted that were in accord with Alliance principles."[40] The agrarian movement, despite its strength, quickly discovered that this strategy was not effective.

After being rebuffed by the party organizations, however, the populist movement in its third-party form made good use of the second point of entry into the system. This occurred in two ways: drawing the major parties closer to populism through electoral competition, and actually fusing with one of the major parties. While these two processes had a similar source (the demonstrated electoral power of the third party), and while the first led in some cases to the second, they were different and often operated in somewhat different ways.

The Populists often succeeded in drawing the majority party at the state level closer to it without fusion; indeed, the most powerful party undertook these changes to avoid falling prey to the movement. This occurred first and most frequently in the South, where the majority Democrats—after largely purging their ranks of Alliancemen and thus virtually forcing the creation of the Populist Party—then proceeded to adopt numerous Populist measures as their own. Hicks estimates that as early as 1892 half of southern Democratic Parties had come out for Populist doctrines, especially free silver and railroad regulation.[41] Western Republicans also took this route to some extent at the state level. Their Nebraska platform had Populist elements as early as 1890 though their gubernatorial candidate was far from a Populist, and in 1892 the Populist threat tilted the internal GOP balance sufficiently to produce control by the proreform faction.[42] However, the national Republican Party, as the majority party in the United States (by a dwindling margin after the 1870s), did not respond to the Populist threat by moving toward the Populists.

To the minority party, Populism presented both threat and opportunity. This produced a second phenomenon, in which greater philosophical compatibility was matched with actual organizational cooperation in the form of fusion. In the South, this took the form of consistent fusion between the Populists and the Republicans. These successes were only temporary, collapsing as the result of anti-Republican and white supremacy sentiment and the difficulties in 1896 of fusing with the Republicans locally and with the Democrats nationally.

The more important fusion, in terms of its long-term impact, was the Populist-Democratic fusion in the western states and at the national level. Here, the victory of the reform forces in the national Democratic Party in 1896 was clearly due to the pressures and opportunities presented by the Populists. Indeed, evidence exists that the Democratic convention chose Bryan over Richard Bland or Horace Boies partially because the Populists had already expressed their dissatisfaction with Bland and Boies, and it is indisputable that the Democratic silver tide had gained great strength from Populist successes—a fact of which the Populists seemed to be well aware.[43] Populist senator William Stewart of Nevada had attended the Democratic convention, and returned to tell the Populists that the Democrats were "as emphatically Populists in their sentiments and actions as yourself. . . . There was nothing left of the Democratic Party at Chicago but the name."[44] The belief that this was the case—and the fear of splitting the silver vote—was crucial in the Populist Party's agreement to fuse.

This agreement had been preceded by years of local Populist-Democratic fusion in the West, which had led in many states (such as Nebraska) to a fundamental and long-lasting realignment of party coalitions.[45] In these states, "local fusion was the bridge by which many Populists gradually moved into the Democratic Party."[46] Such local cooperation, combined with national trends, led Populists and Democrats alike—including Weaver and Bryan—to foresee national fusion as early as 1894.[47]

In sum, "fusion between the Democrats and Populists was not . . . the simple matter of Democratic gain and Populist sacrifice that many historians have depicted."[48] While many Populist radicals decried fusion at the time as a "sellout," they were probably in the minority, and it seems evident that Norman Pollack's appraisal is correct that fusion was an attempt to consolidate the gains of the third party by ensuring the victory of Democratic reformist elements.[49] To the extent that the program of the Populist Party was largely adopted by the Democrats, it is indeed not easy to tell who swallowed whom.

Thus, the third-party route provided a means of influencing the major parties that went well beyond simply challenging them as an independent party. At a minimum, a major party could be forced in the direction of a third party simply as an attempt to preempt support, and at best, that third party could be invited to fuse. Both of these processes may have been helped rather than hindered by the dominance of political "professionals" in the system. For instance, Stanley Parsons discusses a Nebraska Republican state senator by the name of Church Howe who had railroad sympathies but "was first and foremost a professional politician in the Republican party. When the [land] boom collapsed and the storm of populism broke upon the state in 1890, Howe became the first of the Republican politicians to appreciate the need for a change in party policy."[50] Howe quickly took up the issues of railroad reform and free silver.

Likewise, the act of fusion was made more, not less, possible in many cases by the control of major parties by regulars. This can be seen in the reverse case; the most ideological and nonprofessional partisan force in America was the "midroad" Populists, who strenuously objected to fusion and were willing to split even from the main body of the Populist Party to protest it. It stands to reason that major parties dominated by ideology rather than notions of electability would themselves have been less willing to fuse with the Populists. And effective control of nominations by the party leadership made it possible to make deals.

Thus, despite (and in some ways because of) the dominance of party regulars in the convention system, openness was provided—not through initial infiltration, but through third-party pressure. This openness came at a price, however. The clearest requirement levied upon a movement seeking to gain influence with a major party through a third party was for that third party to prove its viability by showing electoral strength. Only then would a major party see a benefit in trying to undercut its strength by imitating it; only then would fusion with it actually hold out the prospect of victory. Thus, not only was access generally denied initially, but a high threshold of strength had to be reached before the third party would be considered anything but an irritant. As Roscoe Martin observed in Texas, the Democrats tried every available means (fair and foul) to eliminate their rival, but "when every alternative had been exhausted and the Populists continued to outrun the charge, the Democrats yet had one last recourse, namely the adoption of the Reform program and the absorption of the Third Party, to which they were forced eventually to resort."[51] This requirement of strength and staying power was a key element of stability in the system.

The practical difficulties involved in third-party campaigns also meant that it would not be easy for movements to create powerful parties. Rather than simply taking over an existing organization, they had to build their own. In the case of the Populists, they had a ready-made organizational base in the Alliance, but even so, they faced great difficulty. The new party also had to compete against major party managers "whose business for a quarter of a century had been to study and to practice the rules of the game of politics."[52] The major parties were liable to use their institutional control of government to cheat third parties out of electoral success.[53] Party loyalties were hard to shake, especially (but not exclusively) in the South. And third parties, while easier to form than they are now (since strict ballot access requirements had not yet been mandated), still faced the difficulties inherent in our electoral system. Thus, movements could not hope to gain influence through the third-party route unless they possessed an enormous reservoir of support.

Finally, because fusion (or the even more mild "pulling") rather than immediate and direct takeover was the most important form of access, another stabilizing feature was added. Reliance on fusion by movement third parties carried with it the risk, borne out in the case of the Greenbackers, that their organizational integrity would ultimately be subsumed by a major party without compensating gains. The Populists managed to avoid this fate: they were subsumed, but only in exchange for a heavy influence in the dominant party. The difference between the two examples lies in the greater strength and viability of the Populists due to the maturation of the movement. Even when movements could force a major party in their direction, they could seldom force it all the way to their position. The major party still maintained a great deal of discretion regarding which movement positions to copy, which to modify, and which to ignore. The Democrats of 1896, as thoroughly influenced by the Populists as any major party by any third party in the long span of the convention system, agreed to free silver, railroad regulation, and a prolabor stance, but not to the "subtreasuries" or government ownership of the railroads. The mixing of two distinct entities inevitably produced a great deal of compromise, in contrast to access to the nomination process itself, which might more likely lead to total capture of the party by a movement.

The Prohibition Movement

The prohibition movement, while much weaker than its populist counterpart, illuminates many of the same points. An antialcohol movement was already evident in parts of the country in the 1850s; it was closely tied to the abolition movement and a host of humanitarian reform issues, and assisted in the formation of the Republican Party.[54] It had some success in the states at that time, and temperance advocates hoped (or even assumed) that the alcohol issue would be the next order of business on the Republican agenda after the Civil War. However, these hopes were disappointed.[55]

A debate ensued in the prohibition movement, as it had in the Alliance, about whether to continue trying to work within the parties or to form a third party. At first, both strategies were tried. A Prohibition Party was created in 1869, running its first presidential ticket in 1872. In the meantime, efforts to infiltrate the major parties (particularly the Republicans) continued until well into the 1880s, but met with minimal success:

> Temperance advocates set out in the 1880s to capture the Republican Party by packing township and precinct conventions. They succeeded in several states, causing disastrous defeats for the GOP. Republican professionals did battle with the prohibitionists at the local level, expelling them from power and withdrawing the party's support for prohibition.[56]

By 1885, longtime prohibition organizer Neal Dow, who had continued to hope for a change in the Republican Party even while running for president on the Prohibition ticket, had given up on the GOP, saying, "They have spit in our faces and kicked us out. I, for one, am out."[57]

This failure to penetrate regular control of a major party led to redoubled efforts for the third party. Like the Populists, that third party often sought success by fusion at the local level, though this brought few victories. Like the Populists, the Prohibition Party faced electoral fraud at the hands of the major parties.[58] And at the presidential level, the party never grew strong enough to force either major party far in its direction.[59] Only once did the Prohibition Party possibly affect a presidential election: in 1884, the Prohibition ticket won 25,016 votes in the decisive state of New York, where Blaine lost to Cleveland by 1,047. The high point of Prohibition electoral strength came in 1892, with 2.2 percent of the vote nationwide. The 1892 election was also noteworthy because the Prohibition platform veered substantially toward populism, indicating that powerful movement third parties could draw in their direction not only the major parties but also third parties weaker than themselves.[60]

After 1892, the Prohibitionist Party steadily lost what electoral strength it had had. In 1896, it too was riven by the great currency question, and "silver Prohibitionists" ran their own ticket when the national party refused to endorse free silver.[61] Factionalism of another sort also consumed the party from that point on, in the debate between those who believed the party must concentrate on the liquor question to the exclusion of almost all else (the "narrow-gauge" faction) and those who believed it must promote a wider reform program (the "broad-gauge" faction).[62] Thus the Prohibition Party, like the Populists, fragmented under the strains on third-party efforts inherent in the American electoral system.

Consistent failure in electoral politics led to a new strategy not seen in the case of the populists, possibly because it had not been necessary. While the Prohibition Party continued to nominate national candidates (and indeed still does), the focus of the prohibition movement shifted to intense nonelectoral lobbying efforts. The Women's Christian Temperance Union and the Anti-Saloon League, elements of the prohibition movement but independent of the party, were crucial in achieving passage of the Eighteenth Amendment. The Anti-Saloon League in particular—not the party—is given credit by most historians for the victory of prohibition.[63] These organizations were pressure groups that "allowed active Democrats and Republicans to remain in their own parties while working for prohibition."[64]

Only in this final development did the prohibition movement depart significantly from the pattern shown in the populist case. The prohibition movement's manifest electoral weakness in comparison to the populists is evident in its performance at each stage of the process: its infiltration efforts fell well short of the Alliance's, its lack of electoral strength made fusion less desirable and mimicry less necessary for each of the major parties, and its outlet to greater influence lay not through amalgamation with a major party but through abandonment of the electoral approach. Nevertheless, the same pattern—and what that pattern says about stability and openness in the convention system—can be seen.[65]

Clearly, a fluid electoral system—in which third-party activity was relatively easy, cross-filing was allowed for fusion, and political leaders could drift in and out of the major parties—was a key complement to the convention system itself. In virtually no case did the route to success lie in takeovers at the caucus level. In the case of the populists, it came through forming a third party, winning enough votes to frighten the major party organizations into making programmatic changes, and persuading that newly friendly organization to voluntarily open the doors of the party to the movement. This process was facilitated when those opposing the organization's shift fled from the scene, as did the gold Democrats. The closed nominating system made this strategy necessary; the open electoral system made it possible. In the case of the prohibition movement, success lay in exiting the electoral (though not political) arena completely.

The Progressives and the Transformation of the Convention System

Understanding from experience the barriers to influence on nominations from even the most broad-based and powerful of popular movements, the populists promoted numerous reforms such as the direct election of presidents, senators, and judges; the initiative, referendum, and recall systems; term limits; proportional representation; and, increasingly, the direct primary. A key tenet of populist doctrine was direct democracy; "the people, not the plutocrats, must control the government."[66] To the populists, these proposals "had the net effect of serving two ends: First, a democratic system of government wherein every man had an equal voice with every other man, was instituted; and second, the Government was strengthened and rendered fit to perform the great services demanded of it by the Populist program."[67]

This program of institutional reform, like reforms to come, emphasized the principle of openness and defined it in such a way as to include a bias for change—specifically, the type of change favored by the program's authors. It was not long before the progressives picked up the banner of openness and carried it to victories their predecessors could have only imagined.

The progressive movement brought together several previous strands of reform: some elements of populist thought, especially regarding antitrust and economic regulation; urban-based political reform like that represented by the liberal Republicans (or "mugwumps"); civil service reform; "muckraking" journalism; "Social Christianity"; and social reforms for the largely immigrant urban populations.[68] Furthermore, the movement infiltrated both major parties with approximately equal success and at approximately the same time, obviating the need for a separate organization except sporadically. Indeed, both parties split into "progressive" and "stand pat" wings, a split that in the opinion of many observers was a more substantive division than the merely "traditional and historical" division between the parties.[69]

The Republican Party was the first to respond, with the return of many western Populists and of the mugwumps, who had fled the soft-money policies of Bryan. Within the Democratic Party were the dominant Bryanites and former Populists, and the Cleveland Democrats, who had also been proreform in many respects; once the divisive silver issue died away, the two reform wings cooperated to help the progressives. The progressives, with supporters in each party, successfully played one party off against the other to move both in their direction.[70]

The progressive program consisted of a combination of procedural and substantive proposals amounting to a "war against privilege and bosses."[71] In short, the progressives promised a fight for direct democracy against what they called the "invisible government," and for the use of the positive powers of government to remedy social ills.[72] The progressive movement was also the driving force behind the introduction of direct primaries and the end of the pure convention system.

The progressive movement proceeded in fairly discernible stages and, while not possessing an organizational structure like the Alliances, did clearly proceed from the bottom up. In the view of Richard Hofstadter and others, the progressive movement was first noticeable in cities as early as the 1890s.[73] Numerous mayors in both parties became early figures in the movement.[74] When progressive mayors met with labor representatives at the National Social and Political Conference in Buffalo in 1899, their call for democracy, redistributive taxation, and control of monopolies "formed the very heart of progressivism" for the next two decades.[75]

Next, at the state level, progressive governors of both parties like Robert La Follette of Wisconsin, Albert Cummins of Iowa, Joseph Folk of Missouri, and Hazel Pingree of Michigan were elected, and implemented large parts of the progressive program. At both the state and local levels, progressive candidates and officeholders clearly benefited from grassroots support marshaled through progressive influence on the Chautauqua clubs, especially in the West.[76]

In turn, the progressives—believing that important problems lay beyond the reach of the states—focused attention on the national level. Theodore Roosevelt's presidency of 1901–1909 was the first taste of national success for the progressives (though Roosevelt was considered an untrustworthy late-comer by some progressives), and his triumphs were largely "due to the pre-liminary work which had been done in the different states."[77] In the meantime, Bryan returned to dominance in the Democratic Party in 1908, on a platform more radical than ever.

By 1912, the forces of progressivism were prepared to make an all-out assault on the major parties. In the Republican Party, sentiment had turned against Roosevelt's handpicked successor, William Howard Taft; in 1909 La Follette and progressive Republican insurgents formed the "National Pro-gressive Republican League." In 1910, thirty-five Democratic progressives had followed suit by forming the "Democratic Federation" with the intent of taking over their party. Progressives in both parties reached a tacit agreement. They would both run a progressive candidate: if they both lost, they would join to form a third party; if they both won, they would stay in their respec-tive parties; and if only one won, the other would bolt to support him.[78]

Democratic progressives coalesced around Woodrow Wilson, while La Follette began a campaign in 1911. Roosevelt, however, returned from a trip to Africa to find Taft vulnerable. His own ambitions were reactivated, and his dislike for La Follette (whom he considered too radical) led him to enter the fray. The Roosevelt–La Follette rivalry bitterly divided the progressive Republicans, though Roosevelt was clearly the more popular nationwide and ultimately became the progressive standard-bearer.[79]

Intertwined with this struggle for party control was the progressive attempt to reform the nominating system, which bore considerable fruit. The presidential nominating system, like the presidency itself, was the great prize. The first presidential primaries were held in 1912 in fourteen states with 40 percent of the delegates. Indeed, many progressive Republican states had passed primary laws precisely as a means of defeating Taft.[80] They almost achieved their purpose. In the states with primaries, Roosevelt won 278 dele-gates, La Follette won 36, and Taft won 48. Only Taft's dominance in the nonprimary states and a well-organized credentials "steamroller" secured his renomination at the national convention.[81] To progressives it seemed as though "before our eyes a nomination was being stolen by gross fraud in brazen defiance of the desire of the mass of the Republican voters throughout the country."[82] Thus rebuffed, Roosevelt and his supporters bolted to form the "Progressive" (or "Bull Moose") Party.

Of course, this "Progressive Party" was truly representative of only the

Republican progressives. In the Democratic Party, the progressives had no need to bolt, having prevailed with Woodrow Wilson, who won the nomination with important help from Bryan. In the general election, Wilson won in a landslide. Roosevelt finished second with 27 percent and eighty-eight electoral votes, and Taft won only 23 percent and eight electoral votes.

This crushing defeat for the "stand pat" Republicans produced a Republican move toward progressivism in much the same way that the elections of 1894 had propelled the Democrats in the direction of populism. In 1916, progressive Charles Evans Hughes won the Republican nomination, ironically without entering any primaries at all. The GOP was, in sum, "chastened by defeat, and forced to recognize the present political tendencies."[83] The Progressive Party, weakened considerably by heavy losses in the 1914 elections, attempted to nominate Roosevelt again, but he declined the nomination. A few die-hard progressives remained independent, and participated in later third-party efforts, but most returned to the Republican Party.[84]

For his part, Wilson secured passage of substantial progressive legislation. He failed, however, to completely transform the presidential nominating system as he had desired; his proposal for a national presidential primary died, and even the growth of state presidential primaries lost momentum by 1920. Wilson had foreseen a plebiscitary system in which individual leaders would fill the role of the parties, and the presidency would be energized by its fully popular grounding. This system, in his view, would provide greater capacity for change.[85] Instead, the "mixed" system evolved when the reform impulse died before the reform itself was completed.

With the entry of the United States into World War I, the progressive movement underwent a transformation. While its fundamental principles and many of its leaders (notably La Follette) remained the same, the composition of its support began to change. Under the pressures of the war and its economic aftermath of inflation, unemployment, and falling crop prices, farmers and labor became more important segments of the progressive coalition.[86]

One new element in the coalition was the Nonpartisan League, a farmers' organization in the populist tradition started in North Dakota in 1915 to promote state ownership of grain elevators and other agricultural facilities. The league had 230,000 members in thirteen western states by 1920, and dedicated itself to achieving political success by controlling the caucuses and primaries of both parties rather than through third-party action. In North Dakota, the league succeeded in 1916 in gaining control of the Republican machinery and winning the governorship and state House.

National headquarters were established in 1917 in Minnesota, which provided another bastion of Nonpartisan League strength; in 1918, the league failed in gubernatorial elections there but won almost half of the state legislature. Lesser successes were also recorded in other states. However, success in North Dakota was overturned when conservative Republicans regained control of the legislature in 1920 and won a recall election against the governor in 1921. In Montana and Colorado, Republicans and Democrats joined forces to defeat league candidates who had taken over one or the other organization, and some states eliminated their primaries. The league suffered loss of membership and organizational vitality after 1920, but served as one of the pillars of the 1924 Progressive Party.[87]

That third-party effort was led by La Follette, and was the first formal alliance of labor with farmers and Socialists. Along with the Nonpartisan League, which had already been working with La Follette for years to reinforce the progressive position in Wisconsin, the backbone of the 1924 party consisted of railroad unions, the Socialist Party, and the so-called Committee of Forty Eight, comprised of former Bull Moose backers who had not surrendered the idea of an independent party after 1916. These groups had come together in 1922 to form the Conference for Progressive Political Action.

The 1924 Progressive Party was occasioned by the apparent failure of the major parties to adhere to progressivism after the war. Like earlier third parties, the 1924 Progressives faced intimidation, organizational hurdles, lack of money, and legal barriers. They also faced new ballot access restrictions; indeed, one scholar has written that state election laws were in 1924 "an almost insuperable obstacle to a new party."[88] Initial ballot access laws, justified by introduction of the Australian ballot, contained low petition requirements and late filing deadlines in a simple effort to ensure "expedient and honest elections—nothing more, nothing less."[89] By the time La Follette ran, high petition requirements and very early filing deadlines were the norm, thus giving legal sanction to a party "duopoly."[90] In the end, La Follette won 17 percent of the vote and Wisconsin's thirteen electoral votes. This was the last effort of the progressive movement to operate outside the boundaries of the major parties, and within a decade it was largely subsumed in the New Deal coalition.

The progressive movement had succeeded in transforming the presidential nominating system (as well as lower-level nominations) in the name of openness through the direct primary. Indeed, it seemed at times as if the achievement of greater direct democracy was their first objective: "If big business was the ultimate enemy of the Progressive, his proximate enemy was the political machine."[91] Social change and political openness were thus inextricably linked in the view of most progressives.[92] Social and economic change did in fact occur, and at least some progressive triumphs must be credited to the new manner of nomination. Furthermore, in many ways their electoral reforms did advance the cause of movements generally. Presidential primaries provided an important outlet for the progressives in the race against Taft—his control of the convention states was nearly complete—and in some states observers noted that "the absence of a presidential primary favored the success of the standpatters."[93] The Nonpartisan League used primaries to good advantage between 1916 and 1920. Moreover, the very issue of primaries (and other devices of direct democracy) became an important progressive weapon in the fight against the party regulars.

Finally, if the experience of the progressives is any guide, the introduction of primaries may have disproportionately aided movements in the majority party. In previous cases, the minority party seemed consistently more vulnerable to movement takeover either in caucuses or through fusion. Such takeovers were universally stymied by the majority party, which was better organized and had greater patronage at its disposal. While on balance movement access remained easier in the minority than majority party, the capacity of movements to operate in the majority party seems to have improved. The progressives still gained control of the Democratic (minority) Party in 1912, when they were shut out of the Republican (majority) Party, but Roosevelt fared better than he would have without primaries. Local examples also provide evidence for this proposition, since the Nonpartisan League temporarily took over the Republican Party in North Dakota and Colorado and the Democratic Party in Montana, all of them local majority parties.

The irony, of course, was that progressives had to gain power through the convention system before they could change it, and one might be tempted to ask why, after having gained power, they considered the change necessary. The dominant strain in progressive thought apparently believed that destruction of the party machinery was the only "permanent cure."[94] Progressives had observed (and some of them had participated in) the temporary rise of movements within major parties, such as the Alliancemen in the South or the Anti-Monopoly Party in Iowa. In these unusual cases, it was not long before the party regulars either co-opted the movement or drove it out. The progressives feared that, without structural change, they might, in time, also be overwhelmed by the superior power of the party organizations. They believed the direct primary offered a way to solidify their position by eliminating the power of the party organizations permanently. Furthermore, the primary promised great gains in areas where the organizations still dominated. Interest and principle coincided.

Nevertheless, there is ample evidence that the contribution of primaries to the nominating system was complex, and that while movements may have been helped by the introduction of some primaries, they were also helped rather than hindered by the progressives' failure to achieve full adoption of their program in the national primary. First, it must be repeated that the progressives frequently used caucuses and other mechanisms of so-called boss control to gain and hold power. The first stirrings of the movement in the cities brought success to progressive mayors who had to win nomination and election without primaries. Governors such as La Follette who introduced primary legislation had already gained their offices through conventions, though sometimes after multiple attempts. Hughes won the Republican nomination in 1916 while entering no primaries at all. And the Nonpartisan League, while emphasizing primaries, gained great victories in the North Dakota caucuses as well, victories that gave it control of the party machinery.[95]

Thus, there were already indications that the old system had contained elements that movements might find useful or even necessary, along with elements that hindered them. That possibility was foreseen by Democratic Alliance governor Ben Tillman of South Carolina, who had agitated for the direct primary until discovering that the convention system was well suited to long-term Alliance control.[96] That likelihood may also have been heightened by the legal reforms of caucus procedures, which, for example, established rules for advance notice, party membership, and vote counting. Although the organization still retained a dominant role in caucuses, the potential for abuse had been reduced in many states and the ability of a well-organized movement to infiltrate the party directly had presumably increased. Some evidence for this possibility can be seen in the fact that it was in the South—where caucus regulation lagged—that the Populists were most fully shut out of the Democratic Party after 1892, and that Taft found the strength that tipped the scales in his favor in 1912.

Just as the old methods could often be turned to progressive advantage, the new methods could and did backfire. While Roosevelt bested Taft in the 1912 Republican primaries, Champ Clark ran neck and neck with Wilson, and some observers even felt he outdid his more progressive rival.[97] The Nonpartisan League was ultimately swept from power through the primaries and, even more ironically, the recall; its control of the party machinery was meaningless in the primaries, and it was thus unable to consolidate its position. In 1924, Calvin Coolidge overwhelmingly won the Republican nomination with a strategy of aggressively confronting opponents in as many primaries as possible; in the end, he crushed California progressive Hiram

Johnson with 68 percent of the nationwide primary vote to Johnson's 29 percent.

The history of progressivism in Wisconsin brings these complexities to light in microcosm. La Follette won nomination in a convention system on his third try. As in past movements under the convention system, the progressives had to show strength and staying power before prevailing, but in 1900, "as support mounted for him and he carried the caucuses and conventions in several key counties, his opponents quit the field."[98] La Follette was renominated by convention twice. His opponents accused him at the 1904 convention of using his control of the state Central Committee to cheat the "stalwarts" out of delegates, of "improperly using the votes of Democrats and Social Democrats to control Republican caucuses," and of arranging convention security so as to physically intimidate the opposition.[99] In the 1904 election—candidates for it had gained nomination through conventions—progressives won a legislative majority for the first time. La Follette had "built and commanded a political machine of unprecedented strength," all before a primary law was passed by the new legislature.[100]

Beginning with the very first primary election in 1906, La Follette experienced a series of political setbacks. His man for governor lost the primary in 1906, as did his man for the Senate in 1908. While winning back some losses in 1910, the progressives lost the gubernatorial primary and legislative dominance in 1914 and 1916, and the crucial Senate primary in 1918. Many defeats were clearly due to progressive factionalism; multiple progressives ran, tearing the movement apart with personal feuds, while the stalwarts concentrated their forces. After rejecting the expedient numerous times as an affront to progressive principles, the progressives finally agreed in 1918 to a preprimary nominating convention.[101] The progressive "anti-boss ideology . . . made it difficult and costly for them to achieve organization and unity."[102] Finally, primaries raised the premium placed on "publicity and promotion in nominating campaigns," and accordingly increased the cost of campaigning and the importance of fund-raising.[103]

Thus, progressivism made great strides in Wisconsin with La Follette as an "extremely astute machine-master," a record copied elsewhere by Hiram Johnson and later by Fiorella LaGuardia,[104] but faltered not least because the primary resulted in the fracturing of its coalition, the gutting of its machinery, and the elevating of the importance of campaign finances.

The relation of the new system to the old was thus not as simple as one might first believe based on the claims of enhanced openness made by the progressives. In the view of Hofstadter, the progressives would have had (and indeed, as he did not point out, largely did have) essentially the same results in the old system as in the new.[105] The old system, while surely more closed than its successor, was not as closed as its critics claimed, especially if one takes into account the ability of strong third parties to influence or fuse with the major parties. It even proved hospitable to the early progressives. And the new system was not as open as its proponents claimed, since primaries could clearly work against movements in both the short and long term, and could not prevent movements like the progressives from being forced into third-party activity on occasion just as they had been before the advent of primaries.[106] At the same time, primaries at the local level seemed to encourage demagoguery and personalism, and gave greater access to extremist organizations like the Nonpartisan League,[107] even though they might just as easily have been defeated in the next primary election. It also seems probable that the majority (and generally governing) party was somewhat more susceptible than it had been to movement disruption. A cost in stability was clearly exacted.

In addition, the broader electoral system had been largely closed to movements insofar as third-party activity was much more difficult, as La Follette discovered to his dismay in 1924. As mentioned, this was partly the result of new ballot access laws and restrictions on cross-filing. It was arguably also the result of the growth of primaries themselves, which tended to bestow state legitimacy on the two major parties and to take the nominating power out of the hands of party leaders who could make deals with third parties when necessity dictated.[108] From this point on, movements would have to contend in a nominating system that was somewhat more open but an electoral system that was much more closed.

Needless to say, this closing of the electoral system increased the importance of openness in nominations and drove outsiders to compete wholly within the major parties. The progressive performance in primaries, and their difficulty in consolidating even those gains they made, provided an early indication that the "mixed" nominating system that emerged would be more favorable not only to stability but perhaps also to openness than would have been the case had the reform impulse carried itself to completion in a national primary. This is a conclusion that can only be explored in greater depth by examining the only full-scale movement to take over a major political party in the "mixed system," the conservatives of 1964.

3

The Conservative Movement
and the Mixed System

I N THE SUMMER OF 1964, SOMETHING HAPPENED
that responsible pundits had thought improbable, if not impossible: a
Republican Party controlled at the presidential level for a quarter-century
by its eastern, more liberal, wing, nominated unabashed conservative Senator Barry M. Goldwater of Arizona for president of the United States.
Goldwater's success was the culmination of an intense organizational effort
spanning two and a half years and of the decade-long growth of the conservative movement itself, both of which had gone largely unnoticed until the Arizona senator's nomination was a near certainty. To Aaron Wildavsky, Goldwater's intraparty victory was a "great mystery"; to Gerald Pomper, an
"earthquake."[1]

How was this victory possible? This is a question of great importance
when assessing not only the mixed system but the reforms that followed it.
Popular movements of the sort backing Goldwater had only rarely succeeded
in so thoroughly capturing a major party. Moreover, the so-called mixed nominating system—mixed between party insider control and direct democratic
influences—under which the campaign of 1964 was fought was later excoriated on the grounds that it provided a major check on such movements.

Under the mixed system, about one-third of the states, usually choosing
about one-third to two-fifths of the delegates, held primaries. The remaining

states chose delegates without a primary, most often by state and local conventions, but sometimes by closed conventions or even party central committee appointment. Furthermore, the plebiscitary impact of the primaries was diluted, though the primaries were important as measures of vote-winning ability and legitimacy.

The reforms were later designed to remove the checks inherent in the mixed system, in place of which "openness" and "participation" were to be the watchwords. The Goldwater nomination muddies these waters, by opening up questions of whether the mixed system was more permeable than has been generally acknowledged and whether later reforms were actually necessary to ensure openness to movements.

The Split Republicans: 1912–1964

Prior to the 1964 nomination campaign, the Republican Party had been the victim of recurrent internecine warfare between its conservative and liberal (also called "progressive," or by the 1950s, "moderate") wings. This split could be traced back to the Taft-Roosevelt split of 1912, when Theodore Roosevelt and his "progressive" backers bolted the Republican Party and ran their third-party campaign.[2]

The split was largely submerged until the 1930s, when the New Deal brought the fissure to the surface again. From 1936 on, the Republican Party was divided between those who resisted the onslaught of the welfare state and those who believed that the only route to Republican survival lay in accommodating it. There was, additionally, a division along isolationist-internationalist lines that largely mirrored the economic division, though this division was blurred after World War II; with the onset of the Cold War, conservatism as represented by Barry Goldwater and Ronald Reagan became staunchly anti-isolationist.[3]

In every contested presidential nominating convention from 1936 to 1960, the liberal wing of the party prevailed, backed by eastern financial power; no candidate who did not meet its approval gained the nomination. Theodore White later remarked that both Thomas Dewey in 1948 and Dwight Eisenhower in 1952 had been "thrust . . . down the throat of hostile Republican conventions."[4] By the end of Eisenhower's presidency, conservative Republicans were in full-scale revolt.

Richard Nixon, who was running as an Eisenhower "modern Republican" in 1960, attempted to placate the dissatisfied conservatives primarily through an assurance to key conservative Republican leaders that he would make no deals with New York governor Nelson A. Rockefeller, who was also seeking the nomination. By the summer of 1960, Rockefeller was out of the running but threatened to refuse his support to Nixon in the fall if his views were not adequately respected. Nixon met with Rockefeller only hours before the convention opened in Chicago (and after the platform had already been drafted), and conceded most of Rockefeller's fourteen platform demands.

Conservatives were enraged by this apparent double cross.[5] A spontaneous movement of delegates and party leaders (especially from the South) sought to nominate Goldwater, who had become the primary national conservative spokesman in eight years as a United States senator. He declined, but addressed the convention as he withdrew from consideration. Goldwater stressed party unity and moved to make Nixon's nomination by acclamation, but also said: "Conservatives, grow up. . . . If we want to take this party back, and I think we can, let's get to work."[6] His address touched off a large demonstration by delegates who felt that they had been betrayed not only in 1960, but for a quarter-century. This demonstration is widely considered the opening shot of the conservative takeover of the Republican Party in 1964.[7]

The Growth of the Conservative Movement

The previous decade had seen the birth and steady expansion of the conservative movement, largely outside the Republican Party. By the mid-1950s, opposition to New Deal liberalism began to coalesce at both the intellectual and popular levels.

There were numerous manifestations of this nascent movement, including the 1953 creation of the Intercollegiate Society of Individualists (changed in 1957 to the Intercollegiate Studies Institute) as a nationwide university organization devoted to disseminating conservative ideas, and the 1955 founding of *National Review*, which soon became the rallying point for varying shades of conservative opinion. *National Review* served as a vehicle for uniting seemingly disparate factions: anticommunists like Whittaker Chambers, classical economic "liberals," and social traditionalists. Thus, beyond intellectually legitimizing the conservative point of view, the magazine served increasingly as an instrument for building a broad conservative coalition.

At the popular level, Young Americans for Freedom was founded in late 1960. YAF would ultimately become the foundation for the Youth for Goldwater organization. And in 1962, the Conservative Party of New York was formed in an effort to force the liberal New York Republican Party to the right.[8]

Thus, a conservative organizational structure—intellectual leadership, the power of the written word, and a committed foot army—was constructed entirely outside the Republican Party. It was not unitary—postwar conservatism was a "series of movements rather than the orderly unfolding of a single force"[9]—but it was coalescing and becoming stronger. As a result, conservative forces within the party itself gained ground.

Despite Eisenhower's proclamation of "modern Republicanism," conservatives continued to firmly control the Republican congressional contingent throughout the Eisenhower years, a position that was only strengthened when John F. Kennedy assumed office.[10] By January 1959, the Republican National Committee was in conservative hands and actually "vented their frustration over the direction of the Republican Party under Ike."[11] Conservatives also gained control of the Young Republicans (1957), the college branch of the YRs (1961), and the National Federation of Republican Women (1962).

Prior to 1964, the Republican Party had been engaged for more than four decades in a "civil war" that was "one of the most fascinating stories of Western Civilization."[12] It was fascinating partly because of the high stakes involved for the party, yet also because the forces arrayed against one another were of "about equal importance" and of roughly equal strength.[13] The liberals had controlled presidential nominations since 1936, with the help of the governors, and the conservatives had controlled the congressional party. Below this level, "outside of the urban Northeast, [conservatives] either held the upper hand or fought on equal terms for control of GOP state organizations."[14] The battle had been in such equilibrium for so long that few expected the balance would be overturned any time soon. Clinton Rossiter remarked confidently in 1963 that "so long as the tides of politics run as they are running today . . . a man who aspires seriously to the Republican nomination for the Presidency must be (or appear to be) a 'Modern Republican.' "[15]

But circumstances had changed in ways that only became fully evident in 1964. First, the liberal presidential strategy of appealing to the urban northern vote, used by Nixon again in 1960 and urged by the liberal Republican Ripon Society, had failed.[16] Conservatives argued, with greater weight after 1960, that the strategy had not worked in five tries (excluding Eisenhower, whose victories, they argued, were due to his universal appeal as a war hero); it was time for a change. Liberal arguments of "electability" based on the old strategy were discredited.[17]

Second, the Republican governors, a traditional bastion of the party's liberal wing, were reeling. In 1952, when they were instrumental in Eisenhower's decisive credentials victory, there were twenty-five Republican governors. By

1964, that number had fallen to sixteen, and many of these had been elected for the first time in 1962 and thus lacked experience or stature.[18]

Third, the balance of power in the party—as in the nation—was shifting inexorably toward the West and the South. In the words of Theodore White, "As the years wore on, the Easterners were almost unaware of how the country was changing."[19] This shifting of power to the more conservative regions of the country led to a relative strengthening of the party's conservative wing. In short, *National Review* columnist Frank Meyer was led to remark after the 1962 midterm elections, with an eye on 1964, that "the center of gravity of the Republican Party has shifted basically to the right."[20]

Perhaps most important, conservatives were organized and energized outside the party in ways they had never been before. This created the opportunity for an alliance between the party's conservative wing and outside forces who were eager to make the Republican Party an unambiguous vehicle for conservatism. For the first time, goaded by the final indignity of Nixon's "Surrender of Fifth Avenue," "the conservatives no longer appear[ed] content to accept the notion that one of their own must take a back seat to a progressive."[21]

Frank Meyer wrote in the *National Review* a month after Nixon's 1960 defeat:

> Conservatives will have to recognize that they have no stake in the Republican Party as such. Which does not mean any underestimation of the importance to conservatives of a struggle to capture control of the Republican Party. The Republican Party is an existing vehicle of the American political system, which, if captured by conservatives, could sweep into its support Southern conservatives and create a new majority of the South, the Midwest, the Mountain States, the Far West, and some smaller states of the East.[22]

The stage was set for the takeover of 1964.

The 1964 Goldwater Nomination Campaign

On October 8, 1961, a group of twenty-two conservatives from across the country met in Chicago to form the nucleus of what later became the "Draft Goldwater Committee." The leaders of the group were William Rusher, former associate counsel to the Internal Security Subcommittee of the United States Senate, John Ashbrook, Ohio congressman and former YR chairman, and F. Clifton White, academician and experienced political operative.

The group gathered with the intention of forming a nationwide grassroots organization sufficiently strong to ensure the nomination of a conservative at the Republican convention of 1964. The group decided not to support any specific candidate until after the 1962 elections; the primary objective was to turn the Republican Party into a conservative instrument.[23] Rusher, Ashbrook, and White pooled their lists of Republican associates—largely from their YR days—as a first step to organization building. The group also decided that secrecy was crucial for the time being. No one outside the expanding organization would discover its existence until over a year later.

The group met again on December 10. A one-year budget of $65,000 was established, and the United States was divided into nine regions, each with a director. The initial objective was to control the precinct caucuses of 1962–1963, which would later have a major impact on national convention delegate selection in most states. Congressional district organizations would be built from the precinct level up. The next month, an office was rented in Suite 3505 of the Chanin Building at Forty-Second Street and Lexington Avenue in New York City. For the next year, what was known to its members as simply the "Suite 3505 Committee" proceeded to build an organization unparalleled in American politics to that time.

For the next year, efforts were concentrated not only on organizing geographically but also on influencing the Republican auxiliary groups. Senate races in Alabama, South Carolina, and Louisiana in the 1962 midterm elections encouraged those seeking a conservative presidential nominee; the conservative southern strategy looked increasingly feasible.[24] The "Suite 3505 Committee" met in December of 1962 to chart strategy and choose a candidate behind whom to throw its considerable and growing weight. The choice quickly centered on Barry Goldwater. Other names were considered, but held in reserve. It was clear that Goldwater was the optimal choice.

The Arizona senator was by 1962 a political figure of substantial stature both within the Republican Party and outside it. Since his first election in 1952, he had gained a reputation as a—if not the—key spokesman for the conservative position. In 1960, his book *Conscience of a Conservative* was published, and sold 3.5 million copies by 1964. Goldwater had also spent years cultivating Republican activists across America. He served three terms as chairman of the Republican Senatorial Campaign Committee, a job that required him to make literally thousands of speeches to fund-raising dinners and rallies. He was by 1963 the most heavily requested speaker on the Republican banquet circuit. He thus made contacts, built up political IOUs, and gained supporters as no other Republican contender was in a position to do.

Perhaps there could be no greater indication of the degree to which the conservatives had already penetrated the party.

Indeed, although trailing Rockefeller in the Gallup polls, Goldwater was doing well in the surveys that mattered most. In polls he showed a deep appeal to the party faithful; he was far ahead among state and county chairmen and delegates to the 1960 convention, many of whom would be returning in 1964.[25] Goldwater was, according to a 1961 *Time* magazine cover story, "the hottest political figure this side of Jack Kennedy."[26]

These facts made Goldwater the man of the moment. Most of the "Suite 3505 Committee" had preferred him from the beginning; now, the decision was formal. An infiltrator leaked news of the meeting, which exploded into the headlines the next day. The untimely publicity had the effect of forcing the committee to speed up its schedule. Worse than that, Goldwater was infuriated, and spent most of January 1963 informing the committee that he wanted no part of a presidential campaign. It was hardly clear whether the committee would have a candidate.

Facing lack of support from the intended candidate, the committee decided in February 1963 to make one final gamble. A "Draft Goldwater Committee" would be formed in April, with or without Goldwater's permission or support. Texas Republican chairman Peter O'Donnell would be the chairman, on the grounds that Goldwater would find it difficult to harshly repudiate him. The gamble worked; the Draft Goldwater Committee was unveiled, and Goldwater, while not endorsing the effort, did not renounce it.

For the rest of 1963, the committee rode the crest of a growing Goldwater tide. Polls showed Goldwater narrowing the gap with Rockefeller until Rockefeller, who had divorced in 1961, married Margaretta ("Happy") Murphy, a mother of four who had herself divorced only weeks before. Within a month, Goldwater had surged into the lead. Rockefeller's remarriage "had the effect of emancipating those rank-and-file Republicans who had really wanted Goldwater all along," but had previously supported Rockefeller on grounds of electability.[27]

The Draft Committee was on schedule with its organizational plan. An example could be seen in the state of Washington, a convention state where the Republican Party was controlled at the top level by Rockefeller supporters. In June 1963, White found a state organizer—a businessman by the name of Luke Williams from Seattle—and gave him the task of filling Washington's precinct caucuses with solid Goldwater supporters. Of fifty-five hundred precincts, only twenty-five hundred had actually been organized by the party. Williams filled the remainder by the end of the year. Washington sent twenty-four delegates to San Francisco in 1964; twenty-two of them voted for Barry Goldwater. While moderate governor Dan Evans would challenge them, conservatives remained a powerful force in the state party machinery thereafter.[28] This pattern was repeated across the Pacific and Rocky Mountain regions.

The South was a different story, since in many southern states the Republican Party machinery was simply nonexistent. Goldwater organizers in the South had not to take over the party, but literally to create it. To whatever degree organization did exist, at the level of state chairmen, it was already in the hands of Goldwater partisans. It was to Goldwater's manifest advantage to build the party in the South, since not only his nomination but his general election strategy depended heavily on southern votes. Alabama's state Republican chairman John Grenier was made southern regional director. Grenier had overthrown the "patronage oriented incumbent party leadership" in the previous year with the help of the state Young Republicans.[29] By 1964, Grenier had overseen, for example, the organization of sixty-four of Alabama's sixty-seven counties, which produced thirty thousand volunteers in the general election. Grenier was not the only southern state chairman to work officially for Goldwater. Mississippi state chairman Wirt Yerger was his state's Goldwater chairman, and the entire South Carolina state central committee simultaneously reconstituted itself as the state's Draft Goldwater Committee. The Republican Party in the South in 1964 was less the "Republican Party" than the "Goldwater Party."[30]

Finally, in the Midwest, the third pillar of conservative strength, the party was generally strong and well organized. Success required a combination of grassroots organization and heavy negotiation with party leaders, many of whom were leaning toward Goldwater but required greater proof of his electoral appeal.[31]

At a Republican National Committee meeting in late June 1963, the Draft Goldwater representatives were very well received. Rowland Evans and Robert Novak remarked in their next column that "the aggressive post-war club of conservative young Republicans from the small states of the West and South are seizing power, displacing the Eastern party chiefs who have dictated Republican policy and candidates for a generation."[32]

By September, Goldwater—who was not even clearly a candidate yet— was at 56 percent among Republican voters, 71 percent among state chairmen, and 85 percent among county chairmen.[33]

Goldwater was doing well within the party in no small degree because he was shaping up as an increasingly formidable opponent to the president. A Goldwater-Kennedy race would be run on clear liberal vs. conservative lines, a division that would be accentuated by their backgrounds: Kennedy, the wealthy Massachusetts Harvard graduate, against Goldwater, the plain-speaking Arizona populist. The nature of this hypothetical contest also gave greater credibility to proposals for the western and southern strategy, which was formally articulated in William Rusher's *National Review* article, "Crossroads for the GOP," in spring of 1963.[34]

By November 1963, Goldwater had been featured by *Time*, *Newsweek*, and *U.S. News and World Report* as a strong challenger to Kennedy. *Time* reported in a survey of the fifty states that Goldwater seemed ahead in twenty-eight, with Texas a toss-up and two southern states with unpledged electors who would also probably vote for Goldwater; according to *Time*, "Goldwater could give Kennedy a breathlessly close contest."[35] Goldwater was already at 44 percent in a head-to-head race, according to a poll taken in October 1963, and he actually led Kennedy in the South 54 to 34 percent.[36] In fact, "In Texas and other Southern and Southwestern states during 1963, [Clif] White had the unprecedented experience of seeing entire Democratic county committees stage 'resignation rallies' and join the Republican Party en masse to work for Goldwater."[37]

Kennedy's assassination in November 1963 suddenly changed the entire political landscape. Goldwater's recently kindled enthusiasm for the race ended, and he informed his wife Peggy at the beginning of December that he had decided against running.[38] His status as front-runner within the party also collapsed in the face of Kennedy's assassination. Many Republicans believed that Lyndon Johnson negated the most attractive aspects of a Goldwater candidacy. The new president was also from a southwestern state—with five times Arizona's electoral votes. He could not easily be targeted as a big-city liberal. He, too, came from a modest background, and had no Ivy League cast to him. In short, Johnson would so muddy the lines of demarcation necessary for Goldwater's success that victory would be impossible.[39]

Nevertheless, Clif White's organization was as strong as before, and still growing. A meeting between a deeply reluctant Goldwater and the Draft Goldwater Committee on December 8 settled the question when Goldwater's supporters convinced him that it was his duty to run.[40] On January 3, 1964, Goldwater officially announced his candidacy at his home near Phoenix. The Draft Goldwater Committee had succeeded in accomplishing what may have been one of the few genuine drafts in American history: "a rare case of spontaneous ideological fervor imposing its energies on a reluctant candidate."[41] The campaign proceeded along the strategic lines White had first laid out two years before. Intense grassroots organization down to the precinct level would continue in all cases. The battle would be won in the convention states, but the mixed system required entry in at least a few contested primaries. The campaign picked New Hampshire, in order to build momentum and because of its reputation for conservatism; Oregon; and California, which was the last primary in the country and gave all eighty-six of its delegates to the victor. Other less seriously contested primaries would also be entered. At this stage, Rockefeller was the only other announced candidate.

From a lead of three to two over Rockefeller in New Hampshire, Goldwater steadily slipped as a result of ill-advised campaign statements on social security and nuclear weapon control in NATO. When the polls closed on March 10, Goldwater finished second—but Rockefeller finished third. The winner was United States ambassador to South Vietnam and 1960 Republican vice presidential candidate Henry Cabot Lodge, who had run a shoestring write-in campaign. The pundits declared Goldwater dead, not realizing that while he had lost fourteen delegates in New Hampshire, he had garnered fifty-four in various state conventions that same week.[42]

Similarly, the Arizona senator quietly picked up hundreds of delegates at state and congressional district conventions around the country over the next three months. The primaries—even the uncontested primaries—got the lion's share of public attention, but the organizational steamroller begun two and a half years before proceeded. Goldwater won 60 percent of the Illinois primary, with write-ins for Maine senator Margaret Chase Smith coming in second. He won the Texas primary with 75 percent of the vote; Rockefeller was put on the ballot by the pro-Goldwater Texas Republican Party against his wishes, and received 5 percent. Goldwater prevailed in Nebraska with 49 percent (write-ins for Nixon were heavy) and most other primary states until Oregon in May.

Where possible, deals were made. Governor James Rhodes of Ohio and Representative John Byrnes of Wisconsin became favorite sons largely at the instigation of the Goldwater campaign, in order to keep other Republicans out of their states. Those delegations were loaded with Goldwater supporters.[43] The campaign worked completely through the regular party in New Jersey, and ended in San Francisco with a surprising twenty of the state's forty votes.

Where necessary, however, the Goldwater organization flexed its muscles. At the Kansas state convention in April, pro-Rockefeller governor John Anderson was defeated in his own campaign for a delegate position, an incident that had the effect of taming anti-Goldwater governors around the country.[44] In Multnomah County, Oregon, the Goldwater precinct organization succeeded in ousting the pro-Rockefeller county leadership, a feat frequently repeated elsewhere.[45]

By the time of the Oregon primary, Goldwater already had 400 solid delegates out of 655 needed, with the probability of as many as 150 more before California. When Goldwater's strategists realized that Rockefeller was prepared to sink vast resources into Oregon to try to revive his campaign, and that the field would be too crowded to permit a clear Goldwater-Rockefeller showdown, the campaign pulled out of active campaigning to concentrate on California. Lodge, still a noncandidate, led for most of the way. However, Rockefeller was the only candidate actively operating in Oregon, and came from behind to win. Lodge withdrew, and the road was open to a showdown in California.

In contrast to the situation in Oregon, Goldwater and Rockefeller had the field to themselves in California. The stakes were high: a Goldwater victory would assure his nomination by winning him eighty-six more delegates and proving his electoral viability to cautious Midwestern party leaders, while a Rockefeller victory seemed the liberals' best (and last) realistic hope of blocking him. Rockefeller started with a lead and was able to pour virtually limitless funds into the race.

Arrayed against the professionalism of the Rockefeller campaign was a massive Goldwater volunteer network. To get on the ballot, candidates had to submit thirteen thousand petition signatures within one month of March 4. It took Rockefeller's professionals all of the month to do it. Goldwater's volunteers had thirty-six thousand signatures by noon on March 4, and eighty-five thousand within two days. Much of the volunteer organization was built around pro-Goldwater Young Republican forces; of ten thousand petition-collecting doorbell ringers in Los Angeles County, eight thousand were YRs, and YR state chairman Robert Gaston was actually placed in charge of Orange, San Bernadino, and Santa Barbara Counties.[46] Three weeks before the primary, eight thousand volunteers canvassed six hundred thousand homes in promising locales, mostly in southern California, and identified three hundred thousand Goldwater supporters.[47] On election day, ninety-five hundred Goldwater volunteers recontacted identified supporters in Los Angeles County alone, ten thousand in the rest of southern California, and five thousand in northern California. Rockefeller's volunteer force numbered two thousand in the entire state of California.[48]

Two days before the primary, "Happy" Rockefeller had a baby, bringing the remarriage issue back into the headlines. Goldwater won pulling away, with 51.4 percent of the vote. The day after the California primary, White counted (but did not admit to) 665 delegates—10 more than needed to nominate. State leaders inclined to support Goldwater but waiting for evidence of his electability joined the bandwagon. It is not clear whether the victory in California was absolutely necessary for Goldwater's nomination—he would still have been well ahead in delegates, perhaps insurmountably so—but it did end all realistic possibility of a successful "stop Goldwater" effort.[49] Goldwater himself felt it was necessary, and was prepared to withdraw if he failed.[50]

The eastern wing of the party desperately sought a way to block Goldwater's nomination. The Republican governors who met at the National Governors' Conference in Cleveland in the first week of June hoped to repeat the performance of 1952, when the Dewey-led governors had united to give momentum to Ike's credentials challenge. Rockefeller was out of the running; Michigan's George Romney considered a run but backed away; William Scranton of Pennsylvania dawdled until deciding to run only a month before the convention. Scranton inherited Rockefeller's staff and resources, and spent over $800,000 in an effort to woo delegates. He visited Illinois, and came away with no delegates to Goldwater's fifty-eight. Elsewhere, he picked up a few, but seldom more than two or three at a time. He could have won every remaining uncommitted delegate, and still lost the nomination. Facing Goldwater's speeding bandwagon, he was far from accomplishing even that. By the opening of the convention, polls showed Scranton ahead of Goldwater in a head-to-head race among Republican voters by margins as great as sixty to thirty-four; Scranton and the eastern party leadership were becoming increasingly strident in its assaults on the Arizona senator; the press was excoriating Goldwater daily. Nevertheless, Goldwater's previous delegate support held, and the Ohio and Wisconsin favorite sons released their delegates to vote for him.

On July 14 at the Cow Palace, Goldwater received 883 votes on the first ballot—only 1 short of White's final delegate prediction—to Scranton's 214. It was the best performance up to that time on the first ballot of a contested Republican convention. Goldwater received 292 of 303 southern votes, and 329 of 390 votes west of the Mississippi River. He thus gained all but 34 of the delegates necessary for nomination from the South and West. His victory was not entirely sectional: New Jersey gave him half its delegation, he won the Midwest, and he was shut out in only three states.

What Theodore White called the "coup d'état" in San Francisco was complete. Furthermore, it would not be reversed. Despite the party's landslide defeat in November, "the liberal wing would not again control the presidential Republican party."[51] The 1964 alliance between the "Taftite Midwest" and the "populist West and South" became a permanent fixture in Republican nominating politics; 1964 was "a decisive stage in the realignment of factional forces within the GOP."[52]

The liberals succeeded in forcing the removal of Goldwater's RNC chairman, Dean Burch of Arizona, in January 1965 but were unable to obtain a liberal replacement. The RNC itself remained in conservative hands.[53] Furthermore, the party at large remained conservative at the grassroots level. Goldwater as a candidate—or the caricature of Goldwater portrayed by both his Republican opponents and Lyndon Johnson—had frightened many Republican voters. Even after his electoral destruction, however, 65 percent of Republican voters were willing to call themselves "conservatives" to only 14 percent "liberal" and 21 percent "moderate."[54] Conservatism was undoubtedly even stronger among party activists. It was a common mistake by commentators both before and immediately after the election to conflate Goldwater and the conservative movement, and to assume that the defeat of the first would mean the extinction of the second. William Rusher was closer to the truth when he said: "There was a substratum of truth to Goldwater's resentful feeling that he had, in a way, been *used* by the conservative movement."[55]

Goldwater's campaign and the conservative movement had in fact used each other. By November 1964, 3.9 million Americans had volunteered for Goldwater—1.4 million more than had volunteered for Johnson, and far more than had ever volunteered for a Republican presidential candidate before.[56] Furthermore, Goldwater raised a record amount of money from small contributors. Although the RNC had begun a small-donor direct mail program in 1962, it was Goldwater's campaign that first used the technique on a massive—and massively successful—basis.[57] The Goldwater volunteer and contributor lists served as the basis for the explosion of conservative organizing in the 1960s and 1970s. And the grassroots activists who took over much of the Republican Party at the precinct level in 1964 did not simply drop out of politics. This had been Goldwater's objective from the beginning, to "remake" the face of Republicanism. In his words, "We'd lose the election but win the party."[58]

After the defeat of 1964, a reformulated conservatism emerged that avoided frontal assault on the New Deal, and whose chief spokesman (Ronald Reagan) possessed "all the Goldwater virtues with none of his flaws."[59] The Republicans gained forty-seven House seats and eight governorships in the next midterm election. Those gains, while widely distributed among the party's factions, came primarily as a result of popular disaffection with Lyndon Johnson and implicitly vindicated at least portions of Goldwater's 1964 campaign. Polls even at the time of Goldwater's candidacy had indicated wide popular support for many of his positions, and party candidates in 1966 rode to victory on many of the same positions.[60]

In 1968, conservative dominance of the party was reconfirmed. The 400,000-member YRs backed Ronald Reagan, the 500,000-member National Federation of Republican Women remained in conservative hands, and even the Republican Governors' Conference—once the liberal bastion—elected Reagan as its chairman. Nixon won the nomination with a clearly right-of-center campaign. This time, in order to secure his victory, he had to make deals not with Nelson Rockefeller but with Barry Goldwater, Strom Thurmond, and John Tower, who held virtual veto power over his vice presidential choice and kept the southern delegates in line. He still had only twenty-five votes to spare, and it is likely that only Thurmond's loyalty to Nixon prevented Reagan from gaining enough southern support to stop Nixon on the first ballot.[61]

Nixon's fall victory was won with a modified version of Goldwater's 1964 Sunbelt strategy, which became codified in Kevin Phillips's 1969 book *The Emerging Republican Majority*.[62] Nixon thus won the presidency in 1968 largely with Goldwater's people, Goldwater's delegates, and Goldwater's strategy.[63] In short, the campaign of 1968 "demonstrated the utter failure of the Republican liberals' efforts to recapture control of the party."[64] Nixon's 1968 victory in fact accelerated the process: the breakup of the New Deal coalition evident in 1968 had "totally undermined the traditional liberal Republican argument that the GOP could only succeed electorally by submerging its policy differences with the Democrats."[65]

By 1980, "time had erased the old hatreds among Republicans. For the most part, the Republican Party, as Goldwater and Taft had meant it to be, was the party of the conservatives."[66] It was a sign of the conservative victory that Barry Goldwater defiantly repeated at the 1984 Republican National Convention the line that had so thoroughly enraged the Rockefeller wing of the party twenty years earlier—"extremism in the defense of liberty is no vice; moderation in the pursuit of justice is no virtue"—and received a triumphant, almost universal, ovation.

Movements and the Mixed System

Goldwater's 1964 victory and the ascent of the Republican conservatives took place in "an unreformed party. . . . The success of the insurgency . . . was not achieved through the transformation of a closed-party delegate-selection process but through use of that process for its own ends."[67] This takeover occurred not in spite of, but in large part because of, the nature of the mixed system. The system worked to the benefit of the conservative movement largely because the movement was not simply an outside movement but rather an alliance between an outside movement and an already strong faction within the party—the sort of sympathetic institutionalized group whose support movements often require. The system had a bias in favor of organization, but the movement was strong enough organizationally to compete with the party on its own terms.

Perhaps most important, Goldwater did substantially better in the convention states than in the primary states by virtually any measurement. He won 73 percent of the delegates in the caucus/convention states, and had a plurality of delegates in twenty-six of those thirty-five states (or 74 percent). Goldwater gained only 62.6 percent of delegates from primary states and, while far outdistancing his nearest rival, won only 38 percent of the popular vote in the primaries. He won delegate pluralities in only 61 percent of primary states (eleven of eighteen) and popular vote pluralities in only 39 percent (seven of eighteen). Observers consistently noted Goldwater's relative weakness in the primary states.[68] Furthermore, his most notable setbacks were the result of primary defeats in New Hampshire and Oregon.

There is a logic to the better performance of movements in convention states; Paul David noted before Goldwater's nomination that primaries could have the effect of closing out "activists with a concern for public policy," and that, therefore, properly structured caucuses could serve the cause of party change far better.[69] The experience of the progressives had often pointed in this direction, and Goldwater's experience in 1964 confirmed the thesis. The nonprimary states were perfect targets for the long-term strategies of Clif White. Most delegates from these states were chosen in processes that ultimately depended upon the precinct caucuses, a device relatively easy for a determined movement to control, especially in areas with weak party organization.

Furthermore, in contrast to contesting costly primaries, organizing at the precinct level was something that could be done from a distance with minimal resources; indeed, some progressives turned against primaries not long after their adoption precisely because of the importance of money in primary campaigns.[70] The Suite 3505 Committee, with a 1962 budget of sixty-five thousand dollars, an actual income of less than half that, and a full-time staff of two—but with the latent ideological support of tens of thousands of potential activists—was perfectly suited to conduct the sort of grassroots organizing campaign that would bear its greatest fruit in precinct caucuses and subsequent conventions. This was especially important considering the financial resources of Rockefeller, who sank $5 million of his own into the race but had little to show for it because most delegates were chosen by means not susceptible to the effects of heavy campaign spending.

In short, success in the caucuses depended upon organization and intensity, thus playing to the greatest strengths of the movement. The Goldwater campaign "was a mass campaign . . . which made its weight felt not in the public forums of politics but in its back rooms"—the old-fashioned way.[71] For his part, Rockefeller realized what was happening, saying, "I've got to get to the Republicans in the primaries and circumvent the Goldwater people who dominate state and local organizations."[72]

Nevertheless, building from this strong base of convention states, Goldwater did benefit from the California primary: "[Goldwater] needed a spectacular victory against a formidable opponent, such as Rockefeller, in the 'make or break' California primary, to remove doubts from convention delegates that he could win a popular, grass-roots decision when all the chips were on the table. . . . Victory caused a veritable stampede to his side."[73]

California made Goldwater's nomination unstoppable and broke down all remaining barriers except for the very hard core of the party's suddenly beleaguered liberal wing. In this sense, the mixed system was working just as its proponents argued it should: in order to prove his legitimacy and his voter appeal to Midwest party leaders, Goldwater's victory in California was essential. This outcome was made possible by the weak party system promoted by California progressives;[74] while the success of the progressive national primary scheme would almost certainly have hurt Goldwater's cause, California stands as an example of how scattered progressive successes did provide some important outlets to movements.

In many ways the mixed system—given the steadily rising costs of primary campaigning—had found an optimal number and arrangement of primaries. The system required few enough primaries that movements were not automatically blocked due to insufficient funds. However, there were enough primaries that movements still had to demonstrate substantial fund-raising capacity—often, because of their nature as movements, from previously untapped sources of financial power. Accordingly, movements had to develop financial strength without which long-term success within the party could never be attained, regardless of primary outcomes. The Goldwater campaign, for example, had to raise $2 million just for the California primary, but was able to enter few enough primaries that its total preconvention fund-raising of $5.5 million was sufficient.

Above all, the key to Goldwater's survival in the primaries lay in the primary structure dominant in the mixed system. It is important to recall that the plebiscitary impact of the primaries was diluted in the mixed system by a substantial disconnection between primary performance and accumulation of delegates in primary states. This disconnection was the result of two basic mechanisms: plurality elections (rather than proportional representation) and the prevalence of separate delegate elections. Goldwater took full advantage of both.

California's winner-take-all primary, for example, gave him all eighty-six of the state's delegates after he defeated Rockefeller by only three percentage points. In separate delegate selection, Illinois gave Goldwater fifty-six of its fifty-eight delegates, though he had won only three-fifths of the vote in the nonbinding preference survey; similar results were obtained in Nebraska (49 percent of the vote, all sixteen delegates), South Dakota (one-third of the vote, twelve of fourteen delegates), and West Virginia (100 percent vote for Rockefeller, ten of fourteen delegates for Goldwater). Thus, Goldwater was able to use the superior cohesiveness of the movement to win plurality elections and the superior organization of the movement to win separate delegate elections. In the end, he was able to translate 38 percent of the primary vote nationwide into 62 percent of the delegates from primary states.

Three other features of the mixed system seemed to help. First, Goldwater was aided by the traditional discretion of the convention in the mixed system. While his delegates were firmly committed prior to the convention, which was an uncommon situation in pre-1964 convention politics, the convention as a whole clearly operated outside the plebiscitary dictates of the modern system. As noted, Goldwater was behind Scranton by as much as 60 to 34 percent among Republican identifiers, according to a Gallup poll published on the eve of the convention, and barely held his own in a four-man race (Goldwater 22 percent, Nixon 22, Lodge 21, Scranton 20). The convention of 1964, however, operated in a system that acknowledged the legitimacy of indirect procedures even when the result did not necessarily coincide with mass popular opinion, and thus was not constrained by Goldwater's relative lack of support among nonactivists.

Second, the heavy influence exerted by party regulars in the mixed system actually aided Goldwater in many respects. The system required any movement seeking access to already have a substantial base of support among party leaders and workers. This clearly represented a barrier to the entrance of a movement, but the benefits of inside party support could outweigh the costs involved in obtaining it. Under the post-1968 reform system, party leaders may support a candidate but can do much less to help him or her; under the mixed system, those elements of the party disposed to help actually had the power to help. While this assistance under a reformed system might be irrelevant for purposes of the nomination itself, it becomes highly relevant later in two ways. First, even if party help is not necessary for nomination, good relations with the party may be necessary for election. Second, a movement by nature wants not merely the nomination but long-term control of the party, which requires deeper support within the party.

A movement in the mixed system had to reach a minimum threshold of "regular" support to have any hope of succeeding, but it is likely that Goldwater—operating from a position as three-time chairman of the Republican Senatorial Campaign Committee and as the de facto national spokesperson for what was probably the philosophical majority in the party—passed that threshold years before he ran for president. It may be no accident that in some parts of the country Goldwater's success actually coincided with a relative resurgence in 1964 of the state and local party organizations, which Gerald Pomper called "again dominant" after years of decline.[75]

Indeed, the relationship of the conservatives to the party machinery provides several lessons about openness in the mixed system, not the least of which is that movements had to have some party support, but such support could not be procured overnight. It required gradual persuasion through electoral successes or actual replacement of the party structure through penetration. This is why the Suite 3505 Committee had to first organize not for the 1964 delegate caucuses but for the 1962–1963 caucuses that led to the election of party officers. Thus movements had to exhibit staying power and organizational expertise well in advance of the nominating contest itself. If they could pass these tests, they might be rewarded with control of the party itself rather than merely a presidential nomination.

Third, Barry Goldwater was sought out and drafted by the conservative movement. The mixed system, much more than the reform system seems to be, was open to "draft" efforts of this nature.[76] This greater openness can be seen theoretically, since several features of the mixed system seem logically to make drafts more possible, including greater delegate discretion and greater reliance on low-cost caucus organization rather than primaries. It can also be seen empirically, insofar as the once fairly common draft has not occurred in either party in any of the six postreform nomination contests.

The strongest movements can take over a party and hand that party to the candidate of their choice; weaker movements are consigned to wait until an ambitious political figure chooses to take the risk of attempting to harness their energies. By making drafts easier, the mixed system benefited strong movements that would otherwise have had fewer points of entry into the nominating system. The conservative movement could not have succeeded in 1964 had it been unable to focus on Goldwater's nomination campaign, which was dependent, needless to say, on Goldwater's reluctant participation. Only a draft could secure that participation.

A variety of party rules (and even traditions) not essential to the existence of the mixed system also benefited the conservatives. Chief among these were the apportionment formulae governing both the selection of delegates and membership on the Republican National Committee. The Republican National Committee did not actively provide assistance to Goldwater but was sympathetic, and failed to act as it might have as any sort of brake on the conservative takeover. This was largely because the formula for membership "overrepresented small and mainly conservative western states at the expense of the liberal heartland in the metropolitan Northeast."[77] The formula, which has been little changed by the Republicans since 1964, has continually come under fire by the liberal wing of the party.[78] Delegate apportionment was similarly biased, based initially on population but also on the awarding of bonus delegates to states that performed well in recent elections. Overall, the delegate apportionment rules favored small states and conservative states; since the small states were, by and large, also the conservative states, the effect was multiplied. In 1952, southern and western delegates were 38 percent of the total, in 1964 43.4 percent; from 1940 to 1964 northeastern delegate strength fell from 32.2 percent to 26.6 percent.[79] Furthermore, Republican Party rules long favored the selection of large numbers of delegates by congressional district, not subject to instruction by state conventions. This undoubtedly made the takeover easier, since it came from the bottom up and the congressional district convention was closer to the bottom than any level except (and on rare occasion including) the county.[80]

Additionally, the decentralized structure of the party offered multiple points of entry for a movement. Auxiliaries like the National Federation of Republican Women and the Young Republicans provided an alternative route to early penetration of the party apparatus. This was especially true of the YRs, who by nature had a high turnover rate of members and leaders, and were thus more susceptible to rapid change. The YRs were thus doubly attractive as a target: easy to control by a movement that was adequately organized and endowed with a coherent and appealing philosophy, and extraordinarily useful as foot soldiers once captured. Indeed, the Draft Goldwater organizers began their efforts in 1961 by pooling lists of contacts from their YR days. If the center was at first resistant, it was possible within the Republican Party of the early 1960s to begin the enterprise by chipping away at the periphery.

The continuing dominance of the conservatives after 1964 was largely due to external factors such as growing public disillusionment with the Great Society and other liberal programs, evident especially from 1966 on; but the rules clearly worked to further this entrenchment. The RNC remained in conservative hands due in no small part to the apportionment method. Furthermore, because takeover in the mixed system had to occur at the precinct level, it was difficult if not impossible for the liberals—who remained outorganized—to seize control. In many parts of the United States, the Republican Party had been an empty house, and the conservatives had moved in. The takeover was thus far more than the transient exercise that many pundits assumed; it was, in a very real way, the remaking of the Republican Party. Had the liberals possessed the same organizational skills, grassroots enthusiasm, and philosophical appeal, and had they struck first, the conservative drive might have been mitigated. By striking first with these new tactics of organization, and by applying them intelligently to an increasingly favorable environment, conservatives helped ensure their own success for a generation.

Conservative dominance at the precinct level continued to work its way up, finally affecting even the gubernatorial branch of the party. In 1964, only four of the nation's sixteen Republican governors supported Barry Goldwater. By 1968, thirteen out of twenty-five could be counted as conservatives. This deprived the liberal wing of its last reliable bastion. The assault on this bastion was not premeditated or centrally planned. It was the simple, and inevitable, result of the fact that the liberals had "neglected the basic rule of politics, which calls for cultivating the grass roots."[81] When the liberals lost the precinct, they could not long hold on at higher levels.

Finally, the conservatives benefited from an interaction between the electoral strategy they had played the major role in developing, on the one hand, and the RNC and delegate apportionment formulae on the other. The conservative strategy, which proved so eminently viable after 1964, made the South and West the Republican electoral base. This had the effect of vastly increasing the stature of the more conservative elements of the party. Western and southern states exhibited a major increase in their contributions to the RNC, sometimes doubling their nationally mandated fund-raising quotas, while New York and other liberal strongholds showed a marked decline.[82] The strategic shift also had the effect of further increasing southern and western delegate strength at future conventions, a shift that was continually aided by population movement to the Sunbelt.[83] Thus, the strategy formulated by the Goldwater campaign in 1964 had the circular effect of reinforcing conservative dominance of the party at the presidential level. It is little wonder that liberal party leaders attacked the new strategy so vehemently.[84]

The Biases of the Mixed System

It is reasonable to conclude, based on the 1964 nomination campaign of Barry Goldwater, that the mixed system was biased toward particular kinds of outside forces. First, it is clear that Goldwater did not need the support of some elements of the party, and did need the support of others—and that there was a structure to those needs. There are four basic levels of the modern party: first, at the highest level, the elected officials of the party (and, by extension, the resources available to them, such as whatever patronage workers they control); next, the party "regulars," that is, its organizational leaders (e.g., state and county chairmen); third, actual or latent grassroots activists at the precinct level; and last, at the broadest level, its registered voters or voters who identify themselves with the party.

Goldwater needed, and received, the support of the two middle layers, the "regulars" and the "activists." He had long been a favorite of the largely conservative party workers due to his service as chairman of the RSCC and his extensive speaking schedule. He also inspired the growing movement of conservative activists who won the nomination for him at the precinct level. Within the party, at both levels he represented the aspirations of those who had felt betrayed by successive liberal-dominated conventions. Outside the party he represented the aspirations of many citizens who were prepared to involve themselves in politics for the first time. It was the cooperation of these two forces that secured his nomination and that maintained conservative control of the Republican Party after 1964.[85]

Conversely, Goldwater and the conservative movement did not need, and largely did not receive, the support of the highest level or the lowest. The organized resistance to Goldwater's nomination was centered among the Republican governors. The normally conservative congressional wing tended to be supportive, but its influence in presidential nominations was traditionally minimal, and this remained so in 1964.[86]

Similarly, at the opposite end of the scale, the masses of Republican voters never gave Goldwater over 35 percent at any time after John F. Kennedy's assassination.[87] However, such support was not necessary for convention victory. What may have been necessary for the long-term conservative takeover of the party, and was in any case very helpful, was the conservative predisposition of those voters. As noted, a January 1965 poll showed that 65 percent of Republican voters still considered themselves "conservatives." Republican voters also supported some of Goldwater's most controversial positions, such as escalation in Vietnam.[88] If Republicans at large did not flock to Barry Goldwater as a candidate, they hardly rejected the core of his philosophy.

In any case, the mixed system in 1964 did create barriers to movement access insofar as it required significant inside party support. The system also required that the outside movement be well developed before making a serious challenge for power; the conservative movement had percolated for over a decade, growing steadily at the intellectual and popular levels before prevailing in 1964. The system was open enough to permit access once those two conditions were met.

Once it developed such strength, a movement could not be stifled from the top alone. Nor did the system impose the equally stiff obstacle of requiring explicit support from the majority of the party's mass voters—a requirement that could have proven insurmountable. By definition, a "movement" attempts to change the status quo within the party and the nation; it hopes to gain control of the party machinery and use it to alter the nature of the party by catalyzing latent and unformed majorities. The movement's candidates therefore seldom have clear majority support until after the movement actually prevails. Indeed, not only was Goldwater able to win the nomination despite his poor showing in the polls, but more concretely, he was able to use the plurality-based primary system to translate only 38 percent of the primary vote into 62 percent of the delegates from primary states. A system that requires majority support at the level of the mass voter would likely be more closed to movement success than was the mixed system.

Beyond the types of support required ("regular" and "activist") and not required (top and bottom levels), other things can be said about the nature of successful movements under the mixed system. Most important, it is clear that the conservative movement was forced to develop new strategies and engage in active party building in order to achieve victory both in 1964 and after.

The strategic innovations of the conservatives substantially altered the nature of the nominating system without any formal change. The extraordinarily early start, over three years before election day, was unavoidable in the sort of campaign that the conservatives pioneered and that has since become standard. In contrast to past nomination campaigns, Goldwater's forces concentrated not on persuading existing delegates but on obtaining the election of delegates who were already firmly committed and could not be stampeded.

The novelty and effectiveness of this approach was not clear to Goldwater's opponents or to long-time political commentators until well after San Francisco. As Theodore White said in retrospect, "The Republican convention in San Francisco was to mark the end of old-style organizational control of a national convention. Barry Goldwater's managers had locked up state delegation after state delegation before the convention ever gathered."[89] By late 1963, Clif White had already won delegates in forty states.[90]

The predominant use of caucuses and conventions for delegate selection required movements to organize at the precinct level. Thus, in order to win in 1964, the conservatives had to make a major contribution to party organization. This was true in states such as Washington, where the Goldwater forces manned the 55 percent of the state's precincts that had previously stood empty. It was even more true in the South, where the strength of the modern Republican Party is in no small part a product of Goldwater's campaign.

Nor was party building confined to precinct organization. Prior to 1964, the financial power of the nation had been steadily shifting, along with the population, from the East (especially New York) to the South and West. New financial centers had grown up in Miami, Dallas, Houston, Denver, and Los Angeles, without being noticed—or effectively mined—by the political world. The Goldwater campaign and the conservative movement, which were largely sectional at the beginning, took advantage of the opportunity and successfully cultivated the new centers of financial power. These new sources of campaign funding were augmented by the innovation of direct mail, which took substantial power out of the hands of large contributors and put it into the hands of mass-based small contributors. As a result, the "eastern Establishment" lost the financial leverage that had long provided its winning edge. After 1964, the Republican Party "built on Goldwater's lists to become the most successful direct mail fund-raising enterprise in American politics."[91]

Thus, both in financial and organizational respects, the conservatives gained their success only by mobilizing dormant Republican potential, particularly in the South and West. The conservatives won the party, but because the mixed system emphasized the role of the party in the nominating process, they had to pay the party back by developing new sources of party strength.

Due to many of the same factors, it was easier for movements to succeed in transforming the minority party than the majority party. In any system, the minority party establishment is more vulnerable to ideological attack, since the very fact that the minority is the minority lends credence to demands for a changed approach. In 1964, previous liberal Republican presidential defeats strengthened the conservative challenge. Furthermore, the minority party was less uniformly organized than the majority party and had more organizational posts open.[92] If Washington state Republicans had already filled all or most of its fifty-five hundred precincts, the party would have been much more difficult to take over. The existence of the one-party South, a major factor in the Democrats' national majority status, was a standing invitation for a movement to build a southern Republican Party in its image from the ground up.

The decline of the Republican governors to a postwar low of sixteen also clearly contributed to the success of the conservative movement. The role of the governors should not be underestimated. Nelson Polsby pointed out that "decentralized [i.e., nongubernatorial] state parties . . . became happy hunting grounds" for movements.[93] Furthermore, when governors were present at national conventions, they served in the powerful post of delegation chairman 80 percent of the time.[94] Goldwater did worst in states with an unfriendly Republican governor, and best in the few states with a friendly Republican governor and the states with Democratic governors.[95]

Finally, unlike the party holding presidential power, the "out" party (often but not always the nation's minority party) had no central party leadership of significance. The national committee was ineffective, and the "titular leader" was seldom powerful—a weakness magnified after 1962 by Nixon's gubernatorial defeat in California.[96] In many respects, then, the minority party was much more susceptible to power vacuums that could be filled by vigorous movements. The mixed system—which relied heavily on the party leadership—thus smiled more graciously on minority party movements that met the other requirements than on similar movements in the majority party. It may not be a coincidence that no "movement candidate" gained the Democratic Party's presidential nomination until George McGovern, who won after the first reforms and after the Democratic majority coalition had shattered in 1968.[97]

If this is true, then the mixed system's treatment of movements served as a self-correcting device for two-party balance: the minority party was structurally more open to movements, which themselves could triumph only by revitalizing and rebuilding the party through philosophical and technical innovation, making it once again a viable force. This process may take several years. Whatever the short-term result in 1964, the conservative takeover of the Republican Party—which provided the party with organizational revitalization (in the South, virtual invention), large-scale volunteer mobilization, new fund-raising technologies and massive donor lists, and the winning Sunbelt strategy—was a primary factor in the party's recovery from "half-party" status in 1964 to the victory in five of six presidential elections between 1968 and 1988.

Openness and Stability in the Mixed System

In short, the mixed system clearly established barriers to the entry of movements, but maintained a generally workable balance between the claims of openness and stability through a complex interaction of its components. The mixed system did impose certain restraints on movements. It required that successful movements be long-lasting and broadly based. It required successful movements to gain the support of, and work with, substantial segments of the existing party; furthermore, movements had to convince at least some party regulars (through primaries or abstract persuasion) that they were electorally viable. And the system extracted a quid pro quo from successful movements: extensive party building and mobilization of new sources of party strength. In short, the system maintained party stability by forcing movements to reach a high threshold of external and party support and maintained governing stability by more heavily insulating the majority (and hence generally governing) party.

However, once these conditions were met, the system was both more open than the system that preceded it and more open than its own later critics acknowledged. The preponderant use of caucuses could actually work to the benefit of well-organized movements. In 1964, it was the caucuses that provided Goldwater with his greatest strength and, just as important, that served as the foundation for conservative control of the party over the long term.

On the other hand, the primaries nearly derailed Goldwater's campaign in New Hampshire and Oregon, and his overall primary performance was substantially worse than his performance in caucuses. Only the dominance of plurality rules and separate delegate elections—as well as the limited number of head-to-head contests—saved Goldwater from being destroyed by the primaries, although California played an important positive role by persuading some hesitant party leaders that he had broad vote-getting power. Only in New York, the last state that permits "cross-filing," did a "Conservative Party" arise to fulfill the function filled by third parties in the convention system.[98]

In all other states the route of purely internal infiltration was taken with success, which would have been highly unlikely in the old system. And the viability of the infiltration route provided the conservatives with a confidence in the loyalty of "their" people in the party, which movements could never have when a party's conversion rested more fully on strategic calculations by unchanged party leaders. In short, the experience of 1964 confirmed the notion that the mixed system was both more open than the convention system and more open, paradoxically, than the system the progressives preferred. The conservatives would likely have failed to gain entry in a system totally controlled by the party organization through conventions and unregulated caucuses, but probably also would have failed to win the nomination for Goldwater, and almost certainly would have failed to take long-term control of the party, in a system of primaries alone.

Furthermore, the mixed system was flexible enough to permit substantial movement access via drafts as well as by factors below the systemic level, such as party decentralization and apportionment formulae that advantaged movements developing new electoral strength. The system was also malleable enough to allow for movement-driven innovations in the process itself that improved movement prospects, such as the Draft Goldwater Committee's early start and delegate search techniques. Finally, the nature of the system introduced an element of openness and innovation to the party system as a whole, by giving greater opportunities to movements in the minority party, which could serve to rejuvenate the party and provide a balancing "hidden hand." The mixed system shared this last characteristic with the convention system, though the gap between openness in the majority and minority parties had almost certainly shrunk somewhat.

Thus the mixed system, as observed in action in 1964, was indeed open to movements, provided they passed a series of tests that showed their strength. The mechanisms necessary for stability and those necessary for openness to actual takeover (as opposed to initial access) by strong movements could actually complement each other. The dominance of caucuses at once imposed hurdles and promised great rewards if the hurdles could be overcome. The primaries, designed to promote openness, had the effect in the mixed system of both permitting and forcing movements to prove their vote-getting ability to party leaders. The importance of party leaders in the system provided peer review and forced movements to engage in party building if they wanted to replace the existing elite, but also ensured that, once victorious, the movement could actually consolidate its position and gain something from victory over the long term.

These realities indicate the complexities involved in the concepts of openness and stability. Openness to initial access by movements clearly stands apart from openness to actual success by movements; the ability to compete is not the ability to prevail. This can be seen, for instance, in the way that caucuses established high thresholds of strength but were well suited to movements that passed the threshold. Additionally, openness to success in the short term—that is, ability to win the nomination—must be considered separately from potential for long-term success, or the ability to take over the party as a long-term instrument of the movement's philosophy and program.

The convention system was so closed to initial access that movements were driven from party ranks and forced to take up the banner of a third party. In the mixed system movements were not driven out but were forced to attain a high degree of strength before seriously challenging for power. Both systems were open to movement success, but only if the movement proved to have great electoral potential and organizational capacity; in the mixed system, success came through actual takeover of the major party, while in the convention system it came through an amalgamation between the major and third party or through the usurpation by the major party of the third party's platform. Given success in either system, movements could look forward to some long-term consolidation of their positions, though the manner of success dictated the degree of consolidation. Success in the mixed system was likely to be longer lasting, for the reasons discussed above; it entailed actual takeover of the party machinery, rather than temporary conversion of party regulars.

Thus, while both systems maintained high levels of stability by restricting access through the establishment of high thresholds of strength, the mixed system was more open than the convention system in all respects: movements were not invariably forced into third-party activity, short-term success was more complete because it did not rely on fusion and relied much less on the calculations of regulars, and for the same reasons long-term success was more probable once short-term success was achieved. The higher degree of openness in the nominating system largely compensated for the greater difficulty attending third-party activity due to ballot access restrictions imposed in the early 1900s.

Two questions naturally present themselves. First, what explains the greater permeability of major parties to movements in the mixed system compared to the convention system, despite the mixed system's continued emphasis on conventions and party leadership? While primaries carried with them serious dangers and disadvantages for movements, they could on occasion still serve the purpose that had been intended for them of providing a means of bypassing the regulars. Theodore Roosevelt and Barry Goldwater both used them to that end with at least some degree of success. Furthermore, caucus/convention processes were themselves undoubtedly made somewhat more open by the wave of regulatory legislation at the turn of the century. And the sheer power of the party organizations to control outcomes had weakened, even though in many cases formal nominating structures remained unchanged. Perhaps most important, the power of patronage was greatly curtailed, leading to the atrophy of the political machine. As Reiter notes, the power of the party organizations in the nominating process declined steadily during the period of the mixed system, as measured by indices such as falling percentages of uncommitted delegates, number of favorite son and "dark horse" candidacies, and number of convention ballots required to nominate.[99] Needless to say, movements that wish to overthrow party organizations benefit when the organizational strength of the party to block them has declined.

Second, if the mixed system was more permeable than the convention system, what explains the relative paucity of movements under the mixed system before 1964? Party decline, though a factor throughout, seems to have accelerated in the 1960s. Furthermore, as scholars have noted, the political environment of the 1950s (and one might add, for the most part, the 1940s) was largely nonideological, governed by a degree of consensus that might be considered remarkable by today's standards. Movements, by definition ideological, did not find fertile soil in those times, regardless of the nominating rules. In contrast, the public became markedly more ideological beginning in the 1960s, a phenomenon that undoubtedly both drove and was driven by the conservative movement.[100] Finally, to some degree it took the Goldwater experience of 1964 to illuminate the opportunities that existed for future potential movements. Indeed, the Draft Goldwater effort and the resultant "Goldwater for President" campaign broke new ground with delegate selection strategies that changed the nature of the convention before any changes were effected in the rules.

Large-scale reform of the nominating process was set in motion only four years after Barry Goldwater's nomination, primarily because of cries that the system that the conservatives had used to take over the Republican Party was not open enough to movements. These claims derived in no small part from an undifferentiated view of openness that conflated access and actual success, mistaking high thresholds of organization, support, and staying power for total closure of the system. In 1972, the first election after the reforms began, the "new politics" movement swept George McGovern to the Democratic nomination. Did he owe his nomination to the reforms? Did the reforms bring the openness their supporters promised, or did they inadvertently make more difficult the sorts of movements that supported Goldwater and McGovern?

4

The Triumph of the "New Politics"

W HEN GEORGE MCGOVERN WON THE DEMOCRATIC
nomination for president in July 1972, the political world was
no less amazed than it had been eight years before by the success of Barry Goldwater. At one point, oddsmaker Jimmy the
Greek laid odds of five hundred to one against McGovern being nominated.
In January 1972, McGovern had stood at 3 percent in the Gallup poll among
Democratic voters, and was not fully considered a serious contender by the
media until his first primary victory, in Wisconsin on April 4. McGovern had
swept past the establishment favorite, Senator Edmund Muskie of Maine, and
Hubert Humphrey, who had stepped into the race late but had proven a for-
midable opponent with the help of organized labor.

The South Dakotan's victory had been obtained by harnessing the organizational energy of what had come to be called the "new politics" movement,
a loose coalition of anti–Vietnam War, feminist, environmental, minority, and
reformist forces. This new politics movement had been seen in incipient form
four years earlier, when Eugene McCarthy and Robert Kennedy attempted
unsuccessfully to wrest control of the Democratic Party away from the forces
of Lyndon Johnson and Hubert Humphrey.

McGovern's triumph came in the first election after the reforms in the
Democratic Party's presidential nominating process, which had been imposed

on state parties by the commission that McGovern himself had chaired. These reforms had the effect of substantially removing the official party from the nominating process. McGovern's victory seems to have been the very sort of event that the reformers hoped their efforts might produce. As William Crotty said:

> Once all hope of capturing the nomination [for McCarthy in 1968] had faded, the insurgents spent the last few weeks prior to the 1968 convention marshalling their forces to advocate change. . . .
>
> Most wanted to change national policy and all wanted to change the national leadership. . . . Reform of the party's nominating process became the vehicle through which the eventual policy and leadership changes the reformers held to be so important could be realized.
>
> There was a clear line of development between the [1968 Democratic] insurgents, the McGovern-Fraser Commission, and the Reform Movement that followed. . . . The parentage is unmistakable.[1]

However, McGovern's story is more complicated than it first appears, and turns out on examination to be far from a ringing demonstration of the alleged openness of the new rules. George McGovern may have owed his nomination in 1972 not so much to the reforms as to the fact that the reform system was only partially in place. Strong movements, such as those supporting McGovern and Goldwater before him, were almost certainly hurt more than they were helped by crucial elements of the reforms.

The Rise of the New Politics

Eugene McCarthy in 1968 was the first standard-bearer of the new politics movement, which was centered on antiwar sentiment. That sentiment had grown slowly, but by 1967, the student revolt against the war was in full swing. The antiwar movement actually began entering electoral politics in a scattered way in 1966, primarily by attempting to influence Democratic politics.[2] Liberal Democrats were also concerned with the war and with the apparent scaling back of the Great Society, and began to turn against the Johnson administration.[3] This incipient "new politics" movement shared a great deal with the "new left" in terms of its opposition to the war and its general critique of American society, and can be distinguished not by its direction but primarily by its less radical character and its willingness to work within "the system."[4]

In 1967, the liberal group Americans for Democratic Action was the forum for an ongoing debate over how best to respond to LBJ. One faction preferred to accept the inevitability of a Johnson renomination but to work for a peace plank in the Democratic platform. The other faction, led by Curtis Gans (a former founding member of the new left Students for a Democratic Society), believed that the only way to stop the war was to deprive Johnson of the nomination.[5] Ultimately, with the help of liberal activist Allard Lowenstein, the debate was resolved in favor of the latter course.

Lowenstein was a link between the anti-Johnson intellectuals and the student revolt, being a member in good standing of ADA and a former president of the National Student Association. In the words of Theodore White, no one "understood better than Lowenstein how powerful a force it [the student movement] might become in American politics."[6] In August 1967, Lowenstein virtually single-handedly started the "Dump Johnson" effort by forming three organizations: "Dissenting Democrats," directed toward the antiwar movement, "Concerned Democrats," directed toward Democratic politicians, and a student network.[7] Lowenstein's first recruit was Curtis Gans. Gans's nationwide travels indicated by mid-October that "it was obvious that a nationwide base was actually there, yet still formless and unnamed."[8]

The greatest need was for a candidate who was willing to challenge Johnson.[9] Only McCarthy was willing to make the run, and, after some hesitation, he announced his candidacy on November 30, 1967. In the meantime, organizational efforts proceeded; the National Conference of Concerned Democrats met in December with 460 generally obscure figures attending from forty-two states. Fifteen student headquarters were established in New Hampshire in preparation for the March primary. By election day, as many as 4,500 students had canvassed the state, contacting as many as 60,000 voters.[10] Combined with the shock of the Tet offensive, this organizational effort drew McCarthy to within seven percentage points of the president's vote (49 percent to 42 percent).[11]

In the same way that the Tet offensive had ended in military victory but psychological defeat, Johnson's finish was a tangible victory but a serious setback in the world of perception. New Hampshire emboldened the fledgling movement, leading to redoubled efforts in Wisconsin. McCarthy's "children's crusade" was formidable, with forty-one student headquarters accounting for 800,000 doorbells rung.[12] At the same time, Robert Kennedy entered the race as an antiwar candidate. Behind in the polls and oppressed by the war, Johnson announced two days before the Wisconsin primary that he was no longer seeking renomination. The primaries had successfully been used to drive an unpopular incumbent from office, but this success did not automatically translate into victory for the movement.

Instead, the race split into two parts. In the remaining primaries, McCarthy and Kennedy bitterly fought each other over largely overlapping constituencies.[13] McCarthy won in Pennsylvania and Massachusetts, Kennedy in Indiana and Nebraska, and McCarthy in Oregon. On the day he was assassinated, Kennedy prevailed in California and South Dakota, while McCarthy won in New Jersey.

Meanwhile, Vice President Hubert Humphrey had become the "organization" candidate as the logical successor to Johnson, entering no contested primaries but winning large numbers of delegates in nonprimary states, often with minimal opposition. This success was often facilitated by the ability of the party organization to shut out interlopers and by the outright control over whole delegations exercised by leaders in some states,[14] but the closed nature of caucus/convention states was not the sole cause of this success.

Where McCarthy made strong efforts in caucus states, he often did well. Antiwar activists had been organizing for two years in Colorado, and McCarthy came away with nineteen of thirty-five delegates; in Iowa, McCarthy and McGovern gained a majority of delegates. Elsewhere, McCarthy forces had pockets of great strength and organization, which were parlayed into delegates. For instance, in North Dakota, serious efforts were made in only one of forty state Senate districts, but in that district, 210 of 230 precinct delegates favored McCarthy. And in Minnesota, McCarthy challenged Humphrey, swamping the caucuses in Minneapolis-Saint Paul and winning nearly half of the congressional district delegates but losing the twenty at-large delegates.[15]

These efforts, however, were sporadic in nature. McCarthy and Kennedy concentrated their energies on the primary states largely to the exclusion of the nonprimary states; both were still playing largely by the old rules, hoping to translate primary victories into nonprimary delegates.[16] They had thus not fully grasped the way in which the Goldwater campaign had exposed a new potential dynamic in nomination campaigns. McCarthy later stated that he had intended "to test as thoroughly as I could the entire process of the Democratic party," including nonprimary processes,[17] but key campaign organizer Ben Stavis said: "As the primary campaigns ended, we became more aware of the actual power structure of the Democratic party. The primaries were crucial for establishing McCarthy as a national political figure. But, we suddenly realized, the number of delegate votes determined by these contests was actually quite low, perhaps only a quarter."[18]

Thus, only when the primary season ended with substantial McCarthy success in New York in mid-June did his campaign turn to the task of persuading uncommitted delegates and the political leaders who influenced them. McCarthy also faced the task of winning Kennedy's old delegates, who were a natural part of his coalition but who harbored resentment born of the primary rivalry and thus supported Humphrey by a margin of four hundred to seventy-five.[19] His advisers split on strategy for gaining these delegates. Dissension produced chaos, and the resulting delegate efforts were perfunctory at best.

In an attempt to forestall the loss of Kennedy delegates to Humphrey, and believing McCarthy to be less than a fully serious candidate, McGovern entered the race two weeks prior to the convention. While McGovern may have drained votes from McCarthy, it seems clear in retrospect that Humphrey had the convention under control in any case thanks to the overwhelming support given him in the nonprimary states. Of the 3,099 delegates at the Democratic national convention in 1968, approximately 600 had been chosen prior to New Hampshire (some in processes starting as early as August 1966) and 600 had been chosen by party organizations; the vast bulk of these went to Humphrey.[20] Thus, the key obstacle to McCarthy was not his movement status per se, but the fact that the movement supporting him was still in its infancy, certainly compared to the conservatives in 1964. Where the movement had been active longer, McCarthy was able to compete with the regulars on their own terms.

Humphrey won overwhelmingly on the first ballot, amid attacks that his candidacy was illegitimate because he had not submitted himself to a test of popular support in the primaries (this argument ignored the fact that Humphrey held a fifty-three to thirty-nine lead over McCarthy among Democrats in the August 7 Gallup poll). The minority (antiwar) platform report on Vietnam was likewise defeated. However, a minority report on rules banning the unit rule was narrowly approved by the full convention. The Credentials Committee was also persuaded to include in its report the call for a reform commission and "meaningful and timely" participation, which became the basis for the McGovern-Fraser Commission. Unable to gain control of the party in Chicago, the new politics forces had succeeded in planting two seeds, one procedural and the other organizational. One grew into the most far-reaching systematic transformation of nominating politics in United States history, and the other into the movement that swept George McGovern into the Democratic nomination after four more years of growth and maturation.

The McGovern Nomination

Although McGovern did not officially announce his candidacy until January 1971, he never stopped running after the 1968 convention. His nomination was aided by the fruit of both the seeds planted by the new politics forces in 1968. Procedurally, he was appointed by DNC chairman Fred Harris to head the Commission on Party Structure and Delegate Selection, which—whatever the other consequences of reform on his campaign—was a political blessing. At the same time, veterans of the McCarthy and Kennedy efforts began to coalesce and establish an organizational foundation for a takeover of the Democratic Party.

That organization was the "New Democratic Coalition," which formed in October 1968 in Minneapolis. By the end of 1968, the NDC had organizations in twenty states, built on the foundation created by Lowenstein in the Dump Johnson effort the year before.[21] The movement was further solidified with the 1970 creation of *The New Democrat*, a proreform magazine started by McCarthy and Kennedy supporters.

The NDC gained great strength in some states such as New York (where it had inherited 130 Democratic reform clubs with 25,000 members), California (with 150 clubs), Massachusetts, Wisconsin, and Florida. While it had difficulty reaching out beyond its white, upper-middle-class base, other elements of the new politics movement were becoming organized on their own terms, such as blacks, Chicanos, and feminists. The NDC held its first national convention in February 1970, but collapsed on the national level with twenty thousand dollars in debts a few months later. Nevertheless, it remained important in some of the crucial battleground states.[22] At the same time, it was evident in 1970 that the movement was prevailing in "whatever internal party fights could be identified."[23]

One of the reasons the NDC collapsed on a nationwide basis was that the McGovern Commission had successfully stolen much of its agenda. When McGovern was offered the chairmanship, he was persuaded by advisers that he could use it to build ties to proreform and antiwar Democrats as well as regulars.[24] As time went by, the commission—together with McGovern's continued antiwar activity—"provided platforms and committed followers on which a presidential campaign could be built."[25] The seventeen regional hearings accomplished much in this regard, and, according to Byron Shafer: "One of the major implicit developments in reform politics during the fall of 1969, unmarked by any specific event, was the emergence of the Party Structure Commission—really its headquarters staff, using the commission framework—as the central link for reform forces nationwide."[26]

By the time McGovern left the commission in late 1970, he had laid a solid groundwork for the coalescing of the new politics movement—behind his own candidacy. He announced his candidacy on January 18, 1971, a date that most pundits considered absurdly early. Gary Hart—who had worked for Kennedy in 1968—had been hired in the summer of 1970 to begin national organizing, and an important strategy session was held at the candidate's Maryland retreat in July. At that retreat, it was decided that an early start would be necessary to overcome low name recognition, and that it would be necessary to establish McGovern as the sole candidate on the left. In the words of Hart, "McGovern's natural base within the Democratic Party was its liberal wing and, more specifically, those forces which shaped and supported the Kennedy and McCarthy candidacies in 1968," and McGovern needed to "harness and control those forces to obtain the nomination."[27] Organization would be decentralized, and the early stages of the campaign financed largely by direct mail.[28]

At the beginning of 1972, after a year of organizational work, McGovern stood at 3 percent in the Gallup poll. Edmund Muskie was the consensus front-runner, and had already locked up a vast reservoir of endorsements from state and local party leaders. But in the estimation of McGovern (and Humphrey, who entered the race at the last minute), Muskie's support, though wide, was not deep. In contrast, McGovern had in the movement a "new system of energy":

> In students, in housewives, so much of whose time is their own, the Movement seemed to have developed the manpower equivalent of the old patronage rolls of machine politics. This new political leisure class could man telephones or hit the doorsteps with bodies and skills that overwhelmed both the numbers and the quality of their competitors within the old party.[29]

Muskie's weakness and McGovern's potential strength was first exposed in the New Hampshire primary, which Muskie was expected to win heavily. Instead, he won with less than half the vote (46 percent), and McGovern came in a solid second with 37 percent. Like McCarthy, McGovern had slowed the front-runner in New Hampshire, and like McCarthy, McGovern did it with grassroots organization; up to thirty-eight hundred students came into New Hampshire to canvass in the last three weeks.[30] Despite McGovern's showing, "very few concluded that he had made himself a real challenger" yet.[31] The remainder of the long campaign was punctuated by a series of dramatic primaries.

The Florida primary saw George Wallace win a crushing victory on the busing issue; Muskie finished a poor fourth, and McGovern succeeded in his goal of blunting his only viable threat on the left, Mayor John Lindsay of New York. Muskie finished first in Illinois, which McGovern had largely conceded. Then came a crucial showdown in Wisconsin.

On the strength of massive organization, McGovern won his first primary victory in Wisconsin, with 30 percent of the vote to Wallace's 22 percent and Humphrey's 21 percent. McGovern had established a headquarters in Wisconsin a year and a half before the primary. The campaign had long viewed Wisconsin as the key breakthrough state; Hart called it a "watershed," and McGovern had stated that "if we can't do well in Wisconsin, I don't know any state where we will do well."[32] Victory in Wisconsin "undeniably thrust McGovern to the front of the pack with the emerging Humphrey."[33] From Wisconsin on, "no other metaphor but that of a guerrilla army on the move can describe the upheaval that was to shake and change the entire Democratic Party in the next six weeks."[34]

The McGovern campaign, its credibility established and its fund-raising bolstered by success in Wisconsin, shifted hundreds of organizers from state to state. While McGovern picked up a win in Massachusetts, Humphrey began to gain momentum, winning in Pennsylvania, Ohio, Indiana, and West Virginia (McGovern seriously contested only Ohio). At the same time, Wallace was showing surprising strength in numerous primaries, winning Tennessee, North Carolina, Maryland, and Michigan before being driven from serious consideration by the bullet of a would-be assassin.

McGovern slowed the Humphrey momentum by winning in Nebraska, and then set up the California primary by winning in Oregon. California's winner-take-all primary was held on June 6; Humphrey called it "the ballgame," Hart called it "Armageddon."[35] McGovern had in California 250 paid staff, 230 offices, 34 phone banks, and 50,000 volunteers.[36] He also outspent Humphrey by a margin of two to one. However, his fifteen-to-twenty-point lead dwindled substantially after a series of debates with Humphrey in which the Minnesotan attacked McGovern's 30 percent defense cut and his income redistribution scheme.[37] On election day, McGovern won 44 to 39 percent, thus picking up all 271 of California's delegates. On the same day, he won New Mexico, South Dakota, and the delegate contests (though not preference poll) in New Jersey.

Only the New York primary remained, and it was largely anticlimactic. Republican governor Nelson Rockefeller had refused to accept legislative changes in the New York primary law to bring it into accord with the McGovern-Fraser guidelines, so it was a pure delegate primary with no presidential preference attached to delegate names. Organization was thus crucial, and only McGovern had it, with 215 reform clubs and 30,000 volunteers.[38] Additionally, no candidate but McGovern had even filed statewide slates; Humphrey had filed no delegate slates, partly because his campaign did not understand the new slate-making requirements and partly in hopes that he could win over Muskie or Jackson delegates after they were chosen. However, neither of those candidates fielded full slates either. McGovern won 230 of 248 delegates at the polls, including a nineteen-year-old woman who defeated Averill Harriman.

McGovern's primary strategy had been executed to near perfection. His presence was established in New Hampshire; Florida had weakened Lindsay; Wisconsin had been won, finishing off Lindsay and providing a media break-through; and California had provided the momentum to clean up in New York. He had won by successfully consolidating the left, as it had not been consolidated in 1968, with the help of some state chapters of the NDC. In six primary states—Maryland, Pennsylvania, Florida, New York, Massachusetts, and California—the NDC or affiliated organization held special preprimary conventions to endorse a presidential candidate. In five, it endorsed McGovern; in California, he fell four percentage points short of the 60 percent requirement, but numerous local clubs aided in the campaign.[39]

While the primaries had gained the lion's share of attention, by mid-April "the press began to notice that McGovern was gaining a lead in states where delegates were chosen through conventions rather than primaries."[40] The campaign had set a goal of three hundred delegates (out of one thousand) to be gained in these states. In the end, that goal was surpassed by over one-third. Nonprimary state director Rick Stearns later held that McGovern's margin in Miami was traceable to the extraordinary success of McGovern in the caucus/convention states.[41]

When the credentials committee met in Washington in the last week of June, a coalition of McGovern's opponents voted to give Humphrey 39 percent of California's delegation on the grounds that California's winner-take-all primary violated the 1968 convention's ban on the unit rule. Until the convention restored the lost delegates to McGovern on the first night in Miami, his nomination was in doubt. When he won, it was clear that his victory was "essentially the new-politics revenge for 1968, the culmination of reformist, new-breed activism that represented the mobilization of the anti-war movement."[42]

McCarthy's failure in 1968 had driven the reforms, and McGovern's success four years later was widely taken as a consequence of the reforms. In this view, an oppressive system had guaranteed the defeat of the new politics movement, and alteration of that system had procured its victory. Yet the reform impulse in the Democratic Party had not yet played itself out, and the reform system itself was not fully in place. Less than half of the overall increase in primaries from 1968 to 1980 had occurred, proportional representation had not been mandated, open primaries were still acceptable, and finance reform was yet to come. Thus, the McGovern campaign and the success of the new politics movement in 1972 must be seen in relation both to the system that preceded it and to the full-fledged reform system.

Primaries and Caucuses

In 1964, Barry Goldwater had prevailed on his strength in the caucus states. He received 73 percent of the delegates from caucus/convention states, and only 62 percent from primary states. Furthermore, the greatest challenges to his campaign came in the New Hampshire, Oregon, and California primaries. This success even in the prereform caucuses suggests that well-organized movements could actually gain an advantage from having to compete in a system dominated by caucuses rather than primaries. This possibility in turn suggests that the reform system, which has included a vast growth in primaries, may actually work to the disadvantage of movements.

The role of caucuses and primaries in 1972 was more complex than in 1964. McGovern did better than Goldwater in the primaries in terms of impact on his campaign, delegates won, and delegates won relative to nonprimary states. Goldwater's only crucial primary victory in terms of campaign momentum came in California. McGovern was helped tremendously by good showings in New Hampshire and Ohio and victories in Wisconsin, Nebraska, Oregon, California, and New York. McGovern, alone among presidential contenders between 1936 and 1972, was able to use the primaries as a vehicle to move up substantially in the polls.[43] In the words of Jeane Kirkpatrick, McGovern "could not have gotten off the ground without primaries."[44] At the end of the campaign, there is evidence that McGovern, like Goldwater, translated his California victory into at least some nonprimary delegates as well.[45] Overall, McGovern managed to win 65 percent of the delegates from primary states, as opposed to only 40 percent from caucus/convention states. It is little wonder that McGovern's performance in the primaries has played the predominant role in accounts of the 1972 race.

Three distinctions must be made: between primary delegates and primary votes, between reformed and unreformed primaries, and between old and new primaries. The first distinction, between primary delegates and primary votes, is crucial. While McGovern received 65 percent of primary delegates, he won only 25 percent of the votes cast in the 1972 primaries. Indeed, ironically— given that Humphrey was attacked in 1968 because his opponents had garnered more votes in the primaries—McGovern in 1972 actually received *fewer* primary votes than Humphrey. Furthermore, while McGovern received a plurality of delegates in sixteen of the twenty-three primary states, he won a plurality of popular votes in only eight of the twenty-one that held candidate preference primaries. Like Goldwater, McGovern faced his greatest threats in the primaries. A loss in California would probably have been fatal, and a poor showing in Wisconsin might have ended the struggling campaign earlier.

Thus, McGovern's success in Miami was not due to crushing victories in the primaries, but to an extraordinary capacity to translate low primary votes into high delegate totals. Gary Hart acknowledged the importance of the vote/delegate distinction by identifying as two separate campaign goals a good showing in about half the primaries for the sake of appearance and momentum and the actual winning of delegates through organization.[46] In fact, as late as mid-May, McGovern had actually gained more delegates from the primaries he had lost than from those he had won.[47] Goldwater had turned 38 percent of the primary vote into 62 percent of the delegates from those states, for a healthy "bonus" of 24 percent. McGovern's bonus was 40 percent. This was only possible because delegate outcomes had not yet been fully tied to candidate performance, even though that was a central tenet of the reform movement.

This leads to the second distinction, between reformed and unreformed primaries. As James Lengle and Byron Shafer have shown, "Most primaries offered delegates by (Congressional) District, and Districted primaries maximized McGovern's strength."[48] McGovern's strength in districted primaries paralleled the success Goldwater had in both primaries and caucuses in a Republican Party dominated by districted selection. Proportional representation, which McGovern himself favored and which his reform commission nearly mandated for 1972, would have helped not McGovern but Wallace, and if applied to California as the Credentials Committee had proposed would have denied George McGovern a first-ballot nomination.[49] With a universal scheme of proportional representation in the primaries, McGovern could not have won 65 percent of the delegates with only 25 percent of the votes. On the other hand, McGovern (prior to California) would also have been disadvantaged by a system of statewide winner-take-all primaries only.[50] More generally, as Carol Casey and Kenneth Bode point out, "McGovern won the nomination . . . because in a span of less than a month he won primaries in New York, South Dakota, Oregon, California, Rhode Island, and New Jersey—all essentially unreformed, winner-take-all primaries conducted under the same rules as in 1968—and won thereby nearly half the votes he carried with him into the convention."[51] A more careful look at particular cases illustrates the point. Wisconsin was the first primary McGovern actually won, and was hence crucial. It was still an open primary, in contradiction to the "urging" of the McGovern-Fraser Commission, which the Mikulski Commission later turned into a requirement. There are substantial indications that McGovern benefited from the crossover vote. His Wisconsin director Gene Pokorny deliberately targeted Republican farmers as a potential crossover vote, and a *New York Times*-Yankelovich survey showed that up to one-third of McGovern's vote came from Wisconsin crossovers, as did up to one-half of Wallace's vote. Conversely, Humphrey gained almost no crossover votes, and, by some estimates, might have finished first had Wisconsin been a closed primary.[52] This was a replay of 1968, when McCarthy had been "suspected of having obtained a generous crossover endorsement in Wisconsin."[53] In the other large open primary of 1972, Michigan, this pattern was repeated: Wallace gained half his vote from crossovers, McGovern one-third, and Humphrey virtually none, though this time Wallace was the victor.[54]

As mentioned, California was winner take all for the last time, despite the fact that this went against reform tenets. Indeed, California's representative on the reform commission, Fred Dutton, had quietly defended California's system among reformers by pointing out that California was likely to vote for a new politics candidate and that the proposed reforms would only dilute its strength.[55]

As for New York, it simply ignored guideline B-2 banning pure delegate primaries. In 1968, the "hideously complex" delegate system was "almost tailor-made for the insurgent tactics of the McCarthy operation."[56] By 1972, nothing had changed except that the movement was stronger and the Democratic organization probably weaker than four years before. In the words of Theodore White, "in New York, the old order had collapsed and the state waited for mop-up by McGovern's army. . . . There was no Democratic Party any longer."[57] Superior organization alone could overcome the absence of candidate affiliations next to delegate names on the ballot, and McGovern alone had that organization.

The momentum of Wisconsin and the delegates of California and New York by themselves go a long way toward explaining the nomination of George McGovern. If the unreformed primaries in California and New York are taken out of the calculations, McGovern received only 53.6 percent of delegates from the remaining primary states, an insufficient number to assure him first-ballot victory.

Of course, all primary states changed their rules for delegate slate-making procedures in a way that reduced the impact of the party regulars. The *New York Times* remarked after the selection meetings that in New Jersey, "even the most seasoned Democratic party professionals here will need a score card to keep track of what happened this weekend," and in California, the system was turned topsy-turvy in ways that arguably made it more difficult for the McGovern campaign to be electorally effective.[58] This level of reform, dealing with who the delegates will be, was essentially unconnected to the larger question of how many delegates each candidate received.[59] Upon this second question the nomination turned, and in that sense McGovern's most crucial primaries were indeed "unreformed."

This point leads to the third (and largely overlapping) distinction: between old and new primaries. The primaries most critical to McGovern's success in 1972 had existed under the mixed system as well, including those in New Hampshire, Wisconsin, Nebraska, Oregon, California, and New York. Indeed, the McGovern primary strategy was built around states that had long maintained primaries and would thus be easily understood as significant by the media and by party voters. Many of these states also exhibited a bias in favor of liberal candidates, since the primary was originally adopted and maintained in states with a progressive tradition.[60] While McGovern won 73.4 percent of the delegates from these "old" primaries, he won only 28.2 percent in the six states that held primaries for the first time in 1972. Had he not received a single delegate from the new primaries, he would still have won the nomination (see table 4.1). In other words, the primary strategy he pursued could have been pursued in 1960, and in fact largely had been the primary strategy of the new politics forces in 1968. In 1968, however, those forces were divided and not nearly as effective.

Like his predecessors in the mixed system, and unlike his successors starting with Jimmy Carter, McGovern carefully chose the primaries that he would seriously contest and substantially ignored the rest.[61] The 1972 campaign would be the last time any successful contender could pursue that strategy, and in many respects McGovern's success was due to his ability to pick and choose primaries.[62] To whatever degree McGovern owed his nomination to the momentum and the delegates he won in the primary states, he owed his nomination much more to the primary system that was dying than to the one that was coming into being.

This leaves the question of the relationship of caucus/convention states to primary states. Since the Democratic Party did not require candidate commitments and proportional representation in the caucuses until 1976, the only figure by which to judge support in the caucus states is the percentage of del-

Table 4-1. 1972 McGovern Delegates: Old *vs.* New Primaries

	Delegates Available (N)	*Delegates Won (N)*	*(%)*
Old primaries	1644	1206.3	73.4
New primaries	338	95.5	28.2
Margin of victory		206.35	

egates gained in those states. By that standard, the primary states greatly out-distanced the caucus states (65 percent to 40 percent). However, a more nuanced analysis shows that this point is far from clear.

As noted, George McGovern received only 25 percent of the votes in the primaries and finished second to Hubert Humphrey in primary votes gained.[63] Indeed, McGovern prevailed in eighteen of thirty-two caucus/convention jurisdictions, and surpassed by over one-third what he considered to be a fairly ambitious goal of three hundred delegates (out of one thousand) from the caucus states. By most accounts, the caucuses were at least as easily penetrated by "new politics" activists as were the primaries.

Jeane Kirkpatrick, after acknowledging the importance of primaries to McGovern's effort, said: "It should be noted that McGovern did better in nonprimary than primary states."[64] According to Democratic consultant Joseph Napolitan, one of the keys to McGovern's success was his targeting of nonprimary states,[65] and veteran *New York Times* correspondent R. W. Apple maintained on May 22, 1972, that recent reverses McGovern had experienced in the Washington state conventions constituted "the first time this year in a convention state [that] anti-McGovern elements equalled Mr. McGovern in organization."[66] Joseph Alsop likewise observed that McGovern did "remarkably well in the non-primary states," and explicitly compared him to Goldwater.[67] Overall, McGovern held a consistent and formidable lead in convention state delegates over any rival.[68]

The fact that the McGovern caucus strategy was similar to Goldwater's—and similarly, though not equally, effective—can be seen in caucus successes by McGovern forces in such unlikely places as Vermont, Virginia, Idaho, Kansas, Mississippi, Louisiana, Utah, and Montana. In Vermont, "party regulars were stunned by the strength of the McGovern forces," which ultimately swept all twelve delegates.[69] In Virginia, the new politics forces took over the Democratic Party and sent by some measures the third most liberal delegation of any in Miami.[70] In the South generally, McGovern surprisingly did much better than Wallace. Elsewhere, the story was the same: Democratic Party caucuses were flooded by adherents of the new politics. In short, throughout the spring of 1972, McGovern had "stung Democratic party regulars . . . with a string of surprise victories in nonprimary states."[71] McGovern could count no equivalent string of victories in primary states that could reasonably have been assumed to be hostile.

Furthermore, these successes were gained with less assistance from party insiders than Goldwater had received.[72] And, despite the reforms, dedicated party leaders in some convention states still had the power to thwart the takeover. In Missouri, despite substantial McGovern success at the precinct level, Governor Warren Hearnes ultimately held the McGovern forces to a small fraction of the delegation. Similar maneuvering by a hostile governor succeeded in Kentucky.[73] The fact that the reforms had not totally deprived party leaders of power, and that so few of them supported McGovern, makes it particularly impressive that McGovern was shut out in only one convention state, Washington (home of his rival Henry Jackson).

Finally, a measure of McGovern's success in the nonprimary states can be found in an examination of states that exchanged caucuses for primaries after 1972. There were eight such states: Vermont, Texas, Georgia, Arkansas, Idaho, Kentucky, Nevada, and Montana. Of these, McGovern lost only Arkansas and Kentucky, and Arkansas gave its votes to its favorite son, Wilbur Mills. In these eight states, McGovern won 71.7 percent of the delegates (78 percent without Arkansas), compared to only 40 percent in all convention states.[74] Political leaders in at least two of these states indicated that they moved to primaries because they believed the primary to be *less* vulnerable to takeover, and it seems probable that others did so as well.[75] Only New Mexico moved in the other direction, apparently for reasons having to do with expense, relative lack of exposure, and fear produced by George Wallace's strong showing.[76] Thus, a major driving force behind the increase in primaries in the reform system was probably a calculation by party leaders, based on McGovern's performance, that primaries were less vulnerable to movement takeover than caucuses.

Tennessee provides an opportunity to directly compare McGovern's primary and caucus capacities in the same state. Tennessee was one of the six states that had adopted a primary after 1968, and state law required delegates to vote in accordance with the results of the primary. However, the actual delegate selection was still performed by caucus/convention procedures. George Wallace won a resounding victory in the primary, with 68 percent to Humphrey's 16 percent and McGovern's 7 percent. However, the new politics forces backing McGovern and Shirley Chisholm took over the caucuses and elected the vast majority of delegates. As a result, for several weeks the possibility existed that the Tennessee delegates would vote for McGovern or Chisholm, despite the primary results. The situation was resolved in a manner satisfactory to Wallace, but the point is that McGovern did much better in a caucus setting than a primary setting when most other factors were controlled.[77]

On a broader scale, one might construct an imperfect control by comparing caucus states to those primary states that had been added after 1968. The original primaries were generally held in states with a strong progressive tradition, and were undoubtedly more ideologically predisposed to McGovern than were most other states. New primary states did not have such a progressive tradition, but were rather responding to other factors when they established primaries. They were thus more similar to the remaining caucus states than to the old primary states in many important respects. While McGovern got 40 percent of the delegates from caucus states, he received only 28 percent in new primary states.

Thus, the caucuses appear—in keeping with the Goldwater experience— to have provided McGovern with an important avenue to the nomination, and it is likely that the caucuses were actually more permeable than the primaries. In some states, especially Texas and Virginia, the reforms were probably crucial to reducing resistance to movement penetration.[78] Rick Stearns has said that he believes McGovern would not have won more than 1,195 delegates (239 short of the number needed to win the crucial California challenge) under the 1968 rules, and that most of this difference came from the caucus states.[79] In any case, the reforms clearly reduced the initial hurdle of access to the caucuses for the movement.

However, it is far from clear that McGovern's successes in the caucuses can be attributed primarily to the reforms. Gary Hart says that:

> I never really calculated it [party reform] as an ace in the hole. . . . People like Rick Stearns and myself realized from '68 that there were enough states that were open enough already—and if you did it right and you started early enough, you could get a helluva lot of delegates without changing any rules. Then, when the rule changes came in and they began to be accepted in state after state and by the national party, we realized even more that the procedures that were available already in '68 were just being expanded into more states. And we always felt that the best organization was going to win.[80]

Stearns himself told McGovern in the fall of 1970 (before implementation of the reforms) that "with a certain amount of intelligence and a committed following, you could write your own ticket in the convention states."[81] McGovern's opponents also seemed to downplay the new rules: Humphrey's director of political operations, J. P. Maloney Jr., held that "the convention system in non-primary states in 1972 was the same as 1968 except for one phenomenon—the packing of precinct caucuses."[82] To Maloney, as to Hart, the key was not reform but organization, and the keys to organizational success were intensity and an early start. By the time Humphrey forces had prepared for battle in most convention states, the battle was over. Furthermore, McGovern's failures illuminate the limits of the reform explanation. The fact that McGovern did suffer at the hands of the regulars in states like Kentucky, Washington, Missouri, and Hawaii shows that the reforms had not rendered the regulars incapable of exerting influence in convention settings.

In short, as Keech and Matthews write, "A challenge of the potency of McGovern's would surely have shaken up the process even in the absence of reforms, especially when no other candidate sought out delegates in the non-primary states in the same systematic way."[83] Even if the caucus reforms might have helped movements by reducing the barriers the party could construct, the reform system on balance probably hurt movements, since the number of caucuses was drastically reduced in favor of less easily organized primaries. What was given by one hand was more than taken away by the other.

It is also far from clear that a static analysis comparing McGovern to McCarthy is adequate. Such an analysis ignores the success of Goldwater in unreformed caucuses, as well as the weaknesses of the McCarthy campaign. In particular, McCarthy made only limited efforts in the nonprimary states, and reversed places with McGovern: in 1968, it was Humphrey who diligently worked the nonprimary states and McCarthy who awakened to their importance too late. Furthermore, McCarthy as a candidate was far from the equal of McGovern.[84] In short, to Keech and Matthews, "Senator McCarthy's 1968 effort in the nonprimary states scarcely deserves to be compared with McGovern's."[85] Finally, McCarthy faced the added burden of running against an incumbent president and then his handpicked successor. Despite all of this, McCarthy at times showed great strength in those caucuses that he did vigorously contest.

On balance, then, the new politics movement prevailed in 1972 in a way that tends to confirm the general openness of the mixed system to the success of such movements when they attain sufficient strength and maturity. The primaries acted, as they had in 1968, to bring the movement candidate to the forefront. However, it was the old primaries, not the new, that were crucial, and McGovern would have failed had not the unreformed nature of many primaries allowed him to substantially disconnect delegate strength from primary votes. His strategy of carefully choosing targets of opportunity was a mixed-system strategy. And the manner in which his primary victories were won, as well as the weakness he showed in primary votes, demonstrated the continuing propensity of primaries to act less as a mechanism of openness than as a brake on movements, a hurdle to be overcome.

It took McGovern fifty thousand volunteers and a two-to-one spending advantage to gain a five-point win in California, and ten thousand volunteers to gain a victory in Wisconsin that still might not have occurred without crossover voting. It took thirty-eight hundred volunteers to lose by nine points in New Hampshire. In neighboring Vermont, with the party regulars lined up as solidly for Muskie as they had been in New Hampshire, McGovern swept the caucuses with a fraction of the human and financial resources. Overall, it cost the McGovern campaign seven thousand dollars to win each delegate in California, compared to average of only fifty dollars per delegate in the nonprimary states.[86] The primaries in 1972, like California in 1964, were tests of organization and support rather than an open road to the nomination. In the sudden absence of mediating forces, the voters at large took their cues on electability and seriousness from McGovern's previous victories, just as the regulars once would have done.[87]

As for Goldwater before the reforms, the caucuses provided McGovern with the perfect forum for low-cost takeovers spearheaded by intense and well-organized movement supporters. These takeovers carried with them the same long-term advantages that had been evident in the Republican Party eight years earlier: Stearns remarked at the time that McGovern workers "are in the process of becoming the regular party organization in some of these [nonprimary] states. Two months ago they were setting up telephone banks."[88] In Colorado, new politics activists had taken over the party through caucuses as early as 1966, then delivered increasing delegate majorities to McCarthy in 1968 and McGovern in 1972. They maintained substantial control in the state thereafter, thwarted only by postconvention primaries that were required for those receiving more than 20 percent of the convention vote.[89] In Virginia, the takeover at the caucus level led to the election of a McGovernite state chairman and national committeeman at the state convention.

In both the primaries and caucuses, the key was the organized mobilization of a reservoir of support. In the words of a *New York Times* correspondent:

> Operationally, the race for the 1972 Democratic Presidential nomination matches an established organization with traditional vote-getting techniques against a loose confederation of leaders heavily dependent on the personal drawing power of their candidate.
>
> The organization candidate, with a network of tested political operatives combing the precincts for his last laggard supporter, is Senator George McGovern of South Dakota, more commonly perceived by many of his fellow Democrats as somewhere outside the regular party structure.
>
> The personality candidate, relying on his record, drive, and voter loyalty rather than ward-style organization, is Senator Hubert H. Humphrey of Minnesota.[90]

This general appraisal seems to have been shared by the McGovern campaign itself. Stearns said that the campaign was "not new politics. . . . It is the renaissance of the old politics."[91] Hart concurred, saying, "We've combined the old politics with the new. The old techniques—voter identification, phone banks, canvassing—aren't being used by anyone else this year because no one else can motivate volunteers the way McGovern can."[92] It was not uncommon in 1972 to find references to the McGovern campaign as a "machine" not dissimilar in form (though certainly dissimilar in content) from the more familiar, though decaying, party machines. In the same way, McCarthy's primary successes had come because, in the words of Ben Stavis, "we had created, on an amateur basis, a super-machine."[93]

The mixed system had put a premium on organization; that is why, in normal times, the party organization dominated it. It is also why, in abnormal times, a movement like that which supported Goldwater could use it as a conduit into the heart of the party itself. Hence McGovern's and Goldwater's caucus success; hence also the greater success of McGovern in the old and unreformed primaries. Of course, the degree of movement success depended not merely on its own organization, but on the relation of its organization to the party; where the party was relatively weak, the movement needed to pass a lower threshold of strength than where the party was strong. In any case, the reforms that McGovern had set in motion before 1972 devalued organization—not just that of the party, but any organization. He was fortunate that the reforms were not completed in time to derail his own nomination.

Plebiscitary Nature of System

The reform system is based in no small part on a plebiscitary ethos, which holds as illegitimate any convention decision that does not reflect the will of the party's voters with respect to presidential candidates. A major objection against Humphrey in 1968 was that he was able to attain the nomination while his insurgent opponents outpolled him in the primaries (indeed, he opted to avoid the primary route).

In 1964 the absence of a strong plebiscitary ethos in the mixed system worked to aid the conservative takeover, in that the movement's candidate—though not necessarily his philosophy—was supported by far less than a majority of the party's voters. In 1972, this phenomenon was repeated. As already mentioned, McGovern finished second in primary votes behind Hubert Humphrey, to join Humphrey in 1968 and Adlai Stevenson in 1952 as the only recent candidates to gain the nomination after being outpolled in the primaries. Like Goldwater, McGovern was the first choice of at most 30 percent of his party's voters on the eve of the convention, and one poll actually showed him behind both Humphrey and Wallace. To an even greater extent than Goldwater's, McGovern's nomination resulted in mass defections from his party in November. In short, McGovern's nomination contradicted the plebiscitary ethos the reforms sought to insinuate into the nominating system.

Specifically, the plebiscitary ethos manifests itself in the reform rules that prevent delegate selection processes from beginning prior to the calendar year of the election and that otherwise promote candidate-centered contests. Some of these rules were in effect in 1972, such as the ban on early selection processes and the requirement that primary delegates identify their presidential preference. Others came after 1972, most notably the proportional representation rule in caucuses, which had the effect of requiring delegate candidates even at the precinct level to identify their presidential preferences. It is useful to consider the impact of these concrete plebiscitary devices (or lack thereof) on the McGovern campaign.

The McCarthy forces were aggrieved in 1968 by the early selection of approximately six hundred delegates, most of whom voted for Hubert Humphrey. Furthermore, Epstein argues that the ban on early delegate selection worked to McGovern's advantage by making it harder for the early front-runner to collect delegates.[94] However, the McGovern campaign was the extension of a movement that had begun five years earlier, and it almost certainly could have benefited from early selection of delegates in some nonprimary states. As it was, its successes in nonprimary states were often due to its head start in organizing.[95] Goldwater had similarly benefited, since the Suite 3505 Committee and Draft Goldwater Committee were in the field long before any rivals. It seems likely that well-grounded movements actually would have something to gain from early delegate selection processes; only movements like the 1968 new politics, which had been organizing for less than a year, would consistently be harmed. Early delegate selection did not shut out movements but rather ensured that movements that succeeded had proven staying power. Likewise, the move toward a purely candidate-centered delegate selection process did not favor the mature version of the new politics in 1972.

Finally, while the reforms reduced the power of the regulars in caucuses, they also ensured that the same focused strategies would be used by all candidates, whether or not they represented a movement. All candidates were forced to seek committed delegates at the precinct level; to wait for uncommitted delegates, as the regular candidates used to do as a matter of course, would no longer be possible. Some of the comparative advantage held in a caucus setting by committed supporters of a movement candidate was thus dissipated.

Movements in the Majority Party

Under both the convention system and the mixed system, movements had a much greater chance of penetrating the minority than they did the majority party. This was because those systems were heavily dependent on the party organizations; naturally, where the party was weakest, it was most vulnerable. The experience of the new politics movement supports this proposition, but also indicates that the reforms might have narrowed the gap between majority and minority parties in this respect.

McCarthy's experience in particular shows the greater barriers to majority party movements that exist in the mixed system. Lyndon Johnson as an incumbent had enormous power at his disposal to block challengers, even after he left the race. Theodore White, for example, details the control Johnson exerted over the Chicago convention.[96] Overall, the Democratic Party, as the majority party, was much healthier organizationally, and indeed had gained the reputation from decades in power of being "the politicians' party."[97] At the Republican convention in Miami, "delegates had been sought retail, one by one. In Chicago, they came in wholesale packages, by states."[98] Indeed, before

Robert F. Kennedy himself entered the race, he advised McCarthy to run in the primary in New Hampshire instead of in Massachusetts, since the Democrats were a minority in New Hampshire and hence the party machinery was weaker and more vulnerable.[99] McCarthy in 1968 was attempting to overcome the entrenched advantages of a party organization that had its own incumbent president and had governed America for the better part of the previous four decades.

It also seems sensible to view the McGovern case as partial confirmation of this thesis. Shafer points out that "organized reform factions . . . were usually found in areas where *Republicans* were in the majority."[100] McGovern had delegate pluralities in twelve of fourteen New England and Rocky Mountain states—two areas where the Democratic Party was relatively weak—and did worst in the South, which had defected at the presidential level but was still a Democratic bastion at the local level. However, his strength in the ten largest states showed that he was hardly shut out of other Democratic strongholds. He did not have to run against an incumbent president of his own party or that president's chosen successor, and it is clear in retrospect that the party's majority coalition (and majority status) had already begun shattering in 1968.

It also seems fair to say that the reforms, to the degree that they reduced organizational barriers to movement access, had a disproportionate impact on the majority party and thus narrowed the gap between majority and minority party vulnerability. McGovern's victory came in a party that, despite its other difficulties, held eight more governorships than it had in 1968.

Financing

Like the conservative movement, the new politics movement was heavily dependent on small contributions raised through direct mail. McCarthy copied Goldwater's fund-raising techniques, sending direct mail to lists of antiadministration sources such as the *New York Review of Books, Ramparts* magazine, and the Student Non-violent Coordinating Committee, among others.[101]

In 1972, McGovern went much further, developing what he called "the best political fund-raising apparatus in the nation."[102] In 1970, McGovern spearheaded a fund-raising campaign for Democratic Senate candidates, which netted $1 million for the candidates and forty thousand names for his own lists. He gained an additional fifty thousand names when he appealed for funds on an antiwar television broadcast after the invasion of Cambodia in April 1970. When he announced his candidacy, he did so by sending an eight-page letter to the people on his lists, which brought back $300,000, enough money to fund the campaign through the first half on 1971. A "McGovern for President Club" was created, in which members pledged $10 a month to the campaign; this brought in a guaranteed monthly income of $100,000. And new lists were constantly developed.[103]

Overall, McGovern raised $5 million from 100,000 donors prior to the Democratic convention; including the general election campaign, he raised $38 million, 65 percent of which came from 700,000 small donors.[104] It was direct mail that had kept McGovern afloat in the difficult pre-Wisconsin days, and that had closed off sources of funding for his liberal competitors (like John Lindsay). Just like Goldwater before him, "McGovern opened up a new, very promising source of revenue for his party."[105]

As a result, it might be surmised that McGovern (and Goldwater and McCarthy before him) would have benefited from the 1974 campaign finance rules had these been in effect. Those rules provide federal matching funds for preconvention donations up to $250, provided that at least $5,000 has been collected in this way in each of twenty states. Mass-based movements such as these would have much to gain from a system weighted toward small contributors.[106] To the extent that the system is so weighted, it is more open to movement access.

However, there are several compensating factors both within the finance laws and in the broader nominating system that probably negate much of this advantage, especially for strong—that is, well-organized and broadly based—movements. First, not only does federal finance law provide matching contributions for donations up to $250, it also prohibits individual contributions in excess of $1,000 and contributions by political action committees in excess of $5,000. It is important to remember that even new politics movement–based candidates like McCarthy, Kennedy, and McGovern relied to some extent—sometimes at crucial junctures—on contributions much larger than those now permitted. McCarthy raised large contributions as well as small.[107] Kennedy raised and spent $11 million in eleven weeks, a feat that would have been impossible without some very large contributions.[108] McGovern was tided over not only by direct mail but by large loans that would fall well outside current regulations, and in the crucial primary stretch after Wisconsin, he was bolstered by contributions ranging from $10,000 to $300,000. Stewart Mott of the General Motors fortune pledged to match funds raised for the California primary, netting the McGovern campaign $400,000.[109]

The loss of large contributions might have hurt their opponents even more, and may have been compensated by the federal matching funds, but as outsiders the movement candidates needed these financial resources more than their opponents. In the view of Herbert Alexander, newly emerging political leaders are inherently put at a disadvantage having to "run all over the country getting $1,000 contributions."[110]

Second, it seems likely that movement candidates (and outsiders of any sort) would have been hurt by the state-by-state spending limits attached to federal funding. McCarthy, for example, drove Johnson out of the race by threatening to overwhelm him in Wisconsin, where he not only had a vast base of volunteers but was concentrating his resources so as to outspend the regulars six to one.[111] McGovern likewise concentrated his resources in California, where he spent fully one-half of his preconvention war chest.[112] In 1964, Goldwater had been forced to spend a similar proportion of his money in California. The spending limits would clearly have curtailed the ability of these candidates either to make an early breakthrough or to win a crucial late primary through concentrated spending.

Furthermore, federal campaign finance regulations carry with them a set of onerous reporting requirements which, Nelson Polsby maintains, has combined with the spending limits to dampen grassroots campaigning. In this view, in order to ensure that all regulations are strictly followed, campaigns impose heavy control from the top.[113] This constrains the kind of effective decentralized operation used by the McGovern campaign and other movement campaigns. It is not difficult to imagine what the effects of this regime might have been on movement efforts. The McCarthy campaign drew a great deal of its vigor from the interaction of volunteers with local supporters when those supporters opened their homes as temporary lodging; this also, not incidentally, vastly reduced McCarthy's campaign expenses.[114] Under current rules, this donated room and board would have to be recorded as an in-kind contribution. Could the campaign have kept track of it all? Would it have simply avoided the practice in order to avoid legal wrangling? If so, how would it have replaced the loss with limited funds?

Thus, it is probable that strong movements have not gained as much as one might expect from the finance rules imposed in 1974. Furthermore, when looking outside the finance rules to the broader nominating system, we find that the "new politics" movement was clearly most financially strained by the primaries, as the conservatives had been. Campaigning in primaries has always cost far more than campaigning in caucuses, by a factor that is now between five and fifteen.[115] The new politics forces had to struggle through half again as many primaries as the conservatives, and that figure grew again by half by the end of the decade. The gain won through matching contributions almost surely was more than offset by the additional costs of campaigning imposed by the reform-driven expansion of primaries.

Openness, Stability, and the New Politics

The McGovern campaign demonstrated numerous crucial points about openness and stability in the nominating system. First, primaries helped McGovern more than they helped Goldwater, but McGovern still did not run impressively in them, and the primaries most important to him had existed before the reforms and were still largely unreformed. Second, the caucuses were almost surely more permeable to movements than the primaries, partly because of the reforms but largely because of the inherent nature of caucuses and movements, as Goldwater had shown in 1964. Third, McGovern won with a "mixed-system" strategy of carefully choosing his primary targets, and probably could not have won if he had been forced to run vigorously in all primary states. Above all, he won with superior organization grounded in the new politics movement, which emulated the party and labor organization he sought to displace, and which took full advantage of the residual pro-organization bias of the prereform system.

The parallels with Goldwater are illustrative. Both did best in caucuses and were threatened most in primaries; both relied on heavy organization; both seem to have been aided by the preponderance of districted delegates, while using an occasional winner-take-all primary to strike an important blow; both took full advantage of the disconnection between primary votes and primary delegates. The contrast with McCarthy is also crucial: McCarthy was a reluctant candidate running against an incumbent president, with the aid of a movement not yet organized for a year and with a strategy that did not attend to the nonprimary states until it was too late, even though two-thirds of the delegates were located there. McGovern might not have won in 1968, but it seems even safer to bet that McCarthy would not have won in 1972. It is interesting to note that McCarthy himself believes that the old system was "better than what we have now." While he thinks that McGovern could not have won in 1968 he also believes the South Dakotan could not have won in 1976.[116]

In short, McGovern's campaign was in many ways more at home in the mixed system than in the reform system, and it benefited from the fact that the reforms were only partially in place. Furthermore, the reforms that were most helpful to him—reducing regular influence in the caucuses, for instance—

were the ones that had been implemented, while those that would have hurt him the most were yet to come.

Since the 1972 nomination was won in a system neither fully mixed nor fully reformed, it can best be considered a way station on the road to the full reform system. In 1972, based on McGovern's experience (and Goldwater's before him), some speculative conclusions could be drawn about the future shape of openness and stability in the nominating system.

It could almost certainly be said that the system was more open to initial movement access, insofar as the barrier presented by party regulars was seriously reduced. This, of course, came at the expense of stability, since the lowering of that barrier would invite movements to compete for power that would not have been strong enough to do so before. Peer review was also seriously curtailed in the same way.[117] This reduction of regular party influence probably increased the susceptibility of the majority party to movement takeover, with the attendant threats to governing stability, but it is significant that McGovern's victory still took place in the party out of the White House, a party whose majority status had already substantially faltered. Furthermore, it could be more clearly predicted that openness to movements—especially in terms of potential for actual success, rather than mere access—would suffer on account of numerous reform factors. These include the increase in primaries; the plebiscitary ethos of the system, and its specific manifestations, such as banning early delegate selection and encouraging a candidate-centered caucus system; and the emphasis on proportional representation.

Above all, the reforms constituted an attack on the advantages of organization that movements and parties alike derive, parties in normal times and movements in abnormal. Rick Stearns himself was upset at the propensity of new politics adherents (and of the reforms) to be "anti-organization."[118] The attack on organization inherent in the reforms hurt both movement and party, both openness and stability, in the same way that the mixed system blended and preserved openness and stability through its emphasis on organization. The reforms hurt openness in the sense that movements no longer operated in a system that traded on the organization that was their greatest strength; stability was hurt in the sense that barriers to initial access were reduced and peer review curtailed.

Not only could it be predicted that strong movements—movements that were not doomed from the beginning—would face greater difficulty in achieving the nomination of their candidates in the fully reformed nominating system, but it might be predicted that even success would not prove as useful.

Goldwater won the nomination and gained at the same time control of the party machinery that served the conservatives for a generation. McGovern won the nomination, but the next Democratic nominee was Jimmy Carter, who had led the anti-McGovern forces in the South and had given Henry Jackson's nominating speech in Miami. The McGovern wing of the Democratic Party has exerted serious and often decisive influence on the party in the years since 1972, but its control of the party has been far less secure than conservative dominance of the GOP.

Hence, there are crucial similarities between 1964 and 1972, and crucial differences between what followed 1964 and what followed 1972. The similarities were due to what the 1964 system still shared with the 1972 system. The differences may have at least as much to do with how the more fully reformed system did in fact break with the past.

5

Post-1972 Movements

WHILE THERE HAVE BEEN NO NEW MOVEMENTS of the strength and stature of the new politics or the conservatives since 1972, there have been two lesser movements that have attempted to influence the major parties. In 1984 and 1988, Jesse Jackson attempted to forge a "rainbow coalition" movement that would influence the direction of the Democratic Party, and in 1988, Pat Robertson attempted to harness the energy of the "Christian right" as the opening shot in an ongoing effort to take over the Republican Party. Furthermore, in 1976, Ronald Reagan challenged and nearly defeated an incumbent president of his own party—Gerald Ford—on the strength of an old movement, the conservative, that had already become a predominant force in the party.

This chapter will confirm that movement success is actually stifled by important elements of the reforms. This negative impact is felt disproportionately by stronger movements, while in certain respects weaker movements are actually encouraged. Weaker movements may not be able to win under any system, but the reforms have improved their access. For instance, proportional representation, the reduction of caucuses, and finance rules that limit contributions and expenditures have narrowed the gap between stronger and weaker movements.

Jesse Jackson and the "Rainbow Coalition"

In March 1983, a substantial portion of America's black leadership gathered to consider the question of whether there should be a black candidate vying for the Democratic presidential nomination in 1984. The majority of those present tentatively decided to proceed with a black candidate, though that candidate was not yet named. Organizational work began at once, in a way reminiscent of the Suite 3505 Committee, which began organizing to elect conservative delegates prior to acquiring a candidate. A voter registration drive was launched in twenty-four states with the goal of increasing black turnout by one-fourth.[1]

This decision was prodded by the policies of the Reagan administration and by the Democratic Party's apparent tendency to take black votes for granted and its attempt to move toward the political center after the electoral debacle of 1980. The mayoral victories of Harold Washington in Chicago and Wilson Goode in Philadelphia and Mel King's creditable race in Boston convinced many in the group that a black presidential candidate was not only necessary but viable.[2]

By November 1983, Rev. Jesse Jackson had declared that he would lead the effort. Jackson had been a part of the initial planning group, and had formed an exploratory committee as soon as the final decision of the group to support a black candidate had been made in June. He maintained that he did not intend to go ahead "without the sanction of the group assembled in Chicago."[3] Jackson's decision in November was made only after months of consultation and was supported by a formidable proportion of the Chicago group as well as other black forces (such as the churches).

Jackson had long been active in the civil rights movement, working first with the Southern Christian Leadership Conference in the 1960s and then starting his own Chicago-based organization "People United to Save Humanity" (PUSH) in the early 1970s. When he announced his candidacy, he proclaimed his intention of leading a "rainbow coalition" of minorities and the "dispossessed" of all races.[4] It seems clear that his major objective was not actually to win the nomination but to solidify the black vote, add to it whatever he could from other minorities and white liberals, and wield this bloc as a weapon to move the Democratic Party to the left.[5]

Jackson entered the campaign much later than most of his rivals and had difficulty establishing an efficient campaign organization throughout 1984.[6] Furthermore, a substantial portion of the black leadership preferred the more customary strategy of supporting the best white candidate, who most of them believed to be Walter Mondale. Despite these disadvantages, Jackson had at his disposal much of the lower echelons of the civil rights movement and the vast network of black churches. In the words of Lorn Foster, "The Jackson campaign was an extension of the civil rights movement and can best be understood in that context."[7]

Within two months, 90 percent of black pastors had endorsed Jackson's effort. With 6.8 million members in forty thousand churches, the National Baptist Convention, USA, endorsed him, as did the smaller Progressive National Baptists Convention. This provided Jackson with a ready-made organization outside his own campaign structure, crucial for volunteers, voter registration drives, get-out-the-vote drives, and fund-raising.[8] The candidate raised untold thousands of dollars in visits to churches, and thousands more were raised by pastors on their own.[9]

As 1984 progressed, Jackson settled in as one of three surviving contenders, behind the front-running Mondale and Gary Hart. After a slow start, Jackson picked up strength in the South, ultimately winning caucuses in South Carolina and primaries in Louisiana and the District of Columbia. He finished with 19 percent of the primary vote, behind Mondale with 39 percent and Hart with 36 percent. Jackson won 465.5 of the 4,162 delegates.

In combination with the Hart forces, Jackson succeeded in bringing to a convention vote four platform minority planks, all of which were defeated. His supporters succeeded in modifying platform language on other topics while the platform was being drafted. Finally, under pressure from Jackson that had begun in January, the Democratic Party agreed to review (yet again) its nominating rules. Jackson wanted the elimination of nonproportional representation primaries, the elimination of thresholds in proportional representation primaries, and a requirement that superdelegates be bound to vote in accord with their state's primary results. He also urged the elimination of caucus procedures on the grounds that they were not as democratic as primaries. The resulting "Fairness Commission" took no such drastic steps, but did reduce thresholds from 20 percent to 15 percent and agreed to delay election of superdelegates until after the initial round of primaries.

When Jackson decided to run again in 1988, it quickly became clear that he had substantially succeeded in building the coalition he had promised in 1984. He still possessed the powerful network of black churches that had sustained him in his first campaign, and he had won over most of the black officials and civil rights leaders (along with their organizational resources) who had backed Mondale in 1984.[10] He began the 1984 campaign winning 50–60 percent of the black vote; by the end of that campaign, he was pulling in

85–90 percent, a figure that rose to 95 percent in 1988. Furthermore, his base had expanded to include more Hispanics, Asians, Indians, labor unions, and white liberals such as peace, environmental, and homosexual groups. His "rainbow coalition," which had appeared to media observers in 1984 as a "monochromic rainbow," seemed much closer to reality, and his own campaign organization was much improved.

As a result, rather than finishing a distant third as in 1984, Jackson found himself in a two-man race with Michael Dukakis. His greatest strength again came in the South, where "Super Tuesday" worked to his benefit, much to the chagrin of Southern moderates, who had hoped that the concentration of southern primaries could pull the Democratic ticket to the right.

Overall, he won 29 percent of the primary vote to Dukakis's 42 percent, and his nomination was seen as a real possibility for a brief moment after his victory in the Michigan caucuses. Again, Jackson's platform preferences and vice presidential aspirations were deflected by the Democratic victor, but this time his rules demands were largely met: Dukakis agreed to push the Democratic National Committee to ban all nonproportional primaries and to reduce superdelegates by about 250. The DNC responded by ratifying the former agreement but reversing the latter. It can only be speculated whether the new rules would have benefited Jackson, since he did not seek the nomination in 1992.

It is apparent that the rainbow coalition, even by 1988, was not a movement of the strength of those that propelled Goldwater and McGovern. It was undoubtedly more personalistic than the strongest movements, drawing a great deal of its strength from Jackson himself. To Jackson's issue director Ronald Walters, "The most important ingredient [to the mobilization of the movement] was the emergence of Rev. Jesse Jackson."[11] And its organizational capacity and the breadth of its base were considerably weaker, depending largely on a racial appeal that failed in 1984 to produce even a unified black community.

By 1988, the movement had matured somewhat and not only solidified its black base but reached out much more effectively. It was also better organized. In 1984, Jackson's objective was not to take over the party, but merely to influence it; the greater strength of the movement in 1988 was reflected in the fact that the nomination itself was no longer assumed to be entirely out of reach.

If we keep in mind the relative weakness of the movement, what can be said about the impact of the reforms on openness and stability as seen in the Jackson enterprises? First, despite his call in 1984 to eliminate caucuses altogether, Jackson held his own in caucuses in 1984 and did much better in them in 1988 than he did in primaries, in terms of both delegates and votes. In 1984, he received a mean vote of 17.5 percent in primaries and 9.8 percent in caucuses, but actually won 13.1 percent of the delegates from caucus states to 12.6 percent from primary states.[12] In the three states that held both caucuses and nonbinding primaries, Jackson performed better in the primary in one, slightly better in the caucuses in another, and much better in the caucuses in the third.[13] In 1988, when the rainbow coalition was stronger, Jackson did substantially better in caucuses: he won 29.7 percent of the delegates from primary states, and 38.9 percent of the delegates from caucus states.[14] At the beginning of the 1988 campaign, the *National Journal* predicted that the reduction of caucuses after 1984 could hurt candidates like Jackson; this prediction was almost certainly accurate.[15] Had the same proportion of delegates been chosen by caucus in 1988 as in 1984, and had Jackson's 1988 delegate percentages remained the same, he would have gained an additional forty-eight delegates.[16]

In 1984 Jackson won two primaries, Louisiana and the District of Columbia, and the South Carolina caucuses. In all three states, there were high concentrations of black voters, a situation magnified in Louisiana by the virtual boycott of the primary by white voters. In 1988, Jackson won seven of thirty-seven primaries (or 19 percent of the primaries) and seven of twenty-two caucus states (or 32 percent).[17] His five Super Tuesday primary victories helped him tremendously.[18]

While all of Jackson's primary victories came in the "black belt," he—like McGovern before him—won caucuses in some of the most unlikely places, such as Alaska and Vermont, and placed a close second in others such as Maine, Kansas, and Colorado.[19] Indeed, it was a surprise victory in Michigan—the largest of the caucus states—that made Jackson a front-runner for a few weeks in March and April. Primary defeats in Wisconsin and New York halted his momentum and then finished him off. Dukakis operatives had indeed expressed hope that the fact that Wisconsin was a primary rather than caucus state would work to their benefit because "the intensity of the Jackson support will have limited effect."[20] While Jackson lost to Dukakis 42-29 percent in the primaries, he beat Dukakis 37-32 percent in the first-level popular voting in the seventeen caucus states where such results were tabulated.[21] The low cost of caucuses undoubtedly contributed to Jackson's success; there were numerous examples where Jackson was outspent by Dukakis ten to one but nearly matched his votes.[22] This greater cost-effectiveness in caucuses is at least partially derived from the greater importance of media advertising in primaries. Studies in both 1984 and 1988 showed that Iowa caucus goers, for example, were little affected by the media.[23]

The relative hospitality of caucuses versus primaries to the Jackson campaign can be seen in the three states that in 1988 held both primaries and caucuses—Idaho, Texas, and Vermont. Such comparison is not definitive, since only Texas held its primary and caucus on the same day. Nevertheless, a consistent pattern emerges. Dukakis won all three primaries handily, but lost two of the caucuses to Jackson. In the third, his winning margin was reduced from fifty-seven points to nineteen (see table 5.1).

Jackson's complaints about the caucuses in 1984 were based on certain effects of the caucus structure. Most states conduct first-level caucuses at the precinct level, which often consists of small neighborhoods. Each precinct is assigned a number of delegates that it can elect to the next level of meeting, usually a county or congressional district convention. These delegate allotments are predetermined on the basis of the Democratic voting strength of each precinct. In 1984, when Jackson's campaign was more heavily weighted toward a racial appeal, he succeeded in bringing out unprecedented numbers of black voters. However, because they were highly concentrated geographically, these black voters tended to swamp selected precinct caucuses while leaving many others virtually untouched. Yet each precinct's delegate total remained the same regardless of turnout. Hence, Jackson had a serious vote "surplus" in his strong areas, while he was unable to reach the 20 percent threshold in many others. For instance, Jackson won an estimated plurality of those who attended the Virginia caucuses, but finished third in delegates because his support was highly concentrated in the Tidewater region.[24] In

Table 5-1. 1988 Voting Results: States Using Primaries and Caucuses

	Primary Result (%)		Caucus Result (%)	
Idaho	Dukakis	73	Dukakis	38
	Jackson	16	Uncommitted	29
			Jackson	22
Texas	Dukakis	33	Jackson	40
	Jackson	25	Dukakis	38
	Gore	20	Uncommitted	10
Vermont	Dukakis	56	Jackson	46
	Jackson	26	Dukakis	45

1988, this problem was largely overcome by Jackson, because he was able to significantly broaden his base beyond black voters.[25] This is undoubtedly why his caucus/primary delegate differential grew as the movement became stronger. Thus, not only may caucuses work to the advantage of movements in general, they also work to a certain extent to hinder movements—like the 1984 version of the rainbow coalition—that are so narrowly based that they consist of small and isolated geographical pockets.

It is no accident that the greatest beneficiary of the caucuses in 1984 was Walter Mondale, the only candidate with an organization to match that at Jackson's disposal. Where Jackson used the organizational base of an outside movement, Mondale built his organization around the party regulars and groups strongly encased in the Democratic Party power structure, such as the AFL-CIO and the National Education Association.[26] This confirms the organizational bias of the old system in which caucus/convention processes were dominant. The reforms, as in the McGovern case, undoubtedly reduced the barriers to entry by movements, as did the decay of party organizations themselves, thus facilitating access by weaker movements that could not pass the prereform threshold but could meet the postreform one. In this sense, Jackson probably did better in many individual caucuses after the caucus reforms than he would have done before them. Nevertheless, his successes fit into a consistent pattern of movement candidates in both parties and in both unreformed and reformed caucuses. The stronger position of parties in caucuses as opposed to primaries also clearly remains.

In both 1984 and 1988 Jackson also attacked the existence of nonproportional primaries. Those primaries—the so-called loophole primary that permitted the winner to take all by congressional district, and the "bonus" primary that gave CD winners one delegate for winning before dividing the rest proportionally—helped early winners to more easily translate primary victories into delegate majorities. Jackson was hurt most by these devices, as by the localized nature of caucuses, in 1984. In that year, he won 19 percent of the primary vote but received only 12 percent of the primary delegates. Had there been pure proportional representation, and had there been no "superdelegates," Jackson would have gained an additional 250 or so delegates, still leaving him almost 1,000 behind Mondale.[27]

In 1988, he won 29.1 percent of the primary vote, and turned that into 29.7 percent of the primary delegates. As in the caucuses, the difference between Jackson's 1984 and 1988 primary performance is that Jackson was a much stronger force the second time he ran.[28] In contrast to 1984, he gained more delegates than votes in both bonus primaries and (due to the thresholds he would have eliminated) proportional representation primaries. Only in loophole primaries, which were winner take all by congressional district, did Jackson have a smaller percentage of delegates than of votes.[29]

It is mathematically inevitable that any delegate system that provides a bonus to winners will leave losers with a disproportionately small number of delegates. McGovern, and to a lesser extent Goldwater, took full advantage of such systems to turn relatively small pluralities into impressive primary delegate majorities. Jackson, as the leader of a weaker movement, found himself in 1984 at the wrong end of the equation, a difficulty he overcame as he gained in strength. Had he run in 1992, it is very possible he would have found himself bemoaning the move back to proportional representation that he imposed on the Democratic Party.

It can thus be said that nonproportional primaries (especially districted plurality primaries), like caucuses, work to the relative disadvantage of movements that are narrowly based, poorly organized, and with limited electoral appeal. Conversely, these same devices that serve as barriers to weak movements are mechanisms for openness to movements that are more broadly based and better organized. A system based on proportional representation primaries, with low thresholds, no bonuses, and few caucuses, would provide greater initial access to movements such as the rainbow coalition in 1984 (and to a lesser extent 1988), which are capable under the reforms of gaining enough votes to disrupt the party even though they are incapable under any system of actually winning. As movements grow in strength, the reforms become more of a hindrance than a help, depriving broad-based movements of the opportunities inherent in the caucus system and depriving strong movements, like strong candidates in general, of the capacity to form delegate majorities from less than a majority of votes—a capacity that historically seems especially important to movements, since by definition even strong ones do not constitute a majority in the decisive stages of their takeover attempts.

A sophisticated statistical analysis undertaken by Stephen Ansolabehere and Gary King, examining the candidate bias of different elements of the nominating system, confirms this basic outline. In 1984, the proportional representation primaries were the least biased against Jackson, with the caucuses and nonproportional primaries more biased against him. In 1988, the caucuses were the least biased element, with proportional primaries next and nonproportional primaries most biased.[30]

Jackson also consistently attacked the superdelegates, who represented an attempt by the Democratic Party to reinject the party's elected officials into the presidential nominating system in hopes of preventing disasters like 1972 and 1980. They served this role in 1984 by providing almost all the margin of victory for Mondale, who was clearly the "regular" choice, and in 1988 by overwhelmingly supporting Dukakis once the race narrowed to one between him and Jackson. Jackson received very few "superdelegate" votes in either year. In many ways, then, the superdelegates restored some elements of the prereform system, such as delegate discretion and party influence. Furthermore, although they disappointed initial expectations in 1984 by quickly jumping on the Mondale bandwagon, in 1988 they were seemingly subject to the influence of shifting primary results, as the old party leaders had been.

The combination of the short-lived increase in caucuses in 1984, and the superdelegates and the allowance of primaries that deviated from pure proportional representation in 1984 and 1988, reintroduced some of the advantages that the old system had afforded to strong organization. Superdelegates backed the "party" choice, and the caucuses and non-PR primaries worked to the advantage of broad-based organization in general. Hence the victories of Mondale, who had party support and what one commentator called "the largest, best-organized and, some say, most sophisticated Democratic machine in years,"[31] and Dukakis, who was a scaled-down version of Mondale. Hence also the problems caused for Jackson from these sources. To the degree that the Hunt Commission succeeded in restoring some elements of the old system, the performance of Jackson vis-à-vis those elements, especially in 1984, further suggests the difficulties of initial movement access for weaker movements in the old system.[32]

Finally, Jackson probably benefited from the election finance regime more than did all other campaigns. He was consistently dependent on small contributions; contributions under five hundred dollars accounted for 86 percent of his total fund-raising in 1984 and 88 percent in 1988.[33] While he used direct mail, he was even more dependent on donations collected at campaign appearances and by pastors of black churches.[34] Furthermore, in 1984 he did not have enough money to spend to come close to the state-by-state or national spending limits, though by 1988 his situation had improved to the extent that he actually outspent Dukakis on TV in Pennsylvania and Ohio.[35]

However, several aspects of the 1974 finance regulations were not beneficial to the rainbow coalition effort. Federal law does not permit matching funds to be issued for cash contributions, but a substantial proportion of contributions to Jackson were in cash, as a result of his dependence on spontaneous collections.[36] Additionally, Jackson's late start in 1984 made it difficult for him to qualify for matching funds that year, and only a good showing in the Georgia primary on Super Tuesday in 1984 kept him from losing his matching funds, which were dependent on his not falling below 20 percent on three consecutive primary dates. Nevertheless, on balance it seems clear that Jackson benefited most not only from matching funds but from the contribution and spending limits applied to his chief competitors. Since he, unlike representatives of previous stronger movements, had almost no capacity to raise large contributions or to breach the state spending limits, he lost nothing from those restrictions.[37]

Pat Robertson and the Christian Right

At the same time that Jesse Jackson's rainbow coalition was making a serious run for the Democratic presidential nomination in 1988, Rev. Marion "Pat" Robertson was attempting to win the Republican nomination on the strength of an "invisible army" of conservative evangelical Christians. As a movement, the "Christian right" had first mobilized in the late 1970s and early 1980s, largely as a reaction to the perception that America was in moral decline, and that this decline was abetted by government actions at numerous levels. The Supreme Court was a particular object of obloquy for its decisions on school prayer, pornography, and abortion. These concerns were part of a broader worldview that called for strong national defense, vigorous prosecution of the Cold War against Communism, and limited government.[38]

Social traditionalists had long been a part of the conservative movement, and Goldwater himself had campaigned against the Supreme Court's anti–school prayer decision. These forces did not attain organizational substance and direction of their own until the late 1970s, however. By the 1980 elections, the Christian right had become "a virtual labyrinth of political action committees, lobbies, educational and research foundations, publications, television programs, and churches . . . some ninety organizations."[39] Among the most important of these organizations were Christian Voice and Moral Majority, both of which were mass-based organizations, and the Roundtable, which was an elite organization "to coordinate and provide resources for conservative religious leaders."[40] The antiabortion movement, which has its own network of forces, also largely overlaps the Christian right.[41]

Prior to 1988, the movement focused primarily on influencing electoral politics by supporting candidates friendly to its agenda, such as Ronald Reagan and numerous Senate and House candidates. In 1988, however, television evangelist Pat Robertson became a candidate in an attempt to focus the energies of the movement and turn the Republican Party more fully into an instrument of that movement. Robertson himself started with a large list of contributors to his television show "The 700 Club," and with a viewing audience of millions more for the show and his own Christian Broadcasting Network (CBN). Additionally, Robertson founded in 1981 an organization called Freedom Council to mobilize conservative Christians for grassroots political activity; Freedom Council had fifty thousand members by the time he decided to run. Finally, by 1987, he had received petitions with more than 3 million names on them urging him to run, which served as the basis of his campaign organization in several states.[42]

Despite the potential voting and organizational strength at Robertson's disposal, the forces supporting him in 1988—like those supporting Jackson in the 1980s—were not as strong as the conservative or new politics movements. Most obviously, the Christian right was itself in many ways a subset of the conservative movement.[43] Furthermore, despite his best efforts to present himself as a standard-bearer for the movement, Robertson was unable to consolidate the Christian right behind his candidacy. Robertson was a "charismatic" (a wing of fundamentalism that believes in faith healing and "speaking in tongues"), which repelled many noncharismatic members of the movement. Indeed, he faced stiff competition for conservative Christian support from George Bush, Jack Kemp, and Pete DuPont; the Moral Majority's Jerry Falwell endorsed Bush, and Bush received most of the votes of self-described "fundamentalist" voters in the primaries.[44]

Nevertheless, the Robertson crusade was an important step in the growing political strength of the Christian right and served as the launching pad of the Christian Coalition, which proved an increasingly potent force within the Republican Party of the 1990s. Robertson's campaign once again proved that caucuses are more permeable to movements than are primaries and provide subsequent benefits that primaries cannot. Robertson won no primaries out of the thirty-four in which he was on the ballot, and placed second in five; he finished with 9.1 percent of the total primary vote. His highest total was 21.1 percent in Oklahoma, where he finished third. In the caucus states, he won outright three of ten (Hawaii, Alaska, and Washington), and finished second in another five; his mean first-round caucus result was 27.6 percent, with a high of 81.3 percent in Hawaii; in six of ten, his percentages were higher than his highest primary figure.[45]

Additionally, though Robertson did not place first in the Nevada caucuses, he won the most national convention delegates because his forces concentrated their strength behind "uncommitted" slates that were actually pro-Robertson.[46] And in Michigan, a coalition of Robertson and Kemp supporters took control of the state party after initial precinct meetings in

August 1986, but Robertson was unable to translate this success into a dele-gate victory due to legal maneuverings by Bush and the old-line Republican establishment, and the breakdown of the alliance with Kemp.[47]

Robertson was catapulted to national prominence on the strength of his showing in the Iowa caucuses, where he finished ahead of George Bush. His campaign bogged down when he could not duplicate his caucus successes in the primary states, and the deathblow was inflicted by his failure in South Car-olina and the Super Tuesday primaries, which followed days later. Had his campaign not faltered then, "Robertson would probably have scored even more caucus successes."[48] Robertson workers freely admitted the advantage to be gained in the caucus setting; as one campaign organizer said before the Ohio primary, "I don't think it would be unrealistic for us to win 15–18 del-egates [out of 88]. This would have to be a caucus state for us to win it."[49]

Furthermore, as in the Goldwater case, caucus proceedings provided an avenue for takeover of the party machinery such as precinct captains and state and county party officers. This happened in Michigan, though the success was short-lived. It was also the case in numerous states that held presidential pref-erence primaries but used a caucus/convention system to select delegates and to arrange party affairs. In Georgia, North Carolina, Virginia, Louisiana, and Mississippi, strong efforts were made to take over the caucuses and elect pro-Robertson delegates, even though they would have been bound to vote for Bush on the early ballots, because they would be free to vote for Robertson if later ballots became necessary and could vote their consciences on all platform and rules questions. In North Carolina, Louisiana, and Georgia, the regulars barely maintained control through procedural devices and credentials chal-lenges. In Oklahoma, even though Robertson finished third in the primary, his supporters went far toward taking over the party machinery; Robertson's Oklahoma director Tommy Garrett described his organization as "old-fash-ioned ward heelers" who were in politics for the long haul.[50]

In 1989, Robertson and his allies formed the nationwide "Christian Coalition" organization, which continued the work of influencing the party. The caucuses, used either to determine delegate victories or merely to select actual delegates and organize the party, worked to the relative advantage of the Robertson forces in the establishment of a base from which to proceed.[51] In any event, if one were to construct a hypothetical mix of caucuses and pri-maries in 1988, Robertson's degree of success would have been directly pro-portional to the importance of caucuses in the system.

A more nuanced look at the arrangement of caucuses and primaries also yields interesting conclusions. The relatively nonplebiscitary nature of

Republican caucuses (there is no proportional representation, no requirement to identify candidate preference, and no ban on early selection) seems to have worked in Robertson's favor at least twice. In Michigan, the Robertson forces took advantage of a very early start of the delegate selection process to ambush the party regulars. It was, of course, McCarthy's inability to influence selection in Michigan and other early states that led new politics advocates to believe that such processes were stacked against movements. Robertson backers might have taken over first-round caucuses had they been held in 1988 as well, but on the whole the Robertson case in Michigan seems to confirm that reforms banning early delegate selection can in some cases actually deprive long-lasting movements of the benefits of organizational strength.

In Nevada, as mentioned, the Robertson forces took advantage of Republican rules making it easier to elect uncommitted slates, using them as a "stalking horse" for their candidate. This is also consistent with some previous instances of systemic fluidity working to the advantage of forces that are well organized but not fully inside the corridors of power. In the same way, Goldwater was able to hide behind favorite-son candidacies in Ohio and Wisconsin.

In contrast to the Democrats, Republican primaries are usually plurality-based. Furthermore, at the same time Democratic delegate apportionment moved from an emphasis on at-large delegates to a focus on districted delegates, the Republicans moved in the opposite direction. This fact minimized Robertson's delegate strength, as it would have minimized Jackson's. In neither case were the candidates strong enough to benefit from the winner-take-all system, especially among at-large delegates. Because the balance was more heavily weighted toward proportional representation in the Democratic Party—and because Jackson was a stronger candidate in the primary states to begin with—Jackson had more influence within the councils of his party than Robertson was able to gain. Republican winner-take-all primaries knocked Robertson out of the running fairly early, depriving him of the capacity to influence the Republican Party at the 1988 national convention in the way Jackson influenced his party.[52]

In addition, Robertson faced a hurdle that Jackson was spared, a hurdle reflecting a fundamental difference between reform and nonreform conceptions of the role accorded to electoral minorities. The Republican rules, unlike Democratic rules, require a candidate to have a delegate majority in at least five states before his name can even be placed into nomination.[53] By this rule, Robertson could not have been nominated even had he remained in the race; nor could Jackson have been nominated in either 1984 or 1988.[54] The difference between Jackson's status and Robertson's status is added evidence for the proposition that, while the reforms might render strong movements less capable of ultimately succeeding, they probably do make it easier for weak movements to gain access to the parties and to influence them even in the absence of electoral victory.

The Robertson case also indicates again the degree to which the less-organized—which is to say, generally the minority—party might be more susceptible to takeover by movements. In state after state, Robertson did best in areas where the Republican Party was weak both organizationally and in terms of voter identification. In Iowa, he was primarily successful in blue-collar Democratic counties.[55] In Michigan, "Robertson ran best . . . where the GOP is much weaker, such as the heavily Democratic, blue-collar areas around Detroit and the industrial corridor stretching north from there. In those areas, Robertson's organization overwhelmed the existing GOP establishment, which is small and has little grass-roots presence."[56] In Hawaii, Robertson also "overwhelmed" the small Republican establishment, and in Illinois, he did best in heavily Democratic areas.[57]

Overall, Robertson made a serious effort to activate new voters and contributors. In Iowa, over 70 percent of his precinct workers had never attended a caucus before.[58] A large percentage of his contributors were first-time contributors to political campaigns.[59] And throughout the South, Robertson's forces registered thousands of new Republican voters, many of them former Democrats.[60] This effort, logically, had its greatest effect in areas where the new pro-Robertson Republicans were a larger proportion of all Republicans and where they did not have to contend with a strong party structure. Indeed, his strategy was based largely on targeting such areas.[61]

Robertson also benefited from Democratic crossover voting. Polling indicated that blue-collar Democrats voted heavily for Robertson in Iowa, which held open caucuses.[62] Nationwide, two-fifths of Robertson primary voters considered themselves "independents," as opposed to only one-fifth of the supporters of George Bush and Robert Dole.[63] In contrast, Jesse Jackson received very few crossover votes from Republicans in Wisconsin or elsewhere, despite an apparent effort by Wisconsin's Republican governor Tommy Thompson to encourage such crossovers.[64] Jackson did benefit from open primaries in another way, however. Most southern primaries are open, and in 1988 the disaffection of white southerners from the Democratic Party (speeded in part by Jackson himself) manifested itself in large-scale white Democratic voting in the Republican primaries. This desertion of whites from the Democratic primaries robbed moderate Democrats like Albert Gore and

Richard Gephart of potential votes and worked to the benefit of Jackson, who wound up winning five primaries on Super Tuesday. Open primaries and caucuses can work to the advantage of movements by permitting not only the addition of new voters but the subtraction of old ones, in an interparty dialectic.

Finally, unlike Jackson, Robertson had no difficulty raising money. Indeed, he raised more money than any candidate in either party except George Bush. Most of his money came from small contributors; 89 percent came in sums smaller than five hundred dollars.[65] These contributions were drawn primarily from direct mail lists he had developed in fund-raising for CBN.[66] Because of this existing fund-raising base, Robertson was able to spend 48 percent of the overall spending limit in 1987, compared to only 8 percent by Jackson. By the end of February 1988 Robertson had spent 79 percent of the limit, compared to only 19 percent for Jackson (and only 59 percent for Bush). In the end, Robertson spent 90 percent of national limits, while Jackson spent only 62 percent.[67] It is thus probably true that the Robertson campaign bumped up against the state limits far more often than did Jackson, and that FECA was thus much more of a mixed blessing to Robertson than to Jackson, though Robertson did receive more matching funds than any other Republican candidate in 1988. The Christian right was in a relative sense punished for having a broader base of contributors and a stronger fund-raising capacity than the rainbow coalition.

The Christian right did not expire with Robertson's defeat in 1988. Indeed, by 1992 it was in a far stronger position than the rainbow coalition, which seemed to have largely atrophied due to excessive personalism and failure to ground itself in the party apparatus.[68] Without Jackson as a candidate, the "rainbow" refracted into pieces, with white leftists largely supporting Jerry Brown, radical labor moving between Tom Harkin and Brown, and blacks (ironically) largely supporting Bill Clinton, whose numerous clashes with Jackson became legendary. In the end, the rainbow coalition's intraparty nemesis, the Democratic Leadership Council, won the day. On the other hand, in 1992 the Christian Coalition, which emphasized not Robertson but grassroots organization and local politics, elected at least three hundred delegates to the Republican national convention, controlled the state parties in six states, and claimed to have reached 40 million voters with its literature.[69] On the basis of this strength, the Christian Coalition spent 1992 "applying leverage on the [Bush] White House like classic power brokers."[70] By spring 1993 it had established 750 local chapters with 350,000 members and an annual budget of $8–10 million, raised mostly through very effective direct mail.[71]

Prior to the 1994 elections, the Christian Coalition claimed 1.4 million members, and *Campaigns & Elections* magazine estimated that the Christian right in general was the "dominant" force in eighteen state Republican parties and a "substantial force" in thirteen more.[72]

In the 1996 Republican nomination race, the national leadership of the Christian right remained neutral, while local leaders and voters split their support among Pat Buchanan, Bob Dole, Phil Gramm, and Alan Keyes. For a time, Buchanan was clearly the favorite of at least a plurality, and he benefited from substantial organizational support; according to exit polls, two of every three religious conservatives in the Louisiana caucuses supported Buchanan.[73] In the end, however, Dole owed his primary season success in no small part to his increasingly wide victories among Christian right voters after the South Carolina primary. Again, the movement's focus was on influencing as much of the nomination race as possible and subsequently influencing the party's platform. Christian Coalition executive director Ralph Reed held that the 1996 scenario—Christian right organizers playing an important role in several campaigns—was "so desirable that we couldn't have scripted it better ourselves."[74]

Overall, the movement's successes have been due to dogged precinct organization, and caucus/convention procedures have been disproportionately avenues of success.[75] Altogether, the successes of the Christian right after the 1988 election help to illustrate the general proposition that the prereform system was better for movements: the political movement from the 1980s that carried the greater influence into the 1990s was the one that operated in the less reformed Republican Party, not the one that operated in the more reformed Democratic Party.[76]

Ronald Reagan in 1976

Ronald Reagan's 1976 effort to unseat Gerald Ford is a different sort of case from the rest, insofar as Reagan was the standard-bearer of a conservative movement that had already established itself as the predominant force in the Republican Party in 1964. Indeed, there are many indications that his failure in 1976 was due not to ideological defeat but primarily to the incumbency of Gerald Ford, who himself was a Midwest conservative backed by Barry Goldwater, Strom Thurmond, John Tower, and Clif White.[77] As White later put it, "The Ford-Reagan struggle was more in the nature of a family argument, with conservatives lined up fairly evenly on both sides."[78] Nevertheless, Reagan was the leader of the conservative movement, and Reagan's 1976 campaign was a movement-backed attack on established power, an attempt by an outsider to unseat an incumbent president of his own party. Since the movement backing Reagan was clearly stronger than the other two examined in this chapter, more information can be gleaned about the operation of strong movements after the reforms.

Several facts stand out about the Reagan nomination effort in 1976. First, Reagan did substantially better in caucus states than in primary states. He won 56 percent of the delegates in caucus states and only 43.8 percent of the delegates in primary states. Even when the delegations of West Virginia, Pennsylvania, and New York are excluded—though primary states, they elected noncommitted organization slates without a head-to-head Reagan-Ford contest—Reagan still had only 51 percent of primary delegates.[79] Pomper noted that Reagan did much better in new as opposed to old primary states, but even so he did approximately equally well in new primary states and caucus states.[80]

Second, while a primary-dominated system was not an advantage for Reagan, the existence of some primaries did give his candidacy an important boost. Victories in the North Carolina, Texas, Indiana, Alabama, and Georgia primaries in the middle of the primary season were important in proving voter appeal, halting an early slide, and actually giving Reagan a certain amount of campaign momentum. Indeed, Reagan's campaign manager John Sears pointed out that some caucus successes could be traced to the effects of primary victories.[81] In this way, Reagan's experience mirrors that of Goldwater, who won on his strength in caucus states but was aided by the California primary.

Third, the types of primaries prescribed by the reforms would either not have helped Reagan or would have positively hurt him. A ban on open primaries and caucuses would have clearly hurt his candidacy. Studies indicate that Reagan was the greatest beneficiary of crossover votes throughout the preconvention season, and these votes provided his margin of victory in at least one crucial primary (Indiana).[82]

Furthermore, a regime of proportional representation would not clearly have helped the Reagan candidacy. In 1976, there were eleven Republican proportional representation primaries and sixteen plurality primaries. According to Pomper, had all primaries been conducted under proportional representation rules, Ford would have gained a net of thirty-eight votes; according to David and Ceaser, the net gain would have been seventeen.[83] These are small shifts but not completely insignificant given the closeness of the race. Of course, the strategic calculus might have shifted, prompting Reagan to compete in New York and Pennsylvania and allowing him to pick up minority support in those states.[84] This potential benefit might well have been out-weighed by the equal likelihood that Ford would have made a more serious effort in winner-take-all California, and by the potential disadvantages of being forced by the new dynamic to seriously contest all primaries.

The requirement of running seriously in almost all primaries, implicit in proportional representation, collided directly with the restrictions of FECA. Contribution limits, which were in place for the first time in 1976, seriously hurt both candidates, but hurt Reagan more than Ford because Reagan had to overcome the advantages of Ford's incumbency. Although Sears argued at the time that the proliferation in the number of primaries was beneficial for Reagan, he later attributed Ford's ultimate victory to that proliferation, which necessitated greater spending, combined with the contribution and spending limits contained in FECA.[85] As Michael Malbin pointed out in the *National Journal* at the time, "The spending limit, designed to weaken the power of incumbency, seems to be hurting Reagan instead."[86]

Finally, Pomper confirms the importance of the Republican delegate apportionment formula to the success of the conservative movement. By Pomper's calculations, had the 1952 apportionment still been in place in 1976, Ford would have "won a considerably more comfortable victory" at the convention with 56 percent of the delegates.[87] And the greater vulnerability of the minority party is reemphasized by the evident importance of the lack of Republican governors to Reagan's successes.[88]

Conclusions

The movement campaigns of Jesse Jackson, Pat Robertson, and Ronald Reagan form a pattern that parallels prior experience. Caucuses were more permeable than primaries, some primaries were important for purposes of establishing credibility, and proportional representation was of decreasing utility to movements as they gained in strength. The greater hospitality of caucuses is rendered all the more interesting when one considers that two of the three cases were in the Republican Party, whose caucuses are less "reformed" than those of the Democratic Party, and that one of these Republican cases constituted a challenge to a sitting president. Numerous observers have explicitly discussed Jackson's and Robertson's caucus successes as analogous.[89] Of the three candidates, only Robertson gained no benefit at all from primaries, and all three were helped by open primaries/caucuses, though somewhat differently. One can also see an important tendency on the part of the reforms to improve openness of access to weaker movements but to hinder openness toward actual success by stronger movements.

This does not mean that in a direct competition a weaker movement would defeat a stronger movement under the reform system; such an argument would, of course, be absurd. And, of course, over time a weak movement may turn into a strong movement, like the new politics from 1968 to 1972. This argument does mean, however, that at the margin, stronger movements are in a worse position after the reforms than they were before them, while weaker movements have on balance improved their position (or narrowed the gap) vis-à-vis the stronger movements. In order to see this more clearly, it is necessary to explore more theoretically and systematically what constitutes movement strength or weakness, and how those factors are related to the reforms.

There are seven key dimensions of movement strength: 1) overall voter support; 2) regional (and, in an often intertwined vein, demographic) breadth of voter support; 3) organizational strength; 4) level of intensity; 5) degree of demonstrated staying power; 6) financial strength; and 7) degree of personalism (the more personalist, the weaker the movement *cum* movement). The reforms affected each of these dimensions to some extent.

In terms of overall support, the replacement of plurality contests with proportional representation mathematically takes from the strong and gives to the weak. Stronger movements that already have sufficient support to assemble pluralities are hurt, while weaker movements can now win delegates without winning primaries. Reagan, the strongest of the three candidates studied in this chapter, was probably hurt by proportional representation. Proportional representation strengthened Jackson's hand against the Democratic Party in 1984, but became less useful to him as he became stronger, and might have become a disadvantage had his voting strength grown even a little bit more. In 1988, Robertson was unable to play the role that Jackson played, in no small part because the greater use of plurality rules in the GOP prevents a weak candidate from accumulating delegates, and the five-state rule could have prevented his nomination from even coming to the floor. Caucus reforms similarly had the effect of reducing the threshold of political strength required to have access to caucuses, helping weak movements rather than stronger movements, which could already pass the higher threshold.

The substantial replacement of caucuses with primaries benefits weak movements or disproportionately hurts strong movements in the dimensions of breadth, organization, and intensity. Caucuses were more friendly to Jackson the second time precisely because their localized structure had the effect of minimizing the delegate victories of highly concentrated (in other words, narrowly based) groupings of voters. As Jackson broadened his base, his caucus-to-primary delegate differential grew from 1 percent to 9 percent. Similarly, because organization and intensity are so much more valuable in caucuses than in primaries, those movements that have greater organization and/or intensity have more to lose from the move away from caucuses. The new politics movement was much better positioned to take advantage of caucuses in 1972 than in 1968, when it was in its infancy.

The reforms also disproportionately hurt movements with demonstrated long-term staying power both prior to and following the election. First, by banning early delegate selection, movements that have already existed for some time are prevented from taking advantage of their strength before the bulk of the nomination race gets under way. Goldwater and the conservatives would clearly have been hurt by such a ban, and Robertson took full advantage of the lack of such a rule in the Republican Party in Michigan. While the ban would have helped McCarthy in 1968, it may well have hurt McGovern, who was aided by a more organizationally mature and stronger movement a few years later. Second, movements that continue to exist after the election year in question are hurt by the move away from caucuses, in that an important avenue to long-term party control has been rendered largely nugatory. As the Christian right has proved its staying power and expanded its organizational strength and sophistication after 1988, it has made strides toward control of the party apparatus, especially (but not only) in states where the movement had previously experienced caucus successes. The reduction of caucuses has clearly made the task of party control more difficult. The fact that long-term control is more difficult now thus hurts the Christian right, which has demonstrated greater staying power, much more than it has hurt the rainbow coalition, which has largely atrophied with time.

To some extent, the 1974 FECA rules helped both financially strong and financially weak movements by providing matching federal funds for small contributions. However, by limiting contributions and state-by-state expenditures, FECA also hurt broadly based movements that were strong enough to raise large amounts of money and in large sums. Weaker movements, not capable of such fund-raising, were not hurt in this way. Reagan and Robertson were probably damaged by spending and contribution limits, while Jackson—the weakest of the three in terms of his financial base—was not.

Finally, in terms of personalism, many observers have noted the degree to which the reforms accelerated the personalization of presidential nomination politics in a variety of ways. The presidential selection process as a whole has become radically "candidate centered." It is difficult to believe that the same forces that aided the rise of the unconnected outsiders discussed in the next chapter did not also work to the relative benefit of those movements that suffer from the greatest personalism.

Some movements may be weak in all these dimensions, but others may suffer from only some of these maladies. Different elements of the nominating system and of the reforms will affect different forms of movement strength or weakness. For instance, the Christian right in 1988 suffered from lack of overall support but not financial weakness, poor organization, or inadequate intensity of support. The rainbow coalition suffered from financial weakness, excessive dependence on personalism, and (especially in 1984) lack of regional/demographic breadth. The net result was that the Christian right was more hurt by reforms that reduced caucuses and restricted finances than was the rainbow coalition.

In any event, some reforms have had the effect of simultaneously hurting strong movements and helping weak ones (proportional representation, certain aspects of FECA, and the ban on early delegate selection); others have had the effect of simply helping weak movements (caucus reforms, the reduction of barriers to personalism); and yet others have had the effect of hurting both strong movements and weak movements, but strong movements more (in most respects, the reduction in caucuses). Across every dimension of movement strength, however, the reforms narrowed the gap between weak and strong.

Thus, the reforms seem to have thrown certain barriers in the way of all movements, such as a reduction of caucuses and imposition of closed primaries. Above all, however, they seem to have made ultimate success by strong movements more difficult while making initial access by weak movements easier. Movements that are less broad-based and less well organized, less well financed and less durable, less intense and more personalistic—indeed, less capable of actually gaining the nomination under any system—are nevertheless encouraged to enter the fray and are able to wield influence even in the predictable absence of victory. This consequence of reform may or may not have been anticipated by the framers of the reforms, but it hardly seems salutary. It is overshadowed only when one examines the other beneficiaries of the reforms: candidates who are connected neither to an organized movement nor to the party.

6

The Rise of the
Unconnected Outsiders

I F THE REFORM MODEL OF PRESIDENTIAL NOMINATIONS benefits weaker movements at the expense of stronger movements, it seemingly helps independent personalist candidates most of all. Specifically, these candidates are outsiders but without connection to an organized movement: a phenomenon without independent organization, demonstrated staying power, or name. Two of the most vivid examples of this phenomenon were George Wallace and Jimmy Carter, whom Jeane Kirkpatrick called "total outsiders" in contrast to the "partial outsider" McGovern (and, one might add, Goldwater).[1] While the two southern governors might appear at first glance to have little in common, it is not too difficult to discern a similar subterranean structure undergirding their successes. Wallace and Carter were bracketed by two less extreme examples of the "unconnected outsider," Estes Kefauver—the first of the unconnected outsiders—in 1952–1956 and Gary Hart in 1984. In 1992 and 1996, the phenomenon of the unconnected outsider reached new heights and found new forms.

Whereas the convention system had no place for such outsiders and the mixed system tolerated but ultimately stymied them, the reform system has positively encouraged them. Wallace first posed a real threat of attaining the nomination only after the reforms, and Carter actually did attain the nomination. After Gary Hart, Paul Tsongas, Jerry Brown, David Duke, Pat

Buchanan in 1992, Ross Perot, and Steve Forbes, it is difficult to argue that the new system has not proved much more hospitable than the old to such candidates. This chapter will examine the rise of the phenomenon of the unconnected outsider, while the next chapter will examine outsiderism in the 1990s.

Antecedents of the "Unconnected Outsider"

The rise of the unconnected outsider, though accelerating rapidly in recent years, has antecedents reaching back as far as the turn of the century. In 1904, newspaper publisher William Randolph Hearst sought the Democratic presidential nomination as a first-term congressman, a "political maverick" with little support from the organized party.[2] Hearst's chief campaign weapon was the collection of eight newspapers he owned, all of which were used for self-promotion on a grand scale. His personal fortune also played a part. There were accusations that Hearst had offered to fund the Democratic National Committee to the tune of $1.5 million (in order to "relieve the national committee from the necessity of appealing to the trust magnates"), and Indiana party leaders called his campaign an "open and unblushing effort of a multi-millionaire to purchase the Presidential nomination."[3] In a sense, however, Hearst attempted to run what might today be considered a conventional, well-organized personal campaign. He made a serious and largely successful effort to take over control of the National Association of Democratic Clubs, turning it into a network of Hearst Clubs.[4] In any event, his campaign failed miserably at the Democratic convention of 1904, falling to that of Judge Alton Parker.

A later and more important antecedent to the unconnected outsider was Wendell Willkie, Republican nominee for president in 1940 and unsuccessful candidate for the GOP nomination in 1944. Willkie came out of nowhere in 1940. He was not mentioned as possible presidential material until after a national radio debate with Robert H. Jackson in 1938; he did not change party registration from Democrat to Republican until 1939; he stood at 3 percent in the Gallup poll in early 1940; and he had never run for or held public office. Willkie's nomination campaign was more dependent on media than any previous campaign (with the possible exception of Hearst's); he was literally thrust into the limelight by coverage in *Time, Life, Fortune,* and the *New York Herald-Tribune.* According to political biographer Steve Neal, "More than anything else, it was Willkie's massive and highly favorable exposure in the public prints that made him a national political force."[5] To the extent that

Willkie represented a political outsider running largely on media coverage, he was indeed a prototype of the unconnected outsider of later years.

There are also several reasons, however, why Willkie must be considered merely a foreshadowing of the unconnected outsider, rather than the first of the breed. First, he had tremendous support from the eastern liberal Republican press and Wall Street establishment. His media bonanza was not self-generated, in the manner of subsequent unconnected outsiders, but was the result of support by Henry Luce and other influential publishers, who made a conscious decision to push Willkie. Indeed, the Republican right would long consider the 1940 convention as just another in a line of conventions dominated by the eastern establishment.

Furthermore, Willkie owed his nomination to a combination of two factors alien to future unconnected candidates. Alongside the support of the major media, Willkie's supporters had built a massive grassroots organization. That organization, consisting of at least two thousand clubs, produced 200,000 petition signatures urging Willkie to run in early 1940 and generated nearly 1 million messages to delegates during the convention itself.[6] These messages were targeted in a sophisticated manner designed to bring maximum pressure on the delegates.[7] This pressure from the outside was coupled with an effective inside strategy that gained delegates the old-fashioned way, by winning over state and local party leaders one by one, building momentum by holding delegates in reserve on the first ballot, and even using control of credentials to pack the galleries with Willkie supporters. Willkie did not base his nomination strategy on primaries (he did not compete in any) but on the prospect of emerging triumphant from a deadlocked convention. He won not by bypassing the regulars (as unconnected outsiders try to do) nor by replacing them (as movements try to do) but by convincing them. In the view of Samuel Pryor, a Connecticut Republican boss who was one of the first organization men to support Willkie, "Willkie was nominated by the 'inside' people of the Republican Party at the convention, not by the 'outsiders.'"[8] In the end, Willkie's sixth-ballot nomination in 1940 came about because his opponents Taft and Dewey could not unite and because he was the only nonisolationist candidate before a convention that opened three days after the surrender of France.

Seeking nomination again in 1944, Willkie faced greater hostility from the regulars, who increasingly considered him a clone of Franklin Roosevelt. He contested two primaries, winning New Hampshire by a disappointing margin and being driven from the race by a disastrous defeat in Wisconsin, where he was shut out of delegates. In the summer of 1944, he contemplated the possibility of forming an unabashedly liberal third party after the election, a notion that was conveyed to a reportedly sympathetic FDR.[9] He died that fall.

Two points stand out about the experience of Willkie. He represented the first important but incomplete incarnation of the unconnected outsider. And, in the mixed system of the 1940s, it was only barely possible for even a partial outsider campaign like Willkie's to be successful, when given the benefit of a massive and well-organized outpouring of public and media support and favorable world-historical events. In the absence of those factors four years later, he did not come close. The system was still sufficiently under the control of the party organizations to deprive him of success, even in the primaries.

Estes Kefauver

Less than a decade after Willkie's unsuccessful 1944 bid, the "unconnected outsider" as a candidate type fully emerged with the candidacy of Senator Estes Kefauver of Tennessee. Kefauver was called by one of his biographers "the most authentic—and most successful—maverick in American political history. Indeed, more than any other major political figure of the last generation, he remained free of the long-range sectional, partisan, and organizational commitments that furnish political security but limit the flexibility of most men in public life."[10]

Kefauver made his name through populist antitrust agitation and chairmanship of a special Senate committee on organized crime that met in 1950–1951. Those spectacular hearings were televised and thrust Kefauver into the national limelight; he was "the first person to become a serious presidential contender as the result of massive television publicity."[11] However, the mixed system threw insurmountable barriers in his way, barriers that would come tumbling down after 1968.

When Kefauver chose to run for the Democratic presidential nomination in 1952, President Harry Truman had not yet decided whether to seek reelection. Consequently, Kefauver became the lightning rod for protest votes in the crucial first primary in New Hampshire. His antibossism, the damage done to numerous Democratic machines by revelations uncovered by the crime hearings, and the challenge to Truman served to galvanize bitter opposition to Kefauver by Democratic regulars. Only one of his Senate colleagues endorsed him. His campaigns took the form of a one-man crusade on behalf of "the people" against "bossism," and Kefauver wielded his underdog status as a "standard campaign weapon."[12]

Like Jimmy Carter a quarter of a century later, Kefauver was criticized for being "too much form and too little substance," and for using a "campaign technique that stressed personal contact and a general approach to the issues at the expense of a serious attempt to educate and inform the voters."[13] In a way that foreshadowed the personalistic Carter nomination campaign, emphasis on "personal charm" and "informal gatherings became the trademark of the Kefauver campaign."[14] Kefauver had ties to elements of the liberal wing of the Democratic Party, some of whom (like Hubert Humphrey) supported him in the last stage of his 1952 race.[15] Nevertheless, what factional support he had was mostly in ad hoc alliances with local factions fighting local machines.[16]

Primaries were the centerpiece of Kefauver's strategy in his presidential bids precisely because the party organizations were hostile and he had no outside organization with which to challenge them. In 1952, he did extremely well in the primaries, starting off with an upset victory over Truman in New Hampshire. By the end of the primary season, Kefauver had won twelve of fifteen preference primaries and 64 percent of the primary vote (there were also two pure delegate primaries). One of his defeats came in Florida at the hands of Richard Russell, who had been expected to win so handily that Kefauver's relatively narrow loss was turned by the media into a moral victory.

While most of the primaries were not contested by serious opposition, Kefauver did in numerous cases face favorite-son candidates representing the state's Democratic organization. Kefauver was able to turn his primary victories into front-running status among the public at large: days before the convention opened, polls showed him with 45 percent to Alben Barkley with 18, Adlai Stevenson with 12, Richard Russell with 10, and Averell Harriman with 5.

Despite this primary record and public support, Kefauver was denied the nomination, which instead went to Stevenson. That outcome was a demonstration of the barriers established by the mixed system to his sort of candidacy. In essence, the party organizations retained sufficient strength under the mixed system to override primary success. There were three basic factors underlying Kefauver's failure to translate primary success into nomination.

First, like unconnected outsiders to come, Kefauver did much worse in caucus/convention states than in primaries; he received only 19 percent of the delegates from nonprimary states. In contrast, in addition to his popular vote victories, he received 48.3 percent of delegates from the preference primary states. Kefauver, unlike his successors, faced an environment in which only two-fifths of the convention's delegates were from primary states. As a result, the relative weight of the party organizations, which were able to dominate the caucus states, was vastly greater than it would be after 1968. Kefauver later called for the establishment of a national primary.

Second, even in the primary states, delegate selection was divorced from the presidential preference vote more often than not. In many cases, Kefauver did not even run actual delegate slates. In the words of Keech and Matthews, unlike Goldwater, McCarthy, and McGovern, "Kefauver had no large, enthusiastic corps of amateur politicians to draw upon as delegate candidates."[17] In other words, Kefauver was not attached to an organized movement.

In addition to the many cases in which delegate selection occurred separately from the preference primary, two jurisdictions—New York and the District of Columbia—held pure delegate primaries. Of those one hundred delegates, Kefauver won one on the first ballot, none on the second, and four on the third (after New York's Harriman withdrew). In short, Kefauver had surprising successes in popular votes only to prove unable to translate those successes into actual delegates, as a result of the nonplebiscitary nature and pro-organizational bias of mixed-system primaries.

Finally, the nonplebiscitary nature of the system worked against Kefauver in another way. As was customary under the mixed system, his opponents picked their primaries carefully. Indeed, Stevenson, the eventual nominee, seriously contested no primaries in 1952. This meant that Kefauver's long string of preference primary victories was discounted, since they frequently came against no major competition. And the flexibility of the convention meant not only that Kefauver's high poll standings could be ignored but, more positively, that someone like Stevenson, who had run in no primaries, could be drafted as an alternative.

In short, by reform standards, "the supporters of Estes Kefauver had even more reason than the supporters of Eugene McCarthy to cry foul."[18] As it was, Kefauver became the Democratic front-runner and actually led all candidates on the first two convention ballots. There is no way of knowing with certainty whether he would have won had the reforms been in place, but with many more primaries and a more sure connection between primary votes and delegates, Kefauver would have been in a much stronger position.

Four years later, Kefauver made another attempt at the presidency. As an opening shot, he held another series of televised hearings in 1955. He still was the object of enmity by Democratic regulars, but had also been supplanted by Stevenson as the popular favorite. As a result, his emphasis on primaries was at once still necessary but also even less likely to succeed.[19]

Kefauver won stunning back-to-back primary victories in New Hampshire and in Minnesota, where he was helped tremendously by crossover votes, forcing Stevenson onto the primary trail to a degree the front-runner would have preferred to avoid.[20] Kefauver held his own with Stevenson, at one point reducing a fifty-one to eighteen Stevenson lead in the polls to thirty-nine to thirty-three. Stevenson's victory in the California primary essentially clinched his nomination, and Kefauver bowed out of the race two weeks before the convention. It is clear once again that he did much better in primary than in nonprimary states, and that he had difficulty turning primary votes into delegates.[21]

Estes Kefauver's campaigns in the 1950s foreshadowed the rise of candidates like Jimmy Carter. His failure was due in no small part to the difference between the system under which he ran and the one under which Carter ran. In the mixed system, a personalistic, nonorganizationally based campaign could be blunted by the relative paucity of primaries and the relatively nonplebiscitary nature of those primaries that existed.

George Wallace

George Wallace was the next unconnected outsider to appear on the scene. Running in the mixed system in 1964, he made strong showings in three primaries but won no delegates; facing the same systemic environment four years later, he preferred running as an independent candidate. His greatest success came in 1972, after the reforms, though his success then was blunted by some remaining features of the old system. In 1976, he started strong and was laid low only by Jimmy Carter, another unconnected outsider.

While many observers casually described the following of George Wallace as a "movement,"[22] it cannot be considered such by the criteria outlined in chapter 1. His support was purely personal and seemed not to be transferrable to other candidates. He was not embraced by a preexisting organizational structure that sought him out (or even merely accepted him) as a standard-bearer; even his third party in 1968 was purely his own creation, which fell into disarray as soon as he rejoined the Democratic Party. Indeed, this personalism can be seen in the name given to the phenomenon: the "Wallace movement." Wallace must be considered not the leader of a genuine movement, but rather an independent personalist candidate who amassed a particularly committed following.

The most striking fact about Wallace's political ventures from 1964 to 1976 was his completely consistent preference for primaries over caucuses, a preference reminiscent of Kefauver. When Wallace ran for the first time in

1964, he chose to contest three northern industrial primary states. His objective was to slow passage of the Civil Rights Act of 1964 by demonstrating voter discontent with it, and to encourage the filing of "unpledged elector" slates in southern states to permit the South to hold the balance in the electoral college.[23] When he began, "his outfit consisted of a handful of country boys and a half dozen tough-looking state troopers."[24]

In all three states—Wisconsin, Indiana, and Maryland—Wallace faced favorite-son stand-ins for Lyndon Johnson. In Wisconsin, his campaign began only three weeks before the primary, and was headed by an Oshkosh housewife. By the time the campaign was over, Wallace had shocked the Democratic Party establishment in Wisconsin and around the country by gaining a third of the vote; Governor John Reynolds, the stand-in, had hoped to keep Wallace below 10 percent. Wallace was aided tremendously by Republican crossovers. His Wisconsin votes "were amassed with very little money, no campaign organization, [and] very few forums."[25]

In Indiana, the party machine of Governor Matthew Welsh swung into high gear, but still only barely kept Wallace below 30 percent, again with numerous crossovers. And in Maryland, "the Wallace campaign gave the appearance of a busy, well-run campaign, but, in truth, the campaign was nothing but ten speeches, plus heavy television, radio and newspaper advertising schedules."[26] He won 43 percent of the vote, according to the official count.[27] This near upset constituted "a shock and a disappointment to the state and national Democratic administrations."[28] Wallace, in short, single-handedly succeeded through the primaries in creating fear of a "white backlash" through a whirlwind campaign in three states, despite having "no organization beyond his immediate staff" and Alabama state personnel.[29] His relative success demonstrated the emerging importance of broadcast media; Wallace was a master at "manipulating television's infatuation with visual action, dramatic confrontation, and punchy sound bites."[30] It was also emblematic of the long-term decline of the party machines that once tightly controlled Indiana and Maryland.

While Wallace was backed by the American Independent Party in 1968, that party was purely his own creation. He appointed his own vice presidential nominee, unilaterally declared a platform, and refused to permit candidates to run for lower offices under his party label. A large organizational effort was required to get his name on the ballot in all fifty states. But again, he used Alabama state government as an organizational base; more than half of the forty-one local Wallace petition headquarters in California were staffed by Alabamans.[31] Indeed, Wallace seemed to "regard formal political organization with a vague contempt, as a sign of political effeteness, an absence of vitality—as if he [was] already naturally blessed with what political organization exists to create."[32] Wallace's party was extremely centralized, with power flowing out of Montgomery. In short, "the AIP was not an integrated, functioning party; it existed only as a vehicle for Wallace's candidacy."[33]

Wallace gained much in 1968, however, in terms of exposure and fundraising. He raised $6 million from 750,000 contributors. Wallace benefited from some very large contributions, including at least $250,000 from Bunker Hunt, but 80 percent was raised in sums of $100 or less. And the 1.6 million names he obtained on ballot petitions could be used in the future.[34] Wallace himself was always careful to distinguish between the "party" and the "movement" (more accurately, himself), to leave room for a return to the Democratic Party.

That return occurred in 1972, when Wallace decided to run in the Florida primary while keeping the third-party option open. According to campaign manager Charles Snider, the American Independent Party was "unique" in its degree of personalism; its voters were for Wallace, and if he decided to run as a Democrat, they would go with him.[35] Running on an antibusing theme, he trounced his opposition in Florida with 41.6 percent of the vote; his nearest competitor, Humphrey, had 18.6 percent. At that point, Wallace chose to enter the race fully. The remainder of his campaign was focused entirely on the primaries, and serves in many respects as a counterpoint to the McGovern/new politics effort.

When the 1972 nomination campaign was over, Wallace had won five primaries and finished second in six more, out of twenty-one preference primaries held that year. He garnered 23.5 percent of the primary vote, finishing a close third behind Humphrey (25.8 percent) and McGovern (25.3 percent). Wallace was actually leading the field both in primaries won and votes received in the primaries through the day after his shooting, with five wins and 3.4 million votes to Humphrey's three wins and 2.6 million votes and McGovern's three wins and 2.2 million votes.[36] Many of these successes were achieved with the aid of Republican and independent crossover votes; in Wisconsin and Michigan, for instance, Wallace gained an estimated one-half of his votes from crossovers.[37]

Furthermore, Wallace's showing—as in 1964—was accomplished with minimal organization. Indeed, his organization in 1972 was, if anything, worse than it had been four years earlier. "Other candidates labored over their advance work and prepared for rallies with skill, art, and delegated manpower. George Wallace simply announced a rally—and the crowds turned up to hear the talking."[38] Because his strategy depended so heavily on personalistic and inflammatory appeals to alienated voters rather than on organization, he was able to attain sweeping successes with little effort.

For example, he placed a surprising second in Wisconsin after only eleven campaign appearances in nine days of campaigning.[39] In Pennsylvania, he also finished a surprising second, after a campaign that consisted of a single rally in Pittsburgh.[40] He gained one-third of the vote in West Virginia, despite having virtually no organization and making no campaign appearances.[41] He won the Michigan primary by a large margin due to the busing issue, despite an enormous anti-Wallace campaign by the most organized political force in the state, organized labor.[42] Even after the assassination attempt that left him paralyzed, Wallace finished second with 20 percent of the vote in Oregon through a purely media-oriented campaign.[43]

Primarily because the reforms were still in an embryonic stage in 1972, however, Wallace was thwarted. Lacking organization, he was unable to translate his vote totals into delegates. In Pennsylvania, despite gaining 21 percent of the vote, he finished with only two delegates—because his campaign had filed only four delegate candidates.[44] Elsewhere, nonproportional delegate systems deprived him of success, as in Wisconsin where he had 22 percent but won no delegates because delegates were chosen on a plurality basis by congressional district and he won no districts.[45] Overall, Lengle and Shafer have shown that of the three major candidates in 1972, "only Governor George Wallace [would] derive electoral satisfaction" from primary rules mandating proportional representation; it would have provided him with his largest lead of any allocation scheme.[46]

Wallace's personalistic campaign was a mirror image of McGovern's movement campaign: where McGovern translated 25 percent of the vote into 65 percent of primary delegates, Wallace translated 24 percent of the vote into 15.5 percent of primary delegates. In short, "the Wallace organization was a juggernaut when it came to capturing the popular vote, but an enfeebled stumbling incompetent in the all-important gathering of delegate strength."[47] This could occur only because delegates were still substantially disconnected from vote outcomes. As Keech and Matthews put it, Wallace

> aimed almost exclusively at generating publicity. Little was done to canvass the candidate's potential supporters, to make sure that they voted, or to see that there were pro-Wallace delegates on the ballot for them to vote for once at the polls. But Wallace's popular appeal was so great that he could do very well in popularity contests without campaigning at all. . . . And Wallace was

almost totally unprepared to translate his surprising popular support into delegate votes. In fact, were it not for the primary laws in Maryland, Michigan, North Carolina, and Tennessee which automatically turned his victories into pledged delegate votes, Wallace would have received many fewer delegate votes than he did.[48]

Furthermore, Wallace performed abysmally in the caucus states, to the point that McGovern actually did better in the southern caucuses than he did.[49] He was completely shut out of delegates in Arkansas, Mississippi, Kentucky, Missouri, and Oklahoma; gained only one delegate in Virginia, three in Louisiana, and six in South Carolina; and finished fourth in Georgia with eleven of fifty-three, behind McGovern, Jackson, and Chisholm. As late as June 10, the *National Journal* delegate count listed Wallace as having only three delegates from convention states out of his three hundred and thirty-one delegates nationwide.[50] The bulk of his caucus state delegates ultimately came from the state of Texas, one of the few states where he was able to rely on the remnants of the American Independent Party for organizational support.[51]

The contrast between Wallace's capacity for winning primaries and his inability to win caucuses can be seen not only by comparing primary states with caucus states—he gained 15.5 percent of primary delegates and only 7.1 percent of caucus delegates—but by examining more closely those states that employed both mechanisms. Again, Wallace was a mirror of McGovern. In Tennessee, for example, Wallace won the primary by a huge margin. Tennessee's delegates, though bound by state law to vote for the primary winner, were chosen through a caucus/convention procedure that was dominated not by Wallace supporters but by McGovern and Chisholm supporters, many of whom threatened not to vote for Wallace. Similarly, in Michigan, Maryland, and North Carolina, Wallace won resounding primary victories only to be endangered by delegates chosen through caucuses.

Finally, in contrast to McGovern, Wallace did much better in the new primaries than in the old. In primaries that had been instituted after 1968, Wallace won 54.3 percent of available delegates; in the "old" primaries, he gained only 7.8 percent, just slightly better than in caucus states. Thus, the increasing shift to primaries helped Wallace while hurting McGovern. Overall, had Wallace gained the same percentage of delegates in the southern caucuses as in the southern primaries, and had he gained the same percentage of delegates in the northern primaries as he received votes in those primaries, he would have come to the 1972 Democratic national convention with 850 more delegates, or a total of over 1,200, with only 1,509 needed to receive the nomination.[52] It would hardly be an exaggeration to say that Wallace's success in 1972 was directly related to the degree to which primaries were dominant in the nominating system and the degree to which those primaries were plebiscitary, directly translating votes into delegates.

Thus, Wallace apparently suffered not from the substance of the reforms but from the fact that they had not come to full fruition, and from the fact that his campaign did not understand them.[53] In sum,

> if the Wallace organization had understood and acted upon the rules governing the Democratic Party nominating process, Wallace would have come to the 1972 Miami convention with approximately the same number of delegate votes that George McGovern had. . . . Without question he had arrived on the national scene in a big way, yet his campaign organization was not prepared for his success. . . . The campaign's lack of planning and money, and terribly inept execution, kept Wallace from playing a commanding role at the convention, a role to which he was entitled because of his popular support. What most members of the Democratic Party considered unthinkable—Wallace as the nominee, or Wallace dictating the nominee or perhaps part of the platform—came within a hairbreadth of being reality. It was not the Democratic Party that prevented such an occurrence, but the Wallace organization itself.[54]

It should be no surprise, then, that after 1972 Wallace—like Kefauver before him—called for primaries to replace caucuses nationwide.[55] Nor should it be a surprise that Wallace's hopes of influencing the 1974 midterm Democratic convention were dashed when he was unsuccessful in procuring delegates, almost all of whom were chosen through caucus procedures.[56] And it should not be a surprise that, in the same way that many caucus states had shifted to primaries to avoid a repetition of McGovern-style takeovers, many primary states after 1972 considered a shift back to caucuses to thwart a future Wallace bid. North Carolina, Tennessee, Louisiana, and Michigan tried to get rid of their primaries, but failed; New Mexico, where Wallace finished a close second, did get rid of its primary; and New Jersey closed its primary in anticipation of the Wallace threat.[57] This was not the first time that states had moved from primaries to caucuses to prevent Wallace's success: in 1968, Maryland Democrats had temporarily discontinued their traditional primary out of fear that Wallace's 1964 showing would be repeated.[58]

Furthermore, although some proportional representation supporters advocated it because they saw it as a way to dilute Wallace's strength in winner-take-all states, Wallace himself actually approved the mandating of proportional representation after 1972.[59] Seeing the danger, South Carolina's Democratic state chairman Dan Fowler introduced a resolution to the DNC calling for the elimination of the proportional representation requirement. His effort was unsuccessful.

In preparation for the 1976 race, Wallace and Jimmy Carter began to cross paths. Carter, understanding that his personalistic appeal as a complete outsider also was best suited for primaries, called for a southern regional primary, a call that Wallace endorsed.[60] While Carter portrayed himself as the "responsible" southern alternative to Wallace, he shared many of the characteristics of the Alabaman. Carter's effort could not be considered the manifestation of an existing movement. He built a completely personalistic (though efficient) campaign organization that was basically unconnected to any party structure or movement and cut across diverse interest groups. He was generally devoid of ideology, to the extent that each ideological grouping of voters considered him one of their own. Much like Kefauver and Wallace, Carter relied on broad themes and personal charm rather than issues.

Carter seriously sought the Wallace voter. As a southern, anti-Washington populist, Carter succeeded in his attempt to "undercut the Wallace appeal."[61] It was no accident that Carter's pollster was Pat Caddell, who as George McGovern's pollster in 1972 had argued that Wallace's constituency was open to anyone who could tap the roots of alienation.[62] McGovern had failed because Wallace voters could not overlook his positions on foreign policy and cultural issues, but a candidate—like Carter—who obscured his issue positions could conceivably reach those voters with broader themes.[63]

Thus, Carter, like Wallace, was a free-floating candidate who sought to capitalize on popular alienation. Where Wallace's approach could be called the "hard" approach, since it relied on exploitation of bitterly divisive issues, Carter could be said to employ the "soft" variant, a replacement of issues with fuzzy themes. Indeed, one of the most consistent attacks against Carter by his opponents was that he was avoiding issues, and one of his speechwriters (Bob Shrum) resigned citing the same concern. To fully understand the reforms, one must look at the Wallace and Carter efforts together in 1976, since each candidate's failures often came at the other's hands.

Wallace began the 1976 race in better organizational and financial shape than ever before. Democratic Party insiders were taking Wallace very seriously.[64] However, Wallace faltered. He beat Carter badly in the Mississippi caucuses, which was the first time Wallace had ever actually prevailed in a caucus setting; indeed, before the event, he confessed to his supporters that he would be surprised to win any delegates there. He then went on to take a lead against Carter in the first round of the South Carolina caucuses, and finished a close third in the Massachusetts primary (he won Boston on the strength of the busing issue), giving him hope that he could succeed in northern industrial states.

Wallace had won Florida by a large margin in 1972, and was therefore expected to do so again. However, the busing issue there was dormant in 1976 and Wallace's liberal opponents stayed out of the state, unofficially designating Carter as the dragon slayer. Carter won 34 to 31 percent, showing that he could beat Wallace in the South; that proved a setback from which Wallace never recovered. Carter went on to beat Wallace in the Illinois primary, and soundly defeated him in North Carolina, thus essentially finishing Wallace off as a serious contender. In the words of David S. Broder, Wallace's "claim to speak for the alienated of the South and the nation had been destroyed by his losses to Carter in Florida and North Carolina."[65]

While Wallace improved in the caucuses, winning Mississippi and leading Carter in the first-round caucuses in South Carolina, he still did better in the primary states. As of June 9, the day he informed Carter that he would be leaving the race and endorsing him, Wallace had won 6.3 percent of available primary delegates and only 3.8 percent of caucus state delegates. In terms of actual voting results, Wallace received 12.5 percent of the total primary vote and a mean primary vote of 10.8 percent, but a mean of only 5.5 percent of first-round delegates in caucus states.

As in 1972, Wallace actually benefited from proportional representation. As *Congressional Quarterly* reported, "In the states which have switched from winner-take-all to proportional representation, he [Wallace] has won 94 delegates. Under the old rules he would only have taken 61."[66] Furthermore, had proportional representation been universal, Wallace's delegate total would have jumped from 149 to 254.[67] While one might ascribe this benefit simply to Wallace's poor showing, it is also true that his strategy for winning the nomination depended heavily on the benefits of proportional representation, especially in New York and California.[68] Indeed, prior to the 1976 race, it had been predicted that Wallace would gain from proportional representation because his "strength, more than any other candidate, lay in his popularity"— something that, unlike organization, could be easily spread around.[69]

Finally, the 1974 FECA regime was first implemented in 1976, and Wallace benefited from the new law more than any other candidate.[70] As in his past campaigns, the vast majority of his money came in small contributions through direct mail. In this sense, FECA did make the presidential nominating system more vulnerable to candidates like Wallace (and to movement candidates) who rely on grassroots excitement among common citizens for their financial sustenance. However, Wallace would have been hurt by the spending limits had they been in place prior to 1976. Wallace was in the uniquely propitious position of being able to gain a reliable list through unregulated spending and then receive matching funds for the fruits of that list.[71]

Jimmy Carter

In the end, Wallace was the chief victim of Carter. He became Carter's victim not because Carter was a different type of candidate, but rather because Carter was a similar type of candidate, and simply better at being one. Indeed, wide-ranging opinion holds that Carter among all recent candidates was most clearly advantaged by the reforms, which had also helped Wallace to a lesser extent.[72]

Carter's candidacy can be traced back to a memo written for him by Hamilton Jordan one day before the 1972 general election, in which Jordan told Carter: "Your candidacy should be an effort to encompass and expand on the Wallace constituency and populist philosophy by being a better qualified and more responsible alternative to George Wallace. . . . I would hope you could gain his support if he saw in your candidacy an extension and continuation of his earlier efforts."[73]

This objective was repeated in a revised 1974 strategy memo.[74] While the attempt to corral Wallace voters generally took the "soft" appeal to alienation, Carter was not beyond occasional lapses into the "hard" appeal, such as a remark, prior to the Pennsylvania and Michigan primaries where he hoped to pick up Wallace supporters, about maintaining the "ethnic purity" of neighborhoods.[75] In the end, Carter succeeded in capturing and softening the Wallace appeal to the extent that the Wallace message "sounded at times like a translation of Jimmy Carter into the vulgar."[76] Carter also expanded the appeal, and by emphasizing broad themes rather than divisive issues brought blacks and some liberals into his fold as well.

Jimmy Carter resembled Wallace in more than the general constituency he sought to sway and the personalism of his campaign. Like Wallace, Carter did much better in the primaries than in the caucuses. As of June 9, the *National Journal* reported that Carter had won 41.4 percent of primary delegates but only 25.7 percent of caucus delegates. In actual votes, he received 39 percent of total primary votes and a mean primary vote of 40.4 percent, but a mean of only 20.5 percent of first-round delegates in the twenty-two caucus/convention states.

Thus, like Wallace, Carter did only approximately half as well in the caucuses as in the primaries. It is true that he bested Wallace in the caucuses in absolute terms. Furthermore, though he lost to Wallace in Mississippi and in the first round in South Carolina, he launched his campaign with a critical success in Iowa and fought to an important tie with Fred Harris in the latter's home state of Oklahoma. This greater level of success can be attributed to a superior personal organization, especially in Iowa, where Carter began creating an organization a year in advance of the caucuses. Nevertheless, while his personal organization was better than Wallace's (and most other candidates') even in Iowa "analysts noted that Carter won . . . on personal charm and individual contact."[77]

Furthermore, it is clear that his organization was not as good as the party organization in most caucus states. In contrast to 1972, when the party was often overwhelmed by the new politics movement, in 1976 caucus states produced a large number of uncommitted delegates. This was partly the result of the 15 percent threshold, which encouraged supporters of candidates receiving less than 15 percent to join together in an officially uncommitted slate, but it was substantially the result of deliberate efforts by party leaders to elect uncommitted delegations. All together, Carter was outdone by uncommitted (generally party) forces in nineteen of twenty-two caucus states.

As with Kefauver and Wallace in years past, Carter's bonanza came in the primary states. Primaries in New Hampshire, Florida, North Carolina, Pennsylvania, Wisconsin, and Ohio all played a crucial role in his ultimate victory. Furthermore, as with Wallace in 1972, Carter did best in those primaries that had been recently instituted, indicating that the change in nominating system clearly worked to his benefit.[78] As with the caucus states, his successes were partially a reflection of the personal organization he had built over the previous two years.

However, the key factor was clearly not organization but personal appeal. Carter won Wisconsin in a manner much more reminiscent of Wallace than of McGovern, implanting a campaign organization there only twenty-eight days before the primary.[79] And where Carter was well organized, his organization often failed to save him from the late-season onrush of Edmund G. (Jerry) Brown and, to a lesser extent, Frank Church. In Rhode Island, for example, Carter had had an organization present for over a year, but lost to Brown's hastily assembled organization and campaign of heavy media.[80] Brown, running the same sort of thematic campaign as Carter's but representing a "fresh face" after months of Carter dominance, also won in Maryland with media but virtually no campaign organization, though he did benefit from the assistance of Governor Marvin Mandel's organization.[81] Indeed, "many were convinced that if Brown had started in New Hampshire with everyone else, the nomination would have been his, not Carter's."[82] And Church won his first victory in Nebraska with "a final blitz of the same kind of personalized campaigning that had made Carter famous."[83] Thus, Carter was fortunate to escape the late-season challenges of Brown and Church, who began to beat him at his own game even without the benefit of a personal organization.

The effects of proportional representation on Carter's candidacy are difficult to untangle. As Pomper showed, and as one might expect, Carter (as the strongest candidate) would likely have been hurt by a system of universal proportional representation.[84] This is especially true in the primaries, but may not have been so true in the caucuses, where he was probably helped.[85] Furthermore,

> if the focus is shifted from individual candidates to ideological tendencies, a very different conclusion begins to emerge regarding the effects of proportional representation on Carter's candidacy. What might be called the center-right of the party (Carter and Wallace) did better with proportional rules than without; the center-left (Jackson, Brown, Udall, and Church) did more poorly. . . . The damage to Carter under proportional representation was inflicted more by Wallace than by any other candidate; but Wallace's delegates had no place to go except Carter.[86]

Finally, while FECA seemed not to benefit Carter as greatly as Wallace, it did apparently drive him toward a strategy of small contributions which he might not otherwise have chosen.[87] Carter concentrated on regional finance committees for most of his money, but relied on direct mail for one-third of his funds. He raised enough in small contributions to receive more matching funds in the crucial period through mid-March than any of his competitors except Wallace and Jackson.[88] Thus, FECA matching funds helped both unconnected outsiders in 1976 more than most other candidates.

Gary Hart

Gary Hart ran in 1984 as an antiestablishment maverick, despite being a ten-year veteran of the United States Senate. He ran a largely thematic campaign calling for "new ideas" and ridiculing the old labor-based Democratic coalition represented most forcefully by the eventual nominee, Walter Mondale. Hart made a strenuous effort to replace that coalition with a new one comprised largely of affluent professionals and intellectuals, and relied heavily on independent crossover votes in New Hampshire, Wisconsin, and elsewhere.[89] Hart had been intimately connected with the new politics movement, but in 1984 was clearly not the standard-bearer of any outside movement.

Hart performed better in primaries than in caucuses by almost any standard, despite the fact that most remaining caucus states were in his native West. However, this disparity was not as great as in the cases of Wallace, Carter, and Kefauver. Hart received 34.4 percent of the delegates from primary states and 32.2 percent of the delegates from caucus states.[90] He achieved a mean of 39.3 in primary states, besting Mondale's primary mean of 37.4, but was defeated by Mondale in mean first-level caucus results (39.4 to 35.5).[91] And, while he actually won five more primaries than Mondale (sixteen versus eleven), Mondale and Hart both won thirteen caucus jurisdictions.

The best test of relative strength came in states that held both caucuses and primaries. In Wisconsin, Hart narrowly won the primary but lost the caucuses by a large margin to Mondale. In Vermont, Hart won the primary with 71 percent of the vote, but won the caucuses only 49 to 33 percent. Finally, in Idaho, Hart won both contests handily, but saw his lead shrink by four percentage points in the caucuses (see table 6.1). Hart subsequently joined Jesse Jackson in denouncing the caucus system as unfair. In the view of observers, Mondale owed his nomination in no small part to the "crucial margin of safety" provided by his caucus strength, which was itself the result of a superior organization built around old-line party and labor forces.[92]

The second half of Mondale's "safety net" consisted of his hammerlock on the superdelegates. In no fewer than five states, superdelegates transformed Hart delegate majorities into Mondale majorities.[93] Early superdelegate elec-

Table 6-1. 1984 Voting Results: States Using Primaries and Caucuses

	Primary Result (%)		Caucus Result (%)	
Wisconsin	Hart	46	Mondale	60
	Mondale	43	Hart	30
Vermont	Hart	70	Hart	49
	Mondale	20	Mondale	43
Idaho	Hart	58	Hart	58
	Mondale	30	Mondale	34

tion also had the effect of helping to brake Hart's momentum after New Hampshire.[94] Overall, Mondale won the vast majority of superdelegates, to the point that without superdelegates he would have had only 57 delegates in excess of the number needed for nomination.[95]

Hart was also seriously disadvantaged by the large-scale reintroduction by the Hunt Commission of plurality elections through loophole and bonus primaries. Had pure statewide proportional representation been in effect, Hart would have gained 58 delegates; more important, Mondale would have lost 454 delegates, pulling him well below the number needed to nominate and reducing Hart's gap at the end of June from 796 to 284.[96] Indeed, Mondale opened up his delegate lead during a crucial stretch in March and April by winning numerous large industrial state primaries that used loophole or bonus primaries.[97] In these primaries, Mondale's organization permitted him to win delegates disproportionate to his strength. Hart, conversely, was hurt not merely by the mathematical fate that inevitably befalls weaker candidates in plurality systems; he was hurt, as were Wallace and Carter, by his distribution of strength.[98]

Thus, Mondale largely owed his victory—and Hart his defeat—to the reintroduction of such mixed-system forms as an increase in caucuses, greater use of plurality elections, and reestablishment of an important delegate role for party regulars. Conversely, Hart owed his close race to the extent to which the reforms were still in place, with the exception of the open primary ban, which worked against him. In essence, the superdelegates and other party forces accomplished against Hart what the regulars accomplished against Kefauver: they served to block an unconnected outsider from a nomination that might have been in reach had the system been constructed more fully on reform lines.

Finally, Hart was helped by FECA. He raised 68 percent of his funds in sums smaller than five hundred dollars, in contrast to Mondale, who raised barely half that way. In a seven-man Democratic field, only Jesse Jackson was more dependent on small contributions.[99]

The Unconnected Outsiders and the Reforms

The mixed system, with a relative paucity of primaries, a disconnection of primary votes from delegates, and a generally substantial role for the party, tended to hinder unconnected outsiders like Kefauver and Wallace. Conversely, the reforms have played to the strengths of such candidates.

For both George Wallace and Jimmy Carter, the primary presented a mechanism for openness that the caucuses did not. This was due to a confluence of factors: neither of them had the organizational capacity to consistently succeed in the caucuses, and both of them had the personal appeal to otherwise disconnected voters to be able to transcend organization in the primaries. In Wallace's case, this appeal was issue-based but apparently not transferrable to others, and led to extreme divisiveness. Numerous observers reported how violence seemed to follow Wallace around campaign appearances as a matter of course, due to the degree to which he was capable of inflaming emotions; in the words of political biographer Dan T. Carter, "Wallace often teetered along a razor's edge of violence."[100] Jimmy Carter appealed to substantially the same alienated constituency, but through largely content-free themes rather than dangerous rhetoric. Upon reaching office, he exhibited grave difficulties in governing, even given a Congress dominated by his own party.[101]

The other examples of this phenomenon also benefited from primaries. Kefauver based his campaigns almost entirely on primary efforts, and in 1952 came reasonably close to winning the nomination. He was stopped only by the superior power of the party organization within the mixed system. Hart, probably the least "outside" of the outsiders, still did somewhat better in primaries than caucuses.

Furthermore, besides the general role of primaries, proportional representation seems on balance to have been to the benefit of Wallace, Carter, and Hart. For this, there is a logical explanation that goes beyond the simple benefits derived from proportional representation by those who cannot attain a plurality. Organization is a discrete phenomenon; it consists of a carefully constructed network of individuals who are capable of mobilizing forces in a specific geographic area. If that area extends over an entire state, then winner-take-all system by state works to the benefit of such organization. If, as is more likely, those areas are smaller, then districted primaries are best. This is why districted primaries were so beneficial to McGovern and Goldwater.

On the other hand, alienation, the stock-in-trade of the unconnected outsider as a class, is at once ephemeral, fickle, and universal. So is public bedazzlement at successful execution of the "popular arts" in general. This is why George Wallace could win 21 percent in Pennsylvania in 1972 after making one campaign stop, or 22 percent in Wisconsin after only eight days of organizing. It is why Jimmy Carter could come out of nowhere in 1976, and then, at the edge of success, be nearly derailed by Jerry Brown, who came from even farther out of nowhere. A system of proportional representation rewards lack of organization, especially when that shortcoming is coupled with charismatic appeals to the mass public. It is no accident that Wallace depended so heavily on media and personal appearances, or that Carter relied so heavily on personal charm and made "far more extensive use of polls than either of his principal opponents."[102]

Similarly, in a more general sense, the nonplebiscitary aspects of primaries in the mixed system worked to the manifest disadvantage of Wallace and Kefauver. In both cases, the candidates were able to achieve great success in winning primary votes, but were unable to turn votes into delegates because they were organizationally incapable of prevailing in (or often of even contesting) the separate delegate selection procedures. Hart was also stymied by the reintroduction of some of these mechanisms in "loophole" primaries in 1984.

Finally, Jimmy Carter showed how the new system virtually requires winners to start early and to run in all primary states. Had a real movement been active in 1976—say, a continuation of the new politics—it would have lost much of the relative advantage of its staying power in the face of Carter's personalistic campaign. No movement confronted with an environment of minimal resources can now hope to succeed by carefully picking and choosing its targets of opportunity, unless extraordinary effort in Iowa or New Hampshire can bring victory and with it the resources to compete elsewhere.[103] Even this prospect is dimmed by the seemingly relentless trend toward "front-loading" major primaries toward the beginning of the primary season. And the reformed campaign finance regime clearly benefits unconnected outsiders, who on average are heavily reliant on small contributions.

The rise of unconnected outsiders has clearly been abetted by changes in communications technology and by the organizational decline of the parties independent of reforms in the nominating system. As the weakening of party organization helped movements, so it helped the unconnected outsiders. Before the reforms, organization control over primaries had slipped sufficiently that Kefauver was able to do well in the primaries that had destroyed Willkie less than a decade before; another decade later, Wallace, an even more improbable candidate, was able to make strong showings against once formidable Democratic party organizations in Wisconsin, Indiana, and Maryland.

Before the rise of the unconnected outsider, Hearst and Willkie had pioneered media-based nomination campaigns, but they could rely only on print media and either owned the newspapers or required powerful publisher allies. Television opened up a whole new avenue of direct appeal to the populace; indeed, television is inextricably linked with the unconnected outsider, and it is little coincidence that the first full example of the species, Kefauver, was launched into national prominence by televised Senate hearings. There have been important nontechnological changes in the character of the media as well, which have benefited the unconnected. Over the course of the first half of the twentieth century, news outlets abandoned the role of party organ for the role of "objective watchdog." In so doing, they replaced a partisan bias openly favoring the regulars of a party (or of a faction of a party)—which worked against the unconnected outsider—with a bias favoring "hot news," the exciting, the extraordinary, and the sensational—a bias that often works to the objective advantage of the unconnected outsider, regardless of the personal preferences of reporters or editors. In this way, George Wallace, though despised by much of the media, drew tremendous benefit from the extensive coverage he received as a phenomenon (Ross Perot would later attain a meteoric rise in early 1992 for the same reason). And the much more recent trend of media decentralization has only worked to help the unconnected further, by offering them a wider range of access—and often a more unmediated form of access—to the public than has ever before been available.

Finally, changes in the structure of public opinion have worked to the advantage of the unconnected outsiders. Most important, by all indications, the proportion of the American electorate that is "alienated"—that feels disconnected, abandoned, and aloof from politics and even society itself—has grown substantially since the 1960s. Some analysts even attribute the long-term decline in voter turnout to this factor.[104] The alienated represent the greatest source of strength for the unconnected outsider, and it stands to reason that electoral opportunities for such outsiders will grow as the number of alienated grows.

All together, circumstances independent of the reforms have led to unprecedented opportunities for ambitious but independent political hopefuls to enter the fray and employ new strategies. This new environment has surely affected both outputs (such candidates had better success) and inputs (since they had better success, they were more likely to try). However, systemic factors have occupied a central place in this transformation. The broader electoral system, while becoming more open after 1968, nevertheless remained less open to third-party candidates than it was in the nineteenth century.[105] Thus, most of the unconnected outsiders were channeled into major party nomination campaigns (George Wallace in 1968 and Ross Perot in 1992 were exceptions, but Wallace also ran within the parties).[106] The nominating system could have responded to the new environment either by inhibiting its negative consequences or by facilitating them; it facilitated them. Indeed, it virtually invited them with a new nominating system that greatly weakened the structural barriers to the dangers posed by the new environment.

The reforms, which sought to open the parties to movements such as the new politics, instead opened the parties much more to individual candidates who are total outsiders unconnected to any autonomous organizational structure and who depend on personal organization and personal—often either divisive or content-free—appeal. It is hardly coincidental that of the four unconnected outsiders between 1952 and 1992, three (Wallace, Carter, and Hart) appeared—or, in the case of Wallace, appeared in their greatest strength—after the reforms, and in the more reformed Democratic Party. Nor is it a coincidence that the phenomenon of unconnected outsiders has only gained momentum, veritably exploding in the 1990s. It is fairly evident that this is not the sort of openness desired by the framers, let alone the critics, of the reforms. It is also probable that the cause of stability is damaged by so clearly reducing the barriers to personalistic candidates without attaining compensating benefits for either movements or parties.

7

Outsiderism in the 1990s

THE ELECTIONS OF 1992 AND 1996 FEATURED AN unusually large number of "outsiders," most of whom were "unconnected" to some degree. If Estes Kefauver was the first example of the archetype and Jimmy Carter represented its coming of age in the reform system, 1992 was the year it went wild. The events of 1992 and 1996 demonstrated three interrelated trends.

First, the theme of outsiderism became a more useful, and hence more frequently used, tool. In the 1992 Democratic race, three of the five candidates tried to position themselves as "outsiders"; in the 1996 Republican race, five of nine.[1] Being an "insider," whether president of the United States, Senate majority leader, or mere senator, served as an automatic burden. Given other advantages, candidates could overcome that burden; and outsiderism carried with it limitations as well as advantages. Nevertheless, not only outsiders but the theme of outsiderism became central to nomination campaigns to an unprecedented degree.

The second trend, clearly connected to the first, was that outsiderism as a phenomenon became diffused to a degree not seen before. Almost every candidate who plausibly could vied to acquire the title of "outsider," even candidates like Bill Clinton in 1992 and Lamar Alexander in 1996, whose claims to outsiderism were relatively modest.

Finally, outsiderism in 1992 and 1996 took new forms. The poles of unconnected outsider and movement outsider remained visible, but new mixtures arose. In particular, some candidates who were fundamentally unconnected outsiders showed the capacity and the inclination, either within a campaign or over time, to build coalitions with some elements of an organized movement.

In the 1992 Democratic primaries, Bill Clinton tried with only modest success to run as an outsider, but found himself flanked by two more plausible outsiders in the form of Paul Tsongas and Jerry Brown. In the Republican primaries, President George Bush found himself challenged by the insurgent campaign of Pat Buchanan and the most extreme of the year's outsiders, David Duke. And no discussion of 1992 would be complete without some mention of Ross Perot, who ran an independent campaign but did touch the primaries at least peripherally. None of the unconnected outsiders of 1992 came close to attaining a major party nomination, and Perot got farther from the White House the closer he got to November 3, yet together they produced an election year that was more dominated by the theme of "outsiderism" than perhaps any in recent American history.[2]

Four years later, Buchanan returned, this time supported by a large part of the Christian right, and was joined by publisher Steve Forbes. The two outsiders Buchanan and Forbes, while defeated for the Republican nomination, were both central players in the 1996 campaign, and were indeed the last two major candidates left in the field against Bob Dole. Buchanan heavily influenced the 1996 Republican platform's stand on social issues, and Forbes clearly drove Dole toward the 15 percent tax cut that became the centerpiece of his fall campaign. All together, the outsiders of the 1990s tend to reaffirm many of the observations and concerns already put forth about the nature of the reform system, while indicating some new directions in which outsiderism might move.

Ross Perot

Ross Perot was the most powerful of 1992's outsiders, and the only one fully divorced from the major parties. When Perot announced on Larry King Live on February 20 that he would consider running for president if "the people" put his name on the ballot in all fifty states, it signaled the beginning of one of the most intriguing episodes in American political history. It remains an unanswered question how much of the outpouring of support that enabled Perot to ultimately attain a ballot position in all fifty states was spontaneous and how much was centrally directed from Dallas. In any event, Perot managed from scratch to build an organization around his presidential quest: part citizens uprising, part educational enterprise, and part cult of personality. He was a candidate (for a majority of 1992, a pseudocandidate) in search of a political "movement" to support him and willing to spend a virtually unlimited fortune to create one. This quest continued with Perot's announcement of a third-party effort (the "Reform Party") in the fall of 1995.

Perot based his appeal on an explicit rejection of both the major parties, and indeed almost certainly won as many votes as he did in November 1992 because of the manifest weakness of both George Bush and Bill Clinton. His campaign was thus built on an appeal to the alienated—the mildly alienated, who were simply annoyed with the two major choices, as well as the severely alienated, who had not voted for years and who saw in Perot a savior from the three c's of 1992, corruption, conspiracy, and colorlessness. In this respect, Perot also resembled George Wallace, who ran a personalist campaign directed at the alienated and who in 1968 formed the American Independent Party as his personal tool. In the same way, the Perot phenomenon in 1992 could not be considered a movement in the true sense, since it was wholly personalist, contained no truly independent organization, had at best only the loosest of ideological frameworks, and had not yet proven any degree of staying power.[3]

While Perot ran outside the traditional party structure, his campaign nevertheless touched the 1992 nominating contests. Starting with the April 7 Democratic and Republican primaries in Minnesota, Perot received significant write-in votes in the primaries. By the time the nominating season ended, Perot write-ins had accounted for a mean of 16.5 percent in three Democratic primaries (Minnesota, Washington, and North Dakota) and 9.5 percent in four Republican primaries (Minnesota, Washington, New Jersey, and North Dakota).[4] Indeed, in the last contest of 1992, in North Dakota on June 9, Perot actually received more votes in the Democratic primary than Bill Clinton, the presumptive nominee.[5] When combined with extensive primary exit poll data showing Perot more popular than Clinton in New Jersey and Ohio and more popular than either Clinton or Bush in California, these primary write-ins added tremendously to Perot's momentum. His success in primaries via the write-in route was limited by his late start and restraints on write-in voting in many states, and was in any case symbolic, but certainly proved the relative ease with which an effective unconnected outsider can have an impact in a primary setting. No such impact was recorded in the caucus states, which produced large numbers of votes for uncommitted delegates but virtually none for Perot.[6]

In a broader sense, Perot's efforts in 1992 and after were a sign that the old convention system strategy of influencing the parties by running an alternative general election campaign rather than attempting to take them over directly is not dead. Indeed, it is likely that a number of recent developments have made such a strategy more viable than at any time since the turn of the century. These factors include court-ordered reductions in ballot access restrictions resulting from the Wallace, McCarthy, and Anderson campaigns, declining public loyalty to the two major parties, and the increasingly decentralized nature of the media. Of course, Perot's personal wealth was an important factor in making the strategy viable as well, countering as it did the major party advantages accruing from federal campaign election law.

Perot's ability to win 19 percent of the vote as an independent candidate in November 1992 and to remain a visible force thereafter, clearly influencing the calculations of both parties, could relieve some pressure on the parties to emphasize openness of their nominating systems at the expense of stability. If such a third-party option is indeed viable, then the openness of the major party nominating systems does not represent the sum total of openness in the American electoral system. On the other hand, the Perot experience could frighten the parties into even greater exertions on behalf of open participation, as the Democrats were frightened by the specter of the Chicago riots.[7]

The Democrats in 1992

The two genuine Democratic "outsiders" seemed to obtain approximately the same results, but for different reasons. Paul Tsongas's campaign fit the description of an "unconnected outsider" campaign, lacking organization, staying power, and name. Indeed, his candidacy closely resembled Gary Hart's. A maverick former senator, running against the party orthodoxy and initially taken seriously by few if any party insiders, Tsongas was quoted as remarking to a supporter in New Hampshire that he would have to save the country from the Democrats before he could save it from George Bush. Bill Clinton's success against Tsongas can be ascribed in no small part to the fact that party leaders were much more comfortable with Clinton, despite the reservations they had about his electability, than with Tsongas. Like Hart, the former Massachusetts senator possessed woefully insufficient organization, and was indeed virtually "invisible" in many of the crucial southern primary states.[8] Nevertheless, Tsongas was still supported by an existing ideological and generational faction within the party (indeed, much the same faction that had supported Hart) and—even more than Hart—also had a detailed substantive program to add to his thematic appeal to disaffected voters wanting change. Tsongas may have been an unconnected outsider, but he represented a relatively mild version of the genre. Given his resemblance to Hart, it was not surprising that his performance largely mimicked Hart's.

Through April 7, the last primaries in which Tsongas's candidacy was a major factor, he received a mean primary vote of 24.4 percent in states where he was on the ballot.[9] His mean first-round caucus vote in that same time period was 19.6 percent. While he actually won one more caucus than primary, five versus four, it was clear that his primary success—especially in New Hampshire—was the key factor driving his early momentum. He also benefited more from the crossover vote in open primaries than any other Democrat, and even received nearly 10 percent of the vote in the New Hampshire Republican primary as a write-in.

His lack of organization hurt him most in the caucus states. For example, in Texas, which had both a primary and caucus component to the delegate selection process, observers argued that "Tsongas's organizational liabilities will probably be most costly" in the caucus phase.[10] This turned out to be an accurate prophecy: Tsongas did substantially better in the primary than the caucuses not only in Texas but in Minnesota, the other state to hold both caucuses and a primary while Tsongas was still viable.[11] On the other hand, Tsongas did well in numerous primaries long after formally suspending his campaign on March 19; without effort or organization, he became "the most successful non-candidate in recent years."[12] He thus virtually replicated Gary Hart's performance both in style and outcome.

Jerry Brown can also be said to have done better in primaries than in caucuses, though his case is somewhat ambiguous. He won 17.5 percent of the delegates from primary states and only 11.4 percent from caucus states.[13] He had a total primary vote through the nomination campaign of 20 percent, a mean primary vote of 16.7 percent, and a mean caucus vote of 17.9 percent in states where he was on the ballot. Brown won three caucus states (and finished ahead of all but uncommitted in another) and only two primaries. However, among states that held both caucuses and primaries in 1992, Brown did better in the primaries than in the caucuses in three (Idaho, Minnesota, and Washington), approximately as well in both in one (Texas), and was not on the ballot in the other (North Dakota).[14] In no case did his caucus showing exceed his primary showing (see table 7.1).

Thus, like Tsongas, Brown preferred primaries but was able to do well in some caucuses. Unlike Tsongas, Brown's overall performance was not the result of a consistent, moderate unconnected outsider campaign. Instead, Brown's curious campaign seemed to have a split personality. In the words of one journalist, "[Brown] himself often seems to be in the throes of a political identity crisis."[15]

In most places, he ran as a magnified version of his 1976 and 1980 self—an extreme unconnected outsider wielding a turtleneck, a 13 percent flat tax proposal, a battle cry of "Take Back America," a 1-800 number, and a one hundred dollar contribution limit. Brown also made substantial use of the services of alienation-obsessed consultant Patrick Caddell, going so far as to virtually plagiarize speeches included in a Caddell 1988 book proposal.[16] Before the Ross Perot phenomenon exploded in April 1992, there was even speculation that Brown might run an independent campaign in the fall should he fail to receive the Democratic nomination. In any event, he was waging an uphill battle against a hostile Democratic organization, even in his own California; he conducted "as much a crusade against the established political order as a campaign for the White House."[17] At the same time, in some caucus states he was able to run a movement-style campaign based on the white liberal remnants of the rainbow coalition. The latter phenomenon accounted for his high overall standing in the caucus states.

Brown won the Colorado and Connecticut primaries, both states which have a long-standing streak of political independence making them particularly open to the appeals of unconnected outsiders. Indeed, his campaign received significant notice only after Colorado, and was deemed at least a semiviable threat to Bill Clinton only as a result of Connecticut. For weeks, Brown's fortunes—his ability to knock Clinton out of the race, if not the more unlikely prospect of gaining the nomination himself—were on the verge of receiving a substantial boost in the New York and Wisconsin primaries, though he ultimately lost both on April 7. In his late-starting campaign in 1976, Brown had won five of the six primaries he contested.

Table 7-1. 1992 Jerry Brown Vote Totals in States Using Primaries and Caucuses

	Caucus[a] (%)	Primary (%)
Idaho	8	16.7
Minnesota	8.2	30.6
North Dakota	7.5	—
Texas	8	8
Washington	18.6	23.1

[a]Caucus totals are first-round results except in Texas, where no first-round results were tabulated. Texas figures reflect second-round caucus convention proceedings.

Nevertheless, throughout the primary season, Brown sought to add organizational and voting strength to his campaign by courting organized labor and attempting to entice the rainbow coalition into an alliance. To this end he gained some of Iowa senator Tom Harkin's labor support and openly courted Jesse Jackson, promising prior to the New York primary that he would make Jackson his vice presidential candidate (a promise that may have cost him that primary). After the 1988 race, observers noted an important split in the rainbow coalition. Andrew Kopkind remarked in the *Nation*: "There is continuing tension, and divergence, between the blacks who make up Jackson's mass base and the issue activists who contribute fewer votes to the coalition but have considerable clout by virtue of their ideological sophistication and organizing skills."[18]

Other observers remarked that the latter faction—white leftists—tended to be less wedded to Jackson and more enthusiastic about the abstract idea of a movement.[19] This split in the rainbow coalition clearly manifested itself in 1992. Despite Brown's blandishments, Jackson remained neutral and the black vote went predominantly to Bill Clinton. In many states, however, it is clear that the white liberal portion of the rainbow coalition—environmentalists, peace activists, homosexual rights groups—did indeed back Brown, who claimed to be inventing a "movement" of his own.[20] This support was focused largely in the caucus states and certainly carried the greatest impact there. In places where Jackson had done well primarily on the strength of this part of the rainbow coalition, Brown also did well.

As a result, of the four caucus states where Brown finished ahead of all competing candidates, Jackson had won two (Vermont and Alaska) in 1988 and had finished a respectable second in another (Maine). Indeed, in Vermont much of the rainbow coalition seems to have wound up backing Brown, though with some hesitation.[21] *Congressional Quarterly* observed that, in Maine, Brown had deliberately courted the Jackson forces, and that "Jackson took one-fourth of the Maine caucus vote in 1988, a showing that Brown essentially matched this year. Brown did it by winning where Jackson had won," among antinuclear and rainbow coalition forces.[22] Similarly, in Washington state, Brown tapped into the Jackson base.[23] The two candidates received almost identical percentages in both Vermont (Jackson 45.7, Brown 46.7) and Alaska (Jackson 34.6, Brown 33.1). Overall, of Brown's top ten caucuses (excluding Guam, which did not hold caucuses in 1988), Jesse Jackson had a 25 percent or higher showing in seven of them in 1988. Throughout the nominating season, Brown used Jackson's white base in the caucuses.[24] Hence, Brown was in essence an unconnected outsider in most primaries while still making use of some organized movement support in some caucus states.

Furthermore, Brown survived to the Democratic national convention and carried into it over six hundred delegates, despite having finished first in only five contests, because universal proportional representation had been once again mandated after 1988 at the insistence of Jackson. Like Jackson before him, Brown understood that he was not going to win, but was able to remain in the race anyway with the goal of forcing the party in his direction.[25] At the convention itself, Brown and his supporters threatened party unity in numerous ways. Although his mercurial behavior was surely not completely dependent on his delegate strength, it seems probable that Brown would have been much less capable of posing such a danger to party unity had a system of plurality primaries required him to actually win in order to collect delegates.

The Republicans in 1992

Among the Republican candidates, David Duke was the most extreme unconnected outsider. Duke was notorious for his ties to the Ku Klux Klan and the American Nazi Party, and had run as an obscure candidate for the Democratic nomination for president in 1988 before changing parties and joining the GOP in 1989. As a Republican, he subsequently ran successfully for Louisiana state representative and unsuccessfully for Louisiana governor and United States senator. He was disavowed by the Republican Party, but was frequently able to use his "underdog" status to win votes from alienated voters. He reached his political peak in the fall of 1991, when he made it to the Louisiana runoff election for governor.

Shortly after losing that runoff, he announced his candidacy against George Bush for the Republican presidential nomination. He had no support within the party and no support from any organized political movement. His only support was derived from his ability to tap into atomized voter anger with divisive issue appeals, and hence he closely resembled George Wallace (though with a much more dubious background and much less popular appeal). He was perhaps the ultimate unconnected outsider of 1992.

Although Duke did not do well in any phase of the 1992 nomination campaign, whatever impact he had was made in the primaries. In the thirteen primaries Duke entered before retiring from the race on April 22, he received a mean vote of 3.7 percent. Nowhere did he finish better than a very poor third in a three-man race. His highest showing was in Mississippi, where he received 10.6 percent; he received only 8.8 percent in his own Louisiana, finishing third even among those who had voted for him for governor only a few months before.[26] Even compared to this poor primary showing, Duke by all indications had negligible success in the caucus states. He lacked even the rudiments of organization, and refused even to contest most of the caucuses.[27] His chief role in the 1992 election was to serve as a warning shot, the first and most extreme harbinger of the stronger, more substantial, and more popularly appealing outsiderism to come.

Pat Buchanan also claimed the mantle of "outsider," as an insurgent running a vitriolic and largely unorganized campaign against an incumbent president of his own party. While an argument could be made that Buchanan was simply a factional insurgent from within the Republican Party, he can also sensibly be viewed as an unconnected outsider in 1992. He shared the basic characteristics of such candidates, and his successes, such as they were, were largely the product of an angry but unfocused protest vote that drew almost equally from conservative, moderate, and liberal voters.[28]

Buchanan never won a primary or a caucus state in 1992, but was catapulted to prominence by his unexpectedly strong showing in the New Hampshire primary, where he garnered 37 percent of the vote and held Bush to 53 percent. This moral victory (as the press portrayed it) carried Buchanan to a series of other strong finishes, gaining 30 percent or more in the Colorado, Maryland, and Georgia primaries before beginning a downward slide in South Carolina and the Super Tuesday primaries. While he too never really had a chance to win, he did succeed in forcing George Bush to the right, at least rhetorically. In contrast to his primary showing, Buchanan's caucus showing was very poor. As Rhodes Cook remarked, "The failure of conservative columnist Patrick J. Buchanan to make an imprint in the caucus states has been a significant factor in his inability to mount a more serious challenge to President Bush for the Republican nomination."[29]

Buchanan won no caucus state delegates, and in the few caucus states where the Republican Party officially tabulated first-round caucus results, his showing was abysmal (4.3 percent in Maine, 2.3 percent in Vermont). Indeed, neither Buchanan nor Duke even competed in the Iowa caucuses, a traditional launching point for long-shot candidacies. This confirms the greater utility of primaries to unconnected outsiders. It also confirms the conventional argument that primaries are very useful to insurgents running against incumbent presidents, and hence that a system devoid of primaries might be intolerably closed to insurgents of all varieties. And it implicitly confirms that a system in which primaries are dominant will reduce substantially the "stability gap" between the governing and nongoverning parties by making the governing party much more susceptible to challenges.

Unlike Jerry Brown, Pat Buchanan was unable to accumulate any significant number of delegates, though he actually outperformed Brown in the primaries (Buchanan received 22 percent of the total primary vote, Brown 20 percent). Buchanan also faced this problem in 1996. The cause of this discrepancy was the continued reliance of the Republican Party on nonproportional rules of delegate distribution. Furthermore, Buchanan's name (not to mention Duke's) could not even be placed in nomination in 1992, since he was unable to garner a majority of delegates in five states or more, as party rules require. Perhaps as a result of these Republican rules, while Buchanan moved Bush in his direction he also had limited leverage at the convention and ended up endorsing Bush in a prime-time speech. Brown, on the other hand, maintained his petulance to the end, refusing to endorse either his party's platform or its candidate. This difference may have simply been the difference between Brown and Buchanan, but it seems probable that the difference in institutional circumstances was also a factor.

The Republicans in 1996

As Jerry Brown conducted a split personality campaign in 1992, Pat Buchanan showed the ability over time to turn his quest for the presidency from a largely unconnected protest campaign into a more explicitly ideological, movement-supported campaign. While Buchanan did not personally change in 1996, the structure of his campaign, his message, and his supporters did. New Hampshire Republican officials, for example, noted a substantial difference between Buchanan 1992 and Buchanan 1996, a shift from mining "a protest vote against Bush" to coming in "with a vision of where he wanted to take the country."[30] In the crucial early primaries of 1992, Buchanan did equally well among self-described liberals, moderates, and conservatives; in 1996, he drew his support disproportionately from "conservative" and "very conservative" voters.[31] In 1992, the Christian right, for the most part, supported George Bush against Buchanan; in 1996, the national leadership of the movement remained neutral, and Buchanan tapped into the lower-level organizational resources of the Christian Coalition and prolife groups in most states. In the Louisiana caucuses, he won two of every three religious conservative votes.[32] Only when Bob Dole broke Buchanan's hold on Christian right voters in South Carolina was his ultimate triumph secure.

As a consequence of Buchanan's acquisition of substantial organizational resources, he did far better in caucuses in 1996 than in 1992, while doing approximately the same in primaries. He won three of the seven caucuses in which results were available, held from late January through the end of March (by which time the nomination was decided), including the crucial Louisiana caucuses. In Louisiana, Buchanan had the support not only of parts of the Christian right but of the governor of Louisiana and the state's Dole supporters, who hoped to weaken Dole's rival, Phil Gramm.[33] Buchanan's close second-place finish in Iowa was credited by observers to "a committed, organized religious community [which] provided him the kind of strong organization that makes the difference" in low turnout caucus settings.[34] State party officials in Missouri similarly pointed to strong "organizational ability" as the source of Buchanan's caucus victory, a component mostly lacking in Buchanan's 1992 run.[35] Conversely, after Buchanan won the New Hampshire primary, he did not win another primary in February or March. He received a lower vote percentage in 1996 than in 1992 in eleven of the twenty states that had primaries in both years (of course, he was also facing several opponents in 1996 rather than one main opponent). In the two states that held both caucuses and primaries, Buchanan did substantially better in the caucuses.[36] Overall, Buchanan received a mean vote of 31.0 percent in caucus states and 22.5 percent in primary states through the end of March 1996.

Like Brown in 1992, Buchanan in 1996 spoke of building a "movement" around his campaign, saying: "We want to remake and reshape the Republican Party."[37] Yet in 1996, the organized movement that aided Buchanan was not the newly organized coalition of cultural conservatives and displaced workers that Buchanan envisioned; rather, it was localized portions (ultimately, a minority) of the Christian right that lent themselves to Buchanan's cause. Buchanan's dilemma in 1996 and beyond was that it was the disorganized half of his electoral equation (anxious workers) that held the key to expanding his base, since trade rather than social conservatism was arguably the most salient part of his 1996 campaign. It was on the issue of trade that Buchanan and the other Republican candidates differed in kind rather than simply degree; in the decisive primaries through March, there was a greater difference between Dole and Buchanan voters on the issue of trade than on the issue of abortion.[38]

In 1996, it was publisher Malcom S. "Steve" Forbes who ran the campaign of an unconnected outsider. Never having held elective office, Forbes hoped to ride to the Republican nomination on the basis of a single idea (the flat tax) buttressed by a general theme (economic growth) and driven by a profound distaste for elected officials and "insiders." Financing almost his entire campaign from his family fortune, Forbes in a sense represented the Republican version of Ross Perot: tycoon as avenging outsider, liberated by ample financial resources from the fund-raising obligations and organizational requirements faced by most politicians. *Newsweek* magazine noted that in the age of outsiderism, many voters believe "his complete lack of political qualifications uniquely qualifies him for the job."[39]

Forbes was the last major Republican candidate to enter the race, and rose like the "meteor" of "Federalist 64" with large infusions of advertising money in the first primary states. His early campaign was largely centered on a vigorous (his opponents said vicious) advertising campaign attacking Bob Dole and some other candidates for insiderism; in many states, the media were virtually the only tool of his campaign. For a brief moment in late January, Forbes held a close second place in Iowa polls and actually pulled ahead in New Hampshire. However, he finished a disappointing fourth in the Iowa caucuses and, a week later, fourth in New Hampshire. He came back to win a couple of primaries and even to seize a short-lived lead in delegates, but was never able to fully recover from his early defeats. Several factors contributed to his downfall in Iowa, but the greatest factor was his almost total lack of organization.

The Forbes campaign did not begin organizing in Iowa until late December, and less than a month before the caucuses had only organized seventeen of Iowa's ninety-nine counties.[40] In contrast, his major opponents had been organizing for over a year. In the end, Forbes spent four hundred dollars on advertising in Iowa for every vote he received, which appeared to commentators to "confirm the notion that a strong caucus still depends on a strong local organization."[41] Indeed, Forbes himself "blamed his poor showing on the caucus mechanism."[42] Forbes did reasonably well in some caucus settings, but overall, primaries were clearly his strength. He won two of twenty-one primaries with a mean primary vote of 16.9 percent, while winning no caucuses and gaining a mean caucus vote of 15.2. Above all, his failure in Iowa, after the polls had raised expectations, was a critical blow to his campaign.

Both Forbes and Buchanan benefited substantially from crossover votes in open primaries. Indeed, through March 1996 both Forbes and Buchanan did better among independents and Democrats than among Republicans.[43] Forbes deliberately targeted independent voters and Buchanan targeted blue-collar Democrats, remarking before the Iowa caucuses: "We'll be in stronger country when we come up and Democrats can vote. I think they'll vote for me. The more that come, the better we'll do."[44] It was not coincidence that

Buchanan's strongest primary showings during the decisive period of the campaign came in Wisconsin and Michigan, open primaries that attracted large numbers of crossover voters.

Parties, Primaries, and Caucuses in 1992 and 1996

In 1992, as in years past, the parties proved much more adept at influencing caucuses than primaries. The mean vote for "uncommitted" in all Democratic contests was 10 percent in primaries, 22.8 percent in caucuses.[45] Furthermore, as Bill Clinton's nomination became simultaneously more probable and, due to a continuing spate of negative revelations, less appealing, these figures increased substantially, especially in the caucus states. After mid-March, Democratic primaries registered a mean 12.4 percent "uncommitted" vote, while the uncommitted vote in caucus states jumped to a mean of 36.7 percent. Similarly, while most Republican caucus states did not tabulate first-round results, it is probable that they produced many more uncommitted delegates than did the primaries.[46] A similar pattern emerged in 1996, when the twenty-nine primaries through the end of March (not including the New York pure delegate primary) saw a mean uncommitted/other vote that was about half that in the corresponding caucuses.[47]

Thus, while unconnected outsiders like Tsongas, Brown, Duke, Perot, Buchanan in 1992, and Forbes did better in primaries than in caucuses to varying degrees, the parties as institutions did better in caucuses, either in the form of uncommitted delegates (Democrats 1992, Republicans 1996) or in a combination of uncommitted delegates and delegates secured for the incumbent president (Republicans 1992). Also doing well in caucuses was the movement side to Brown's split personality campaign and Buchanan's movement-oriented 1996 campaign.

Campaign Finance and the Outsiders

The unconnected outsiders of 1992, especially Buchanan and Brown, clearly benefited from FECA. An overwhelming preponderance of their funds (indeed, all of Brown's) came in small contributions from direct mail or televised appeals. The two men received more matching funds than any other candidates but George Bush and Bill Clinton, who did so well only because of the enormous volume of their total fund-raising.[48] Tsongas also received three-fifths of his contributions in sums under five hundred dollars. Although he raised very little money in his presidential race, David Duke financed his state races primarily through very effective small-donor appeals. Had he been a stronger force in 1992, he would almost certainly have benefited significantly from FECA. In both parties, the unconnected outsiders were much more reliant on small donations and on FECA matching funds than were the ultimate nominees (see table 7.2.)

In 1996, Buchanan relied primarily on a direct mail list of approximately 100,000 small donors, largely previous contributors to his 1992 campaign.[49] In the first disbursement of federal matching funds, Buchanan benefited more than anyone except Dole and Gramm, who, like Bush in 1992, had vastly outraised him overall.[50] Forbes also benefited from FECA, though in a different way; because he declined to accept matching funds, he was not bound to FECA spending limits as were his major opponents. He was thus able to spend up to $4 million in some highly targeted states (such as Arizona, which provided him with an important primary victory), and threatened to completely drain Dole's campaign coffers. Had Dole not achieved a decisive breakthrough on "Junior Tuesday" and "Super Tuesday," just as he was on the verge of bumping up against aggregate FECA spending limits, Forbes might have been able to turn his financial advantage into several more victories.[51] This sort of benefit from FECA rules is only available, of course, to the self-financed outsider.

Outsiderism in the 1990s

The reform system has accommodated (if not led to) a veritable explosion of outsiderism in the 1990s. For the most part, these outsiders have been unconnected. There has been no candidate serving as the unalloyed repre-

Table 7-2. 1992 Campaign Finance: Outsiders vs. Nominees

	Contributions <$500 As % of Total Raised	FECA Matching Funds As % of Total Raised
Clinton	38	33
Brown	100	45
Tsongas	60	37
Bush	9	28
Buchanan	83	41

Source: Anthony Corrado, "The Changing Environment of Presidential Campaign Finance," in *In Pursuit of the White House: How We Choose Our Presidential Nominees*, ed. William G. Mayer (Chatham, N.J.: Chatham House, 1996), pp. 230, 233.

sentative of an entire existing movement and no genuinely new movements. Both Jerry Brown and Pat Buchanan have claimed to be building new movements, though in reality they only attached themselves to portions of existing movements. Brown seemingly abandoned his self-proclaimed effort to build a new movement after 1992, though Buchanan vowed to press ahead after 1996. Meanwhile, Perot continued his efforts to build an alternative structure outside the major parties.

As unconnected outsiders in the 1990s, Perot, Tsongas, Forbes, and Duke generally fit the mold of their predecessors, though at least the first three gave greater attention to specific policy prescriptions than did previous examples of this candidate type. Brown and Buchanan showed it was possible to combine types either within a single campaign or across years. In all, Duke and Buchanan did substantially better in primaries than in caucuses in 1992; Forbes in 1996 also did better in primaries, and was largely derailed by his failure in the Iowa caucuses. In an absolute sense, Tsongas, like Hart before him, did better than any of the other unconnected outsiders in caucuses, probably because he and Hart were the least "outside" of the outsiders, but still did slightly better in the primaries than in the caucuses. Brown generally concentrated on primaries, doing well mostly in those caucus states where he could latch onto rainbow coalition support. And Perot used the primaries of both parties to advance his 1992 presidential aspirations in a way that was impossible to replicate in the caucuses.

Buchanan's candidacies present a particularly fascinating and complex instance of outsiderism. Buchanan evolved from a relatively unfocused, unconnected, and disorganized protest candidate in 1992 to the recipient of substantial organizational assistance from elements of the Christian right in almost every state in 1996. Thus, of all the major outsiders in the 1990s, only Buchanan in 1996 can really be said to have fundamentally based his campaign on movement support,[52] and his results corresponded to the pattern of previous movement campaigns; unlike the other outsiders of the 1990s (including himself in 1992), he excelled in caucus settings. Because of the fractionated nature of his movement support (most of the Christian right ultimately went to Bob Dole) Buchanan must, however, be considered a relatively weak movement candidate.

Other outsider patterns were generally confirmed in the 1990s: proportional representation in the Democratic Party greatly benefited Brown, and the lack of proportional representation in the Republican Party hurt Buchanan both times he ran. The ephemeral alienation discussed in the last chapter accounted for Perot's ability to win large numbers of primary votes without even being on the ballot. And while Forbes benefited twice from win-ner-take-all delegate schemes, he was hurt much more often than helped, gain-ing an estimated 31 percent support but receiving no delegates in New York's pure delegate primary, for example.[53] Virtually every outsider candidate in the 1990s benefited from open primaries, and virtually every outsider candidate benefited disproportionately from FECA, even Forbes, though for different reasons than most.

Given the nature of the current nominating system in combination with the continued grassroots decline of parties and the growth of alienation, the continued decentralization of the media, and the ongoing volatility of Ameri-can politics, there is little reason to believe that outsiderism will abate any time soon. Unconnected outsiders will almost surely continue to arise in substan-tial numbers with little warning, with the weakest among them fading away almost as quickly. A few more enterprising or ambitious outsiders, in the mold of Ross Perot or Pat Buchanan, may seek to build a "movement" around themselves, and in the process may at least, like Buchanan, acquire the orga-nized support of portions of an existing movement. It is even possible to imag-ine that Perot and Buchanan—or at least their supporters—might represent the nucleus of a truly new movement, thus far unnamed and inchoate (the "nationalist movement"?). Buchanan, at least, has expressed interest in such an alliance and has explicitly targeted former Perot voters with varying degrees of success.[54] For such an alliance to produce a true movement, rather than a pseudomovement, some inconsistencies or antipathies between the two groups must be resolved, the personalism of the chief protagonists must be overcome and de-emphasized, and some truly independent organizational structure must come into being. The short-lived bid by former Colorado governor Richard Lamm to win the 1996 Reform Party nomination was an indication of how far that party had yet to travel to become something other than a vehicle for Perot's personal ambition. If these forces do obtain autonomous organiza-tional strength and wish to compete within the parties, they must also over-come the bias of the nominating system against organization and for person-alism, which remains the driving force in nominating politics.

While organized movements continue to operate and to exert influence, particularly in less reformed settings like Republican caucuses, the presiden-tial nomination campaigns of the 1990s should erase any remaining doubt that the current system is partial to the unconnected outsider. The proliferation of such outsiders, and of outsiderism as a theme, will likely be looked back upon as one of the most important characteristics of presidential politics in the third decade after the reforms.

8

Conclusion

OUTSIDERS HAVE ALWAYS PLAYED AN IMPORTANT role in American politics. Throughout American history, outsiders have tested the party system and bypassed it by starting third parties: to their supporters, they have carried with them high ideals; to their opponents, dangerous demagoguery. Always they have challenged the structures and ideas of established politics. They are fundamental to political change, and the ways political parties have sought to meet their challenge have been fundamentally intertwined with the mechanisms parties have chosen to nominate their presidential candidates. Outsiders are thus affected by the nominating system, but, in seeking greater openness, they have also driven change in the system more than once. Both within the parties and beyond them, the presidential campaigns of the 1990s demonstrated the enduring—even growing—impact of outsiders and outsiderism on American politics.

Yet the categories we are accustomed to applying—outsiders versus insiders, openness versus stability—are not sufficient. In many ways, they mask important distinctions. Without understanding those distinctions, we cannot come to terms with the challenges posed by outsiders, and thus with the role of change and openness, within the context of presidential nominations. Ultimately, the complexity of openness, stability, and outsiderism itself presents the polity with crucial choices.

The Dimensions of Openness and Stability

The first question we must answer when considering the openness of the presidential nominating system to outsiders is what constitutes openness. Openness and stability can be most easily understood as zero-sum objectives; yet, paradoxically, practitioners of political science from Alexander Hamilton to the Democratic Commission on Delegate Selection and Party Structure have claimed to achieve not just a balance of those values but a blend.[1] This paradox becomes comprehensible when one realizes that openness is not a single value but is made up of at least three dimensions. Openness of initial access is the first, openness to short-term success (winning the nomination) is the second, and openness to long-term success (consolidating control over the party) is the third.

Stability may have a zero-sum relationship to openness, but if openness is a threefold concept then stability is so as well. In that sense, stability in terms of access is simply lack of openness of access; stability in terms of success is merely a lack of openness to success. But this relationship is true only within each dimension: for example, stability in terms of access does not necessarily mean lack of openness in terms of success (unless there is zero access). A given nominating system might block the vast majority of outsiders from obtaining access, but the few who cleared the initial hurdle might have a very good chance of winning. Another system might give access to a larger proportion of outsiders, but might give them only a meager chance of gaining the nomination. It is these distinctions among the dimensions of openness and stability that make a blend of the two values possible. Furthermore, these dimensions are clearly affected in different ways by each component of the nominating system and by different systems in their entirety.

Aside from the three dimensions of openness (and thus stability), there is another element of stability, which has less to do with the ability of outsiders to compete and win than with the terms under which they succeed. To what degree does the nominating system force outsiders to moderate their demands in order to succeed? To what degree does the system insulate the majority or governing party from change more than it does the minority party? These considerations might be called "governing stability," since the primary concern is the effect of outsiders not on the party but on broader regime stability and moderation.

Not All Outsiders Are the Same

The second question to answer when thinking about the openness of the nominating system to outsiders is what constitutes an outsider. At the beginning of this study, it was argued that not all outsiders are the same. Some outsiders are part of or are supported by a broader political movement that possesses independent organization and some evidence of staying power, and indeed is a force with enough autonomous substance to be assigned a name like "conservative movement," "new politics," or "progressive movement." These movements exist on a continuum of strength. Other outsiders are not connected in a substantial way to any movement. This division between movement outsiders and unconnected outsiders was established by definition. While the division is logically and historically defensible, the definition does not by itself explain why the division is important.

This study has identified two reasons why that division is important. First, it is apparent that the two types of outsiders have different characteristics, some (but not all) of which flow out of the definition. Movements, because they seek to take over political parties for the long term, tend to have a longer-range perspective on party affairs. Likewise, because by definition they possess some measure of organization, they may actually be capable of functionally replacing the party organization they seek to defeat. Movements by definition have displayed staying power and some breadth of popular appeal. Issues and questions of political philosophy are their stock-in-trade; as a result, win or lose, they often elevate the standard of public discourse. And since they depend so heavily on organization, movements often have the effect of bringing together large numbers of Americans in a common civic enterprise.

The category of the unconnected outsider is somewhat more difficult to assess, since the candidates who fall within it include a much broader range of styles, from David Duke to Paul Tsongas. Nevertheless, something can be said about this group on average as well. By definition, the unconnected outsiders are not supported by autonomous organization and do not have the capacity to replace the party structure, only to destroy it. Nor do they wish to replace it; as independent candidates, they wish to gain their party's nomination but do not seek to turn the party into a long-term instrument. The unconnected outsiders are accountable to neither party nor movement, and more often than not they rely on either content-free themes (Kefauver, Carter, Hart, Brown, Perot) or extreme divisiveness (Wallace, Duke, Buchanan), directed at the most alienated. These candidates are usually characterized by an almost exclusive reliance on the media, and tend to rely on the exploitation of social atomization. They are no more prone toward ideological extremism than candidates representing movements (indeed, perhaps less so), but their inherent lack of accountability, untempered personalism, short-term frame of reference, and rhetorical styles would seem to make them more prone to demagoguery by virtually anyone's definition. As a class they are, in many respects, similar to the "transient meteors" who, the Founders warned, "sometimes mislead as well as dazzle."[2]

These are, of course, generalizations, and there are exceptions. Paul Tsongas, for example, was acclaimed by most observers for having elevated the debate in the 1992 primaries. Some movements (like the rainbow coalition) are more personalist than others (like the conservative movement or the new politics), and some unconnected outsiders (like George Wallace and Ross Perot) attempt to build personalist pseudomovements around themselves. These two phenomena may at some point shade into each other. Jerry Brown's 1992 campaign had a split personality, and Pat Buchanan showed that the same candidate who began as an unconnected protest candidate could acquire substantial movement support over time.

Nevertheless, the theoretical division of movement outsiders and unconnected outsiders is generally supported by the difference in their practical characteristics.[3] Those differences are not trivial, but carry with them serious issues for the health of the polity. All that political science can do is to try to draw sensible boundaries, to assess the average characteristics of each class, and to determine which, on balance, is preferable if a choice must be made. That a choice can and must be made is a consequence of the second substantive difference between movement outsiders and the unconnected: they are affected differently by the components of the nominating system.

All together, just as there are different dimensions of openness, there are also three axes when thinking about "openness to whom?" The first axis is the one most frequently understood in discussions of openness: insiders versus outsiders, with outsiders including both movements and the unconnected outsiders. The second axis is organization versus nonorganization: the party organization and movements together on one hand, the unconnected outsiders on the other. The third axis is strong versus weak among all candidates. These axes can be identified in nominating systems and in their systemic components.

Components of the Nominating System

Caucuses and Primaries

As Paul-Henri Gurian observed, the fundamental difference between caucuses and primaries is that "in caucus situations, the emphasis is on grassroots organization; in primaries, the emphasis is on advertising and mass media."[4] As a result, caucuses and primaries can both be said to operate along the organization/nonorganization axis and, to a lesser extent, along the strong/weak axis, though with opposite biases. Caucuses benefit organization—both party and movement—while primaries most systematically benefit unconnected outsiders. This notion finds support as well from recent studies of caucus participants, which tend to show both ideological activists and party regulars disproportionately represented.[5] The strongest movements are disproportionately benefited by caucuses, while weaker and less mature movements are helped less and the unconnected are positively hurt. Needless to say, substantial political consequences result from that difference.

Ever since the introduction of direct primaries at the local level in the 1890s, reformers have viewed them as a mechanism for openness, permitting popular forces to bypass an entrenched elite. In many instances, the existence of some primaries has indeed served an important role in assuring access into the nominating system for political movements. However, on balance, movement candidates do less well in primaries than in caucuses. Beyond a certain point, the gains in access from primaries are more than negated by the loss in potential for actual success.

With or without McGovern-Fraser, the nature of caucuses makes them hospitable to movements, though McGovern-Fraser did reduce initial barriers to entry and the structural differences between caucuses and primaries. Goldwater came before 1968, and did what McGovern did after 1968 but with even greater success. McCarthy came before the reforms, leading a movement that had just come into being and running against an incumbent president, and did well in selected caucus states where he had the organization and planning to compete. Jackson did well after the reforms, but Reagan, Robertson, and Buchanan in 1996 did even better in the substantially less reformed Republican caucuses, Reagan against an incumbent president.

Caucuses are, at the same time, more hospitable than primaries to party influence in normal times. The proportion of delegates chosen as uncommitted is consistently much higher in the caucuses, and most (though not all) of this is the result of organized efforts by the local party structure. Thus, caucuses not only block access by weak movements and the unconnected but also retain, even after McGovern-Fraser, a greater degree of organized party influence than do primaries.

On the other hand, caucuses are generally inhospitable to unconnected outsiders. The more extreme their outsiderism, the more this is likely to be true. Some have speculated that this is the result of class differences in the bases of support of, for instance, Wallace and McGovern, rather than a difference inherent in the character of caucuses and primaries. This line of argument falters when one considers the demographic similarities between Wallace supporters, who did not master caucuses, and Robertson supporters, who did.[6] The key difference was the prior organization of Robertson supporters as part of a movement.

Thus, while a smattering of primaries may be important even for strong movements, the greatest beneficiaries of a primary-dominated system are the unconnected outsiders. Movements thrive on two characteristics, both of which are maximized by caucuses and diluted and minimized by primaries: intensity and organization. Movements are characterized by an intensity bred by a sense of urgent purpose. In most cases, movements do less well in primaries because their intensity is diluted and their organization strained. That intensity has its greatest impact in low turnout contests, but turnout in primaries is generally ten to twenty times higher than turnout in caucuses.[7] Movements' organization also gives them an advantage in low turnout contests. A given level of organization will have greater effect in a caucus setting than in a primary, and there are numerous substitutes for organization—especially the media—that can be used in primaries but are not nearly as effective in caucuses. If there is really only one way to win a caucus—organization—there are two ways to win a primary—organization and what the Founders called the "popular arts," with the latter easily capable of overcoming the former. Unconnected outsiders do not have the support of a preexisting organizational structure broader than their own campaign, but they are skilled in the "popular arts" and have special appeal with those citizens who are so alienated or disaffected that their voting constitutes a surprising mobilization of new voters. Such outsiders are capable of rising primarily on the strength of personal appeal and television.

Aside from the short-term benefits—the election of delegates—gained by movements in caucus settings, it is significant that movement victories obtained through caucuses rather than primaries are often accompanied by long-term movement control of the party machinery. Unlike movements, unconnected outsiders are interested only in their own short-term success and not in long-term party control.

In this way, primaries are a mirror image of caucuses, where initial access is made more difficult but strong movements have much to gain. Hence, in relation to movements, primaries do seem to have the moderating and stabilizing influence that has been implied by some writers; they serve foremost as a tough testing ground of electability and popular appeal, and only secondarily as a means of infiltration.[8] This stabilizing influence, however, is absent in relation to the unconnected outsiders (see table 8.1). And systems dominated by caucuses tend to be more permeable to movements in the organizationally weaker—hence generally minority—party. As a result, caucuses, unlike primaries, contribute to governing stability.[9]

Open Primaries

The opening of primaries operates on the insider/outsider axis, consistently providing avenues of openness for outsiders of all sorts, both movements and the unconnected. Movement candidates such as McCarthy, McGovern, Reagan, Robertson, and Buchanan have benefited, as have unconnected outsiders such as Kefauver, Wallace, Hart, Tsongas, and Forbes.[10] The chief losers of open primaries have been the "regulars" such as Hubert Humphrey, Gerald Ford, and Bob Dole, whose greatest base is among traditional party voters.

Proportional Representation

Proportional representation affects both the strong/weak axis and the organization/nonorganization axis, with strong candidates hurt and weak candidates helped and with localized organization hurt to the benefit of ephemeral support. It is a clear instance of improving access but at the same time reducing the potential for ultimate success. In particular, a universal regime of pure PR would make it impossible to construct a majority of delegates from less than a majority of votes. Once thresholds and districted primaries are established, this changes somewhat, more so the higher the threshold. Nevertheless, the general principle underlying PR requires that delegate totals not be greatly out of line with vote totals.

This effect on candidates in general is widely understood, but the importance of it to movements must be emphasized. Because of the nature of movements, the ability to transform a minority of votes into a majority of delegates through organization and intensity is crucial for movement success. Thus, not only does proportional representation hurt strong candidates and help weak ones, but this effect falls especially heavily on movements. As *CQ Weekly Report* observed prior to the 1976 campaign, "The advent of proportional representation has reduced the impact the committed supporters of an insurgent candidate can have in a multi-candidate field."[11]

Naturally, PR conversely helps weak movements and weak candidates (assuming a fairly low threshold to win delegates). It also works to the benefit of those whose success is based less on organization than on ephemeral popular appeal. The importance of organization can be seen further in the advantage that movements and parties both seem to derive from pure delegate primaries in which the candidate's name is not attached to the name of the delegate on the ballot. This sort of primary has traditionally worked to the advan-

Table 8-1. Caucuses and Primaries

Movement Candidates

	Caucus Vote	Caucus Delegates	Primary Vote	Primary Delegates
Goldwater 1964	nr	75%	38%v	62%
McCarthy 1968	nr	12%	39%v	35%
McGovern 1972	nr	40%	25%v	65%
Reagan 1976	nr	56%	51%v	44%
Jackson 1984	10%m	13%	18%m	12%
Jackson 1988	37%v	39%	29%v	30%
Robertson 1988	28%m	–	10%m	–
Buchanan 1996	31%m	–	23%m	–

Unconnected Outsiders

	Caucus Vote	Caucus Delegates	Primary Vote	Primary Delegates
Kefauver 1952	nr	19%	65%v	40%
Wallace 1972	nr	7%	24%v	16%
Wallace 1976	6%m	4%	11%m	6%
Carter 1976	17%m	26%	40%m	41%
Hart 1984	36%m	32%	39%m	34%
Tsongas 1992	20%m	–	24%m	–
Brown 1992	18%m	11%	17%m	18%
Buchanan 1992	nr	–	22%v	–
Duke 1992	nr	–	4%m	–
Forbes 1996	15%m	–	17%m	–

Notes:

v = total votes in all caucuses or primaries nationally

m = mean of state primary or first-round caucus results when on ballot

nr = not reported in most states

Total vote is used when no caucus results are reported or when both caucus and primary results are available in that form for candidates who proceeded through the whole nominating process. Where total caucus votes are not available, or where candidates left the campaign early, mean vote results are used for both caucuses and primaries for comparability. In some of these cases, actual vote totals are available for primaries and are referred to in the relevant chapters. Delegate figures for Carter and Wallace in 1976 are preconvention figures as of June 9, 1976 (See *National Journal*, June 12, 1976). All other delegate figures are from the convention roll call. Jackson and Hart delegate figures in 1984 are adjusted to remove pledged superdelegates. Jackson delegates in 1988 are adjusted to remove pledged superdelegates and to account for Texas's mixed system in which 65 percent of delegates were chosen by primary and 35 percent by caucus; in the absence of official results, Jackson's Texas delegates are divided proportionately, though unofficial evidence indicates that Jackson did better in the caucus portion than the primary portion. Brown 1992 delegates are adjusted to remove pledged superdelegates and to account for Texas' mixed system in which three-quarters of delegates were chosen by primary and one-quarter by caucus; in the absence of official results, Brown's four Texas delegates are divided proportionately. Tsongas 1992 mean votes are for contests through April 7, when he ceased to be a major factor in the race. Duke's 1992 mean primary votes are for the thirteen primaries he entered before withdrawing April 22. Buchanan's 1996 mean votes are for the twenty-eight primaries and seven caucuses he entered through March 26, at which time the Republican nomination was determined. Forbes's mean votes are for the twenty-one primaries and six caucuses he entered through March 12, after which time he withdrew from the race. Buchanan, Duke, Forbes, Robertson, and Tsongas were not viable candidates at the time of the convention.

tage of the party organization. Sufficiently well-organized movements, however, are capable of beating the regulars at their own game in these settings, as in the McCarthy and McGovern efforts in New York. This type of primary is similar to the so-called loophole primary, which was used by some states in the Democratic Party in 1976, 1984, and 1988, in which voters cast ballots directly for the delegates in districted plurality primaries. Party organizations more often succeeded in electing uncommitted delegates in this type of primary than in others (though less than in caucuses), and party-backed candidates like Walter Mondale in 1984 have done especially well there.[12]

On the other hand, proportional representation seems to work to the benefit of unconnected outsiders, who depend on personalist popular appeals rather than organization for success. Wallace, for example, could in 1972 obtain 20 percent of the vote seemingly by simply appearing on the ballot. His strength was not as localized as would be the strength of a candidate more dependent on organization, and he had much more to gain from a rule of proportional representation. In the same way, Perot at the end of the 1992 primary season could win 10 to 20 percent not only without campaigning but without even being on the ballot.

Finally, proportional representation encourages (or even requires) candidates to run in virtually all contested primaries. It is no longer possible to pick and choose primaries for maximum effect. However, the ability to pursue strategies of concentration was very important for Goldwater and McGovern in their successful efforts, and was also important for McCarthy and Robert Kennedy. Even Reagan in 1976 pursued this strategy, but did not always choose his targets well. It stands to reason that movement candidates will be disadvantaged by having to run in all states, for the same reason they are relatively disadvantaged by proportional representation in any given state: they depend on organization, and it is very difficult and very costly to maintain everywhere the sort of organization that primary states require. Even McGovern, who was quite strong, was forced to move hundreds of organizers from state to state. This was possible only because there were a limited number of states to which such attention was directed. Unconnected outsiders thrive in such diffused campaigns, however; Kefauver was the first candidate to use the "run everywhere" strategy, and Carter was the first to win with it.

Plebiscitary Ethos

The plebiscitary, or candidate-centered, ethos has been the philosophical underpinning of reforms since the progressive movement. Indeed, it is the broadest of the reform tenets, encompassing both a general attitude and a number of specific mechanisms. It holds that the rules governing nomination contests should emphasize the importance of public support for individual candidates. This ethos takes the specific form of primaries and proportional representation, but also manifests itself in requirements that delegates identify which candidate they support, in other attempts to reduce delegate discretion, and in the ban on early delegate selection processes. In counterpoise would be an ethos emphasizing delegate flexibility, easier construction of majorities, and the representative rather than popular nature of the process. The plebiscitary ethos as a whole operates on the same axes as proportional representation (strong/weak and organization/nonorganization) and with the same biases.

In general terms, the plebiscitary ethos would clearly have worked against movements and for unconnected outsiders. Two movement candidates—Goldwater and McGovern—won nomination despite low poll standings and mediocre primary results, while Estes Kefauver was denied nomination in 1952 despite very good polls and enormous primary success. The plebiscitary ethos as a general attitude would have rejected (and in some cases did reject) these results as illegitimate.

The specific devices of primaries and proportional representation have already been discussed on their own terms. Weak movements, like the nascent form of the new politics in 1968, may be protected by the ban on early delegate selection, but movements that have exhibited staying power by surviving for several years may be hurt by it.

Thus, movements are deprived of certain important advantages they would otherwise possess. In the attempt to take away the power of parties, a plebiscitary system also takes away the power of other well-organized forces. By focusing purely on the actual candidates and downplaying the deliberative aspects of the nominating process, important tactical flexibility may be damaged. And by holding candidates to a standard of popular majority support, a plebiscitary system may hurt those dynamic forces that are a narrow plurality (or less) but are yet striving to construct a working majority.

Campaign Finance

Federal campaign finance law most clearly affects some combination of the strong/weak axis (restraining the strong to the benefit of the weak) and the insider/outsider axis (helping outsiders of all sorts who are dependent on small donations). Since they are grassroots-based rather than establishment-based, movements tend to rely much more on small contributions than do establishment candidates. As a result, the matching fund provisions of the FECA regime work to the advantage of movement candidates like Reagan in 1976, Jackson in both 1984 and 1988, and Robertson in 1988.

However, several aspects of FECA clearly work to the detriment of movements, especially stronger movements. The one-thousand-dollar limit on individual contributions hamstrings little-known candidates by forcing them to spend an inordinate amount of time fund-raising. The ability to raise large amounts of money is a sign of the breadth of a movement's base; strict contribution limits work much more to the benefit of weaker movements like the rainbow coalition, which are incapable of raising large amounts of money in any case.

Similarly, spending limits also work more clearly to the benefit of weaker movements whose fund-raising capacities are not sufficient to approach the spending limits. Finally, FECA reporting requirements force the curtailment of decentralized and spontaneous grassroots campaign activity. Movements thrive on such activity, so it seems probable that this restraining influence of FECA hurts movement-backed candidates disproportionately.

Each of these potential disadvantages clearly increase as the movement becomes better organized, more broadly based, and more financially healthy. Only the cutoff of federal matching funds when a candidate fails to win 10 percent of the vote on two consecutive primary dates hurts weak movements disproportionately. On balance, FECA increases the access for weaker movements while providing only a mixed blessing for movements that actually stand a chance of winning.

It should also be remembered that in 1976 George Wallace was by far the greatest beneficiary of FECA's matching fund provision, and Ronald Reagan was the greatest victim of its spending limits regime. In 1992, Jerry Brown and Pat Buchanan were among the greatest beneficiaries of matching funds. Unconnected outsiders can take advantage of matching funds at least as well as movements can, and even if they face the same contribution limit and spending limit restraints they are probably less affected by the curtailment of decentralized campaign organization activity, since such activity is hardly their strength.

Systemic Change in American History

How have these components fit together over time? What did the systems produced by these components mean for outsiders and parties, for openness and stability? Where has the evolution of presidential nomination left us today?

The convention system was clearly the most stable and least open of the systems studied. It operated as a whole on the inside/outside axis and the strong/weak axis. While occasional initial infiltration was possible, for the most part the parties were able to maintain control of the nominating process against movements seeking to work from within. Instead, movements had to rely on a third-party strategy, facilitated by the option of fusion, of gaining influence by proving their own electoral strength.

Stability was hence gained not only by limiting access and making movements attain a high threshold of strength but by moderating the terms on which movements could gain success. Once a movement grew strong enough in electoral competition to force its way into a major party, it could consolidate its position for years. And because the convention system was so dependent on party organization and the route to power lay through fusion, the minority party was generally more open than the majority party, both locally and nationally. This characteristic of the system clearly contributed to governing stability as well.

The mixed system that followed operated on the organization/nonorganization axis and the strong/weak axis. Parties still established relatively high barriers to initial access, but once those were breached by a movement of great strength, the movement had a good chance not only of winning the nomination for its standard-bearer but also of consolidating its position in the party. The existence of a few primaries (many of them open) combined with turn-of-the-century caucus reforms to make access easier than it was in the convention system; the predominance of caucuses and plurality/delegate primaries put a premium on organization; the representative and nonplebiscitary nature of the system made it easier for movements to construct delegate majorities from less than a majority of votes. Like the convention system, the mixed system, because it was based on organization and required movements to engage in serious party building, made it more likely that movements could succeed in the minority rather than majority party, though primaries probably reduced this discrepancy somewhat.

On the other hand, unconnected outsiders like Estes Kefauver and George Wallace were systematically stymied. There were a limited number of primaries, there was no guarantee that they could translate primary successes into delegates, and the lack of a plebiscitary ethos made it possible for representative conventions to pass them over despite substantial primary successes. In short, the mixed system was not nearly as closed to strong movements as has been suggested, but was indeed closed to the unconnected.

The system that resulted from the post-1968 reforms is more open to access than were previous systems. The explosion of primaries, the reduction and reform of caucuses, the rise of proportional representation, and even campaign finance reforms guarantee this result. This greater openness of access is consistent with the concerns of the McGovern-Fraser report that access in the mixed system had been unfairly denied.

However, many of these same reforms have made the system less open than the mixed system was to actual success and to long-term consolidation by movements. Thus, the reform system makes it easier for a movement to enter the fray, but more difficult for it to win and more difficult for it to translate its victory into long-term control of the party apparatus. At the same time, the reforms work to the advantage of the unconnected outsiders, who find success in primaries easier and who represent no autonomous force that seeks to turn the party into a durable instrument of its will.

Prior to the reforms, movements could not bypass the party organization; they were forced to combat it on its own terms, but if they had superior organization they could win not only the nomination but with it the party. And because the party influenced nominations so heavily, there was actually something to be gained in taking it over.

The reforms have changed that, by reversing the organizational bias of the mixed system. The organized—that is, parties and movements alike—have been hurt on balance, while the unconnected outsiders have gained. Additionally, the bias of the strong/weak axis has been reversed through proportional representation, the reduction of caucuses, the ban on early delegate selection, and FECA. Stability in terms of success and consolidation is thus obtained vis-à-vis movements by the dominance of primaries in the system and by a plebiscitary ethos that makes it difficult for a minority candidate like Goldwater or McGovern to be nominated.

This stability has three shortcomings. First, the system can more easily prevent movement success, but actually encourages the entry of weaker movements that could not win under any system but are capable under this system of amassing delegates and influencing the party. Second, stability is maintained against movement success because the characteristics of the reform system match up well against the characteristics of movements. Against unconnected outsiders, these systemic characteristics are not up to the task, and the stability that is offered against movements collapses. The position of the Iowa caucuses as the "gatekeeper" of the nominating season may offer some protection, but it is limited indeed; unconnected outsiders can break through in Iowa (Carter did so and Forbes might have done so) and defeat in Iowa does not end all future prospects (the ultimate nominee has won Iowa only four of the nine times since 1972 that a contested race has been tabulated). Finally, the reform system further reduces the relative insulation once enjoyed by the majority party, contributing to a greater potential for governing instability.[13] Thus, the reform system is at once less open to the ultimate success of movements and in many ways less stable than the system it replaced. It is probably no coincidence that no new strong movements have been seen since 1972, while weaker movements and the unconnected have flourished; the institutional environment has almost surely affected not just outcomes but inputs as well.

Outsiders and Nonsystemic Factors

Obviously, the rules governing presidential nominations cannot be discussed in isolation from other political and social factors influencing openness and the extent and nature of outsiderism. Indeed, the beginning of the upsurge in outsiderism after 1960 predated the reforms, and nominating rules cannot bear the full weight of explanation. There are at least four major nonsystemic factors that have interacted with the nominating system: party decline, the disaggregating effect of the modern media, changes in the broader electoral system (most notably rules governing third parties), and the general social and political climate. These factors have had an important impact on outsiderism and on the political calculations of candidates and party leaders.

It is not always easy to sort out the effects of party decline from the effects of changed rules. The organizational decline of the parties began long before 1968, and has benefited outsiders of all varieties. Weaker party organizations throw up lower roadblocks than do stronger parties to movements entering caucuses, with or without the reforms; they also have less capacity to block the rise of the unconnected. Nevertheless, loss of the nominating power must be rated as not only one of the greatest effects, but also as one of the greatest causes, of party decline in the last twenty-five years. And parties in their weakened state are still more capable of influencing caucuses than primaries—which is also still true of movements and still untrue of unconnected outsiders. Thus, the relation of parties, movements, and unconnected outsiders to the basic components of the nominating system has remained constant, even if the threshold for access has been reduced by party weakness.

Second, the nature and impact of the media has dramatically changed the ways in which office is sought and won. The rise of television, the accelerating decentralization of the media, and the ostensible nonpartisanship of the media in the last half of the twentieth century have provided an avenue of access to the political system for unconnected outsiders, who were shut out when there was no alternative to organization. Thus, not only the changed rules but the changed campaign environment works to encourage the entry of the unconnected. Again, however, not only have the media increasingly affected nominations, but the changed manner of nomination has itself enhanced the power of the media, since primaries are much more amenable to media coverage and "horse race" analysis than are caucuses. Unconnected outsiders may be encouraged to run by the availability of the new weapon of the media, but the media are such a useful weapon largely because of the ways the nominating system has changed. Indeed, Larry M. Bartels makes the argument that the whole system is now driven by perceptions of momentum flowing out of the primaries as interpreted by the media, a situation tailor-made for unconnected outsiders.[14]

Third, party openness is related, often inversely, to the openness of the electoral system outside the parties. It is not only party rules that affect the calculations of outsiders, but the availability of the third-party option. The convention system could be as closed as it was because it was relatively easy to bypass with a third party. The mixed system's greater openness helped to compensate for the closed nature of the electoral system after the turn of the century. Today, many legal barriers to third-party ballot access have been reduced as a result of court challenges, and the media have become increasingly decentralized, clearing the path for Ross Perot to run as an independent instead of within the major parties. These calculations will continue to shift, depending on both party rules and political and social factors affecting the third-party option.

Finally, more general social and political changes have worked to encourage the rise of outsiderism. American politics has become more ideological and polarized since the 1960s. Movements, which are by nature ideological, have thus found more fertile ground in the post-1960 era. Likewise, numerous surveys have indicated greater political and social alienation among Americans, also starting in the 1960s. If unconnected outsiders aim largely at appealing to the alienated, their potential audience has grown sharply since 1964.

In each of these cases, nonsystemic factors have clearly influenced the opportunities for outsiders in presidential nominations. The greatest impact would seem to be on their calculations regarding access. Party weakness may lower the threshold of access in ways that encourage the entry of weaker movements and the unconnected; the importance of media may lead more unconnected outsiders to calculate that the reform system favors their entrance; and third-party prospects may determine whether an outsider chooses to gamble on major party nomination. Consideration of these factors, however, cannot be divorced from the nominating rules; seldom do these factors exert one-way influence. Furthermore, once candidates decide to enter, the rules much more unambiguously affect who wins and what they gain with their victory.

Thus, the social and political factors encouraging outsiderism are almost entirely out of the control of the parties, but the parties through their nominating rules can choose how to deal with those factors. The nominating system did not create outsiderism by itself and cannot eliminate it, even if that were deemed desirable, but the system is intertwined with outsiderism. It can either inhibit and restrain or encourage and accelerate outsiderism, and it can try to channel outsiderism in a particular direction.

Outsiders and Openness: What Do We Want?

The openness of the American political system to fundamental change—and the regulation of that change—has been and will continue to be one of the most important issues in American society. The capacity of the political parties to accommodate forces promoting change has been and will continue to be one of the most important avenues for openness in the broader political system. And the presidential nominating system is perhaps the single greatest key to openness within the parties.

The crucial question in presidential nominations then becomes, "What do we want?" It is clear that the three dimensions of openness—access, success, and consolidation—do not come as a package. Different institutional arrangements promote different dimensions of openness. Furthermore, it is clear that the institutional arrangements that we choose must depend on what kind of forces we prefer the system to be open to. Stability likewise consists not of a simple negation of openness, but of choices about what kind of forces to discourage and how to discourage them.

The reform system, on balance, works to the relative advantage of the unorganized and the weak, in a mirror image of the mixed system, which worked disproportionately to the advantage of the organized and the strong. This has meant in practice that weak movement candidates like Jesse Jackson and Pat Robertson have been encouraged, and unconnected outsiders like Jimmy Carter and George Wallace have had unprecedented success. Strong movements, like those that gained victory for Barry Goldwater and George McGovern, have been disadvantaged. Organization was the key to the mixed system; the antiorganization reforms that were meant to hurt the party hurt independently organized forces as well, leaving the field open to those who draw votes not through organization but through intense media appeals and personal charm (see table 8.2). In this sense at least, then, parties and movements are not enemies but rather have a natural community of interest, though it is not clear whether parties understand this. Perhaps they do not; or perhaps parties have understood the post-1968 tradeoffs quite well but have willingly allowed themselves to be weakened, preferring to take their chances with the unconnected rather than accept the risk of losing organizational control to a movement. If so, they have hurt themselves and American politics in the shortsighted pursuit of security. In any event, the community of interest among the organized is real.

All this is certainly not to say that under the reform system there will be no movements, or that there will be no strong movements, or that no movement will ever succeed in nominating its candidate, or that weaker movements will defeat stronger ones. Nor is it to say that any of the three—strong movements, weak movements, or unconnected outsiders—are inevitably good or bad in any absolute sense. The point is that the reform system establishes a new hierarchy among outsiders and helps or hinders those outsiders in ways that fundamentally transform their calculations and that could be decisive in a close-fought nomination race.

This new hierarchy turns on its head not only past systemic bias, but com-

Table 8-2. Characteristics of Nominating Systems

	Convention	Mixed	Reform
Access			
Openness			
To movements	low	medium	high
To unconnected	none	low	high
Success			
To movements	medium	high	low
To unconnected	none	low	high
Consolidation			
Of movements	medium	high	low
Of unconnected	none	none	none
Axis	I/O, S/W	Or/N, S/W	Or/N, S/W
Benefit to	I, S	Or, S	N, W

Notes:
I = Insider
O = Outsider
Or = Organization
N = Nonorganization
S = Strong
W = Weak

mon sense. If there is to be openness, it would seem more healthy, both for the parties and for the polity as a whole, for that openness to express itself in the potential for success by stronger movements that clearly represent a broad base of society, that have proven their staying power, and that have the organizational capacity to functionally replace the party structure they seek to defeat. It would seem less healthy to block such movements in favor of granting easier access to movements that are weaker, more narrowly based, and potentially transient. It would seem still less healthy to favor both easier access and easier success by completely personalist candidates who are unaccountable to either party or movement, who cannot replace the party structure, and who are on average probably more prone to demagoguery. Yet that is precisely the hierarchy of openness that the reform model promotes.

If this hierarchy is not what we want, then we must consider how the elements of the nominating system might be rearranged. The first necessary step is intellectual: we must relegitimize representative, deliberative, organization-based, and non–candidate-centered conceptions of delegate selection. That reconceptualization is not impossible in the American political setting, as can be seen in a similar reconceptualization that took place in the 1820s and 1830s. Then, faced with the collapse of the congressional caucus and the rise of personalism, Martin Van Buren and others deliberately reoriented presidential selection in a pro-organization and antipersonalist direction.[15] It is neither possible nor desirable to restore the pure convention system that was ushered in by that reorientation, but we can at least be assured that the antiorganization and propersonalist trends of the last quarter century are not historically irreversible.

If another reconceptualization of presidential selection should occur along these lines, obvious institutional changes would follow. The proportion of primaries to caucuses would be reduced. Those primaries that remain would emphasize nonproportional delegate selection, particularly winner-take-all selection by congressional district and direct delegate election. Caucuses would ensure both greater influence by party officers and some connection between the presidential nominating system and the selection of those officers. Proportional representation in caucuses would also be abandoned, which would allow parties and strong movements to take advantage of their caucus superiority. Finally, federal finance law would retain the matching fund provision, but would allow larger individual contributions and would increase or eliminate spending limits. Most of these changes would restore the importance of organization, giving the party organization greater influence in normal times and reestablishing a heavy party-building requirement from movements that wish to succeed. Strong candidates and movements would once again be advantaged, and weaker movements and the unconnected more easily blocked.

These changes probably can be made only imperfectly and in increments. No ornate scholarly design will ever take root in its entirety, and this is just as well. The shortcomings of the current system are in no small part a result of such a comprehensive reform gone awry. Conversely, the mixed system, which was in many ways superior, was the result of gradual development. We know that such incremental change is not impossible; as William G. Mayer points out, "Of the 39 states that used a presidential primary for delegate selection for at least one election between 1972 and 1988, fourteen of them have, at one time or another, [at least temporarily] abandoned the primary and adopted a caucus system."[16] Similarly, from 1988 to 1996, most Republican primaries in New England shifted from proportional representation to some form of winner-take-all delegate allocation.[17]

Of course, the nominating system cannot be viewed in isolation from the party system as a whole. To the extent that the caucuses produce less reliable party control than before, because the parties themselves are weaker, stability may require the Democratic Party to maintain a certain number of ex officio delegates. While reestablishment of meaningful caucuses might leave the parties temporarily more vulnerable, it might also prove a catalyst for their renaissance. Furthermore, to the degree that strong state and local parties were tied in American history to strong state and local governments, it is hardly absurd to suppose that the government decentralization now theoretically embraced to some extent by both major parties could ultimately result in a strengthening of state and local parties.

In any event, the reestablishment of a pro-organization bias in presidential nominations is important for parties and movements alike. Although numerous political and social factors are at work, one of the most important in the present equation is that errors have been made by those in the political arena: the reforms have accelerated the worst of the trends, encouraging the unconnected and channeling outsiderism in a fundamentally unconstructive and even dangerous direction. These errors can presumably be reversed by those in the political arena as well. It is possible in this study to perceive potential remedies as well as ills. One can hope for the sake of both openness and stability, of both parties and movements, that such remedies will not sit forever idle.

NOTES

1. Openness, Stability, and the Presidential Nominating System

1. Byron E. Shafer, *Quiet Revolution: The Struggle for the Democratic Party and the Shaping of Post-reform Politics* (New York: Russell Sage Foundation, 1983), p. 28.

2. A third value, securing an able president, has also been important. For the most part, however, in ways that will be seen later, this has not been an independent concern but has been put forward behind arguments for either greater openness or greater stability. See James W. Ceaser, *Presidential Selection: Theory and Development* (Princeton: Princeton University Press, 1979), pp. 10–23, which identifies five objectives for the selection system, all of which fall into one of these three categories: minimize harmful effects of highly ambitious contenders (stability), promote the proper kind of executive leadership (stability), provide for the proper amount of choice and change (tempered openness), ensure legitimate accession (the proper mix of openness and stability), and secure an able president (quality). See also Nelson Polsby, *Consequences of Party Reform* (New York: Oxford University Press, 1983), pp. 168–69.

3. James Ceaser and Andrew Busch, *Upside Down and Inside Out: The 1992 Elections and American Politics* (Lanham, Md.: Rowman & Littlefield, 1993), p. 5. For a more thorough discussion of modern "outsiderism," see pp. 1–10.

4. James Madison, *Notes of Debates in the Federal Convention of 1787* (New York: W.W. Norton, 1987), pp. 307–08.

5. Ibid.

6. See Alexander Hamilton, "Federalist 70," in *The Federalist Papers* (New York: NAL Penguin, 1961); Ceaser, *Presidential Selection*, pp. 72–73. Hamilton discusses the overall balance achieved in "Federalist 68."

7. Judith H. Parris, *The Convention Problem* (Washington, D.C.: Brookings Institution, 1972), p. 3.

8. For a discussion of the operation of the congressional caucus, see Frederick W. Whitridge, "Caucus System," (1883) repr. in Leon Stein, ed., *The Caucus System in American Politics* (New York: Arno, 1974); C. S. Thompson, "The Rise and Fall of the Congressional Caucus as a Machine for Nominating Candidates for the Presidency," repr. in Stein, *The Caucus System;* and Frederick A. Dallinger, *Nominations for Elective Office in the United States* (Cambridge: Harvard University Press, 1897).

9. Martin Van Buren, *Inquiry into the Origin and Course of Political Parties in the United States* (New York: Hurd and Houghton, 1867), pp. 4–5.

10. For discussion of the defects and collapse of the congressional caucus, see Whitridge, "Caucus System," p. 9; M. Ostrogorski, *Democracy and the Organization of Political Parties* (New York: Macmillan, 1908) 2:22; William J. Crotty, *Political Reform and the American Experiment*

(New York: Thomas Y. Crowell, 1977), pp. 198–99; Thomas R. Marshall, *Presidential Nominations in a Reform Age* (New York: Praeger, 1981), pp. 19–22; Gerald Pomper, *Nominating the President* (Chicago: Northwestern University Press, 1963), pp. 16–20.

11. Dallinger, *Nominations for Elective Office*, p. 20.

12. Crotty, *Political Reform*, pp. 199–200.

13. See Pomper, *Nominating the President*, p. 21; Paul T. David, Ralph M. Goldman, and Richard C. Bain, *The Politics of National Party Conventions*, 2d ed. (New York: Vintage, 1964), pp. 60–61; Crotty, *Political Reform*, p. 200.

14. Pomper, *Nominating the President*, p. 29.

15. See Eugene H. Roseboom, *A History of Presidential Elections* (New York: Macmillan, 1970), p. 106. For a discussion of Martin Van Buren's theory of party competition, which emphasized the ability of parties to restrain and channel ambition through the nominating process, see Ceaser, *Presidential Selection*, chap. 3.

16. Modifications from the 1830s to 1860 included the establishment of party platforms, national committees, the two-thirds rule in the Democratic Party, delegate apportionment rules (based on the electoral college), and a practice of permitting states to use their own discretion in the selection of delegates.

17. Walter Dean Burnham, *Critical Elections and the Mainsprings of American Politics* (New York: W.W. Norton, 1970), p. 72; see also James W. Ceaser, *Reforming the Reforms: A Critical Analysis of the Presidential Selection Process* (Cambridge, Mass.: Ballinger, 1982), p. 21.

18. Ostrogorski, *Democracy*, 2:207.

19. James Bryce, *The American Commonwealth* (Chicago: Sergel & Co., 1889), 2:98, 78–85, 93–101; Ostrogorski, *Democracy*, 2:211.

20. See Dallinger, *Nominations for Elective Office*, chap. 5; Ostrogorski, *Democracy*, 2:213–16; C. Edward Merriam, *Primary Elections: A Study of the History and Tendencies of Primary Election Legislation* (Chicago: University of Chicago Press, 1909), pp. 6–7; James W. Davis, *Presidential Primaries: Road to the White House* (New York: Thomas Y. Crowell, 1967), p. 24; V. O. Key, *Politics, Parties, and Pressure Groups*, 4th ed. (New York: Thomas Y. Crowell, 1958), 410.

21. Ostrogorski, *Democracy*, 2:211–13; Bryce, *The American Commonwealth* 2:55–57, 78–85, 93–101.

22. Bryce discusses the importance of electability, including the ability to make all factions of the party reasonably happy, in convention decisions. See *The American Commonwealth*, chap. 70, 2:179–95.

23. Crotty, *Political Reform*, p. 200.

24. Austin Ranney, *Curing the Mischiefs of Faction: Party Reform in America* (Berkeley: University of California Press, 1975), p. 18.

25. Merriam, *Primary Elections*, pp. 9–16.

26. Ranney, *Curing the Mischiefs of Faction*, p. 80; on the importance of the Australian ballot, see also Daniel A. Mazmanian, *Third Parties in Presidential Elections* (Washington, D.C.: Brookings Institution, 1974), pp. 90–100; Leon D. Epstein, *Political Parties in the American Mold* (Madison: University of Wisconsin Press, 1986), pp. 162–67; Merriam, *Primary Elections*, pp. 29–30; Burnham, *Critical Elections*, pp. 74–76.

27. Merriam, *Primary Elections*, pp. 31–67.

28. Dallinger, *Nominations for Elective Office*, p. 197.

29. Ranney, *Curing the Mischiefs of Faction*, pp. 124–25.

30. See Ceaser, *Presidential Selection*, chap. 4.

31. For a contemporary discussion of the drive for presidential primaries, see Louise Overacker, *The Presidential Primary* (New York: Macmillan, 1926).

32. Ceaser, *Reforming the Reforms*, pp. 23–24.

33. Crotty, *Political Reform*, pp. 212–13.

34. John G. Geer, *Nominating Presidents* (Westport, Conn.: Greenwood, 1989), p. 2. Indeed, as Crotty points out, the trend toward the primary was reversed in large part by "the same people who had worked so hard to institute it," partially because they had discovered that the plurality primary, which was the most frequently used system, tended to benefit the most cohesive force—which was most often the local machine. *Political Reform*, pp. 208–09.

35. Geer, *Nominating Presidents*, p. 2. Even in 1944, the Wisconsin primary knocked Wendell Willkie out of contention, though it seemed unlikely at the time that he would be nominated, regardless of the outcome.

36. See Terry Sanford, *A Danger of Democracy* (Boulder: Westview, 1981), pp. 61–65, 73; on the general strengths of the mixed system, see Pomper, *Nominating the President*, pp. 210–16; Ranney, *Curing the Mischiefs of Faction*, p. 137.

37. Ceaser, *Reforming the Reforms*, p. 102.

38. David et al, *The Politics of National Party Conventions*, p. 23.

39. Shafer, *Quiet Revolution*, pp. 13–15.

40. *Mandate for Reform: A Report of the Commission on Party Structure and Delegate Selection to the Democratic National Committee* (Washington, D.C.: Democratic National Committee, April 1970), p. 14; see also David E. Price, *Bringing Back the Parties* (Washington, D.C.: Congressional Quarterly Press, 1984), p. 146.

41. Shafer, *Quiet Revolution*, p. 34; see also pp. 23–34; Polsby, *Consequences of Party Reform*, p. 33; William J. Crotty, *Decision for the Democrats: Reforming the Party Structure* (Baltimore: Johns Hopkins University Press, 1978), pp. 23–27; Theodore H. White, *The Making of the President 1972* (New York: Atheneum, 1973), p. 17.

42. Shafer, *Quiet Revolution*, p. 42.

43. Ibid., p. 73.

44. Ibid., pp. 85, 95. It is interesting to note the estimates of the proportion of reformers on the commission by chief counsel Eli Segal and Al Barkan, the AFL-CIO representative. Segal estimated that 50 percent of the full commission, 70 percent of the executive committee, and 100 percent of the staff were reformers; Barkan estimated that 64 percent of the full commission, 80 percent of the executive committee, and 100 percent of the staff were reform-minded.

45. On the hearings, see White, *1972*, p. 24; Crotty, *Political Reform*, p. 243; idem, *Decision for the Democrats*, pp. 41–58; Shafer, *Quiet Revolution*, pp. 111–12.

46. Shafer, *Quiet Revolution*, p. 117.

47. *Mandate for Reform*, pp. 21–32.

48. Kenneth A. Bode and Carol F. Casey, "Party Reform: Revisionism Revised," in *Political Parties in the Eighties*, ed. Robert A. Goldwin (Washington, D.C.: American Enterprise Institute, 1980), pp. 6–10.

49. Crotty, *Party Reform* (New York: Longman, 1983), p. 47.

50. *Mandate for Reform*, p. 49. It is interesting to note that this justification of reform contains at least a pro forma nod to the principle of stability, by claiming that failure to further open the system will lead to chaos.

51. Shafer, *Quiet Revolution*, pp. 117–18.

52. On the proportional representation debate, see ibid., pp. 149–51, 174–78; Paul T. David and James W. Ceaser, *Proportional Representation in Presidential Nominating Politics* (Charlottesville: University Press of Virginia, 1980), pp. 5–6; White, *1972*, p. 26.

53. See Elaine Cuilla Kamarck, "Structure as Strategy: Presidential Nominating Politics in a Post-reform Era," in *The Parties Respond*, ed. L. Sandy Maisel (Boulder: Westview, 1990), pp. 163–65, 167–68.

54. Shafer, *Quiet Revolution*, p. 6. See also Marshall, *Presidential Nominations*, pp. 55–57.

55. David and Ceaser, *Proportional Representation*, pp. 10–13; Crotty, *Party Reform*, pp. 63–73; Price, *Bringing Back the Parties*, pp. 150–52; Judith Center, "1972 Democratic Convention Reforms and Party Democracy," *Political Science Quarterly* (June 1974): 347. The commission increased the proportion allowed to be appointed by party committees from 10 to 25 percent (though these delegates still had to reflect candidate preferences as determined in primaries or caucuses), restored the use of proxy voting (but limited it to three per voter), and eliminated the controversial requirement for race, sex, and age quotas, which the McGovern Commission had instituted to try to remedy "underrepresentation" of certain demographic groups.

56. See Donald M. Fraser, "Democratizing the Democratic Party," in Goldwin, *Political Parties in the Eighties*, p. 123; Ranney, *Curing the Mischiefs of Faction*, pp. 205–06.

57. Bode and Casey, "Party Reform," pp. 16–18.

58. Fraser, "Democratizing the Democratic Party," p. 123.

59. Polsby, *Consequences of Party Reform*, p. 59; Austin Ranney, *The Federalization of Presidential Primaries* (Washington, D.C.: American Enterprise Institute, 1978), p. 3.

60. George McGovern, *Grassroots* (New York: Random House, 1977), 153.

61. Ranney, *The Federalization of Presidential Primaries*, p. 3; Fraser, "Democratizing the Democratic Party," p. 123.

62. Ranney, *The Federalization of Presidential Primaries*, p. 3; Polsby, *Consequences of Party Reform*, p. 62.

63. Edward C. Banfield, "Party 'Reform' in Retrospect," in Goldwin, *Political Parties in the Eighties*, p. 30.

64. See ibid., pp. 32–33; Ranney, *Curing the Mischiefs of Faction*, pp. 120, 139; Austin Ranney, *Participation in American Presidential Nominations, 1976* (Washington, D.C.: American Enterprise Institute, 1977); Shafer, *Quiet Revolution*, p. 117; James W. Ceaser, "Political Change and Party Reform," in Goldwin, *Political Parties in the Eighties*, pp. 97–98; James W. Ceaser, "The Theory of the Presidential Nominating Process," in Kenneth W. Thompson, ed., *The Presidential Nominating Process* (Lanham, Md.: University Press of America, 1983), 1:8–9; Jeane Jordan Kirkpatrick, *Dismantling the Parties* (Washington, D.C.: American Enterprise Institute, 1978), pp. 2–3; Marshall, *Presidential Nominations*, pp. 45–50.

65. The argument was that party members' right to "full and meaningful participation" was diluted when others were also allowed to vote.

66. See Ranney, *Curing the Mischiefs of Faction*, pp. 2–3; Crotty, *Political Reform*, pp. 256–57; Polsby, *Consequences of Party Reform*, p. 54; David E. Price and Albert Beveridge, "The Political and Nominating Process," in Thompson, *The Presidential Nominating Process*, 3:40.

67. William G. Mayer, "Caucuses: How They Work, What Difference They Make," in *In Pursuit of the White House: How We Choose Our Presidential Nominees*, ed. William G. Mayer (Chatham, N.J.: Chatham House, 1996), pp. 116–17.

68. Marshall, *Presidential Nominations*, p. 48.

69. See David and Ceaser, *Proportional Representation*, p. 14.

70. Polsby, *Consequences of Party Reform*, p. 54.

71. See Marshall, *Presidential Nominations*, p. 42; and Epstein, *Political Parties*, pp. 103–04, which holds that the two parties' nominating systems are basically the same.

72. Ceaser, *Reforming the Reforms*, p. 102.

73. Polsby, *Consequences of Party Reform*, p. 29.

74. See ibid.; Banfield, "Party 'Reform' in Retrospect"; Ceaser, *Reforming the Reforms;* idem, "The Theory of the Presidential Nominating Process"; Austin Ranney, "Candidates, Coalitions, Institutions, and Reforms," in Thompson, *The Presidential Nominating Process*, vol. 1; Sanford, *A Danger of Democracy;* Kirkpatrick, *Dismantling the Parties;* James L. Sundquist, "The Crisis of Com-

petence in Government," in *Setting National Priorities: Agenda for the 1980s*, ed. Joseph A. Pechman (Washington, D.C.: Brookings Institution, 1980), pp. 539–40; Parris, *The Convention Problem*, p. 56; Thomas E. Cronin and Robert D. Loevey, "Putting the Party as Well as the People Back in Presidential Picking," in Thompson, *The Presidential Nominating Process*, 1:62–63; Herbert E. Alexander, "Money and the Presidential Nominating Process," in Thompson, *The Presidential Nominating Process*, 3:60–61, 77; Douglas Cater, "The History of the Presidential Nominating Process," in Thompson, *The Presidential Nominating Process*, 1:30–31; David et al, *The Politics of National Party Conventions*, pp. 333–35; Wilson Carey McWilliams, "Down With Primaries," *Commonweal*, July 1, 1976; Henry E. Brady and Richard Johnston, "What's the Primary Message: Horse Race or Issue Journalism?" in *Media and Momentum: The New Hampshire Primary and Nomination Politics*, ed. Garry R. Orren and Nelson W. Polsby (Chatham, N.J.: Chatham House, 1987), pp. 127–86.

75. *The Official Proceedings of the Democratic National Convention 1972.*

76. Crotty, *Party Reform*, p. 234; see also Crotty, *Political Reform*, p. 252. Geer and Shere similarly argue that the direct primary is the best (though perhaps not only) mechanism for ensuring healthy intraparty competition and access for insurgent groups. See John G. Geer and Mark E. Shere, "Party Competition and the Prisoner's Dilemma: An Argument for the Direct Primary," *Journal of Politics* (August 1992): 741–61.

77. See Bode and Casey, "Party Reform," esp. pp. 13–15; Crotty, *Political Reform*, p. 222; Geer, *Nominating Presidents*, pp. 5–8, 15–30; Barbara Norrander, "Ideological Representativeness of Presidential Primary Voters," *American Journal of Political Science* (August 1989): 570–87.

78. See esp. Howard L. Reiter, *Selecting the President* (Philadelphia: University of Pennsylvania Press, 1985); Fraser, "Democratizing the Democratic Party."

79. Ceaser, "Political Change and Party Reform," p. 99.

80. See S. J. Duncan-Clark, *The Progressive Movement* (Boston: Small, Maynard, 1913), p. 38.

81. Crotty, *Party Reform*, pp. 47–48.

82. John Wilson, *Introduction to Social Movements* (New York: Basic Books, 1973), p. 8. See also Roberta Ash, *Social Movements in America* (Chicago: Markham, 1972), p. 1.

83. See discussion of the Greens in Ferdinand Muller-Rommel, *New Politics in Western Europe* (Boulder: Westview, 1989), pp. 14–16; and Rudolf Heberle, *Social Movements: An Introduction to Political Sociology* (New York: Appleton-Century-Crofts, 1951), pp. 8–9.

84. Martin Kolinsky and William E. Paterson, eds., introduction to *Social and Political Movements in Western Europe* (New York: St. Martin's, 1976), p. 21; Wilson, *Introduction to Social Movements*, p. 11.

85. Heberle, *Social Movements*, pp. 8, 9–11; Wilson, *Introduction to Social Movements*, pp. 11–13.

86. Mayer N. Zald and John D. McCarthy, *The Dynamics of Social Movements* (Cambridge, Mass.: Winthrop, 1979), p. 3.

87. Robert H. Salisbury, "Political Movements in American Politics: An Essay on Concept and Analysis," *National Journal of Political Science* 1 (1989): 18; and Wilson, *Introduction to Social Movements*, pp. 8–9.

88. See Lawrence Goodwyn, *The Populist Moment* (New York: Oxford University Press, 1978), p. xviii.

89. Salisbury, "Political Movements in American Politics," pp. 21, 19.

90. Of course, their goal is to become the majority at some point. It is also important to remember that it is possible for the majority to sympathize with a movement or its candidates without identifying itself as part of the movement. It could be argued that movements might theoreti-

cally be a majority, even at the moment they originate, but in practice that has not been the case in American history. Indeed, the birth of a movement that already represents a majority—or the continuing survival for a long time of a movement that has become the majority—might, almost by definition, be the sign of a real breakdown of democratic majoritarianism. Movements seek fundamental change in the political/social order. If a majority movement comes into being, it is because the existing order is radically unsatisfactory to a majority; if such a movement lasted very long, it would only be because the change it sought had not yet been achieved. These outcomes would indicate nothing less than a serious crisis of democratic governance.

91. Ranney, *Curing the Mischiefs of Faction,* p. 61.

92. John H. Aldrich, *Before the Convention: Strategies and Choices in Presidential Nomination Campaigns* (Chicago: University of Chicago Press, 1980), p. 2.

2. Movements in the Pure Convention System

1. Fusion could be accomplished in a number of ways, and could reflect varying degrees of equality between the partners. For instance, at the presidential level it might be manifested not merely in the nomination of the same candidate by both parties but by the splitting of the ticket (presidential nominee from one party and vice presidential from the other) and agreement to split elector positions. Agreements on electors and most other forms of fusion were arranged on a largely ad hoc basis at the local level. There is even a recorded case of two-party fusion across states, when in 1890 Democrats and Farmers' Alliance legislators agreed to split the Senate seats up for election in Illinois and South Dakota. See Goodwyn, *The Populist Moment,* pp. 240–41.

2. Ibid., p. vii.

3. Ibid., p. 136; see also pp. 114–15.

4. J. Rogers Hollingsworth, *The Whirligig of Politics: The Democracy of Cleveland and Bryan* (Chicago: University of Chicago Press, 1963), pp. 3–5. See also Paul W. Glad, *McKinley, Bryan, and the People* (Philadelphia: J.B. Lippincott, 1964), pp. 36–43; James W. Sundquist, *Dynamics of the Party System* (Washington, D.C.: Brookings Institution, 1973), pp. 93–96; Roscoe Martin, *The People's Party in Texas* (Austin: University of Texas Bulletin Number 3308, 1933), pp. 18–20.

5. Sundquist, *Dynamics of the Party System,* pp. 97–98.

6. Fred E. Haynes, *Third Party Movements with Special Reference to Iowa* (Cedar Rapids: Torch, 1916), pp. 94–100, 103–04, 203–04; Howard P. Nash Jr., *Third Parties in American Politics* (Washington, D.C.: Public Affairs Press, 1959), pp. 148–50.

7. Haynes, *Third Party Movements,* p. 121.

8. Ibid., pp. 153–54, 164–69.

9. Ibid., pp. 199–200; Martin, *The People's Party in Texas,* p. 21; Sundquist, *Dynamics of the Party System,* pp. 108–09.

10. Additionally, the "National Agricultural Wheel" in the South had 500,000 members. On the Alliances, see Goodwyn, *The Populist Moment,* chaps. 2–4.

11. Ibid., pp. 66–69.

12. Sundquist, *Dynamics of the Party System,* pp. 117, 115–116; Goodwyn, *The Populist Moment,* 139.

13. John D. Hicks, *The Populist Revolt* (Minneapolis: University of Minnesota Press, 1931), p. 141.

14. Haynes, *Third Party Movements,* p. 238; see also Hollingsworth, *The Whirligig of Politics,* pp. 7–8.

15. Sundquist, *Dynamics of the Party System,* p. 119.

16. See Hicks, *The Populist Revolt,* pp. 181–185, 247; Goodwyn, *The Populist Moment,* pp. 155, 158–163.

17. Martin, *The People's Party in Texas*, pp. 36–44, 142–46; Goodwyn, *The Populist Moment*, pp. 145–49.

18. Robert F. Durden, *The Climax of Populism: The Election of 1896* (Lexington: University of Kentucky Press, 1965), p. 8.

19. Hicks, *The Populist Revolt*, p. 149.

20. See, for example, Gene O. Clanton, *Kansas Populism* (Lawrence: University of Kansas Press, 1969), pp. 43, 54–55; Stanley B. Parsons, *The Populist Context* (Westport, Conn.: Greenwood, 1973), pp. 54, 57–58, 64, 79.

21. Hollingsworth, *The Whirligig of Politics*, p. 8; Glad, *McKinley, Bryan, and the People*, pp. 62–65; Sundquist, *Dynamics of the Party System*, pp. 121–23; Mazmanian, *Third Parties*, p. 51.

22. Glad, *McKinley, Bryan, and the People*, p. 149; Henry Minor, *The Story of the Democratic Party* (New York: Macmillan, 1928), p. 380; Norman Pollack, *The Populist Response to Industrial America* (Cambridge: Harvard University Press, 1962), chap. 5; Durden, *The Climax of Populism*, p. 14.

23. Glad, *McKinley, Bryan, and the People*, p. 83. See also Hollingsworth, *The Whirligig of Politics*, pp. 10–17.

24. Hollingsworth, *The Whirligig of Politics*, p. 30; see also pp. 19–29.

25. Nash, *Third Parties in American Politics*, p. 194.

26. Hollingsworth, *The Whirligig of Politics*, p. 36.

27. Ibid., p. 37.

28. Ibid.

29. Glad, *McKinley, Bryan, and the People*, p. 127.

30. Hollingsworth, *The Whirligig of Politics*, pp. 38, 43.

31. Anna Rochester, *The Populist Movement in the United States* (New York: International, 1943), p. 102.

32. Sundquist, *Dynamics of the Party System*, p. 142, 138–39; see also Hollingsworth, *The Whirligig of Politics*, pp. 54–57; Minor, *The Story of the Democratic Party*, p. 389.

33. Sundquist, *Dynamics of the Party System*, pp. 138–39. This was not a universally held opinion of Bryan; some historians such as Goodwyn rate him as essentially a conservative reformer who co-opted a radical movement.

34. On the fusion debate within the Populist Party, see Martin, *The People's Party in Texas*, pp. 239–46; Durden, *The Climax of Populism*, pp. 24–65; Hicks, *The Populist Revolt*, pp. 356–69; Pollack, *The Populist Response*, pp. 104–05, 119–31; C. Vann Woodward, *Tom Watson: Agrarian Rebel* (New York: Oxford University Press, 1963), pp. 288–301.

35. It is not clear how much the gold Democrats actually contributed to Bryan's defeat; the clearest example of their influence came in Kentucky, where they won 5,084 votes and McKinley beat Bryan by only 277. Durden, *The Climax of Populism*, p. 127.

36. Martin, *The People's Party in Texas*, p. 266.

37. Hollingsworth, *The Whirligig of Politics*, pp. 106, 113; see also Sundquist, *Dynamics of the Party System*, p. 139; Hicks, *The Populist Revolt*, p. 378.

38. See Woodward, *Tom Watson*, pp. 370–486. Most important, between 1895 and 1904, Watson did an about-face on the question of white supremacy. Even before abandoning the Populist Party, Watson reversed his previous position against Negro disenfranchisement, and soon became one of the leading racial demagogues of the South.

39. Glad, *McKinley, Bryan, and the People* p. 207; and Haynes, *Third Party Movements*, pp. 382–86.

40. Hicks, *The Populist Revolt*, p. 141.

41. Ibid., p. 247.

42. Parsons, *The Populist Context*, pp. 9, 90.

43. Durden, *The Climax of Populism*, pp. 19–20. Populists' understanding of their role in bringing the Democratic shift can be seen in the keynote address of North Carolina senator Marion Butler at the 1896 Populist convention (p. 31).

44. Ibid., p. 24.

45. Parsons, *The Populist Context*, p. 93. See also Hicks, *The Populist Revolt*, pp. 256–59; Worth Robert Miller, *Oklahoma Populism* (Norman: University of Oklahoma Press, 1987), chap. 8; Thomas A. Clinch, *Urban Populism: Free Silver in Montana* (Missoula: University of Montana Press, 1970).

46. Durden, *The Climax of Populism*, p. 165.

47. Pollack, *The Populist Response*, pp. 119–32.

48. Durden, *The Climax of Populism*, pp. 88–89.

49. Pollack, *The Populist Response*, pp. 104–05; see also Durden, *The Climax of Populism*. The debate over fusion continues to this day, with authors such as Goodwyn holding that fusion was the result of manipulation by a minority centered in Populist Party officeholders. Goodwyn, *The Populist Moment*, pp. 247–63.

50. Parsons, *The Populist Context*, p. 9.

51. Martin, *The People's Party in Texas*, p. 238.

52. Ibid., p. 136.

53. See ibid., pp. 184–87, 232–37; Goodwyn, *The Populist Movement*, pp. 188–96.

54. Roger C. Storms, *Partisan Prophets: A History of the Prohibition Party* (Denver: National Prohibition Foundation, 1972), pp. 1–3; Steven J. Rosenstone, Roy L. Behr, and Edward H. Lazarus, *Third Parties in America* (Princeton: University of Princeton Press, 1984), p. 75.

55. Rosenstone et al, *Third Parties in America*, pp. 75–76; Storms, *Partisan Prophets*, pp. 2–3.

56. Richard J. Jensen, ed., *Grass Roots Politics* (Westport, Conn.: Greenwood, 1981), p. 54.

57. Storms, *Partisan Politics*, p. 9.

58. Ibid., p. 8.

59. Rosenstone et al, *Third Parties in America*, point out that "fears of large-scale defections led the major parties to make platform concessions, but the Democrats and Republicans soon learned that the number of temperance voters was small and that the ire of drinkers—particularly immigrant drinkers—was a greater political concern" (p. 77); see also D. Leigh Colvin, *Prohibition in the United States* (New York: George H. Doran, 1926), chap. 10.

60. Storms, *Partisan Politics*, p. 21; Henry C. Ferrell, *Prohibition, Reform, and Politics in Virginia, 1895–1916* (repr. from *Studies in the History of the South, 1875–1922* 3 [1966]), p. 178. In some locales, at least a part of the constituency and even leadership of the Populist and Prohibition parties overlapped, such as in Texas, where the Populist Party "refused to espouse the cause of prohibition actively" but "was filled to overflowing with preachers and . . . the old Prohibitionist E. L. Dohoney was prominent in its councils." Martin, *The People's Party in Texas*, p. 107.

61. Rosenstone et al, *Third Parties in America*, p. 77; Colvin, *Prohibition in the United States*, pp. 256–57.

62. See Storms, *Partisan Politics*, p. 23.

63. See Jensen, *Grass Roots Politics*, p. 55; Rosenstone et al, *Third Parties in America*, p. 78; *Guide to U.S. Elections* (Washington, D.C.: Congressional Quarterly Press, 1974), p. 184. See in general James H. Timberlake, *Prohibition and the Progressive Movement 1900–1920* (Cambridge: Harvard University Press, 1966); K. Austin Kerr, *Organized for Prohibition: A New History of the Anti-saloon League* (New Haven: Yale University Press, 1985); Joseph R. Gusfield, *Symbolic Crusade: Status Politics and the American Temperance Movement*, 2d ed. (Urbana: University of Illinois Press, 1986), p. 120. Colvin is a rare dissenter, attacking the Anti-saloon League for undercutting the Prohibition Party; Colvin, *Prohibition in the United States*, pp. 380–405.

64. *Guide to U.S. Elections*, p. 184.

65. For discussion of the prohibition movement at the local level, see Ferrell, *Prohibition, Reform, and Politics;* Gilman M. Ostrander, *The Prohibition Movement in California, 1848–1933* (Berkeley: University of California Press, 1957); Robert Smith Bader, *Prohibition in Kansas* (Lawrence: University Press of Kansas, 1986); Paul E. Isaac, *Prohibition and Politics: Turbulent Decades in Tennessee, 1885–1920* (Knoxville: University of Tennessee Press, 1965); Lewis L. Gould, *Progressives and Prohibitionists: Texas Democrats in the Wilson Era* (Austin: University of Texas Press, 1973).

66. Hicks, *The Populist Revolt*, p. 406.

67. Martin, *The People's Party in Texas*, p. 54.

68. For a discussion of the components of the progressive movement, see Sundquist, *Dynamics of the Party System*, p. 156; Richard Hofstadter, *The Progressive Movement, 1900–1915* (Englewood Cliffs: Prentice-Hall, 1963), pp. 7–8; Richard Hofstadter, *The Age of Reform* (New York: Alfred A. Knopf, 1955), pp. 164–72; Stanley P. Caine, "The Origins of Progressivism," in Lewis L. Gould, ed., *The Progressive Era* (Syracuse: Syracuse University Press, 1974); John J. Broesamle, "The Democrats from Bryan to Wilson," in Gould, *The Progressive Era*, pp. 86–92; Benjamin Parke De Witt, *The Progressive Movement* (1915; reprint Seattle: University of Washington Press, 1968), pp. 26–35; Kenneth Campbell MacKay, *The Progressive Movement of 1924* (New York: Columbia University Press, 1947), chap. 1.

69. Fred E. Haynes, *Social Politics in the United States* (New York: Houghton Mifflin, 1924), p. 181.

70. Hollingsworth, *The Whirligig of Politics*, pp. 238–40; Sundquist, *Dynamics of the Party System*, pp. 158–62; Everett Carll Ladd Jr., *American Political Parties: Social Change and Political Response* (New York: W.W. Norton, 1970), p. 129.

71. Haynes, *Social Politics*, pp. 418–19.

72. Hofstadter, *The Progressive Movement*, pp. 4–5; see also Duncan-Clark, *The Progressive Movement.*

73. Hofstadter, *The Progressive Movement*, p. 9; Haynes, *Social Politics*, pp. 172–81.

74. Haynes, *Social Politics*, pp. 173–78.

75. Caine, "The Origins of Progressivism," p. 31.

76. Haynes, *Social Politics*, p. 172.

77. Haynes, *Third Party Movements*, p. 408; see also pp. 392, 408–19.

78. De Witt, *The Progressive Movement*, p. 38–39, 41, 69–70.

79. For a discussion of the Roosevelt–La Follette split in 1911–1912, see Amos R. E. Pinchot, *History of the Progressive Party 1912–1916* (New York: NYU Press, 1958), pp. 131–57; De Witt, *The Progressive Movement*, p. 76; Lewis L. Gould, "Republicans Under Roosevelt and Taft," in Gould, *The Progressive Era*, p. 79; Haynes, *Social Politics*, p. 186.

80. See Overacker, *The Presidential Primary*, p. 16.

81. David et al, *The Politics of National Party Conventions*, p. 205; Mazmanian, *Third Parties*, pp. 56–57; Haynes, *Third Party Movements*, pp. 428–29; De Witt, *The Progressive Movement*, pp. 81–82.

82. Pinchot, *History of the Progressive Party*, p. 165.

83. De Witt, *The Progressive Movement*, p. 4.

84. See Pinchot, *History of the Progressive Party*, pp. 182, 212–13, 219–23; Jensen, *Grass Roots Politics*, p. 55.

85. Ceaser, *Presidential Selection*, pp. 172–74.

86. For the effects of the war on progressivism, see Herbert F. Margulies, *The Decline of the*

Progressive Movement in Wisconsin 1890–1920 (Madison: State Historical Society of Wisconsin, 1968), pp. 250–57; MacKay, *The Progressive Movement of 1924*, chap. 1 (esp. p. 20).

87. On the Nonpartisan League, see Haynes, *Social Politics*, pp. 299–330; MacKay, *The Progressive Movement of 1924*, pp. 47–53.

88. MacKay, *The Progressive Movement of 1924*, pp. 171–94.

89. Mazmanian, *Third Parties*, p. 91.

90. Ibid., pp. 90–92; Rosenstone et al, *Third Parties in America*, pp. 20–22.

91. Hofstadter, *The Age of Reform*, p. 254.

92. Duncan-Clark, *The Progressive Movement*, p. 38.

93. Haynes, *Third Party Movements*, p. 468.

94. Hofstadter, *The Age of Reform*, pp. 256–62.

95. See Haynes, *Third Party Movements*, pp. 310–13.

96. Hicks, *The Populist Revolt*, p. 408.

97. Clark won five contests and 42 percent of the vote, while Wilson won five contests and 45 percent of the vote. *Guide to U.S. Elections*, p. 314; for the assessment of their overall performances, see De Witt, *The Progressive Movement*, pp. 40–41. On the first ballot, Clark won 157 delegates from primary states to Wilson's 154; in nonprimary states, Clark had 283.5 delegates to Wilson's 170. *Guide to U.S. Elections*, p. 148.

98. Margulies, *The Decline of the Progressive Movement*, p. 49.

99. Ibid., pp. 71–74; see also Haynes, *Social Politics*, p. 171.

100. Margulies, *The Decline of the Progressive Movement*, pp. 80–81.

101. See ibid., chaps. 3–6; Ranney, *Curing the Mischiefs of Faction*, pp. 25–27.

102. Margulies, *The Decline of the Progressive Movement*, p. 99.

103. Hofstadter, *The Age of Reform*, p. 265.

104. Ibid., 267–68.

105. Ibid., p. 264.

106. The two cases, 1912 and 1924, are somewhat different, in that in 1912 the progressives were driven into bolting despite the results of the primaries whereas in 1924 the primary results contributed to the bolt. The second case more clearly shows the potential of a primary-dominated system (or national primary) to defeat movements. De Witt, *The Progressive Movement*, provides further evidence for the importance of third parties even in the early mixed system, holding that the third-party threat in 1912 was crucial in persuading Democratic regulars to allow Wilson to win the nomination (p. 83).

107. The Nonpartisan League–dominated legislature in North Dakota even passed a bill outlawing criticism of the league's industrial program. Haynes, *Social Politics*, pp. 326–27.

108. See Epstein, *Political Parties*, pp. 173, 244–45.

3. The Conservative Movement and the Mixed System

1. Aaron B. Wildavsky, *The Revolt Against the Masses and Other Essays on Politics and Public Policy* (New York: Basic Books, 1971), p. 246; and Pomper, *Nominating the President*, p. 267.

2. Robert J. Donovan, *The Future of the Republican Party* (New York: Signet, 1964), p. 16; Theodore H. White, *The Making of the President 1960* (New York: Atheneum, 1961), p. 65.

3. After World War II, the conservative wing largely rejected isolationism in favor of what became known as the "New Nationalism," which was firmly globalist but placed greater emphasis on unilateral rather than collective action, and which manifested itself in attacks on the United Nations and foreign aid programs. Nicol C. Rae, *The Decline and Fall of the Liberal Republicans from 1952 to the Present* (New York: Oxford University Press, 1989), p. 52. See also Conrad

Joyner, *The Republican Dilemma: Conservatism or Progressivism* (Tucson: University of Arizona Press, 1963), p. 79.

4. Theodore H. White, *The Making of the President 1964* (New York: Atheneum, 1965), p. 164.

5. Nixon, for his part, denied the agreement was a surrender and claimed that "Rockefeller was the one doing the surrendering." According to Nixon, he gave up nothing, since he was not personally bound by the platform itself. While Rockefeller could no longer deny him the nomination, Nixon's key goal was apparently to gain Rockefeller's support in November. See Richard M. Nixon, *Six Crises* (New York: Warner, 1979), pp. 373–74; Nelson Polsby and Aaron Wildavsky, *Presidential Elections*, 4th ed. (New York: Charles Scribner's Sons, 1976), p. 96.

6. White, *1960*, pp. 214–25.

7. Idem, *1964*, pp. 93–94; F. Clifton White, *Suite 3505: The Story of the Draft Goldwater Movement* (New York: Arlington House, 1967), p. 19; Nick Thimmesch, *The Condition of Republicanism* (New York: W.W. Norton, 1968), p. 27.

8. William A. Rusher, *The Rise of the Right* (New York: William Morrow, 1984), pp. 89, 129–34; M. Stanton Evans, *The Future of Conservatism* (New York: Holt, Rinehart, and Winston, 1968), p. 112.

9. Paul Gottfried and Thomas Fleming, *The Conservative Movement* (Boston: Twayne, 1988), p. 32.

10. Evans, *The Future of Conservatism*, p. 119.

11. David W. Rheinhard, *The Republican Right Since 1945* (Lexington: University Press of Kentucky, 1983), p. 150.

12. White, *1964*, p. 65.

13. Joyner, *The Republican Dilemma*, p. 95.

14. George H. Mayer, *The Republican Party 1854–1966* (New York: Oxford University Press, 1966), p. 529.

15. Clinton Rossiter, *The American Presidency* (New York: Time Inc., 1963), p. 229.

16. See Lee W. Huebner and Thomas E. Petri, eds., *The Ripon Papers 1963–68* (Washington, D.C.: National, 1968) pp. 5, 8, 12–13.

17. Nelson Polsby, "Strategic Considerations," in *The National Election of 1964*, ed. Milton C. Cummings Jr. (Washington, D.C.: Brookings Institution, 1966), pp. 84–85. See also Mayer, *The Republican Party*, p. 529.

18. John H. Kessel, *The Goldwater Coalition* (New York: Bobbs-Merrill, 1968), pp. 38–39.

19. White, *1964*, p. 72.

20. Frank S. Meyer, *The Conservative Mainstream* (New Rochelle, N.Y.: Arlington House, 1969), p. 253.

21. Joyner, *The Republican Dilemma*, pp. 91–92.

22. Meyer, *The Conservative Mainstream*, p. 241.

23. White, *Suite 3505*, pp. 31–41.

24. Louis M. Seagull, *Southern Republicanism* (New York: John Wiley & Sons, 1975), p. 85.

25. White, *Suite 3505*, p. 78.

26. "Salesman for a Cause," *Time*, June 23, 1961, pp. 12–16.

27. Michael Kramer and Sam Roberts, *"I Never Wanted to Be Vice-president of Anything!": An Investigative Biography of Nelson Rockefeller* (New York: Basic Books, 1976), p. 270.

28. White, *1964*, pp. 140–41.

29. Seagull, *Southern Republicanism*, p. 89.

30. White, *1964*, pp. 142–43, 99–100. See also Earle Black and Merle Black, *The Vital South: How Presidents Are Elected* (Cambridge: Harvard University Press, 1992), pp. 126–31.

31. White, *1964*, pp. 143–44.

32. Quoted in White, *Suite 3505*, p. 165.

33. Ibid., pp. 213, 223, 240.

34. William A. Rusher, "Crossroads for the GOP," *National Review*, February 12, 1963.

35. "Box Score for '64: Can Anybody Beat Kennedy?" *Time*, October 4, 1963, pp. 35–36. See also "'Draft Goldwater' Move Starts—Its Meaning," *U.S. News & World Report*, April 29, 1963, pp. 42–45.

36. Thimmesch, *The Condition of Republicanism*, p. 32; Michael Miles, *The Odyssey of the American Right* (New York: Oxford University Press, 1980), p. 292.

37. Rusher, *The Rise of the Right*, p. 156.

38. Barry M. Goldwater, *With No Apologies* (New York: Berkley Books, 1979), p. 161.

39. William R. Keech and Donald R. Matthews, *The Party's Choice* (Washington, D.C.: Brookings Institution, 1976), p. 83.

40. Goldwater, *With No Apologies*, p. 164.

41. Evans, *The Future of Conservatism*, p. 120.

42. White, *1964*, pp. 107–16; White, *Suite 3505*, pp. 280–98.

43. Davis, *Presidential Primaries*, pp. 138–43. As early as spring 1963, the Draft Goldwater Committee had been trying to drum up favorite sons in the primary states, so Rockefeller's primary drive would be derailed while their organizational superiority in the convention states could be brought to bear; Robert D. Novak, *The Agony of the GOP 1964* (New York: Macmillan, 1965), p. 133.

44. White, *Suite 3505*, pp. 308–10.

45. White, *1964*, p. 120.

46. Thimmesch, *The Condition of Republicanism*, p. 34.

47. Kessel, *The Goldwater Coalition*, p. 87.

48. See Lee Edwards, *Goldwater: The Man Who Made a Revolution* (Washington, D.C.: Regnery, 1995), pp. 216–28; White, *1964*, p. 132.

49. Clif White thinks Goldwater would have won anyway, as does Rusher, who says that it was "flatly and mathematically impossible" for Goldwater to lose the nomination even had he lost California.

50. Goldwater, *Goldwater* (New York: Doubleday, 1988), p. 170. On the importance of California, see also Polsby and Wildavsky, *Presidential Elections*, p. 108; Rae, *Decline and Fall*, pp. 57–58.

51. Rae, *Decline and Fall*, p. 46.

52. Ibid., pp. 46, 77.

53. Stephen Hess and David S. Broder, *The Republican Establishment: The Present and Future of the G.O.P.* (New York: Harper & Row, 1967), p. 42; see also Rae, *Decline and Fall*, pp. 83, 87.

54. White, *Suite 3505*, p. 417.

55. Rusher, *The Rise of the Right*, p. 172.

56. Stanley Kelley Jr., "The Presidential Campaign," in Cummings, *The National Election of 1964*, p. 47.

57. Herbert E. Alexander, "Financing the Parties and Campaigns," in Cummings, *The National Election of 1964*, pp. 179–80.

58. Goldwater, *Goldwater*, pp. 117, 154.

59. See Gottfried and Fleming, *The Conservative Movement*, pp. 30–32; Theodore H. White, *The Making of the President 1968* (New York: Pocket, 1970), p. 42; Evans, *The Future of Conservatism*, pp. 264–65.

60. According to Nick Thimmesch, "Ironically, while a majority of Americans didn't like Goldwater, they favored most of his views"; polls showed that this was the case regarding cuts in welfare (55 percent in favor), opposition to more spending if it added to the debt (74 percent), opposition to further federal encroachment on the states (54 percent), calls for reduced union influence in government (57 percent), a more moderate pace in civil rights policy (68 percent), support for a firmer stand against the Soviets (54 percent), cuts in foreign aid (63 percent), and fear of the growth of the federal government (only 35 percent said it was *not* getting too big). Thimmesch, *The Condition of Republicanism*, p. 54.

A 1964 Harris Poll showed popular support for Goldwater's position on school prayer (88 percent), government internal security requirements (94 percent), and right to work (64 percent); 60 percent said that welfare was demoralizing and 60 percent said that government was getting too powerful. A 1964 Opinion Research poll showed support for cutting foreign aid (63 percent) and getting tougher with the Soviet Union (45 percent in favor versus 38 percent against); 68 percent said that stronger action should be taken against North Vietnam and Cuba, and 78 percent agreed that stopping the spread of Communism should be the nation's number one goal. Evans, *The Future of Conservatism*, pp. 60–61, 64, 65.

61. F. Clifton White and William J. Gill, *Why Reagan Won: A Narrative History of the Conservative Movement 1964–1981* (Chicago: Regnery Gateway, 1981), pp. 122–23; Black and Black, *The Vital South*, pp. 132–37. In addition, 20.7 percent of Nixon's delegates claimed to have been influenced by Goldwater's endorsement. Goldwater, *With No Apologies*, pp. 212–13. See also *Guide to U.S. Elections*, p. 207: "In order to head off the defection to Reagan of his more conservative supporters, Nixon seemed to take a sharp tack to the right the day before the balloting" on issues such as school busing, states rights, and strict constitutional construction.

62. Kevin P. Phillips, *The Emerging Republican Majority* (New Rochelle, N.Y.: Arlington House, 1969).

63. For discussion of Nixon in 1968, see Gottfried and Fleming, *The Conservative Movement*, p. 32; Price, *Bringing Back the Parties*, p. 30; Hess and Broder, *The Republican Establishment*, p. 407; White and Gill, *Why Reagan Won*, pp. 107–11; Rae, *Decline and Fall*, pp. 91–96; White, *1968*, pp. 61–64; 166–68, 171–72, 299.

64. Rae, *Decline and Fall*, p. 88.

65. Ibid., p. 197.

66. Theodore H. White, *America in Search of Itself: The Making of the President 1960–1980* (New York: Warner, 1983), p. 302.

67. Rae, *Decline and Fall*, p. 77.

68. Keech and Matthews, *The Party's Choice*, pp. 194–95; *Guide to U.S. Elections*, pp. 169, 340–42. Furthermore, in two of Goldwater's seven primary victories, "unpledged" actually had a higher vote total.

69. David et al, *The Politics of National Party Conventions*, pp. 225–27, 328–29.

70. See Crotty, *Political Reform*, pp. 211–13; Hofstadter, *The Age of Reform*, p. 265.

71. Pomper, *Nominating the President*, p. 273.

72. Quoted in Thimmesch, *The Condition of Republicanism*, p. 34.

73. Davis, *Presidential Primaries*, pp. 67, 90.

74. Rae, *Decline and Fall*, p. 52.

75. Pomper, *Nominating the President*, pp. 272–73.

76. This meaning of a "draft" is not restricted to action begun at the convention itself, but can include efforts by groups over a period of time to convince a potential candidate to enter the race. The key is that the initiative lies with the group or movement rather than the candidate. On the importance of draft options, see David et al, *The Politics of National Party Conventions*, p. 325.

77. Rae, *Decline and Fall*, p. 68.

78. See Josiah Lee Auspitz, "Will the GOP Make a Place for Lugenia Gordon?" *Washington Post*, March 14, 1989.

79. Rae, *Decline and Fall*, p. 73; Black and Black, *The Vital South*, p. 128.

80. On the importance of congressional district delegates, see David et al, *The Politics of National Party Conventions*, pp. 216, 166–78; White, *Suite 3505*, p. 49.

81. Harold Faber, ed., *The Road to the White House: The Story of the 1964 Election by the Staff of the New York Times* (New York: McGraw-Hill, 1965), p. 81.

82. Alexander, "Financing the Parties," p. 184.

83. Parris, *The Convention Problem*, pp. 34–35. By 1968, the South/West bloc accounted for 46.3 percent of all convention delegates; by 1984, 51 percent.

84. For the importance of demographics to conservative success, see Phillips, *The Emerging Republican Majority*, pp. 26, 42; Rae, *Decline and Fall*, p. 49; Rusher, *The Rise of the Right*, p. 169; Evans, *The Future of Conservatism*, pp. 61–62.

85. Byron E. Shafer, *Bifurcated Politics: Evolution and Reform in the National Party Convention* (Cambridge: Harvard University Press, 1988), p. 37.

86. Only 32 Republican representatives had been delegates in 1960 compared to 136 Democratic representatives. David et al, *The Politics of National Party Conventions*, p. 242.

87. His level of support among Republican voters after the assassination rested consistently around 30 percent. See Angus Campbell, "Interpreting the Presidential Victory," in Cummings, *The National Election of 1964*, p. 265.

88. James McElvoy III, *Radicals or Conservatives? The Contemporary American Right* (Chicago: Rand McNally, 1971), pp. 81–82.

89. White, *America in Search of Itself*, p. 175; see also Novak, *The Agony of the GOP 1964*, pp. 345–46; Paul Tillett, "The National Conventions," in Cummings, *The National Election of 1964*, p. 38.

90. Goldwater, *Goldwater*, p. 146.

91. James W. Ceaser, "Political Parties—Declining, Stabilizing, or Resurging?" in *The New American Political System* (2d rev. ed.), ed. Anthony King (Washington, D.C.: American Enterprise Institute, 1990), p. 104.

92. Tillett, "The National Conventions," p. 39.

93. Polsby, "Strategic Considerations," p. 95.

94. David et al, *The Politics of National Party Conventions*, p. 250.

95. Keech and Matthews, *The Party's Choice*, pp. 195–96; also Reiter, *Selecting the President*, p. 45.

96. David et al, *The Politics of National Party Conventions*, pp. 107–10; Davis, *Presidential Primaries*, p. 71.

97. In regard to minority party susceptibility, see also Reiter, *Selecting the President*, p. 115; Aaron Wildavsky, "The Goldwater Phenomenon: Purists, Politicians, and the Two-party System," *Review of Politics* (July 1965): 392.

98. Mazmanian, *Third Parties*, p. 116.

99. See Reiter, *Selecting the President*, chap. 2; see also Martin P. Wattenberg, *The Decline of American Political Parties, 1952–1980* (Cambridge: Harvard University Press, 1984); Polsby and Wildavsky, *Presidential Elections*, pp. 115–16.

100. The proportion of the American electorate that could be classified as "ideologues" grew from 12 percent in 1956 to 27 percent in 1964, before leveling off in the low 20s after 1968. See Angus Campbell et al, *The American Voter* (New York: John Wiley and Sons, 1960), p. 249; John C. Pierce, "Ideology, Attitudes, and Voting Behavior of the American Electorate: 1956, 1960, 1964," Ph.D. diss., University of Minnesota, 1969, p. 63; Paul Hagner and John C. Pierce, "Conceptualization and Consistency in Political Beliefs, 1956–1976," paper presented at the annual

meeting of the Midwest Political Science Association, 1981, p. 29; Norman H. Nie and Kristi Andersen, "Mass Belief Systems Revisited: Political Change and Attitude Structure," *Journal of Politics* (September 1974).

4. The Triumph of the "New Politics"

1. Crotty, *Party Reform*, pp. 47–48.
2. Aurthur Herzog, *McCarthy for President* (New York: Viking, 1969), pp. 15–21.
3. For a discussion of the disaffection of liberal intellectuals, see ibid., chap. 2; Herbert S. Parmet, *The Democrats: The Years After FDR* (New York: Macmillan, 1976), pp. 264–65; for a discussion of the scatterings of dissent among local Democratic Party leadership, see White, *1968*, p. 90.
4. On the new politics-new left split, see Parmet, *The Democrats*, p. 264; White, *1968*, pp. 89, 263–76; Ben Stavis, *We Were the Campaign: New Hampshire to Chicago for McCarthy* (Boston: Beacon, 1968), p. 78; Carl Oglesby, "An Open Letter to McCarthy Supporters," in *The New Left: A Documentary History*, ed. Massimo Teodori (Indianapolis: Bobbs-Merrill, 1969). For summaries of new politics philosophy, see George McGovern, "The New Politics," in *The New Politics: Mood or Movement?*, ed. James A. Burkhart and Frank J. Kendrick (Englewood Cliffs: Prentice-Hall, 1971); and Adlai Stevenson III, "Politics: The Old and New," in *The New Politics: Mood or Movement?*, ed. James A. Burkhart and Frank J. Kendrick (Englewood Cliffs: Prentice-Hall, 1971); Lewis Chester, Godfrey Hodson, and Bruce Page, *An American Melodrama: The Presidential Campaign of 1968* (New York: Viking, 1969), p. 376. For discussion of the development of the movement itself, see Stephen C. Schlesinger, *The New Reformers: Forces for Change in American Politics* (Boston: Houghton Mifflin, 1975); Stewart Burns, *Social Movements of the 1960s: Searching for Democracy* (Boston: Twayne, 1990).
5. See Herzog, *McCarthy for President*, pp. 21–23; Chester et al, *An American Melodrama*, p. 62.
6. White, *1968*, p. 88.
7. Chester et al, *An American Melodrama*, p. 63; Parmet, *The Democrats*, p. 266.
8. White, *1968*, p. 91.
9. Chester et al, *An American Melodrama*, pp. 64–67.
10. White, *1968*, p. 107.
11. It is interesting to note, however, that postelection surveys showed that up to 60 percent of McCarthy's voters voted against Johnson because he wasn't prosecuting the war vigorously enough. Richard J. Scammon and Benjamin J. Wattenberg, *The Real Majority* (New York: Coward, McCann & Geoghegan, 1970), p. 91.
12. White, *1968*, pp. 148–50.
13. Kennedy had offered McCarthy a deal whereby the two would divide the primaries between them in order to avoid splitting the antiwar vote; McCarthy, philosphically skeptical of backroom deals and particularly irritated at Kennedy for having entered the race, refused. Chester et al, *An American Melodrama*, pp. 132–33.
14. For examples, see *Mandate for Reform*, pp. 17–32; Schlesinger, *The New Reformers*, p. 2.
15. Eugene McCarthy, *The Year of the People* (Garden City: Doubleday, 1969), chap. 11; Chester et al, *An American Melodrama*, p. 201.
16. Kennedy, for instance, remarked that he would have to "win some primaries to show the pols." Parmet, *The Democrats*, p. 251. See also Dennis Wainstock, *The Turning Point: The 1968 United States Presidential Campaign* (Jefferson, N.C.: McFarland, 1988), pp. 79–80; McGovern, *Grassroots*, p. 113; Stavis, *We Were the Campaign*.
17. McCarthy, *The Year of the People*, p. 176.

18. Stavis, *We Were the Campaign*, p. 150.

19. Wainstock, *The Turning Point*, p. 115.

20. Chester et al, *An American Melodrama*, p. 548.

21. Parmet, *The Democrats*, pp. 289–91; Schlesinger, *The New Reformers*, pp. 109–10.

22. For a discussion of the NDC, see Schlesinger, *The New Reformers*, pp. 4–7, 114–118; Parmet, *The Democrats*, p. 291.

23. White, *1972*, pp. 45–46. Hart also comments on the general maturation of the new politics movement between 1968 and 1972: Gary Warren Hart, *Right from the Start: A Chronicle of the McGovern Campaign* (New York: Quadrangle, 1973), p. 88.

24. McGovern, *Grassroots*, p. 136.

25. Ibid., p. 159. See also Schlesinger, *The New Reformers*, pp. 8–9, on how the reforms succeeded in stimulating various new politics constituencies to respond and organize.

26. Shafer, *Quiet Revolution*, pp. 158–59. See also, Gordon L. Weil, *The Long Shot: George McGovern Runs for President* (New York: W.W. Norton, 1973), p. 35.

27. Hart, *Right from the Start*, p. 5.

28. Ibid., 16–19, 36; White, *1972*, pp. 42–44. On general strategy, see Ernest R. May and Janet Fraser, eds., *Campaign '72: The Managers Speak* (Cambridge: Harvard University Press, 1973), pp. 33–34, 73; Hart, *Right from the Start*, pp. 54–55; Weil, *The Long Shot*, pp. 17, 20, 35.

29. White, *1972*, p. 45.

30. Hart, *Right from the Start*, pp. 122–23.

31. May and Fraser, *Campaign '72*, p. 9.

32. Hart, *Right from the Start*, pp. 6, 137; "Campaign Highlights," *CQ Weekly Report*, March 25, 1972, p. 653. See also Weil, *The Long Shot*, p. 64.

33. Hart, *Right from the Start*, p. 144.

34. White, *1972*, p. 101.

35. Ibid., p. 129; Hart, *Right from the Start*, p. 181.

36. Hart, *Right from the Start*, p. 182; White, *1972*, pp. 129–36; "Campaign '72: California Presidential Primary," *CQ Weekly Report*, May 27, 1972, p. 1194.

37. See Hart, *Right from the Start*, p. 108; Weil, *The Long Shot*, pp. 114–18; White, *1972*, pp. 131–36; "McGovern-Humphrey Debates," *CQ Weekly Report*, June 3, 1972, p. 1265. More generally, see Andrew J. Glass, "Effective Media Campaign Paved Way for McGovern Win in California," *National Journal*, June 10, 1972, pp. 966–74.

38. White, *1972*, pp. 136–37.

39. Schlesinger, *The New Reformers*, pp. 118–27; see also Weil, *The Long Shot*, p. 57; and Richard Dougherty, *Goodbye, Mr. Christian: A Personal Account of McGovern's Rise and Fall* (Garden City: Doubleday, 1973), p. 103. On the general consolidation of the left, see Aurthur H. Miller, Warren E. Miller, Alden S. Paine, and Thad A. Brown, "A Majority Party in Disarray: Policy Polarization in the 1972 Election," *American Political Science Review* (September 1976): 756. It is ironic that, according to Schlesinger, many of these conventions were "stacked" with little advance notice and were firmly controlled from the top down; Schlesinger, *The New Reformers*, p. 120.

40. May and Fraser, *Campaign '72*, p. 12.

41. Richard G. Stearns, "Reforming the Democrats' Reforms," *Washington Post*, December 3, 1972, p. B3.

42. Parmet, *The Democrats*, p. 296.

43. See James R. Beniger, "Winning the Presidential Nomination: National Polls and State Primary Elections 1936–1972," *Public Opinion Quarterly* (Spring 1976): 30.

44. Kirkpatrick, *Dismantling the Parties*, p. 7. See also Malcolm E. Jewell, "A Caveat on the Expanding Use of Presidential Primaries," *Policy Studies Journal* (Summer 1974): 279; Jeffrey L.

Pressman and Denis G. Sullivan, "Convention Reform and Conventional Wisdom: An Empirical Assessment of Democratic Party Reforms," *Political Science Quarterly* (Fall 1974): 542.

45. See Pressman and Sullivan, "Convention Reform," p. 542; for a specific example in Connecticut, see R. W. Apple, "McGovern Gains 41 Votes in Elections of Five States," *New York Times*, June 5, 1972, p. 26.

46. Hart, *Right from the Start*, p. 104.

47. Keech and Matthews, *The Party's Choice*, p. 203.

48. James I. Lengle and Byron E. Shafer, "Primary Rules, Political Power, and Social Change," *American Political Science Review* (March 1976): 25.

49. Ibid., p. 30.

50. Ibid.

51. Bode and Casey, "Party Reform," p. 12.

52. Dougherty, *Goodbye, Mr. Christian*, p. 98; "Cross-over a Key Factor," *New York Times*, April 5, 1972, p. 1; "Times Study Finds Voters Liked McGovern on Taxes," *New York Times*, April 6, 1972, p. 1. In May and Fraser, *Campaign '72*, both McGovern delegate counter Rick Stearns and Humphrey campaign director Jack Chestnut agree with this interpretation (pp. 97, 118). David Adamany's data show that McGovern's margin was actually diminished by crossover voting, but also indicate that McGovern won a plurality of crossover votes—33.3 percent to Wallace's 29.0 percent, with Humphrey far behind. David Adamany, "Cross-over Voting and the Democratic Party's Reform Rules," *American Political Science Review* (June 1976): 539.

53. Parmet, *The Democrats*, p. 267. In fact, Adamany estimates that McCarthy won nearly 70 percent of the crossover vote in Wisconsin in 1968. Adamany, "Cross-over Voting," p. 539.

54. See Jack Rosenthal, "Survey Ties Issues, Not Shooting, to Wallace Victory," *New York Times*, May 17, 1972, p. 30; see also Gary D. Wekkin, *Democrat Versus Democrat: The National Party's Campaign to Close the Wisconsin Primary* (Columbia: University of Missouri Press, 1984), pp. 36–39.

55. McGovern, *Grassroots*, p. 150.

56. Chester et al, *An American Melodrama*, pp. 405–06. Also see Wainstock, *The Turning Point*, p. 116.

57. White, *1972*, pp. 136–38.

58. "Clutter of Dems Vying for National Delegate Posts," *New York Times*, April 9, 1972, p. 79; William Cavala, "Changing the Rules Changes the Game: Party Reform and the 1972 California Delegation to the Democratic National Convention," *American Political Science Review* (March 1974): 27–42.

59. These reforms did change substantially the composition of the delegation in 1972 in terms of demography and the political and government experience of the delegates. See John W. Soule and Wilma E. McGrath, "A Comparative Study of Presidential Nominating Conventions: The Democrats 1968 and 1972," *American Journal of Political Science* (August 1975): 501–17; Pressman and Sullivan, "Convention Reform."

60. Rick Stearns in May and Fraser, *Campaign '72*, pp. 96–97.

61. See Leon D. Epstein, "Political Science and Presidential Nominations," *Political Science Quarterly* (Summer 1978): 184–86.

62. See Joseph Kraft, "McGovern in Front," *Washington Post*, April 27, 1972, p. A23; Marshall, *Presidential Nominations*, p. 176; Pressman and Sullivan, "Convention Reform," p. 560.

63. It is a fascinating irony that this ratio almost precisely reversed the successes of the insurgent forces at the Chicago convention of 1968, where they received only 28.5 percent of the delegates while having won 69.3 percent of the primary votes.

64. Kirkpatrick, *Dismantling the Parties*, p. 7. See also Polsby and Wildavsky, *Presidential Elections*, p. 114; Keech and Matthews, *The Party's Choice*, p. 204.

65. Christopher Lydon, "McGovern's Route to the Top," *New York Times*, June 11, 1972, p. 56.

66. R. W. Apple, "Jackson and Muskie Cling to Support in Home States," *New York Times*, May 22, 1972, p. 40.

67. Joseph Alsop, "1972's Goldwater," *Washington Post*, May 17, 1972, p. A15. For similar observations, see William Chapman, "McGovern Holds Edge in Caucuses," *Washington Post*, April 9, 1972, p. A3; Rowland Evans and Robert Novak, "Behind Humphrey's Surge," *Washington Post*, April 27, 1972, p. A23; Norman Miller, "Democratic Reforms: They Work," *Wall Street Journal*, May 16, 1972, p. 24; May and Fraser, *Campaign '72*, p. 12; Weil, *The Long Shot*, p. 56; Hart, *Right from the Start*, pp. 106–07, 168.

68. "1972 Delegates from Non-primary States," *National Journal*, July 1, 1972, p. 1090. Two weeks before the convention, McGovern had 375.9 convention state delegates, while Humphrey had only 89.3 and Muskie, who was no longer actively in the race, 98.6.

69. R. W. Apple, "Jackson and Muskie," p. 40; see also "A Vermont McGovern Gain," *New York Times*, April 21, 1972, p. 44.

70. David and Ceaser, *Proportional Representation*, pp. 227–30.

71. Andrew H. Malcolm, "Dakotan Falls Short of Goal in Missouri," *New York Times*, May 25, 1972, p. 50.

72. See Donald R. Matthews, "Presidential Nominations: Process and Outcomes," in *Choosing the President*, ed. James David Barber (Englewood Cliffs: Prentice-Hall, 1974), p. 60.

73. See Hart, *Right from the Start*, p. 168; William Chapman, "McGovern, Wallace Fight for Delegates in Missouri," *Washington Post*, June 11, 1991, pp. A1, A16; Malcolm, "Dakotan Falls Short"; "Kentucky Picks Delegates," *New York Times*, June 4, 1972, p. 52. Overall, Hart claims that in early June seven key governors still had influence over 233 uncommitted convention state delegates; Hart, *Right from the Start*, p. 195.

74. The initial roll call of Texas gave Wallace fifty-two delegates to McGovern's forty-one, but it immediately changed the figures to add fifteen delegates to McGovern's total. See *Official Proceedings of the Democratic National Convention 1972*, pp. 391–92.

75. See Ceaser, *Presidential Selection*, p. 275; Fraser, "Democratizing the Democratic Party," p. 125. Bode and Casey hold that Georgia and Texas moved to primaries in 1976 to help favorite sons, but that begs the question of why favorite sons would be advantaged by primaries instead of caucuses; it seems sensible to presume this perceived advantage was derived from a belief by party leaders that they could more easily influence primaries than caucuses. See Bode and Casey, "Party Reform," pp. 16–17.

76. Bode and Casey, "Party Reform," p. 17; Philip Crass, *The Wallace Factor* (New York: Mason Charter, 1976), pp. 219–20.

77. See "Wallace's Tennessee Prize Is in Doubt," *New York Times*, April 30, 1972, p. 41; Bill Kovach, "Confident Wallace Insists on Delegates' Allegiance," *New York Times*, May 4, 1972, p. 30; "Tennessee Spurs Wallace Backers," *New York Times*, May 6, 1972, p. 14.

78. See R. W. Apple, "Texas Convention Is Still Big, but All Else Is Different," *New York Times*, June 14, 1972, p. 36; Martin Waldron, "Rank and File Seize Convention in Texas," *New York Times*, June 14, 1972, p. 36; R. W. Apple, "Texas Proves that the New Delegate Guidelines Work," *New York Times*, June 16, 1972, p. 22; Helen Dewar, "New Democratic Party Rules Making a Difference," *Washington Post*, May 22, 1972, p. A20. In general, see Kirkpatrick, *Dismantling the Parties*, p. 8.

79. Stearns, "Reforming the Democrats' Reforms," p. B3. See also Jonathan Cottin, "Stearns: He More Than Filled His Quota," *National Journal*, July 1, 1972, p. 1091, where Stearns says: "My ideas couldn't have worked for McGovern if not for the reform commission."

80. Hart, in May and Fraser, *Campaign '72*, p. 40.

81. Jonathan Cottin, "McGovern Swept Convention States on Work of Silent Majorities," *National Journal*, July 1, 1972, p. 1084.

82. Ibid., p. 1086.

83. Keech and Matthews, *The Party's Choice*, p. 210.

84. White, *1968*, p. 331; Herzog, *McCarthy for President*, pp. 219–22; Chester et al, *An American Melodrama*, pp. 82, 559; Stavis, *We Were the Campaign*, pp. 51–53, 168–69.

85. Keech and Matthews, *The Party's Choice*, p. 210.

86. Lydon, "McGovern's Route," p. 56.

87. See Beniger, p. 30. Geer argues a similar case, that in general primaries serve to provide voters with cues on electability, and hence have not changed as much in their purpose as has been thought. Geer, *Nominating Presidents*.

88. Cottin, "McGovern Swept Convention States," p. 1085.

89. Alan Ware, "The End of Party Politics? Activist-Officeseeker Relationships in the Colorado Democratic Party," *British Journal of Political Science* (April 1979): 237–50.

90. Warren Weaver Jr., "McGovern and Humphrey: A Contrast in Organization," *New York Times*, May 21, 1972, p. 58.

91. Cottin, "McGovern Swept Convention States," p. 1084.

92. Patrick Anderson, "The Taste of Success," *New York Times Magazine*, May 14, 1972, pp. 13–14.

93. Stavis, *We Were the Campaign*, p. 28.

94. Epstein, "Political Science and Presidential Nominations," p. 182.

95. See Cottin, "McGovern Swept Convention States."

96. White, *1968*, pp. 338–39.

97. Ibid., 80–81.

98. White, *1972*, p. 329.

99. Chester et al, *An American Melodrama*, p. 83.

100. Shafer, *Quiet Revolution*, p. 131.

101. See Schlesinger, *The New Reformers*, p. 195; Parmet, *The Democrats*, p. 276.

102. McGovern, *Grassroots*, p. 261.

103. See Hart, *Right from the Start*, pp. 24, 36–42, 73, 119; McGovern, *Grassroots*, p. 163, 166, 177.

104. Schlesinger, *The New Reformers*, pp. 195–99.

105. Ibid., p. 199.

106. See Epstein, "Political Science and Presidential Nominations," p. 190; Ranney, "Candidates, Coalitions, Institutions, and Reforms," 1:79; Schlesinger, *The New Reformers*, pp. 199–200.

107. Chester et al, *An American Melodrama*, p. 136.

108. Alexander, "Money and the Presidential Nominating Process," 3:67.

109. See "McGovern's Funds Grow from a Trickle to a Flood," *New York Times*, May 4, 1972, p. 30; Hart, *Right from the Start*, pp. 36, 119.

110. Alexander, "Money and the Presidential Nominating Process," p. 77; see also Polsby and Wildavsky, *Presidential Elections*, p. 87.

111. Chester et al, *An American Melodrama*, pp. 136–37.

112. See "Campaign '72: California Presidential Primary," p. 1194, which estimates McGovern's spending in California at $2.5 million.

113. See Polsby, *Consequences of Party Reform*, pp. 79–80.

114. See White, *1968*, pp. 107, 148; Stavis, *We Were the Campaign*, p. 75.

115. See Cronin and Loevy, "Putting the Party Back," pp. 62–63; William Crotty and John

S. Jackson III, *Presidential Primaries and Nominations* (Washington, D.C.: Congressional Quarterly Press, 1985), p. 183.

116. Eugene McCarthy, "The President, the Public, and the Nominating Process," in Thompson, *The Presidential Nominating Process*, 1:40–41.

117. Polsby, *Consequences of Party Reform*, p. 114.

118. Stearns, "Reforming the Democrats' Reforms," p. B3.

5. Post-1972 Movements

1. See Diane M. Pinderhughes, "The Articulation of Black Interests by Black Civil Rights, Professional, and Religious Organizations," in *The Social and Political Implications of the 1984 Jesse Jackson Presidential Campaign*, ed. Lorenzo Morris (New York: Praeger, 1990), p. 125.

2. For the debate within the black leadership, see ibid., p. 125; Lucius J. Barker, "Jesse Jackson's Candidacy in Political-social Perspective: A Contextual Analysis," in *Jesse Jackson's 1984 Presidential Campaign*, ed. Lucius J. Barker and Ronald W. Walters (Urbana: University of Illinois Press, 1989), pp. 9–14; Ronald W. Walters, "The Emergent Mobilization of the Black Community in the Jackson Campaign for President," in Barker and Walters, *Jesse Jackson's Campaign*, pp. 38–41; Marguerite Ross Barnett, "The Strategic Debate Over a Black Presidential Candidate," *PS* (Fall 1983): 489–91; Thomas H. Landers and Richard M. Quinn, *Jesse Jackson and the Politics of Race* (Ottawa, Ill.: Jameson, 1985), pp. 188–89.

3. Walters, "Emergent Mobilization," p. 43.

4. For Jackson's conception of the rainbow coalition, see Jesse Jackson, "The Rainbow Coalition Is Here to Stay," *Black Scholar* (September/October 1984): 72–74.

5. See Ronald Smothers, "The Impact of Jesse Jackson," *New York Times Magazine*, March 4, 1984, p. 46; Dom Bonafede, "Though He Won't Win the Nomination, Jackson Will Leave His Political Mark," *National Journal*, March 24, 1988, pp. 562–65; Richard Corrigan, "Jackson's Guessing Game: What Does He Want and What Will Mondale Give Him?" *National Journal*, July 14, 1984, p. 1348; Frances M. Beal, "U.S. Politics Will Never Be the Same," *Black Scholar* (September/October 1984): 13.

6. See Lorn S. Foster, "Avenues for Black Political Mobilization: The Presidential Campaign of Reverend Jesse Jackson," in Morris, *Implications of the Jackson Campaign*, esp. pp. 210–11; Milton Coleman, "Late-starting Jackson Campaign Begins to Gain Some Altitude," *Washington Post*, February 1, 1984, p. A3.

7. Foster, "Avenues," p. 205.

8. East Saint Louis Mayor Carl Officer held that Jackson's organization came from the network of black churches, saying that the Jackson campaign itself was "99 percent crusade and 1 percent organization." Ronald Smothers, "Jackson Attracts Crowds, but Planning Is Erratic," *New York Times*, January 15, 1984, p. 21.

9. For the general importance of black churches to Jackson, see Pinderhughes, "The Articulation of Black Interests," pp. 128–34; Foster, "Avenues," p. 210; Kenneth D. Wald, "Ministering to the Nation: The Campaigns of Jesse Jackson and Pat Robertson," in *Nominating the President*, ed. Emmet H. Buell Jr. and Lee Sigelman (Knoxville: University of Tennessee Press, 1991), p. 137; Gerald M. Boyd, "Black Churches a Mainspring of Jackson's Efforts," *New York Times*, February 14, 1984, p. 24; Bill Peterson, " 'Big Church' Provides Jackson a Political Base," *Washington Post*, April 3, 1984, p. A3.

10. See "Jackson and the Mayors," *National Journal*, February 13, 1988, p. 376.

11. Walters, "Emergent Mobilization," p. 51. On the question of personalism, see also Bonafede, "Though He Won't Win the Nomination," p. 563; Foster, "Avenues," pp. 207–09;

Linda Williams and Lorenzo Morris, "The Coalition at the End of the Rainbow," in Barker and Walters, *Jesse Jackson's 1984 Presidential Campaign,* p. 246; for a highly critical account, see Adolph Reed, *The Jesse Jackson Phenomenon: The Crisis of Purpose in Afro-American Politics* (New Haven: Yale University Press, 1986), p. 71, where he accuses the Jackson campaign of lacking "a structure of meaning deeper than superficial candidate packaging."

12. This calculation excludes unpledged "superdelegates."

13. In Idaho, he received 2.4 percent of the caucus vote and 5.7 percent of the primary vote; in Vermont, 14.0 percent of the caucus vote, 7.8 percent of the primary vote; in Wisconsin, 10.2 percent of the caucus vote, 9.9 percent of the primary vote.

14. Again, this excludes unpledged superdelegates. It also divides Jackson's delegates from Texas proportionately, with 65 percent assumed to have been won in the primary and 35 percent in the caucuses (in 1988 Texas had a dual process and allocated its delegates in this manner). This method of calculation actually understates Jackson's success in caucuses, since unofficial tabulations clearly showed him doing better in the caucus proceedings in Texas than in the primary, but no Texas records were available to show the actual delegate breakdown.

15. "New Rules for Delegates," *National Journal,* February 27, 1988, p. 516.

16. This, of course, is a very rough and speculative form of measurement, based on a static analysis. Other factors could have easily intervened, such as individual state characteristics. There are also ways in which the benefits to Jackson from more caucuses might be disguised. For instance, just as Jackson gained momentum from the caucuses in Michigan, he would have stood a much better chance of winning the next crucial state, Wisconsin, had it held caucuses instead of a primary. Such a victory might have produced momentum that would have increased subsequent delegate totals in both caucus and primary states.

17. The total number of states comes to over fifty because of D.C., various United States territories, and three states that held both nonbinding primaries and caucuses.

18. See Emmet H. Buell Jr. and James W. Davis, "Win Early and Often: Candidates and the Strategic Environment of 1988," in Buell and Sigelman, *Nominating the President,* p. 22.

19. See William A. Schneider, "Caucuses, Not Primaries, Need Fixing," *National Journal,* July 9, 1988, p. 1838.

20. Jack W. Germond and Jules Witcover, "Jackson's Next Chance," *National Journal,* April 2, 1988, p. 910.

21. Rhodes Cook and Dave Kaplan, "In 1988, Caucuses Have Been the Place for Political Passion," *CQ Weekly Report,* June 4, 1988, p. 1525.

22. See Dick Kirschten, "Jackson's More-for-less Campaign," *National Journal,* March 5, 1988, p. 618.

23. See Adam Clymer, "Poll Finds Organization Led to Mondale Victory," *New York Times,* February 21, 1984, p. 21; Alan I. Abramowitz, Ronald B. Rapoport, and Walter Stone, "Up Close and Personal: The 1988 Iowa Caucuses and Presidential Politics," in Buell and Sigelman, *Nominating the President,* pp. 65–68.

24. Dick Kirschten, "Democrats Weigh Party Rules Changes to Meet Jesse Jackson's Demands," *National Journal,* May 12, 1984, pp. 924–26; "'Backroom' Party Caucuses Draw Fire from Mondale Foes," *CQ Weekly Report,* June 2, 1984, p. 1315; Paul Taylor, "Jackson's Votes Diluted in South," *Washington Post,* March 20, 1984, pp. A1, A6.

25. See Cook and Kaplan, "Caucuses Have Been the Place."

26. Cook and Kaplan discuss the two basic approaches to caucuses—movement-style organization and party-based organization—and clearly identify Jackson with the former and Mondale and (to a lesser extent) Dukakis with the latter. It is interesting to note that even in 1984, Jackson's Michigan coordinator acknowledged that "blacks and campus liberals to whom Jackson appeals are

easy to identify and that getting them to the low-visibility caucuses is like organizing for a march or demonstration. Mondale's campaign is equipped for such a drill, but none of the others." Jack W. Germond and Jules Witcover, "Jackson Aims at Share of Michigan Prize," *National Journal*, February 11, 1984, p. 287.

27. "The Democratic Campaign: What If?" *CQ Weekly Report*, June 23, 1984, p. 1505; "1984 Democratic Party Rules Pad Mondale Delegate Lead," *CQ Weekly Report*, June 23, 1984, pp. 1504–05.

28. See Michael Oreskes, "Jackson Campaign, Up from Chaos, Gets the Most Out of Fewest Dollars," *New York Times*, March 27, 1988, p. 26, where the writer attributes Jackson's improved delegate-to-vote differential to his "new efficiency."

29. "How States Allocated Democratic Delegates in 1988," *CQ Weekly Report*, July 2, 1988, p. 1800.

30. Stephen Ansolabehere and Gary King, "Measuring the Consequences of Delegate Selection Rules in Presidential Nominations," *Journal of Politics* (May 1990): 609–22.

31. Bernard Weinraub, "Smooth Mondale Drive Was Polished for a Decade," *New York Times*, February 8, 1984, sec. 2, p. 10.

32. See Josiah Lee Auspitz, "Party Rules," in *The 1984 Election and the Future of American Politics*, ed. Peter W. Scramm and Dennis J. Mahoney (Durham: Carolina Academic Press, 1987), pp. 148–49 and p. 164. Auspitz argues that issue-oriented activists can take a larger role with proportional representation and low thresholds.

33. See Anthony Corrado, "The Changing Environment of Presidential Campaign Finance," in Mayer, *In Pursuit of the White House*, pp. 232–33.

34. See for instance "Jackson Sets Sights on a Super Sunday," *Washington Post*, January 19, 1988, p. A4.

35. "Jackson's Negative Ads," *Washington Post*, May 1, 1988, p. A15.

36. Robert C. Smith, "From Insurgency Toward Inclusion: The Jackson Campaigns of 1984 and 1988," in Morris, *The 1984 Jesse Jackson Presidential Campaign*, p. 218.

37. See Clyde Wilcox, "Financing the 1988 Prenomination Campaigns," in Buell and Sigelman, *Nominating the President*, pp. 94–95; see also Buell and Davis, "Win Early and Often," *Primaries*, p. 13.

38. See Samuel S. Hill and Dennis E. Owen, *The New Religious Political Right in America* (Nashville: Abingdon, 1982), chap. 7; Dan Morgan, "Evangelicals Are a Force Divided," *Washington Post*, March 8, 1988, pp. A1, A9; John C. Green and James L. Guth, "The Christian Right in the Republican Party: The Case of Pat Robertson's Supporters," *Journal of Politics* (February 1988): 150–65.

39. Hill and Owen, *The New Religious Right*, p. 51.

40. Ibid., p. 69; see, in general, chap. 4.

41. It should be noted, however, that this overlap is far from complete: in particular, Catholics play a major role in the prolife movement, and there is a significant representation in the movement of otherwise left-leaning individuals such as pacifists, death penalty opponents, and even a small coterie of feminists.

42. Buell and Davis, "Win Early and Often," p. 25; David E. Rosenbaum, "Robertson Backers Eager for Southern Test," *New York Times*, February 13, 1988, p. 9.

43. Pastor and Stone have shown that the new activists in Robertson's 1988 campaign did significantly differ from Bush and Dole supporters both demographically and in their degree of social conservatism. See Gregory S. Pastor and Walter J. Stone, "Candidate-centered Sources of Party Change: The Case of Pat Robertson, 1988," paper presented at the Western Political Science Association annual meeting, Portland, Oregon, March 1995. Nevertheless, Green and Guth argue that

even the new people brought into the Republican Party by the Robertson campaign are from "proto-Republican" groups, that they tend to agree with "mainstream" Republicans on economics and foreign policy issues, that they seek not a fundamental reorientation of the Republican agenda but simply an expansion of it to give greater emphasis to social issues, and that they are similar enough to current Republicans "to suggest their eventual assimilation into the right wing of the GOP." Green and Guth, "The Christian Right."

44. Morgan, "Evangelicals Are a Force Divided," pp. A1, A9; Bob Benenson, "Pat Robertson: The Anatomy of a Candidacy," *CQ Weekly Report*, May 14, 1988, p. 1268; Rhodes Cook, "Bush-Dole Nomination Contest Is No Watershed Event for GOP," *CQ Weekly Report*, January 23, 1988, p. 155; Wald, "Ministering to the Nation," pp. 134–35.

45. It is necessary to use mean rather than actual proportion because some Republican caucus states reported first-round delegate percentages but not turnout.

46. See "Undecided Voters Key in Nevada's Caucus Voting," *National Journal*, February 27, 1988, p. 551.

47. Rhodes Cook, "GOP's View of Delegate Rules Invites Procedural Shenanigans," *CQ Weekly Report*, February 6, 1988, p. 249.

48. Cook and Kaplan, "Caucuses Have Been the Place," p. 1523.

49. "Robertson Backers Hooked on Politics in Buckeye State," *National Journal*, March 5, 1988, p. 617.

50. David Maraniss, "Oklahoma and the Robertson Difference," *Washington Post*, February 29, 1988, p. A1.

51. See Bob Benenson, "Robertson's Cause Endures Despite His Defeat," *CQ Weekly Report*, May 14, 1988, pp. 1267–73. For a case study of a Kentucky county takeover, see James A. Barnes, "Anatomy of a Robertson Takeover," *National Journal*, March 26, 1988, p. 824. An example of this process at work in reverse can be seen in a case study of the Jackson campaign in the Maryland primary in 1984, where Jackson finished a strong second but had little or no effect on the party structure thereafter. See Alvin Thornton and Frederick C. Hutchinson, "Traditional Democratic Party Politics and the 1984 Maryland Jackson Presidential Campaign: A Case Study," in Barker and Walters, *Jesse Jackson's 1984 Presidential Campaign*, pp. 196–202. For a discussion of post-1988 party assimilation by both the Christian right and rainbow coalition, see Allen D. Hertzke, *Echoes of Discontent: Jesse Jackson, Pat Robertson, and the Resurgence of Populism* (Washington, D.C.: Congressional Quarterly Press, 1993), chap. 5.

52. Buell and Davis, "Win Early and Often," p. 7; see also Kamarck, "Structure as Strategy," p. 178.

53. This rule was first adopted by the 1976 Republican national convention to be applied in 1980, with a threshold of three states; in 1980 the convention voted to require five states beginning in 1984.

54. It should be noted that such a rule would be even more difficult to overcome in the Democratic Party, because proportional representation would make it less likely that a candidate could achieve a majority of delegates even in states he won, and because superdelegates are added to the delegate totals of the states from which they come.

55. Rhodes Cook, "Iowa's Stars Take a Back Seat in New Hampshire," *CQ Weekly Report*, February 13, 1988, pp. 287–88.

56. Cook, "GOP's View of Delegate Rules," p. 249.

57. "Robertson Scores in Hawaii, Blocked in Kansas," *CQ Weekly Report*, February 6, 1988, p. 281; Rhodes Cook, "Democrats Falter in Key Index: No One Shows a Broad Appeal," *CQ Weekly Report*, March 19, 1988, p. 741.

58. T. R. Reid and Bill Peterson, "Robertson's Recruits," *Washington Post*, February 8, 1988, pp. A1, A6.

59. Charles R. Babcock, "Mailing Lists of '88 Contributors Are Future Assets for Kemp, Robertson," *Washington Post*, March 13, 1988, p. A14.

60. T. R. Reid, "Heartened by Iowa, Robertson Prepares for Sharper Scrutiny," *Washington Post*, February 10, 1988, pp. A1, A14; Dick Kirschten, "The GOP's Wild Card," *National Journal*, February 27, 1988, p. 522.

61. See Rhodes Cook, "Bids of Jackson and Robertson Are Uphill, but Bear Watching," *CQ Weekly Report*, October 3, 1987, p. 2387; Kirschten, "The GOP's Wild Card."

62. Reid, "Heartened by Iowa," pp. A1, A14.

63. E. J. Dionne Jr., "Robertson Republicans Stand Out," *New York Times*, February 27, 1988, p. 8.

64. Analysis of Super Tuesday primary voters indicated that Robertson was the only Republican candidate who would have gained from all primaries being open (he would have had 11 percent in that case, compared to 8 percent if all primaries had been closed). Jackson would have had 25 percent if all primaries were closed, 24 percent if all were open. Priscilla L. Southwell, "Open Versus Closed Primaries: The Effect on Strategic Voting and Candidate Fortunes," *Social Science Quarterly* (December 1991): 789–96.

65. Duane M. Oldfield, "The Christian Right in the Presidential Nominating Process," in Mayer, *In Pursuit of the White House*, p. 264.

66. Babcock, "Mailing Lists," p. A14.

67. Wilcox, "Financing," p. 113.

68. See Andrew Kopkind, "Strategies for Now—And Next Time," *Nation*, September 25, 1989, pp. 297–314, on the dangers of grassroots decay resulting from the rainbow coalition's 1989 restructuring, which placed greater top-down control in the hands of Jesse Jackson.

69. See "Rise of the Religious Right," *New Leader*, September 21, 1992, p. 4; James L. Guth, John C. Green, Lyman A. Kellstedt, and Corwin E. Smidt, "God's Own Party: Evangelicals and Republicans in the '92 Election," *Christian Century*, February 17, 1993, pp. 172–76; "Republicans Court Religious Right," *Christian Century*, August 26–September 2, 1992, p. 770.

70. Joe Conason, "The Religious Right's Quiet Revival," *Nation*, April 27, 1992, p. 553.

71. Robert Sullivan, "An Army of the Faithful," *New York Times Magazine*, April 25, 1993, p. 34.

72. See Oldfield, "The Christian Right," p. 254; John F. Persinos, "Has the Christian Right Taken Over the Republican Party?" *Campaigns & Elections* (September 1994): 22. For an in-depth examination of the role of the Christian right in the 1994 elections, see Mark J. Rozell and Clyde Wilcox, *God at the Grass Roots: The Christian Right in the 1994 Elections* (Lanham, Md.: Rowman & Littlefield, 1995).

73. Richard L. Berke, "Buchanan Wins in Louisiana in Blow to Gramm Campaign," *New York Times*, February 7, 1996, pp. 1, 17.

74. "Not My Echo, My Shadow and Me," *National Journal*, January 1996, p. 11.

75. See Douglas Usher, "Republican Rules and Religious Right Takeovers," paper prepared for the annual meeting of the Midwest Political Science Association, Chicago, Illinois, April 19, 1996.

76. For instance, Christian Coalition forces completely dominated the 1992 delegate selection in Iowa (winning forty-two of forty-six delegates) and won a majority in Alaska, where Robertson had done very well in the caucuses four years earlier. Similarly, of five states that were identified by James M. Wall as having coalition members as party leaders, three (Alaska, Washington, and Minnesota) are caucus states where Robertson did well in 1988. See Sullivan, "An Army of the Faithful," p. 34; James M. Wall, "Organizing the Precincts," *Christian Century*, April 21, 1993, pp. 419–20.

77. See Reiter, *Selecting the President*, pp. 103–04; Thomas R. Marshall, *Presidential Nominations in a Reform Age* (New York: Praeger, 1981), pp. 181–82.

78. White and Gill, *Why Reagan Won*, p. 162.

79. See David and Ceaser, *Proportional Representation*, pp. 283–84; see also Crotty and Jackson, *Presidential Primaries and Nominations*, pp. 96–97.

80. Gerald Pomper, "New Rules and New Games in Presidential Nominations," *Journal of Politics* 41 (1979): 789–92. Reagan received 58.8 percent of new primary state delegates and 56 percent of caucus state delegates.

81. Michael Malbin, "The Campaign Bonanza Awaits the Winners of the 'Big Casino,'" *National Journal*, May 29, 1976, p. 751.

82. See Geer, *Nominating Presidents*, pp. 116–17.

83. Pomper, "New Rules and New Games," p. 793; this does not include Pennsylvania and New York, which had no head-to-head preference contest. David and Ceaser, *Proportional Representation*, pp. 54–56. In fact, the actual mix of proportional and nonproportional primaries maximized Reagan's strength; he would also have been hurt by a universal system of districted or statewide winner-take-all primaries. Pomper, "New Rules and New Games," pp. 796–97. Ansolabehere and King confirm that Reagan would not have been helped if all primaries had been proportional. Ansolabehere and King, "Measuring the Consequences," pp. 609–22.

84. See David and Ceaser, *Proportional Representation*, p. 56.

85. Jonathon Moore and Janet Fraser, *Campaigning for President: The Managers Look at '76* (Cambridge: Ballinger, 1977); see also Bruce F. Freed, "Federal Funds Prop Up Debt-laden Candidates," *CQ Weekly Report*, February 14, 1976; Dom Bonafede, "Kinks in the Campaign Finance Law," *National Journal*, June 12, 1976, p. 828.

86. Michael Malbin, "When It Comes to Campaign Finance, Is It Better Red than Dead?" *National Journal*, May 15, 1976, p. 655.

87. Pomper, "New Rules and New Games," pp. 799–802.

88. See Malbin, "The Campaign Bonanza," p. 751.

89. See Buell and Davis, "Win Early and Often," p. 33; Wald, "Ministering to the Nation," p. 142; Cook and Kaplan, "Caucuses Have Been the Place." p. 1523.

6. The Rise of the Unconnected Outsiders

1. Kirkpatrick, *Dismantling the Parties*, p. 23.

2. W. A. Swanberg, *Citizen Hearst* (New York: Charles Scribner's Sons, 1961), p. 213.

3. Ibid., pp. 214–15.

4. See ibid., p. 209; Oliver Carlson and Ernest Sutherland Bates, *Hearst, Lord of San Simeon* (New York: Viking, 1936), p. 142.

5. Steve Neal, *Dark Horse: A Biography of Wendell Willkie* (Garden City: Doubleday, 1984), p. 85. For similar analysis, see Donald Bruce Johnson, *The Republican Party and Wendell Willkie* (Urbana: University of Illinois Press, 1960), p. 104–05; Ellsworth Barnard, *Wendell Willkie: Fighter for Freedom* (Marquette: Northern Michigan University Press, 1966), p. 165.

6. Neal, *Dark Horse*, pp. 70–71, 107; Johnson, *The Republican Party*, p. 83.

7. Johnson, *The Republican Party*, p. 90.

8. Ibid., p. 107.

9. Neal, *Dark Horse*, pp. 315–18.

10. Joseph Bruce Gorman, *Kefauver: A Political Biography* (New York: Oxford University Press, 1971), p. 3.

11. Keech and Matthews, *The Party's Choice*, p. 43; see also Gorman, *Kefauver*, chaps. 5–6.

12. Gorman, *Kefauver*, p. 137.

13. Ibid., pp. 218, 230.

14. Ibid., pp. 124, 132.

15. See Charles L. Fontenay, *Estes Kefauver: A Biography* (Knoxville: University of Tennessee Press, 1980), esp. p. 217.

16. See ibid., pp. 202, 205; David et al, *The Politics of National Party Conventions*, p. 259.

17. Keech and Matthews, *The Party's Choice*, pp. 186–87.

18. Reiter, *Selecting the President*, p. 152.

19. See Keech and Matthews, *The Party's Choice*, p. 62.

20. David et al, *The Politics of National Party Conventions*, pp. 204–05.

21. See Gorman, *Kefauver*, pp. 261–62; and chap. 15 in general.

22. See for instance Seymour Martin Lipset and Earl Raab, *The Politics of Unreason: Right Wing Extremism in America 1790–1970*, 2d ed. (New York: Harper & Row, 1978), p. 547.

23. See Bill Jones, *The Wallace Story* (Northport, Ala.: American Southern, 1966), p. 173; "Alabama Governor Files in Wisconsin," *New York Times*, March 7, 1964.

24. Wayne Greenhaw, *Watch Out for George Wallace* (Englewood Cliffs: Prentice-Hall, 1976), p. 20.

25. Jones, *The Wallace Story*, p. 176.

26. Ibid., p. 263; see also Jody Carlson, *George C. Wallace and the Politics of Powerlessness: The Wallace Campaigns for the Presidency, 1964–1976* (New Brunswick: Transaction, 1981), pp. 34–38.

27. According to Wallace, Governor J. Millard Tawes later confided that Wallace had actually won the Maryland primary but that the party organization had misreported results to prevent his victory. Crass, *The Wallace Factor*, p. 71; see also Jones, *The Wallace Story*, pp. 304–05.

28. Ben A. Franklin, "Brewster Victor, Wallace Has 43% in Maryland Vote," *New York Times*, May 20, 1964, p. 1.

29. Carlson, *George C. Wallace*, pp. 43, 70.

30. Dan T. Carter, *The Politics of Rage* (New York: Simon & Schuster, 1995), p. 209.

31. Ibid., p. 312.

32. Marshall Frady, *Wallace* (New York: NAL, 1968), p. 12.

33. Carlson, *George C. Wallace*, p. 74; see also Carter, *The Politics of Rage*, p. 300.

34. Richard W. Boyd, "Electoral Trends in Postwar Politics," in Barber, *Choosing the President*, p. 197; Carter, *The Politics of Rage*, pp. 335–38.

35. Ken Ringle, "Wallace Running, but as a Democrat: Social Issue," *Washington Post*, January 14, 1972, p. A1. Snider seemed to be correct; at least in North Carolina, there was evidence that many American Independent Party members changed their registration to Democratic to vote for Wallace in the 1972 North Carolina primary. "Campaign '72: North Carolina Primary May 6," *CQ Weekly Report*, April 29, 1972, p. 950.

36. Carlson, *George C. Wallace*, p. 148.

37. See "Cross-over a Key Factor," p. 1; "Times Study Finds Voters Liked McGovern on Taxes," p. 1; Rosenthal, "Survey Ties Issues," p. 30.

38. White, *1972*, p. 96. While this seems to have been basically true, it may be somewhat hyperbolic. For an account of Wallace advance work in Oregon, see "Building Crowds for Wallace," *National Journal*, June 3, 1972, p. 927.

39. Carlson, *George C. Wallace*, pp. 145–46.

40. Ibid., p. 147.

41. Crass, *The Wallace Factor*, p. 19.

42. See Rowland Evans and Robert Novak, "Message From Michigan," *Washington Post*, May 19, 1972, p. A23; Crass, *The Wallace Factor*, p. 191.

43. Wallace Turner, "Wallace Tally in Oregon Shows Voter Discontent," *New York Times,* May 25, 1972, p. 50.

44. See Andrew J. Glass, "Political Organization Adds Needed Muscle for Humphrey and McGovern Victories," *National Journal,* April 29, 1972, p. 714.

45. See Carlson, *George C. Wallace,* p. 147.

46. Lengle and Shafer, "Primary Rules," p. 30.

47. See Crass, *The Wallace Factor,* p. 22; Keech and Matthews, *The Party's Choice,* p. 206.

48. Keech and Matthews, *The Party's Choice,* p. 206.

49. See Chapman, "McGovern Holds Edge in Caucuses," p. A3; Keech and Matthews, *The Party's Choice,* p. 209; Thomas R. Marshall, *Presidential Nominations in a Reform Age* (New York: Praeger, 1981), p. 177.

50. "Democratic Convention Countdown: Current Delegate Standing," *National Journal,* June 10, 1972, p. 1005.

51. See William Chapman, "McGovern, Wallace Split Texas Delegates," *Washington Post,* May 8, 1972, p. A1. See also R. W. Apple, "McGovern and Wallace Show Strength in Texas Race," *New York Times,* April 16, 1972, p. 38, where the writer points out that Wallace "has not done well in similar efforts in other states, notably Georgia and South Carolina, largely because his campaign de-emphasizes organization."

52. Greenhaw, *Watch Out for George Wallace,* p. 54.

53. See Crass, *The Wallace Factor,* pp. 192–93; May and Fraser, *Campaign '72,* pp. 43, 99–100; Carlson, *George C. Wallace,* p. 149. In this sense, Wallace was also a mirror image of McGovern, who was helped not by the substance of the reforms so much as by knowledge of them and by the fact that they were only partially implemented.

54. Crass, *The Wallace Factor,* p. 19.

55. Carlson, *George C. Wallace,* p. 193.

56. Crass, *The Wallace Factor,* pp. 216–17; Carlson, *George C. Wallace,* p. 189.

57. See Crass, *The Wallace Factor,* pp. 219–20; Carlson, *George C. Wallace,* pp. 197, 202–06; White, *America in Search of Itself,* pp. 287–88; Jules Witcover, *Marathon: The Pursuit of the Presidency 1972–1976* (New York: Viking, 1977), p. 169.

58. Bode and Casey, "Party Reform," p. 16.

59. See Rhodes Cook, "New Primary Rules Make Little Difference," *CQ Weekly Report,* June 5, 1976, p. 1421; Crass, *The Wallace Factor,* p. 225.

60. Crass, *The Wallace Factor,* p. 221.

61. Lipset and Raab, *The Politics of Unreason,* p. 522; also p. 531. In Wisconsin, for example, "Carter was the chief beneficiary of the Wallace collapse"; Rhodes Cook, "Wisconsin: A Long Night for Udall," *CQ Weekly Report,* April 10, 1976, p. 814.

62. Greenhaw, *Watch Out for George Wallace,* pp. 48–50.

63. *New York Times*-Yankelovich surveys in 1972 in Florida, Wisconsin, and Pennsylvania showed some similarity between Wallace and McGovern voters in degree of alienation, but also showed deep ideological and issue differences. Wallace voters, it would seem, were alienated by different things than were McGovern voters. "Alienated-voter Theory Doubted," *New York Times,* April 28, 1972, p. 23.

64. For a general account of Wallace's improved 1976 campaign, see Jules Witcover, "Wallace Machine," *Washington Post,* May 4, 1975, p. A1; Carlson, *George C. Wallace,* pp. 195–97; Greenhaw, *Watch Out for George Wallace,* pp. 56–60.

65. David S. Broder, "Endorsements Clinch Carter Victory," *Washington Post,* June 10, 1976, p. A1.

66. Cook, "New Primary Rules," p. 1421.

67. Pomper, "New Rules and New Games," p. 793.

68. Greenhaw, *Watch Out for George Wallace*, p. 64.

69. Carlson, *George C. Wallace*, pp. 185–186.

70. See Witcover, *Marathon*, p. 165.

71. For a discussion of Wallace's 1976 finance situation, see Michael Malbin, "Supreme Court's Ruling on Election Law Causes Confusion," *National Journal*, February 7, 1976, pp. 167–68; Freed, "Federal Funds," p. 318. For Wallace in 1972, see Jonathan Cottin, "Democrats Tap Fresh Financial Sources but Encounter Money-raising Problems," *National Journal*, May 13, 1972, pp. 803–07; for 1968, see Boyd, "Electoral Trends," p. 197.

72. See Polsby, *Consequences of Party Reform;* Crotty, *Political Reform*, pp. 272–73; Ranney, "Candidates, Coalitions, Institutions, and Reforms," 1:76; McCarthy, "The President, the Public," 1:40; Price and Beveridge, "The Political and Nominating Process," 3:38.

73. Witcover, *Marathon*, pp. 110–11.

74. Ibid., p. 136.

75. Kandy Stroud, *How Jimmy Won: The Victory Campaign from Plains to the White House* (New York: William Morrow, 1977), pp. 277–81.

76. Ibid., p. 262.

77. Rhodes Cook, "Iowa Caucuses: An Early Triumph for Carter," *CQ Weekly Report*, January 24, 1976, p. 189.

78. Pomper, "New Rules and New Games," pp. 789–90.

79. Witcover, *Marathon*, pp. 260, 274–80.

80. See Stroud, *How Jimmy Won*, p. 303; Witcover, *Marathon*, p. 342; "June 1: A Warmup for the Final Week," *CQ Weekly Report*, June 5, 1976, p. 1422.

81. See Witcover, *Marathon*, pp. 332–36; Stroud, *How Jimmy Won*, p. 300. Witcover renders an ambiguous verdict on the importance of Mandel's help; the machine wielded a "still-effective whip" but was in some disarray because of Mandel's mounting legal troubles.

82. Stroud, *How Jimmy Won*, p. 298.

83. Witcover, *Marathon*, p. 329.

84. Pomper, "New Rules and New Games," pp. 794–95.

85. David and Ceaser, *Proportional Representation*, p. 50.

86. Ibid., p. 50.

87. See Epstein, *Political Parties*, p. 282.

88. See Malbin, "Better Red than Dead?" p. 650.

89. See "The Independent Vote That Made All the Difference," *New York Times*, March 4, 1984, sec. 4, p. 1; Geer, *Nominating Presidents*, p. 118.

90. This calculation excludes unpledged superdelegates.

91. *Congressional Quarterly* maintained that Hart had also actually won more first-level caucus votes than his opponents, but it seems impossible to state this with certainty since numerous states reported vote percentages but only estimated turnout, and four others (including Texas) did not report turnout at all. See "First-round Results of Democratic Caucuses," *CQ Weekly Report*, June 2, 1984, p. 1317.

92. "'Backroom' Party Caucuses," p. 1315; "Democratic Nominating Rules: Back to Drawing Board for 1988," *CQ Weekly Report*, June 30, 1984, pp. 1568–69.

93. "Party Rules Pad Mondale Delegate Lead," pp. 1504–05.

94. Richard E. Cohen, "Congressional Super Delegates Flex New Presidential Ticket-making Muscle," *National Journal*, July 14, 1984, p. 1352.

95. Priscilla Southwell, "The 1984 Democratic Nomination Process," *American Politics Quarterly* (January 1986): 35.

96. "The Democratic Campaign: What If?" p. 1505.

97. See Anthony Corrado, "Party Rules Reform and Candidate Nomination Strategies: Consequences for the 1990s," paper presented at the annual meeting of the American Political Science Association, Washington D.C., August 29–September 1, 1991, pp. 4–5.

98. See Glen E. Thurow, "The 1984 Democratic Primary Election: Issues and Image," in *The 1984 Election and the Future of American Politics*, ed. Peter W. Schramm and Dennis Mahoney (Durham: Carolina Academic Press, 1987), p. 44. Hart, it turns out, did best in states that actually were governed by proportional representation and lost states that were governed by plurality or bonus rules, which had the effect of minimizing his strength.

99. Corrado, "The Changing Environment," p. 232.

100. Carter, *The Politics of Rage*, pp. 362–63; see also Crass, *The Wallace Factor*, pp. 1–17.

101. See Polsby, *Consequences of Party Reform*, chap. 3; see also Ranney, "Candidates, Coalitions, Institutions, and Reforms," 1:76.

102. Robert Walters, "The Pols and the Polls—Taking the Pulse of the People," *National Journal*, May 1, 1976, p. 597. See also Stroud, *How Jimmy Won*, p. 310: Carter "possessed magnetic Southern charm coupled with a mesmerizing influence on small crowds. One on one he was irresistible." On Wallace, see for instance "Building Crowds for Wallace," p. 927.

103. For a discussion of Carter's "run everywhere" strategy and its relation to proportional representation, see Witcover, *Marathon*, pp. 196–97.

104. See Ruy A. Teixeira, *The Disappearing American Voter* (Washington, D.C.: Brookings Institution, 1992), chap. 2.

105. After 1968, a series of Supreme Court decisions reduced considerably the number of petition signatures that states could require for ballot access and shortened filing deadlines. Despite these decisions, third parties still faced greater roadblocks than in the 1800s. First, prior to the 1890s advent of the Australian ballot, there were generally no ballot access requirement at all because ballots were not printed by the state. Second, today all states but New York still prohibit "cross-listing," a device necessary for the party fusion that was an important part of third parties' access to the electoral system. Finally, third parties still face a formidable disadvantage at the presidential level in the form of automatic public financing of the major parties' campaigns.

106. The impact of the environmental factors can be seen in the changing character of third candidates over time. Just as unconnected outsiders have become more common within the parties, this type of candidate has supplanted the traditional movement-centered third party. In the 1800s and midway through the twentieth century, third candidates truly represented "third parties" that had autonomous organization, a platform, and control over nominations. Since 1968, the most important "third parties" have been independent candidates who have essentially nominated themselves, established their own platforms, chosen their own vice presidential candidates, and, at most, attempted to build a personalist "party" around themselves. Wallace, Anderson, and Perot all fit this mold.

7. Outsiderism in the 1990s

1. Among 1992 Democrats, Jerry Brown, Bill Clinton, and Paul Tsongas tried to claim the title of outsider (Tom Harkin and Bob Kerrey did not), while in 1996, Lamar Alexander, Pat Buchanan, Steve Forbes, Alan Keyes, and Morry Taylor did so (leaving Bob Dole, Bob Dornan, Phil Gramm, and Richard Lugar).

2. See Ceaser and Busch, *Upside Down and Inside Out*.

3. Of course, forces that appeared to be transient, disconnected, and personalist at the time may endure and be transformed into genuine movements. If United We Stand America or the Reform Party proclaimed by Perot in the fall of 1995 takes on an independent organizational life of

its own, continues to attract grassroots support, nominates its own candidates, and sharpens its issue appeal, it may ultimately qualify as a movement.

4. See "1992 Democratic Primary Results," Democratic convention special issue, *CQ Weekly Report*, July 4, 1992, p. 69; "1992 Republican Primary Results," Republican convention special issue, August 8, 1992, p. 63.

5. Neither Clinton nor Perot were on the ballot, so all votes for either man were write-ins.

6. For example, Perot received .8 percent in the Vermont Republican caucuses on March 31.

7. That is, the Chicago riots resulting from Humphrey's nomination in 1968, not the NBA championship in 1992. See *Mandate for Reform*, p. 49, where the McGovern-Fraser Commission defends its recommendations on the grounds that failure to open the Democratic Party could lead to "third or fourth parties, or the anti-politics of the street."

8. William Booth, "Stranger to Georgia, Tsongas Bears Burden of 'Massachusetts Thing,'" *Washington Post*, February 20, 1992, p. A14; David S. Broder, "Tsongas Forced to Play Organizational Catch-up," *Washington Post*, March 8, 1992, p. A19.

9. Tsongas officially suspended his campaign on March 19, but remained an inactive but viable candidate through the New York, Wisconsin, Minnesota, and Kansas primaries on April 7. Indeed, he finished ahead of Jerry Brown in New York. After that round of primaries, he ended speculation that he might reenter the race actively.

10. Broder, "Tsongas Forced to Play."

11. In Minnesota, Tsongas had 7.6 percent in the first-round caucuses (March 3) and 21.3 percent in the primary (April 7). In Texas, where both the primary and first-round caucuses were held on March 10, Tsongas received approximately 8 percent in the second round of the caucus process (first-round result were not tabulated statewide) and 19.2 percent in the primary.

12. Rhodes Cook, "Front-runners Face Good News, Bad News in Final Phase," *CQ Weekly Report*, May 16, 1992, p. 1377.

13. This calculation excludes unpledged superdelegates and is adjusted to reflect the mixed system in Texas.

14. Again, it must be emphasized that this is only a rough method of comparison, since none but Texas hold their primary and caucus proceedings on the same day, and since all but Texas have nonbinding primaries, which receive less even attention from all candidates than do primaries where delegates are actually at stake. Also, the results in Texas are not first-level results, which were not tabulated statewide, but rather results from the next level (county/state Senate conventions).

15. Richard L. Berke, "Insider, Outsider, Brown Runs on Contradictions," *New York Times*, April 3, 1992, p. 13.

16. See David Von Drehle, "Gov. Brown Runs on Old Script," *Washington Post*, March 30, 1992, p. A1. Also, on the topic of Brown's outsider campaign, see Lou Cannon, "Brown Relishes Outsider's Role," *Washington Post*, February 6, 1992, p. A1.

17. Cook, "Front-runners Face Good News, Bad News," p. 1377. See also Lou Cannon, "Fearful Clinton Backers in California Seek to Use Party Machine Against Brown," *Washington Post*, March 26, 1992, p. A23.

18. Kopkind, "Strategies for Now—And Next Time," p. 313.

19. Mae M. Ngai, "Whither the Rainbow?" *Nation*, December 18, 1989, p. 738.

20. See Lou Cannon, "Brown Vows He Would Back Clinton," *Washington Post*, April 12, 1992, p. A25.

21. Maralee Schwartz, "Brown Takes Lead Among Vermont Democrats," *Washington Post*, April 1, 1992, p. A8. Although Brown received support, local observers also maintained that he had not inspired the same devotion as Jackson had.

22. See Rhodes Cook, "Super Tuesday Tone to Be Set in Early Southern Face-offs," *CQ Weekly Report*, February 29, 1992, p. 486.

23. Rhodes Cook, "Clinton, Brown Taste First Wins; Bush-Buchanan Duel Rolls On," *CQ Weekly Report*, March 7, 1992, p. 562.

24. Rhodes Cook, "Clinton Left Behind in Caucuses," *CQ Weekly Report*, April 4, 1992, p. 899.

25. See James M. Perry, "Brown's Chaotic California Salad of a Campaign Proves Surprisingly Tasty as He Looks Beyond '92," *Wall Street Journal*, March 17, 1992.

26. E. J. Dionne Jr. and Ann Devroy, "Buchanan Urged to Quit," *Washington Post*, March 11, 1992, p. A1.

27. Duke's organizational malaise is discussed by Rhodes Cook, "Duke Fading," *CQ Weekly Report*, February 15, 1992, p. 369.

28. See E. J. Dionne Jr., "GOP Challenger Exceeds Projections," *Washington Post*, February 19, 1992, p. A1.

29. Rhodes Cook, "Caucuses Undercut Buchanan Bid," *CQ Weekly Report*, May 16, 1992, p. 1378.

30. Rhodes Cook, "GOP Faces Uncharted Terrain in Wake of Buchanan Upset," *CQ Weekly Report*, February 24, 1996, p. 441. For a discussion of the increased sharpness of Buchanan's message in 1996, see James A. Barnes, "The Firebrand," *National Journal*, January 6, 1996, p. 10.

31. See "Voters in the Republican Primaries," *New York Times*, March 31, 1996, p. A12. Through the March 26 primaries, 38 percent of self-described "very conservative" voters supported Buchanan while 19 percent of self-described "liberal" or "very liberal" voters did so.

32. Richard L. Berke, "Buchanan Wins in Louisiana," pp. 1, 17.

33. Buchanan won delegates or nonbinding straw polls in caucuses in Louisiana, Alaska, and Missouri, and lost Minnesota, Wyoming, Washington, and Iowa. Hawaii and Utah did not make results available.

34. Adam Nagourney, "A Strong Second-place Gives Heart to Buchanan," *New York Times*, February 13, 1996, p. A19.

35. "For Buchanan, Early Gains in Missouri," *New York Times*, March 11, 1966, p. A9.

36. Those states were Louisiana (44 percent caucus, 32.7 percent primary) and Washington state (28 percent caucus, 21 percent primary).

37. James Bennet, "Buchanan Keeps Campaigning, for the Issues and for the Fun of It," *New York Times*, March 7, 1966, p. A1, A17; William Schneider, "Can't Live With 'Em Or Without 'Em," *National Journal*, March 30, 1996, p. 746.

38. See "Voters in the Republican Primaries," p. A12. Exit polls indicated that Buchanan lost to Dole among voters of both positions on both abortion and trade. On abortion, he lost by forty points among prochoice voters and by fourteen points among prolife voters, leaving a gap of twenty-six points. On trade, he lost by fifteen points among protectionist voters and by forty-seven points among pro–free trade voters, leaving a larger gap of thirty-two points.

39. Jonathan Alter, "Can You Really Buy a Caucus?" *Newsweek*, January 22, 1996, p. 38.

40. Ibid., p. 38.

41. Elizabeth Kolbert, "Ads for Forbes Played Role in Outcome but Not the One He Intended," *New York Times*, February 14, 1996, p. B8.

42. Rhodes Cook, "Dole's Shaky Lead Faces Test in Volatile New Hampshire," *CQ Weekly Report*, February 17, 1996, p. 400.

43. See "Voters in the Republican Primaries," p. A12. Buchanan received 21 percent among Republicans, 28 percent among independents, and 29 percent among Democrats; Forbes received 10 percent among Republicans, 11 percent among Democrats, and 15 percent among independents.

44. James Bennet, "A Gleeful Buchanan Takes Message to Iowa," *New York Times*, February 9, 1996, p. A26. See also Jack W. Germond and Jules Witcover, "San Diego Won't End Buchanan

Effort," *National Journal*, March 16, 1996, p. 613; Rhodes Cook, "Midwestern Enclaves Suggest Dole Has Work to Do," *CQ Weekly Report*, March 23, 1996, pp. 810–13.

45. The caucus figure is 26.3 percent if one includes the anomalous 87 percent uncommitted vote in American Samoa.

46. Cook, "Caucuses Undercut Buchanan Bid," p. 1378.

47. Numerous states reported "uncommitted" and "other" together, so it is not entirely clear how much of the vote represented each category. Overall, uncommitted/other vote averaged 9.7 percent in six caucuses (excluding Louisiana) and 5.1 percent in primaries.

48. See Corrado, "The Changing Environment," pp. 230, 233; "Brown Tops Matching Funds List," *New York Times*, May 29, 1992, p. 19; Steven A. Holmes, "The Checks Are in the Mail, and Made Out to Buchanan," *New York Times*, February 24, 1992, p. 16.

49. Barnes, "The Firebrand," p. 9.

50. See Nagourney, "A Strong Second-place Gives Heart to Buchanan," p. A19; Rhodes Cook and Jonathan Salant, "Presidential Primary Focuses on Federal Funding," *CQ Weekly Report*, January 6, 1996, p. 64.

51. Jonathan D. Salant, "Dole's Outlays May Pose Problems," *CQ Weekly Report*, March 9, 1996, p. 638.

52. Alan Keyes in 1996 also fit the category of candidates who were highly reliant on movement support, but he was never particularly visible or viable.

53. See Adam Nagourney, "A Region Not Likely to Be Heavily Contested in '96," *New York Times*, March 9, 1996, p. 9.

54. Buchanan showed success in Perot strongholds in the earliest primary states in 1996, and through March had done better among Perot voters than among either Clinton voters or Bush voters. On the other hand, numerous Perot strongholds supported Dole instead. See "Voters in the Republican Primaries"; Cook, "GOP Faces Uncharted Terrain," p. 441; Rhodes Cook, "Dole Supreme in Week of Wins; 'Super Tuesday' Comes Next," *CQ Weekly Report*, March 9, 1996, p. 642.

8. Conclusion

1. In "Federalist 68," Alexander Hamilton explains at length how the presidential selection system would blend popular input (openness) with protections against demagoguery (stability); the McGovern-Fraser Commission report argues that only greater openness and participation can forestall chaos and even violence.

2. John Jay, "Federalist 64," in *The Federalist Papers*.

3. Even Pat Buchanan provides some evidence of this difference. As a movement-backed candidate in 1996, he formulated a more focused and coherent message and seemed to take a longer view on party affairs, claiming in early 1996 that he was unlikely to undertake a third-party bolt not only because it would help Bill Clinton but because it would hurt the long-term prospects of the movement.

4. Paul-Henri Gurian, "The Influence of Nomination Rules on the Financial Allocations of Presidential Candidates," *Western Political Quarterly* (September 1990): 682.

5. See Mayer, "Caucuses: How They Work," pp. 133–36.

6. See Richard Cohen, "They're Hunkering Below the Radar Line," *Washington Post*, February 11, 1988, p. A27.

7. This results in differences between caucus and primary participants. See Thomas R. Marshall, "Turnout and Representation: Caucuses Versus Primaries," *American Journal of Political Science* (February 1978): 169–82.

8. Geer contends that, contrary to assumptions, primary voters are generally more moderate

than the party following as a whole. Additionally, Geer holds that previous primary performance can have a powerful effect on later primary performance, so that in a sense reform system primary voters are affected by primaries much the same way that party regulars were affected by the smaller number of primaries in the mixed system. Bartels buttresses the latter argument by emphasizing the importance of early primary performance to later primary outcomes. Geer, *Nominating Presidents*, pp. 15–27, 78–83, 106. See also Larry M. Bartels, *Presidential Primaries and the Dynamics of Public Choice* (Princeton: Princeton University Press, 1988).

9. Because caucus and primary states are not randomly distributed geographically or ideologically, a simple comparison of caucus state versus primary state performance by candidates is not entirely satisfactory. William G. Mayer has accordingly made an important attempt to correct for these imbalances by controlling results for region, ideology, home state of the candidate and his opponents, and a variety of other demographic variables, depending on the campaign. See Mayer, "Caucuses: How They Work." I have not made use of these figures for several reasons. Controlling for these factors in any race prior to 1972 is problematic because so few primaries were seriously contested. For instance, in 1964 only three of the seventeen Republican primaries were serious tests of candidate strength: New Hampshire, Oregon, and California. An attempt to control for region would be seriously skewed in such a situation. Once the nomination campaign became fully plebiscitary and serious candidates contested most or all primaries, such statistical controls are theoretically much more valid, but nevertheless difficult to construct practically. For example, the ideological control constructed by Mayer relies on various measures of state ideology, but it is the ideology of the relevant political party in each state that is crucial for nominating purposes, not the ideology of the state as a whole. Idaho, for example, ranks near the top of a variety of scales of conservatism, but the Democratic Party of Idaho is quite liberal, having produced Senator Frank Church and caucus victories for George McGovern in 1972, Gary Hart in 1984, Michael Dukakis in 1988 (with Jesse Jackson placing a credible second), and Tom Harkin in 1992. There are also numerous instances in which particular state contests ought to be treated like a candidate's home state, though they are not. For example, Robert Dole's 1988 campaign in Iowa cannot be analyzed without understanding his status as "Iowa's third senator," a position that a simple control for region cannot sufficiently capture. That year, Michael Dukakis of Massachusetts likewise benefited in neighboring New Hampshire. It is not always clear even in which regional category states should be placed; Texas, for instance, which accounts for a large number of delegates in both parties, could reasonably be placed in either the South (as Mayer does) or the West.

In any event, in post-1972 races, Mayer's exercise in constructing a set of statistical controls basically confirms my argument. Mayer's analysis showed unconnected outsiders remaining unchanged or doing even worse in caucus versus primary delegate showings after controlling: Jimmy Carter remained steady in 1976, Gary Hart lost another ten to eleven percentage points in caucuses versus primaries in 1984, and Jerry Brown lost three points and Paul Tsongas two points in 1992. On the other hand, Jesse Jackson's movement campaigns gained six percentage points in 1984 and nine to ten points in 1988 in caucuses over primaries after controlling. The only exception was Ronald Reagan in 1976, who Mayer's analysis showed to have done slightly better in primaries than caucuses. Robertson, Buchanan, and Duke were not studied. Mayer argues out that in most cases since the reforms, differences between caucus and primary showings are not statistically significant, whether or not they are controlled. In a case like the 1976 Reagan-Ford contest, of course, a "statistically insignificant" difference can nevertheless determine the nomination.

10. Indeed, the reformers who pushed the Mikulski Commission into banning open primaries in 1974 clearly had George Wallace on their minds. See Wekkin, *Democrat Versus Democrat*, pp. 34–42.

11. "Rules and Rigors of Year's Record Primaries," *CQ Weekly Report*, January 31, 1976, p. 225.

12. David and Ceaser, *Proportional Representation*, pp. 38–39; Corrado, "Party Rules Reform."

13. Of course, there is an ongoing debate over whether it can be said that there is a majority party today, and indeed whether American politics will ever again see a stable majority party as in the past. This "dealignment" thesis cannot be satisfactorily addressed in these pages, however, and past experience must, for the time being, remain the guide.

14. Bartels, *Presidential Primaries*.

15. See Ceaser, *Presidential Selection*, chap. 3.

16. See Mayer, "Caucuses: How They Work," p. 117.

17. See Rhodes Cook, "GOP's Rules Favor Dole, If He Doesn't Stumble," *CQ Weekly Report*, January 27, 1996, p. 229.

BIBLIOGRAPHY

"1972 Delegates from Non-primary States." *National Journal,* July 1, 1972.

"1984 Democratic Party Rules Pad Mondale Delegate Lead." *CQ Weekly Report,* June 23, 1984.

"1992 Democratic Primary Results." Democratic Convention Special Issue, *CQ Weekly Report,* July 4, 1992.

"1992 Republican Primary Results." Republican Convention Special Issue, *CQ Weekly Report,* August 8, 1992.

Abramowitz, Alan I., Ronald B. Rapoport, and Walter Stone. "Up Close and Personal: The 1988 Iowa Caucuses and Presidential Politics." In *Nominating the President,* edited by Emmet H. Buell Jr. and Lee Sigelman. Knoxville: University of Tennessee Press, 1991.

Adamany, David. "Cross-over Voting and the Democratic Party's Reform Rules." *American Political Science Review* (June 1976).

"Alabama Governor Files in Wisconsin." *New York Times,* March 7, 1964.

Aldrich, John H. *Before the Convention: Strategies and Choices in Presidential Nomination Campaigns.* Chicago: University of Chicago Press, 1980.

Alexander, Herbert E. "Financing the Parties and Campaigns." In *The National Election of 1964,* edited by Milton C. Cummings Jr. Washington, D.C.: Brookings Institution, 1966.

———. "Money and the Presidential Nominating Process." In *The Presidential Nominating Process,* edited by Kenneth W. Thompson. Vol. 3. Lanham, Md.: University Press of America, 1984.

"Alienated-voter Theory Doubted." *New York Times,* April 28, 1972.

Alsop, Joseph. "1972's Goldwater." *Washington Post,* May 17, 1972.

Alter, Jonathan. "Can You Really Buy a Caucus?" *Newsweek,* January 22, 1996.

Anderson, Patrick. "The Taste of Success." *New York Times Magazine,* May 14, 1972.

Ansolabehere, Stephen, and Gary King. "Measuring the Consequences of Delegate Selection Rules in Presidential Nominations." *Journal of Politics* (May 1990).

Apple, R. W. "McGovern and Wallace Show Strength in Texas Race." *New York Times,* April 16, 1972.

———. "Jackson and Muskie Cling to Support in Home States." *New York Times,* May 22, 1972.

———. "McGovern Gains 41 Votes in Elections of Five States." *New York Times,* June 5, 1972.

——. "Texas Convention Is Still Big, But All Else Is Different." *New York Times*, June 14, 1972.

——. "Texas Proves that the New Delegate Guidelines Work." *New York Times*, June 16, 1972.

——. "Finding the Formula." *New York Times*, March 6, 1996.

Ash, Roberta. *Social Movements in America*. Chicago: Markham, 1972.

Auspitz, Josiah Lee. "Party Rules." In *The 1984 Election and the Future of American Politics*, edited by Peter W. Schramm and Dennis J. Mahoney. Durham: Carolina Academic Press, 1987.

——. "Will the GOP Make a Place for Lugenia Gordon?" *Washington Post*, March 14, 1989.

Babcock, Charles R. "Mailing Lists of '88 Contributors Are Future Assets for Kemp, Robertson." *Washington Post*, March 13, 1988.

"'Backroom' Party Caucuses Draw Fire from Mondale Foes." *CQ Weekly Report*, June 2, 1984.

Bader, Robert Smith. *Prohibition in Kansas*. Lawrence: University of Kansas Press, 1986.

Bain, Richard C., and Judith H. Parris. *Convention Decisions and Voting Records*. Washington, D.C.: Brookings Institution, 1973.

Banfield, Edward C. "Party 'Reform' in Retrospect." In *Political Parties in the Eighties*, edited by Robert A. Goldwin. Washington, D.C.: American Enterprise Institute, 1980.

Barker, Lucius J. "Jesse Jackson's Candidacy in Political-social Perspective: A Contextual Analysis." In *Jesse Jackson's 1984 Presidential Campaign*, edited by Lucius J. Barker and Ronald W. Walters. Urbana: University of Illinois Press, 1989.

Barnard, Ellsworth. *Wendell Willkie: Fighter for Freedom*. Marquette: Northern Michigan University Press, 1966.

Barnes, James A. "Anatomy of a Robertson Takeover." *National Journal*, March 26, 1988.

——. "Eyeing the Rules." *National Journal*, June 18, 1988.

——. "The Firebrand." *National Journal*, January 6, 1996.

Barnett, Marguerite Ross. "The Strategic Debate Over a Black Presidential Candidate." *PS* (Fall 1983).

Bartels, Larry M. *Presidential Primaries and the Dynamics of Public Choice*. Princeton: Princeton University Press, 1988.

Beal, Frances M. "U.S. Politics Will Never Be the Same." *Black Scholar* (September/October 1984).

Benenson, Bob. "Pat Robertson: The Anatomy of a Candidacy." *CQ Weekly Report*, May 14, 1988.

——. "Robertson's Cause Endures Despite His Defeat." *CQ Weekly Report*, May 14, 1988.

Beniger, James R. "Winning the Presidential Nomination: National Polls and State Primary Elections 1936–1972." *Public Opinion Quarterly* (Spring 1976).

Bennet, James. "A Gleeful Buchanan Takes Message to Iowa." *New York Times*, February 9, 1996.

——. "Still Loud and Unbowed." *New York Times*, March 7, 1996.

———. "Buchanan Keeps Campaigning, for the Issues and for the Fun of It." *New York Times*, March 11, 1996.

Berke, Richard L. "Insider, Outsider, Brown Runs on Contradictions." *New York Times*, April 3, 1992.

———. "Buchanan Wins in Louisiana in Blow to Gramm Campaign." *New York Times*, February 7, 1996.

"Bitter Infighting Could Spell Trouble for Georgia GOP." *Washington Post*, August 21, 1988.

Black, Earle, and Merle Black. *The Vital South: How Presidents Are Elected*. Cambridge: Harvard University Press, 1992.

Bode, Kenneth A., and Carol F. Casey. "Party Reform: Revisionism Revised." In *Political Parties in the Eighties*, edited by Robert A. Goldwin. Washington, D.C.: American Enterprise Institute, 1980.

Bonafede, Dom. "The Thrill Returns." *National Journal*, April 3, 1976.

———. "Kinks in the Campaign Finance Law." *National Journal*, June 12, 1976.

———. "Though He Won't Win the Nomination, Jackson Will Leave His Political Mark." *National Journal*, March 24, 1988.

Booth, William. "Stranger to Georgia, Tsongas Bears Burden of 'Massachusetts Thing.'" *Washington Post*, February 20, 1992.

"Box Score for '64: Can Anybody Beat Kennedy?" *Time*, October 4, 1963.

Boyd, Gerald M. "Black Churches a Mainspring of Jackson's Efforts." *New York Times*, February 14, 1984.

Boyd, Richard W. "Electoral Trends in Postwar Politics." In *Choosing the President*, edited by James David Barber. Englewood Cliffs: Prentice-Hall, 1974.

Brady, Henry E., and Richard Johnston. "What's the Primary Message: Horse Race or Issue Journalism?" In *Media and Momentum: The New Hampshire Primary and Nomination Politics*, edited by Garry R. Orren and Nelson W. Polsby. Chatham, N.J.: Chatham House, 1987.

Broder, David S. "Endorsements Clinch Carter Victory." *Washington Post*, June 10, 1976.

———. "Tsongas Forced to Play Organizational Catch-up." *Washington Post*, March 8, 1992.

Broder, David S., and William Booth. "Harkin Lowers His Sights, Targeting 3 Caucus States." *Washington Post*, February 27, 1992.

Broesamle, John J. "The Democrats from Bryan to Wilson." In *The Progressive Era*, ed. Lewis L. Gould. Syracuse: Syracuse University Press, 1974.

"Brown Tops Matching Funds List." *New York Times*, May 29, 1992.

Brownstein, Ronald. "Democratic Rules Pact Could Change Nature of 1988 Primary Campaign." *National Journal*, June 30, 1984.

Bryce, James. *The American Commonwealth*. Chicago: Sergel & Co., 1889.

Buell, Emmet H., Jr., and James W. Davis. "Win Early and Often: Candidates in the Strategic Environment of 1988." In *Nominating the President*, ed. Emmet H. Buell Jr. and Lee Sigelman. Knoxville: University of Tennessee, 1991.

"Building Crowds for Wallace." *National Journal*, June 3, 1972.

Burnham, Walter Dean. *Critical Elections and the Mainsprings of American Politics*. New York: W. W. Norton, 1970.

Burns, Stewart. *Social Movements of the 1960s*. Boston: Twayne, 1990.

"Bush-Robertson War Is Over, But Word Hasn't Reached Soldiers." *National Journal*, May 28, 1988.

Caine, Stanley P. "The Origins of Progressivism." In *The Progressive Era*, edited by Lewis L. Gould. Syracuse: Syracuse University Press, 1974.

"Campaign '72: California Presidential Primary." *CQ Weekly Report*, May 27, 1972.

"Campaign '72: North Carolina Primary May 6." *CQ Weekly Report*, April 29, 1972.

"Campaign Highlights." *CQ Weekly Report*, March 25, 1972.

Campbell, Angus. "Interpreting the Presidential Victory." In *The National Election of 1964*, edited by Milton C. Cummings Jr. Washington, D.C.: Brookings Institution, 1966.

Campbell, Angus et al. *The American Voter*. New York: John Wiley and Sons, 1960.

Cannon, Lou. "Brown Relishes Outsider's Role." *Washington Post*, February 6, 1992.

———. "Fearful Clinton Backers in California Seek to Use Party Machine Against Brown." *Washington Post*, March 26, 1992.

———. "Brown Vows He Would Back Clinton." *Washington Post*, April 12, 1992.

Carlson, Jody. *George C. Wallace and the Politics of Powerlessness: The Wallace Campaigns for the Presidency, 1964–1976*. New Brunswick: Transaction, 1981.

Carlson, Oliver, and Ernest Sutherland Bates. *Hearst, Lord of San Simeon*. New York: Viking, 1936.

Carmines, Edward G., and James A. Stimson. *Issue Evolution: Race and the Transformation of American Politics*. Princeton: Princeton University Press, 1989.

Carter, Dan T. *The Politics of Rage: George Wallace, the Origins of the New Conservatism, and the Transformation of American Politics*. New York: Simon & Schuster, 1995.

Cater, Douglas. "The History of the Presidential Nominating Process." In *The Presidential Nominating Process*, edited by Kenneth W. Thompson. Vol. 1. Lanham, Md.: University Press of America, 1983.

"Caucuses: Light Turnout, Many Uncommitted." *CQ Weekly Report*, July 10, 1976.

Cavala, William. "Changing the Rules Changes the Game: Party Reform and the 1972 California Delegation to the Democratic National Convention." *American Political Science Review* (March 1974).

Ceaser, James W. *Presidential Selection: Theory and Development*. Princeton: Princeton University Press, 1979.

———. "Political Change and Party Reform." In *Political Parties in the Eighties*, edited by Robert A. Goldwin. Washington, D.C.: American Enterprise Institute, 1980.

———. *Reforming the Reforms: A Critical Analysis of the Presidential Selection Process*. Cambridge, Mass.: Ballinger, 1982.

———. "The Theory of the Presidential Nominating Process." In *The Presidential Nominating Process*, edited by Kenneth W. Thompson. Vol. 1. Lanham, Md.: University Press of America, 1983.

———. "Political Parties—Declining, Stabilizing, or Resurging?" In *The New American Political System*, edited by Anthony King. 2d rev. ed. Washington, D.C.: American Enterprise Institute, 1990.

Ceaser, James, and Andrew Busch. *Upside Down and Inside Out: The 1992 Elections and American Politics*. Lanham, Md.: Rowman & Littlefield, 1993.

Center, Judith. "1972 Democratic Convention Reforms and Party Democracy." *Political Science Quarterly* (June 1974).

Chapman, William. "McGovern Holds Edge in Caucuses." *Washington Post*, April 9, 1972.

——. "McGovern, Wallace Split Texas Delegates." *Washington Post*, May 8, 1972.

——. "McGovern, Wallace Fight for Delegates in Missouri." *Washington Post*, June 11, 1972.

Chester, Lewis, Godfrey Hodson, and Bruce Page. *An American Melodrama: The Presidential Campaign of 1968*. New York: Viking, 1969.

Clanton, Gene O. *Kansas Populism*. Lawrence: University of Kansas Press, 1969.

Clendinen, Dudley. "Computer-aided Black Network Won Louisiana for Jackson." *New York Times*, May 7, 1984.

Clinch, Thomas A. *Urban Populism: Free Silver in Montana*. Missoula: University of Montana Press, 1970.

Cloud, David S. "For Jackson, the Promise of Something Greater." *CQ Weekly Report*, July 2, 1988.

"Clutter of Dems Vying for National Delegate Posts." *New York Times*, April 9, 1972.

Clymer, Adam. "Poll Finds Organization Led to Mondale Victory." *New York Times*, February 21, 1984.

Cohen, Richard E. "Congressional Super Delegates Flex New Presidential Ticket-making Muscle." *National Journal*, July 14, 1984.

——. "They're Hunkering Below the Radar Line." *Washington Post*, February 11, 1988.

Coleman, Milton. "Late-starting Jackson Campaign Begins to Gain Some Altitude." *Washington Post*, February 1, 1984.

Colvin, D. Leigh. *Prohibition in the United States*. New York: George H. Doran, 1926.

Conason, Joe. "The Religious Right's Quiet Revival." *Nation*, April 27, 1992.

Cook, Rhodes. "Iowa Caucuses: An Early Triumph for Carter." *CQ Weekly Report*, January 24, 1976.

——. "Wallace in Mississippi: 'We Thrashed Them.'" *CQ Weekly Report*, January 31, 1976.

——. "Caucus Report: Carter vs. the Uncommitted." *CQ Weekly Report*, April 10, 1976.

——. "Wisconsin: A Long Night for Udall." *CQ Weekly Report*, April 10, 1976.

——. "New Primary Rules Make Little Difference." *CQ Weekly Report*, June 5, 1976.

——. "Bids of Jackson and Robertson Are Uphill, but Bear Watching." *CQ Weekly Report*, October 3, 1987.

——. "Bush-Dole Nomination Contest Is No Watershed Event for GOP." *CQ Weekly Report*, January 23, 1988.

——. "GOP's View of Delegate Rules Invites Procedural Shenanigans." *CQ Weekly Report*, February 6, 1988.

——. "Iowa's Stars Take a Back Seat in New Hampshire," *CQ Weekly Report*, February 13, 1988.

——. "Democrats Falter in Key Index: No One Shows a Broad Appeal." *CQ Weekly Report*, March 19, 1988.

——. "Pressed by Jackson Demands, Dukakis Yields on Party Rules." *CQ Weekly Report*, July 2, 1988.

——. "Duke Fading." *CQ Weekly Report*, February 15, 1992.

——. "Super Tuesday Tone to Be Set in Early Southern Face-offs." *CQ Weekly Report*, February 29, 1992.

——. "Clinton, Brown Taste First Wins; Bush-Buchanan Duel Rolls On." *CQ Weekly Report*, March 7, 1992.

——. "Clinton Left Behind in Caucuses." *CQ Weekly Report*, April 4, 1992.

——. "Front-Runners Face Good News, Bad News in Final Phase." *CQ Weekly Report*, May 16, 1992.

——. "Caucuses Undercut Buchanan Bid." *CQ Weekly Report*, May 16, 1992.

——. "GOP's Rules Favor Dole, If He Doesn't Stumble." *CQ Weekly Report*, January 27, 1996.

——. "Dole's Shaky Lead Faces Test in Volatile New Hampshire." *CQ Weekly Report*, February 17, 1996.

——. "GOP Faces Uncharted Terrain in Wake of Buchanan Upset." *CQ Weekly Report*, February 24, 1996.

——. "Dole Supreme in Week of Wins; 'Super Tuesday' Comes Next." *CQ Weekly Report*, March 9, 1996.

——. "Midwestern Enclaves Suggest Dole Has Work to Do." *CQ Weekly Report*, March 23, 1996.

Cook, Rhodes, and Dave Kaplan. "In 1988, Caucuses Have Been the Place for Political Passion." *CQ Weekly Report*, June 4, 1988.

Cook, Rhodes, and Jonathan Salant. "Presidential Primary Focuses on Federal Funding." *CQ Weekly Report*, January 6, 1996.

Corrado, Anthony. "Party Rules Reform and Candidate Nomination Strategies: Consequences for the 1990s." Paper presented at the annual meeting of the American Political Science Association, Washington, D.C., August 29–September 1, 1991.

——. "The Changing Environment of Presidential Campaign Finance." In *In Pursuit of the White House: How We Choose Our Presidential Nominees*, edited by William G. Mayer. Chatham, N.J.: Chatham House, 1996.

Corrigan, Richard. "Jackson's Guessing Game: What Does He Want and What Will Mondale Give Him?" *National Journal*, July 14, 1984.

Cottin, Jonathan. "Democrats Tap Fresh Financial Sources but Encounter Money-raising Problems." *National Journal*, May 13, 1972.

——. "McGovern Swept Convention States on Work of Silent Majorities." *National Journal*, July 1, 1972.

——. "Stearns: He More Than Filled His Quota." *National Journal*, July 1, 1972.

"Countdown for Delegate Race." *National Journal*, June 12, 1976.

Crass, Philip. *The Wallace Factor*. New York: Mason Charter, 1976.

Cronin, Thomas E., and Robert D. Loevy. "Putting the Party as Well as the People Back in President Picking." In *The Presidential Nominating Process*, edited by Kenneth W. Thompson. Vol. 1. Lanham, Md.: University Press of America, 1983.

"Cross-over a Key Factor." *New York Times*, April 5, 1972.

Crotty, William J. *Political Reform and the American Experiment*. New York: Thomas Y. Crowell, 1977.

———. *Decision for the Democrats: Reforming the Party Structure*. Baltimore: Johns Hopkins University Press, 1978.

———. *Party Reform*. New York: Longman, 1983.

Crotty, William J., and John S. Jackson III. *Presidential Primaries and Nominations*. Washington, D.C.: Congressional Quarterly Press, 1985.

Dallinger, Frederick A. *Nominations for Elective Office in the United States*. Cambridge: Harvard University Press, 1897.

David, Paul T., and James W. Ceaser. *Proportional Representation in Presidential Nominating Politics*. Charlottesville: University Press of Virginia, 1980.

David, Paul T., Ralph M. Goldman, and Richard C. Bain. *The Politics of National Party Conventions*. 2d ed. Washington, D.C.: Brookings Institution, 1964.

Davis, James W. *Presidential Primaries: Road to the White House*. New York: Thomas Y. Crowell, 1967.

De Witt, Benjamin Parke. *The Progressive Movement*. 1915. Reprint Seattle: University of Washington Press, 1968.

"The Democratic Campaign: What If?" *CQ Weekly Report*, June 23, 1984.

"Democratic Convention Countdown: Current Delegate Standings." *National Journal*, May 27, 1972.

"Democratic Convention Countdown: Current Delegate Standings." *National Journal*, June 10, 1972.

"Democratic Convention: New Faces and New Rules." *CQ Weekly Report*, July 8, 1972.

"Democratic Nominating Rules: Back to Drawing Board for 1988." *CQ Weekly Report*, June 30, 1984.

"The Democrats: Old Guard Under Attack." *CQ Weekly Report*, June 24, 1972.

Dewar, Helen. "New Democratic Party Rules Making a Difference." *Washington Post*, May 22, 1972.

"Different Systems Yield Different Results." *CQ Weekly Report*, June 4, 1988.

Dionne, E. J., Jr. "Robertson Republicans Stand Out." *New York Times*, February 27, 1988.

———. "GOP Challenger Exceeds Projections." *Washington Post*, February 19, 1992.

Dionne, E. J., Jr., and Ann Devroy. "Buchanan Urged to Quit." *Washington Post*, March 11, 1992.

Donovan, Robert J. *The Future of the Republican Party*. New York: Signet, 1964.

Dougherty, Richard. *Goodbye, Mr. Christian: A Personal Account of McGovern's Rise and Fall*. Garden City: Doubleday, 1973.

"'Draft Goldwater' Move Starts—Its Meaning." *U.S. News & World Report*, April 29, 1963.

Duncan-Clarke, S. J. *The Progressive Movement*. Boston: Small, Maynard, 1913.

Durden, Robert F. *The Climax of Populism: The Election of 1896*. Lexington: University of Kentucky Press, 1965.

Edsall, Thomas B. "Robertson Forces Seeking to Control State Parties." *Washington Post*, February 14, 1988.

Edwards, Lee. *Goldwater: The Man Who Made a Revolution*. Washington, D.C.: Regnery, 1995.

Epstein, Leon D. "Political Science and Presidential Nominations." *Political Science Quarterly* (Summer 1978).

———. *Political Parties in the American Mold*. Madison: University of Wisconsin Press, 1986.

Evans, M. Stanton. *The Future of Conservatism*. New York: Holt, Rinehart, and Winston, 1968.

Evans, Rowland, and Robert Novak. "Behind Humphrey's Surge." *Washington Post*, April 27, 1972.

———. "Message from Michigan." *Washington Post*, May 19, 1972.

Faber, Harold, ed. *The Road to the White House: The Story of the 1964 Election by the Staff of the New York Times*. New York: McGraw-Hill, 1965.

Faw, Bob, and Nancy Skelton. *Thunder in America*. Austin: Texas Monthly Press, 1986.

Ferrell, Henry C. *Prohibition, Reform, and Politics in Virginia, 1895–1916*. Reprinted from *Studies in the History of the South, 1875–1922* 3 (1966).

"First-round Results of Democratic Caucuses." *CQ Weekly Report*, June 2, 1984.

Flint, Jerry M. "Michigan Campaigning, Student Style." *New York Times*, May 17, 1972.

Fontenay, Charles L. *Estes Kefauver: A Biography*. Knoxville: University of Tennessee Press, 1980.

"For Buchanan, Early Gains in Missouri." *New York Times*, March 11, 1996.

Foster, Lorn S. "Avenues for Black Political Mobilization: The Presidential Campaign of Reverend Jesse Jackson." In *The Social and Political Implications of the 1984 Jesse Jackson Presidential Campaign*, edited by Lorenzo Morris. New York: Praeger, 1990.

Frady, Marshall. *Wallace*. New York: NAL, 1968.

Franklin, Ben A. "Brewster Victor, Wallace Has 43% in Maryland Vote." *New York Times*, May 20, 1964.

Fraser, Donald M. "Democratizing the Democratic Party." In *Political Parties in the Eighties*, edited by Robert A. Goldwin. Washington, D.C.: American Enterprise Institute, 1980.

Freed, Bruce F. "Federal Funds Prop Up Debt-laden Candidates." *CQ Weekly Report*, February 14, 1976.

"Gallup Poll Finds McGovern Lagging." *New York Times*, April 9, 1972.

Geer, John G. *Nominating Presidents*. Westport, Conn.: Greenwood, 1989.

Geer, John G., and Mark E. Shere. "Party Competition and the Prisoner's Dilemma: An Argument for the Direct Primary." *Journal of Politics* (August 1992): 741–61.

Germond, Jack W., and Jules Witcover. "Jackson Aims at Share of Michigan Prize." *National Journal*, February 11, 1984.

———. "Jackson's Pull May Not Show in Delegate Count." *National Journal*, February 27, 1988.

———. "Jackson's Next Chance." *National Journal*, April 2, 1988.

———. "Now the Dukakis Bandwagon Can Start Rolling." *National Journal*, April 23, 1988.

———. "San Diego Won't End Buchanan Effort," *National Journal*, March 16, 1996.

Glad, Paul W. *McKinley, Bryan, and the People*. Philadelphia: J. B. Lippincott, 1964.

Glass, Andrew J. "Political Organization Adds Needed Muscle for Humphrey and McGovern Victories." *National Journal*, April 29, 1972.

———. "Effective Media Campaign Paved Way for McGovern Win in California." *National Journal*, June 10, 1972.

Goldwater, Barry M. *Goldwater*. New York: Doubleday, 1988.

———. *With No Apologies*. New York: Berkley Books, 1979.

Goodwyn, Lawrence. *The Populist Moment*. New York: Oxford University Press, 1978.

"GOP 'Pros' Split on 'Gate' Effect, Like Reagan in '76." *Gallup Opinion Index* (March 1974).

Gorman, Joseph Bruce. *Kefauver: A Political Biography*. New York: Oxford University Press, 1971.

Gottfried, Paul, and Thomas Fleming. *The Conservative Movement*. Boston: Twayne, 1988.

Gould, Lewis L. *Progressives and Prohibitionists: Texas Democrats in the Wilson Era*. Austin: University of Texas Press, 1973.

———. "Republicans Under Roosevelt and Taft." In *The Progressive Era*, edited by Lewis L. Gould. Syracuse: Syracuse University Press, 1974.

Grasmick, Harold S. "Rural Culture and the Wallace Movement in the South." *Rural Sociology* (Winter 1974).

Green, John C., and James L. Guth. "The Christian Right in the Republican Party: The Case of Pat Robertson's Supporters." *Journal of Politics* (February 1988).

Greenhaw, Wayne. *Watch Out for George Wallace*. Englewood Cliffs: Prentice-Hall, 1976.

Guide to U.S. Elections. Washington, D.C.: Congressional Quarterly Press, 1975.

Gusfield, Joseph R. *Symbolic Crusade: Status Politics and the American Temperance Movement*. 2d ed. Urbana: University of Illinois Press, 1963.

Guth, James L., John C. Green, Lyman A. Kellstedt, and Corwin E. Smidt, "God's Own Party: Evangelicals and Republicans in the '92 Election." *Christian Century*, February 17, 1993.

Hagner, Paul, and John C. Pierce. "Conceptualization and Consistency in Political Beliefs, 1956–1976." Paper presented at the annual meeting of the Midwest Political Science Association, 1981.

Hamilton, Alexander. "Federalist 68." *The Federalist Papers*. New York: NAL Penguin, 1961.

———. "Federalist 70." *The Federalist Papers*. New York: NAL Penguin, 1961.

Hart, Gary Warren. *Right from the Start: A Chronicle of the McGovern Campaign*. New York: Quadrangle, 1973.

Haynes, Fred E. *Social Politics in the United States*. New York: Houghton Mifflin, 1924.

———. *Third Party Movements with Special Reference to Iowa*. Cedar Rapids: Torch, 1916.

Heberle, Rudolf. *Social Movements: An Introduction to Political Sociology*. New York: Appleton-Century-Crofts, 1951.

Hertzke, Alan. *Echoes of Discontent: Jesse Jackson, Pat Robertson, and the Resurgence of Populism.* Washington, D.C.: Congressional Quarterly Press, 1993.

Herzog, Aurthur. *McCarthy for President.* New York: Viking, 1969.

Hess, Stephen, and David S. Broder. *The Republican Establishment: The Present and Future of the G.O.P.* New York: Harper & Row, 1967.

Hicks, John D. *The Populist Revolt: A History of the Farmers' Alliance and the People's Party.* Minneapolis: University of Minnesota Press, 1931.

Hill, Samuel S., and Dennis E. Owen. *The New Religious Political Right in America.* Nashville: Abingdon, 1982.

Hofstadter, Richard. *The Age of Reform.* New York: Alfred A. Knopf, 1955.

———. *The Progressive Movement 1900–1915.* Englewood Cliffs, N.J.: Prentice-Hall, 1963.

Hollingsworth, J. Rogers. *The Whirligig of Politics: The Democracy of Cleveland and Bryan.* Chicago: University of Chicago Press, 1963.

Holmes, Steven A. "The Checks Are in the Mail, and Made Out to Buchanan." *New York Times,* February 24, 1992.

"How States Allocated Democratic Delegates in 1988." *CQ Weekly Report,* July 2, 1988.

Huebner, Lee H., and Thomas E. Petri, eds. *The Ripon Papers 1963–68.* Washington, D.C.: National, 1968.

"The Independent Vote That Made All the Difference." *New York Times,* March 4, 1984.

Isaac, Paul E. *Prohibition and Politics: Turbulent Decades in Tennessee 1885–1920.* Knoxville: University of Tennessee Press, 1965.

Jackson, Jesse. "The Rainbow Coalition Is Here to Stay." *Black Scholar* (September/October 1984).

"Jackson and the Mayors." *National Journal,* February 13, 1988.

"Jackson's Negative Ads." *Washington Post,* May 1, 1988.

"Jackson Sets Sights on a Super Sunday." *Washington Post,* January 19, 1988.

"The Jackson Vote: A Comparison." *CQ Weekly Report,* March 19, 1988.

Jay, John. "Federalist 64." *The Federalist Papers.* New York: NAL Penguin, 1961.

Jenkins, Kent, Jr. "Robertson Exhorts N. Virginia Backers to Carry Fight into GOP Caucuses." *Washington Post,* March 25, 1988.

Jensen, Richard J. *Grass Roots Politics.* Westport, Conn.: Greenwood, 1983.

Jewell, Malcolm E. "A Caveat on the Expanding Use of Presidential Primaries." *Policy Studies Journal* (Summer 1974).

Johnson, Donald Bruce. *The Republican Party and Wendell Willkie.* Urbana: University of Illinois Press, 1960.

Jones, Bill. *The Wallace Story.* Northport, Ala.: American Southern, 1966.

Joyner, Conrad. *The Republican Dilemma: Conservatism or Progressivism.* Tucson: University of Arizona Press, 1963.

"June 1: A Warmup for the Final Week." *CQ Weekly Report,* June 5, 1976.

Kamarck, Elaine Cuilla. "Structure as Strategy: Presidential Nominating Politics in a Post-reform Era." In *The Parties Respond,* edited by L. Sandy Maisel. Boulder: Westview, 1990.

Keech, William R., and Donald R. Matthews. *The Party's Choice*. Washington, D.C.: Brookings Institution, 1976.

Kelley, Stanley, Jr. "The Presidential Campaign." In *The National Election of 1964*, edited by Milton C. Cummings Jr. Washington, D.C.: Brookings Institution, 1966.

"Kentucky Picks Delegates." *New York Times*, June 4, 1972.

Kerr, K. Austin. *Organized for Prohibition: A New History of the Anti-saloon League*. New Haven: Yale University Press, 1985.

Kessel, John H. *The Goldwater Coalition*. New York: Bobbs-Merrill, 1968.

Key, V. O. *Politics, Parties, and Pressure Groups*. 4th ed. New York: Thomas Y. Crowell, 1958.

Kirkpatrick, Jeane Jordan. *Dismantling the Parties*. Washington, D.C.: American Enterprise Institute, 1978.

Kirschten, Dick. "Democrats Weigh Party Rules Changes to Meet Jesse Jackson's Demands." *National Journal*, May 12, 1984.

———. "The GOP's Wild Card." *National Journal*, February 27, 1988.

———. "Jackson's More-for-less Campaign." *National Journal*, March 5, 1988.

Kolbert, Elizabeth. "Ads for Forbes Played Role in Outcome but Not the One He Intended." *New York Times*, February 14, 1996.

Kolinsky, Martin, and William E. Paterson, eds. *Social and Political Movements in Western Europe*. New York: St. Martin's, 1976.

Kopkind, Andrew. "Strategies for Now—And Next Time." *Nation*, September 25, 1989.

Kovach, Bill. "Confident Wallace Insists on Delegates' Allegiance." *New York Times*, May 4, 1972.

Kraft, Joseph. "McGovern in Front." *Washington Post*, April 27, 1972.

Kramer, Michael, and Sam Roberts. *"I Never Wanted to be Vice-president of Anything!": An Investigative Biography of Nelson Rockefeller*. New York: Basic Books, 1976.

Ladd, Everett Carll, Jr. *American Political Parties: Social Change and Political Response*. New York: W.W. Norton, 1970.

Landers, Thomas H., and Richard M. Quinn. *Jesse Jackson and the Politics of Race*. Ottawa, Ill.: Jameson, 1985.

Lardner, George, Jr. "Preachers, Phone Banks Talk Up Jackson." *Washington Post*, May 5, 1984.

Lauer, Robert H., ed. *Social Movements and Social Change*. Carbondale and Edwardsville: Southern Illinois University Press, 1976.

Lengle, James I., and Byron E. Shafer. "Primary Rules, Political Power, and Social Change." *American Political Science Review* (March 1976).

Lipset, Seymour Martin, and Earl Raab. *The Politics of Unreason: Right Wing Extremism in America, 1790–1970*. 2d ed. New York: Harper & Row, 1978.

Lydon, Christopher. "McGovern's Route to the Top." *New York Times*, June 11, 1972.

MacKay, Kenneth Campbell. *The Progressive Movement of 1924*. New York: Columbia University Press, 1947.

Madison, James. *Notes of Debates in the Federal Convention of 1787*. New York: W.W. Norton, 1987.

Malbin, Michael. "Supreme Court's Ruling on Election Law Causes Confusion." *National Journal*, February 7, 1976.

———. "When It Comes to Campaign Finance, Is It Better Red Than Dead?" *National Journal*, May 15, 1976.

———. "The Campaign Bonanza Awaits the Winners of the 'Big Casino.'" *National Journal*, May 29, 1976.

Malcolm, Andrew H. "Dakotan Falls Short of Goal in Missouri." *New York Times*, May 25, 1972.

Mandate for Reform: A Report of the Commission on Party Structure and Delegate Selection to the Democratic National Committee. Washington, D.C.: Democratic National Committee, April 1970.

Maraniss, David. "Oklahoma and the Robertson Difference." *Washington Post*, February 29, 1988.

Margulies, Herbert F. *The Decline of the Progressive Movement in Wisconsin 1890–1920.* Madison: State Historical Society of Wisconsin, 1968.

Marshall, Thomas R. *Presidential Nominations in a Reform Age.* New York: Praeger, 1981.

Martin, Roscoe. *The People's Party in Texas.* Austin: University of Texas Bulletin Number 3308, 1933.

Matthews, Donald R. "Presidential Nominations: Process and Outcomes." In *Choosing the President,* edited by James David Barber. Englewood Cliffs: Prentice-Hall, 1974.

May, Ernest R., and Janet Fraser, eds. *Campaign '72: The Managers Speak.* Cambridge: Harvard University Press, 1973.

Mayer, George H. *The Republican Party 1854–1966.* New York: Oxford University Press, 1966.

Mayer, William G. "Caucuses: How They Work, What Difference They Make." In *In Pursuit of the White House: How We Choose Our Presidential Nominees,* edited by William G. Mayer. Chatham, N.J.: Chatham House, 1996.

Mazmanian, Daniel A. *Third Parties in Presidential Elections.* Washington, D.C.: Brookings Institution, 1974.

McCarthy, Eugene. "The President, the Public, and the Nominating Process." In *The Presidential Nominating Process,* edited by Kenneth W. Thompson. Vol. 1. Lanham, Md.: University Press of America, 1983.

———. *The Year of the People.* Garden City: Doubleday, 1969.

McElvoy, James III. *Radicals or Conservatives? The Contemporary American Right.* Chicago: Rand McNally, 1971.

McGovern, George. *Grassroots.* New York: Random House, 1977.

———. "The McGovern Reforms and After." In *The Presidential Nominating Process: Change and Continuity in the 1980s,* edited by Kenneth W. Thompson. Vol. 4. Lanham, Md.: University Press of America, 1985.

———. "The New Politics." In *The New Politics: Mood or Movement?* edited by James A. Burkhart and Frank J. Kendrick. Englewood Cliffs: Prentice-Hall, 1971.

"McGovern-Humphrey Debates." *CQ Weekly Report,* June 3, 1972.

"McGovern Shows Strength in Missouri." *New York Times,* April 20, 1972.

"McGovern's Funds Grow from a Trickle to a Flood." *New York Times,* May 4, 1972.

McWilliams, Wilson Carey. "Down With Primaries." *Commonweal*, July 1, 1976.

Merriam, C. Edward. *Primary Elections: A Study of the History and Tendencies of Primary Election Legislation.* Chicago: University of Chicago Press, 1909.

Meyer, Frank S. *The Conservative Mainstream.* New Rochelle, N.Y.: Arlington House, 1969.

Miles, Michael. *The Odyssey of the American Right.* New York: Oxford University Press, 1980.

Miller, Aurthur H., Warren E. Miller, Alden S. Paine, and Thad A. Brown. "A Majority Party in Disarray: Policy Polarization in the 1972 Election." *American Political Science Review* (September 1976).

Miller, Norman. "Democratic Reforms: They Work." *Wall Street Journal*, May 16, 1972.

Miller, Worth Robert. *Oklahoma Populism.* Norman: University of Oklahoma Press, 1987.

Minor, Henry. *The Story of the Democratic Party.* New York: Macmillan, 1928.

Moore, Jonathon, and Janet Fraser, eds., *Campaigning for President: The Managers Look at '76.* Cambridge: Ballinger, 1977.

Morgan, Dan. "Evangelicals Are a Force Divided." *Washington Post*, March 8, 1988.

Muller-Rommel, Ferdinand. *New Politics in Western Europe.* Boulder: Westview, 1989.

Nagourney, Adam. "A Strong Second-place Gives Heart to Buchanan." *New York Times*, February 13, 1996.

———. "A Region Not Likely to Be Heavily Contested in '96." *New York Times*, March 9, 1996.

Nash, Howard P., Jr. *Third Parties in American Politics.* Washington, D.C.: Public Affairs Press, 1959.

Neal, Steve. *Dark Horse: A Biography of Wendell Willkie.* Garden City: Doubleday, 1984.

"New Rules for Delegates." *National Journal*, February 27, 1988.

Ngai, Mae M. "Whither the Rainbow?" *Nation*, December 18, 1989.

Nie, Norman H., and Kristi Andersen. "Mass Belief Systems Revisited: Political Change and Attitude Structure." *Journal of Politics* (September 1974).

Nixon, Richard M. *Six Crises.* New York: Warner, 1979.

Norrander, Barbara. "Ideological Representativeness of Presidential Primary Voters." *American Journal of Political Science* (August 1989): 570–87.

"Not My Echo, My Shadow and Me." *National Journal*, January 6, 1996.

Novak, Robert D. *The Agony of the GOP 1964.* New York: Macmillan, 1965.

O'Brien, Tim. "McGovern Gains Delegates: Virginia Strength." *Washington Post*, June 12, 1972.

The Official Proceedings of the Democratic National Convention 1972.

Oglesby, Carl. "An Open Letter to McCarthy Supporters." In *The New Left: A Documentary History,* edited by Massimo Teodori. Indianapolis: Bobbs-Merrill, 1969.

Oldfield, Duane M. "The Christian Right in the Presidential Nominating Process." In *In Pursuit of the White House: How We Choose Our Presidential Nominees,* edited by William G. Mayer. Chatham, N.J.: Chatham House, 1996.

Oreskes, Michael. "Jackson Campaign, Up from Chaos, Gets the Most Out of Fewest Dollars." *New York Times*, March 27, 1988.

Ostrander, Gilman M. *The Prohibition Movement in California, 1848–1933*. Vol. 2. Berkeley: University of California Press, 1957.

Ostrogorski, M. *Democracy and the Organization of Political Parties*. New York: Macmillan, 1908.

Overacker, Louise. *The Presidential Primary*. New York: Macmillan, 1926.

Parmet, Herbert S. *The Democrats: The Years After FDR*. New York: Macmillan, 1976.

Parris, Judith H. *The Convention Problem*. Washington, D.C.: Brookings Institution, 1972.

Parsons, Stanley B. *The Populist Context*. Westport, Conn.: Greenwood, 1973.

Pastor, Gregory S., and Walter J. Stone. "Candidate-centered Sources of Party Change: The Case of Pat Robertson, 1988." Paper presented at the annual meeting of the Western Political Science Association, Portland, Oregon, March 1995.

Perry, James M. "Brown's Chaotic California Salad of a Campaign Proves Surprisingly Tasty as He Looks Beyond '92." *Wall Street Journal*, March 17, 1992.

Persinos, John F. "Has the Christian Right Taken Over the Republican Party?" *Campaigns & Elections* (September 1994).

Peterson, Bill. "'Big Church' Provides Jackson a Political Base." *Washington Post*, April 3, 1984.

Phillips, Kevin P. *The Emerging Republican Majority*. New Rochelle, N.Y.: Arlington House, 1969.

Pierce, John C. "Ideology, Attitudes, and Voting Behavior of the American Electorate: 1956, 1960, 1964." Ph.D. diss., University of Minnesota, 1969.

Pinchot, Amos R. E. *History of the Progressive Party 1912–1916*. New York: NYU Press, 1958.

Pinderhughes, Diane M. "The Articulation of Black Interests by Black Civil Rights, Professional, and Religious Organizations." In *The Social and Political Implications of the 1984 Jessse Jackson Presidential Campaign*, edited by Lorenzo Morris. New York: Praeger, 1990.

Plissner, Martin, and Warren Mitofsky. "The Changing Jackson Voter." *Public Opinion* (July/August 1988).

Pollack, Norman. *The Populist Response to Industrial America: Midwestern Populist Thought*. Cambridge: Harvard University Press, 1962.

Polsby, Nelson. *Consequences of Party Reform*. New York: Oxford University Press, 1983.

———. "Strategic Considerations." In *The National Election of 1964*, edited by Milton C. Cummings Jr. Washington, D.C.: Brookings Institution, 1966.

Polsby, Nelson, and Aaron Wildavsky. *Presidential Elections*, 4th ed. New York: Charles Scribner's Sons, 1976.

Pomper, Gerald. *Nominating the President: The Politics of Convention Choice*. Chicago: Northwestern University Press, 1963.

———. *Nominating the President: The Politics of Convention Choice*. 2d ed. New York: W.W. Norton, 1966.

———. "New Rules and New Games in Presidential Nominations." *Journal of Politics* 41 (1979).

Pressman, Jeffrey L., and Denis G. Sullivan. "Convention Reform and Conventional

Wisdom: An Empirical Assessment of Democratic Party Reforms." *Political Science Quarterly* (Fall 1974).

Price, David E. *Bringing Back the Parties.* Washington, D.C.: Congressional Quarterly Press, 1984.

Price, David E., and Albert Beveridge. "The Political and Nominating Process." In *The Presidential Nominating Process,* edited by Kenneth W. Thompson. Vol. 3. Lanham, Md.: University Press of America, 1984.

Rae, Nicol C. *The Decline and Fall of the Liberal Republicans from 1952 to the Present.* New York: Oxford University Press, 1989.

Ranney, Austin. "Changing the Rules of the Nominating Game." In *Choosing the President,* edited by James David Barber. Englewood Cliffs: Prentice-Hall, 1974.

———. *Curing the Mischiefs of Faction: Party Reform in America.* Berkeley: University of California Press, 1975.

———. *Participation in American Presidential Nominations, 1976.* Washington, D.C.: American Enterprise Institute, 1977.

———. *The Federalization of Presidential Primaries.* Washington, D.C.: American Enterprise Institute, 1978.

———. "Candidates, Coalitions, Institutions, and Reforms." In *The Presidential Nominating Process,* edited by Kenneth W. Thompson. Vol. 1. Lanham, Md.: University Press of America, 1983.

Reed, Adolph. *The Jesse Jackson Phenomenon: The Crisis of Purpose in Afro-American Politics.* New Haven: Yale University Press, 1986.

Reid, T. R. "Heartened by Iowa, Robertson Prepares for Sharper Scrutiny." *Washington Post,* February 10, 1988.

Reid, T. R., and Bill Peterson. "Robertson's Recruits." *Washington Post,* February 8, 1988.

Reiter, Howard L. *Selecting the President: The Nominating Process in Transition.* Philadelphia: University of Pennsylvania Press, 1985.

"Republicans Court Religious Right." *Christian Century,* August 26–September 2, 1992.

Rheinhard, David W. *The Republican Right Since 1945.* Lexington: University Press of Kentucky, 1983.

Ringle, Ken. "Wallace Running, but as a Democrat: Social Issue." *Washington Post,* January 14, 1972.

"Rise of the Religious Right." *New Leader,* September 21, 1992.

Roberts, Ron E., and Robert Marsh Kloss. *Social Movements: Between the Balcony and the Barricade.* Saint Louis: C.V. Mosby, 1974.

"Robertson Backers Hooked on Politics in Buckeye State." *National Journal,* March 5, 1988.

"Robertson Mounts Effort to Dominate Southern Delegates." *National Journal,* February 20, 1988.

"Robertson Scores in Hawaii, Blocked in Kansas." *CQ Weekly Report,* February 6, 1988.

Rochester, Anna. *The Populist Movement in the United States.* New York: International, 1943.

Rogin, Michael. "Politics, Emotion, and the Wallace Vote." *British Journal of Sociology* (March 1969).

Roseboom, Eugene H. *A History of Presidential Elections*. New York: Macmillan, 1970.

Rosenbaum, David E. "Robertson Backers Eager for Southern Test." *New York Times*, February 13, 1988.

Rosenstone, Steven J., Roy L. Behr, and Edward H. Lazarus. *Third Parties in America*. Princeton: Princeton University Press, 1984.

Rosenthal, Jack. "Survey Ties Issues, Not Shooting, to Wallace Victory." *New York Times*, May 17, 1972.

Rossiter, Clinton. *The American Presidency*. New York: Time Inc., 1963.

Rozell, Mark J., and Clyde Wilcox. *God at the Grass Roots: The Christian Right in the 1994 Elections*. Lanham, Md.: Rowman & Littlefield, 1995.

"Rules and Rigors of Year's Record Primaries." *CQ Weekly Report*, January 31, 1976.

Rusher, William A. "Crossroads for the GOP." *National Review*, February 12, 1963.

———. *The Rise of the Right*. New York: William Morrow, 1984.

Salant, Jonathan D. "Dole's Outlays May Pose Problem." *CQ Weekly Report*, March 9, 1996.

"Salesman for a Cause." *Time*. June 23, 1961.

Salisbury, Robert H. "Political Movements in American Politics: An Essay on Concept and Analysis." *National Journal of Political Science* 1 (1989).

Sanford, Terry. *A Danger of Democracy*. Boulder: Westview, 1981.

Scammon, Richard J., and Benjamin J. Wattenberg. *The Real Majority*. New York: Coward, McCann & Geoghegan, 1970.

Schlesinger, Arthur M., Jr., ed. *History of American Presidential Elections 1789–1968*. Vol. 4. New York: Chelsea House, 1971.

Schlesinger, Stephen C. *The New Reformers*. Boston: Houghton Mifflin, 1975.

Schneider, William A. "Caucuses, Not Primaries, Need Fixing." *National Journal*, July 9, 1988.

———. "Can't Live With 'Em Or Without 'Em." *National Journal*, March 30, 1996.

Schram, Martin. *Running for President 1976: The Carter Campaign*. New York: Stein and Day, 1977.

Schwartz, Maralee. "Brown Takes Lead Among Vermont Democrats." *Washington Post*, April 1, 1992.

Seagull, Louis M. *Southern Republicanism*. New York: John Wiley & Sons, 1975.

Shafer, Byron E. *Quiet Revolution: The Struggle for the Democratic Party and the Shaping of Post-reform Politics*. New York: Russell Sage Foundation, 1983.

———. *Bifurcated Politics: Evolution and Reform in the National Party Convention*. Cambridge: Harvard University Press, 1988.

Smelser, Neil. *Theory of Collective Behavior*. New York: Free Press, 1963.

Smith, Gordon. "Social Movements and Party Systems in Western Europe." In *Social and Political Movements in Western Europe*, edited by Martin Kolinsky and William E. Paterson. New York: St. Martin's, 1976.

Smith, Robert C. "From Insurgency Toward Inclusion: The Jackson Campaigns of 1984 and 1988." In *The Social and Political Implications of the 1984 Jesse Jackson Presidential Campaign*, edited by Lorenzo Morris. New York: Praeger, 1990.

Smothers, Ronald. "Jackson Attracts Crowds, but Planning Is Erratic." *New York Times*, January 15, 1984.

———. "The Impact of Jesse Jackson." *New York Times Magazine*, March 4, 1984.

Soule, John W., and Wilma E. Mcgrath. "A Comparative Study of Presidential Nominating Conventions." *American Journal of Political Science* (August 1975).

Southwell, Priscilla. "The 1984 Democratic Nomination Process." *American Politics Quarterly* (January 1986).

———. "Open Versus Closed Primaries: The Effect on Strategic Voting and Candidate Fortunes." *Social Science Quarterly* (December 1991): 789–96.

"State Caucuses Should End, Jackson Says." *Washington Post*, March 15, 1984.

Stavis, Ben. *We Were the Campaign: New Hampshire to Chicago for McCarthy*. Boston: Beacon, 1968.

Stearns, Richard G. "Reforming the Democrats' Reforms." *Washington Post*, December 3, 1972.

Stevenson, Adlai, III. "Politics: The Old and New." In *The New Politics: Mood or Movement?* edited by James A. Burkhart and Frank J. Kendrick. Englewood Cliffs: Prentice-Hall, 1971.

Storms, Roger C. *Partisan Prophets: A History of the Prohibition Party*. Denver: National Prohibition Foundation, 1972.

Stroud, Kandy. *How Jimmy Won: The Victory Campaign from Plains to the White House*. New York: William Morrow, 1977.

Sullivan, Robert. "An Army of the Faithful." *New York Times Magazine*, April 25, 1993.

Sundquist, James L. *Dynamics of the Party System*. Washington, D.C.: Brookings Institution, 1973.

———. "The Crisis of Competence in Government." In *Setting National Priorities: Agenda for the 1980s*, edited by Joseph A. Pechman. Washington, D.C.: Brookings Institution, 1980.

Swanberg, W. A. *Citizen Hearst*. New York: Charles Scribner's Sons, 1961.

Taylor, Paul. "Jackson's Votes Diluted in South." *Washington Post*, March 20, 1984.

"Tennessee Spurs Wallace Backers." *New York Times*, May 6, 1972.

Teixeira, Ruy A. *The Disappearing American Voter*. Washington, D.C.: Brookings Institution, 1992.

Thimmesch, Nick. *The Condition of Republicanism*. New York: W.W. Norton, 1968.

Thompson, C. S. "The Rise and Fall of the Congressional Caucus as a Machine for Nominating Candidates for the Presidency." Reprinted in *The Caucus System in American Politics*, edited by Leon Stein. New York: Arno, 1974.

Thornton, Alvin, and Frederick C. Hutchinson. "Traditional Democratic Party Politics and the 1984 Maryland Jackson Presidential Campaign: A Case Study." In *Jesse Jackson's 1984 Presidential Campaign*, edited by Lucius J. Barker and Ronald W. Walters. Urbana: University of Illinois Press, 1989.

Thurow, Glen E. "The 1984 Democratic Primary Election: Issues and Image." In *The 1984 Election and the Future of American Politics*, edited by Peter W. Schramm and Dennis J. Mahoney. Durham: Carolina Academic Press, 1987.

Tillett, Paul. "The National Conventions." In *The National Election of 1964*, edited by Milton C. Cummings Jr. Washington, D.C.: Brookings Institution, 1966.

Timberlake, James H. *Prohibition and the Progressive Movement 1900–1920*. Cambridge: Harvard University Press, 1966.

"Times Study Finds Voters Liked McGovern on Taxes." *New York Times,* April 6, 1972.

Turner, Ralph, and Lewis Killian. *Collective Behavior.* Englewood Cliffs: Prentice-Hall, 1957.

Turner, Wallace. "Wallace Tally in Oregon Shows Voter Discontent." *New York Times,* May 25, 1972.

"Undecided Voters Key in Nevada's Caucus Voting." *National Journal,* February 27, 1988.

Usher, David. "Republican Rules and Religious Right Takeovers." Paper prepared for the annual meeting of the Midwest Political Science Association, Chicago, Illinois, April 18–20, 1996.

Van Buren, Martin. *Inquiry into the Origin and Course of Political Parties in the United States.* New York: Hurd and Houghton, 1867.

"A Vermont McGovern Gain." *New York Times,* April 21, 1972.

Von Drehle, David. "Gov. Brown Runs on Old Script." *Washington Post,* March 30, 1992.

"Voters in the Republican Primaries." *New York Times,* March 31, 1996.

Wainstock, Dennis. *The Turning Point: The 1968 United States Presidential Campaign.* Jefferson, N.C.: McFarland, 1988.

Wald, Kenneth D. "Ministering to the Nation: The Campaigns of Jesse Jackson and Pat Robertson." In *Nominating the President,* edited by Emmet H. Buell Jr. and Lee Sigelman. Knoxville: University of Tennessee Press, 1991.

Waldron, Martin. "Rank and File Seize Convention in Texas." *New York Times,* June 14, 1972.

Wall, James M. "Organizing the Precincts." *Christian Century,* April 21, 1993.

"Wallace's Tennessee Prize Is in Doubt." *New York Times,* April 30, 1972.

Walters, Ronald W. "The Emergent Mobilization of the Black Community in the Jackson Campaign for President." In *Jesse Jackson's 1984 Presidential Campaign,* edited by Lucius J. Barker and Ronald W. Walters. Urbana: University of Illinois Press, 1989.

———. "The Issue Politics of the Jesse Jackson Campaign for President in 1984." In *The Social and Political Implications of the 1984 Jesse Jackson Presidential Campaign,* edited by Lorenzo Morris. New York: Praeger, 1990.

Ware, Alan. "The End of Party Politics? Activist-Officeseeker Relationships in the Colorado Democratic Party." *British Journal of Political Science* (April 1979).

Wattenberg, Martin P. *The Decline of the American Political Parties, 1952–1980.* Cambridge: Harvard University Press, 1984.

Wayne, Stephen J. *The Road to the White House 1996.* New York: St. Martin's, 1996.

Weaver, Warren Jr. "McGovern and Humphrey: A Contrast in Organization." *New York Times,* May 21, 1972.

Weil, Gordon L. *The Long Shot: George McGovern Runs for President.* New York: W.W. Norton, 1973.

Weinraub, Bernard. "Smooth Mondale Drive Was Polished for a Decade." *New York Times,* February 8, 1984.

Wekkin, Gary D. *Democrat Versus Democrat: The National Party's Campaign to Close the Wisconsin Primary*. Columbia: University of Missouri Press, 1984.

White, F. Clifton. *Suite 3505: The Story of the Draft Goldwater Movement*. New Rochelle, N.Y.: Arlington House, 1967.

White, F. Clifton, and William J. Gill. *Why Reagan Won: A Narrative History of the Conservative Movement 1964–1981*. Chicago: Regnery Gateway, 1981.

White, Theodore H. *The Making of the President 1960*. New York: Atheneum, 1961.

———. *The Making of the President 1964*. New York: Atheneum, 1965.

———. *The Making of the President 1968*. New York: Pocket, 1970.

———. *The Making of the President 1972*. New York: Atheneum, 1973.

———. *America in Search of Itself: The Making of the President 1960–1980*. New York: Warner, 1983.

Whitridge, Frederick W. "Caucus System." 1883. Reprinted in *The Caucus System in American Politics*, edited by Leon Stein. New York: Arno, 1974.

Wilcox, Clyde. "Financing the 1988 Prenomination Campaigns." In *Nominating the President*, edited by Emmet H. Buell Jr. and Lee Sigelman. Knoxville: University of Tennessee Press, 1991.

Wildavsky, Aaron. "The Goldwater Phenomenon: Purists, Politicians, and the Two-party System." *Review of Politics* (July 1965).

———. *The Revolt Against the Masses and Other Essays on Politics and Public Policy*. New York: Basic Books, 1971.

Williams, Linda, and Lorenzo Morris. "The Coalition at the End of the Rainbow." In *Jesse Jackson's 1984 Presidential Campaign*, edited by Lucius J. Barker and Ronald W. Walters. Urbana: University of Illinois Press, 1990.

Wilson, James Q. *Political Organizations*. New York: Basic Books, 1973.

Wilson, John. *Introduction to Social Movements*. New York: Basic Books, 1973.

Witcover, Jules. "Wallace Machine." *Washington Post*, May 4, 1975.

———. *Marathon: The Pursuit of the Presidency 1972–1976*. New York: Viking, 1977.

Woodward, C. Vann. *Tom Watson: Agrarian Rebel*. New York: Oxford University Press, 1963.

Zald, Mayer N., and John D. McCarthy. *The Dynamics of Social Movements*. Cambridge, Mass.: Winthrop, 1979.

INDEX

Adams, John Quincy, 4
AFL-CIO, 114. *See also* labor, organized
Alexander, Lamar, 152
alienation. *See* unconnected outsiders
American Independent Party (AIP), 136–37, 139, 154. See also Wallace, George
Americans for Democratic Action (ADA), 83
Anderson, John (1964 governor of Kansas), 62
Anderson, John (1980 presidential candidate), 155
anti-abortion movement, 117, 161
Anti-Masonic Party, 5
Anti-Monopoly Party (previously Reform Party, 1870s), 30, 49
anti-nuclear groups, 158
anti-Vietnam War movement, 9, 81–86, 90, 103
Ashbrook, John, 57–58
Australian ballot, 6, 48

Barkley, Alben, 133
Bland, Richard, 39
Bland Bill, 35
Boies, Herbert, 39
Brown, Edmund G. (Jerry), 23, 129, 166, 170–71; and 1976 campaign, 144–45, 148, 157; and 1992 campaign, 153, 156–59, 161–62; and fundraising, 164–65, 178; and primaries and caucuses, 156–58, 164, 166; and proportional representation, 159, 161, 166; and rainbow coalition, 122, 157–58, 166
Bryan, William Jennings, 35–40, 45–47
Buchanan, Patrick J. (Pat), 23, 129–30, 166–67, 170–72; and 1992 campaign, 160–61; and 1996 campaign, 123, 153, 161–63; and Christian right movement, 123, 153, 161–62, 166; and fundraising, 164–65, 178; and open primaries, 163–64, 174; and Ross Perot, 167; and primaries and caucuses, 123, 160, 162, 164,

166, 172; and proportional representation, 161, 166; and Republican Party, 160
Bull Moose Party. *See* Progressive Party
Burch, Dean, 65
Bush, George, 118–19, 122, 153–55, 159–61, 165
Byrnes, John, 62

Caddell, Patrick (Pat), 141, 157
Calhoun, John, 4
Carter, Jimmy, 23, 93, 107, 129, 141–49, 151–52, 170, 183; and fundraising, 145; and primaries and caucuses, 141–48, 180; and proportional representation, 145, 176; and reforms, 143–44; and George Wallace, 135, 141–45
caucuses: as convention nominating system "primaries," 5–6, 50–51; cost of, 67, 70, 98, 104–05, 112; Democratic vs. Republican, 14, 119–20, 125; and media, 113, 171, 182; in mixed nominating system, 8, 78, 84; and movements, 27, 67–68, 75, 77, 95, 105, 114–15, 118, 128, 171–74; and political parties, 50, 67, 114, 116, 119, 127, 144, 164, 172, 181, 186; in reform nominating system, 11–15, 18, 94, 96–97, 100–01, 105–06, 108, 115, 126–27, 172, 179–80; and stability, 160–61, 171–74; state regulation of, 6, 50, 79, 179; structure of, 113; and unconnected outsiders, 27, 171–74. *See also specific candidates and movements*
Chambers, Whittaker, 55
Chautauqua Clubs, 45
Chisholm, Shirley, 96, 139
Christian right movement, 22–23, 108, 117–23, 127–28; and "700 Club," 118; and Pat Buchanan, 123, 153, 161–62, 166; and caucuses, 119–20, 123, 127; and Christian Broadcasting Network (CBN), 118, 122; and Chris-

Christian right movement *(Cont.)*
    tian Coalition, 118–19, 122–23, 161; and con-
    servative movement, 117–18; and Moral
    Majority, 117–18; and Republican Party, 117,
    120–23, 127. *See also* Falwell, Jerry; Reed,
    Ralph; Robertson, Marion G.
Church, Frank, 144–45
civil rights movement, 21, 109–11
Clark, Champ, 50
Clay, Henry, 4
Cleveland, Grover, 33–35, 37, 43, 45
Clinton, Bill, 122, 152–55, 157–58, 164–65
Commission on Delegation Selection and Party
    Structure (1969–70). *See* McGovern-Fraser
    Commission
Congressional caucus system of presidential nomi-
    nation, 4–5, 185
conservative movement, 22–23, 52–80, 85, 108,
    123, 171; and Christian right movement,
    117–18; growth of, 55–57; and mixed nomi-
    nating system, 66–76; and Republican party,
    55–59, 64–66, 71–76, 107; and sunbelt strat-
    egy, 57, 61, 66, 72; and Young Americans for
    Freedom (YAF), 55
Conservative Party of New York, 55, 77
Constitutional Convention of 1787, 1–3
convention system of presidential nomination,
    4–7, 27–52, 178–79, 185; criticisms of, 6, 52;
    and mixed nominating system, 79–80, 101;
    and movements, 27–52, 178–79; origins of,
    4–5; openness in, 5, 7, 27–29, 40–44, 52,
    78–79, 178–79; political parties in, 5–6,
    28–29, 34, 38, 40–44, 49, 79, 101, 179; and
    third parties, 27, 29, 38, 40–42, 44, 52, 79,
    155, 179, 182; and progressives, 6–7, 28–29,
    45–52; stability in, 28–29, 41, 43–44, 79,
    178–79; and unconnected outsiders, 28, 129
Coolidge, Calvin, 50–51
Coxey's Army, 35
Crawford, William, 4
Cummins, Albert, 45

demagogues, 1, 3, 16, 52, 170–71, 185
Democratic National Convention: of 1832, 5; of
    1892, 33; of 1896, 36–37, 39; of 1904, 130;
    of 1952, 134; of 1956, 135; of 1968, 1, 9, 11,
    85–86, 101–02; of 1972, 89–90, 107,
    139–40; of 1974, 140; of 1984, 110; of 1992,
    159, 161
Democratic Party: and anti-Vietnam War move-
    ment, 82–83; and Bimetallic Democratic
    National Committee, 36; and blacks, 109; and
    Jerry Brown, 157, 159; and Bill Clinton, 155;
    and Democratic Federation, 46; and Demo-
    cratic Leadership Council (DLC), 122; and
    Democratic National Committee (DNC),
    9–10, 12, 111, 130, 141; and "Dump John-
    son" movement, 83; and Farmers' Alliance,
    32–34; and Estes Kefauver, 132–34; and
    Grange parties, 30; majority, collapse of in
    1968, 76, 106; and National Association of
    Democratic Clubs, 130; and National Confer-
    ence of Concerned Democrats, 83; New
    Democratic Coalition (NDC), 86, 89; and
    new politics movement, 82–88, 92, 95, 102,
    107; and Nonpartisan League, 48–49; and
    populists, 30, 33, 35–37, 39–42, 45, 47; and
    progressive movement, 45–47, 49; and prohi-
    bitionist movement, 43; and rainbow coalition,
    108–11, 122–23, 126; reform clubs of (1972),
    86, 89, 102, 122; and reforms, post-1968,
    14–16, 82, 93, 151; and silver issue (1890s),
    33, 35–37, 39, 42, 44–45; in South (1964),
    61, 76; and Paul Tsongas, 155; and George
    Wallace, 136–37, 140–41. *See also* Fairness
    Commission; Hunt Commission; McGovern-
    Fraser Commission; Mikulski Commission;
    superdelegates
depression of 1893, 34–35
Dewey, Thomas, 54, 64, 131
direct primaries. *See* primaries
Dole, Robert J. (Bob), 123, 153, 161–63,
    165–66, 174
Dow, Neal, 42
Draft Goldwater Committee, 57, 59–61, 71, 78,
    80, 101. See also Suite 3505 Committee
Dukakis, Michael, 111–13, 116
Duke, David, 23, 129, 153, 159–61, 164–66, 170
DuPont, "Pete," 118
Dutton, Fred, 92

Eighteenth Amendment to U.S. Constitution, 43
Eisenhower, Dwight D., 54, 56, 64
elections, U.S. national: of 1872, 42; of 1873, 30;
    of 1878, 31; of 1880, 34; of 1882, 31; of
    1884, 43; of 1890, 32; of 1892, 34, 43; of
    1894, 35; of 1896, 37–38, 43; of 1904, 130;
    of 1912, 46–47, 50, 54; of 1914, 47; of 1916,
    49–50; of 1924, 48, 50–52; of 1952, 56, 100;
    of 1960, 56; of 1962, 51, 58, 76; of 1964, 65;
    of 1966, 65–66, 82, 98; of 1968, 66, 76; of
    1972, 13; of 1980, 109, 117; of 1992, 155
Electoral College, 3, 23
environmentalists, 81, 111, 158
Evans, Dan, 60
Fairness Commission (1984), 110

Falwell, Jerry, 118
Farmers' Alliance, 31–33, 38, 41–43, 45, 49–50
Federal Election Campaign Act Amendments of 1974 (FECA), 13, 16, 108, 167, 177–80; and 1992 outsider campaigns, 164–65; and 1996 outsider campaigns, 165; and Jimmy Carter, 145; and future reforms, 185; and Gary Hart, 147; and Jesse Jackson, 116–17, 122, 178; and movements, 103–05, 127–28, 177–78; and new politics movement, 103–05; and outsiders, 104; and rainbow coalition, 178; and Ronald Reagan, 125, 178; and Pat Robertson, 122, 178; and third parties, 155; and unconnected outsiders, 149, 167, 178; and George Wallace, 142–43
Federalist, 64, 163
Federalist Party, 4
feminists, 81, 86
Folk, Joseph, 45
Forbes, Malcolm S. (Steve), 23, 130, 153, 162–63, 166; and fundraising, 165; and media, 163; and open primaries, 163, 174; and plurality primaries, 167; and primaries and caucuses, 163, 166, 180
Ford, Gerald, 108, 123–25, 174
Founding Fathers, 2–3, 25, 171, 173
Fowler, Dan, 141
Fraser, Donald, 9, 12

Gans, Curtis, 83
Garrett, Tommy, 119
Gaston, Robert, 63
Gephardt, Richard, 122
Goldwater, Barry M., 27, 54, 111, 115, 117, 129, 183; and 1960 Republican national convention, 55; and 1964 campaign, 53, 58–80, 176; and 1968 campaign, 66; and 1976 campaign, 123–24; and caucus/convention states, 59–60, 62–63, 67–68, 70, 75, 77, 172; and Christian right movement, 119, 127; and fundraising, 65, 67–68, 75; and new politics movement, 81–82, 84, 90–91, 94–96, 99, 101–03, 105–07; and nonproportional primaries, 69, 71, 74, 77, 115, 148; and popular standing, 59–61, 64, 66, 73–74, 177, 180; and primaries, 62–64, 67–69, 77; and Republican Senatorial Campaign Committee (RSCC), 58, 70, 73; and San Francisco convention, 64; and volunteers, 63, 65. See also Draft Goldwater Committee; Suite 3505 Committee
Goode, Wilson, 109
Gore, Albert (Al), 121
Gramm, Phil, 123, 162, 165

Grange (also Patrons of Husbandry), 30–32
Greenback-Labor Party (also National Party), 31
Greenback Party (also National Independent Party), 30–31, 34, 41
Grenier, John, 60

Hamilton, Alexander, 169
Harding, Warren G., 17
Harkin, Tom, 122, 158
Harriman, Averill, 89, 133–34
Harris, Fred, 10, 86, 144
Hart, Gary, 155–56, 166; and 1972 campaign, 87–88, 96–97, 99; and 1984 campaign, 23, 110, 129, 145–49, 151, 170; and fundraising, 147; and open primaries, 146–47, 174; and primaries and caucuses, 146–48; and proportional representation, 147–48; and reforms, 147. See also McGovern, George; new politics movement
Hearnes, Warren, 95
Hearst, William Randolph, 130, 149
Hogg, James Stephen, 33
homosexual groups, 111, 158
Howe, Church, 40
Hughes, Charles Evans, 47, 50
Hughes, Harold, 9
Humphrey, Hubert H., 133; and 1968 campaign, 9–10, 81, 84–85, 91, 100; and 1972 campaign, 81, 87–89, 91–92, 94, 96–97, 99–101, 137; and open primaries, 174
Hunt, Bunker, 137
Hunt Commission (1981–82), 147

Intercollegiate Studies Institute (also Intercollegiate Society of Individualists), 55

Jackson, Andrew, 4–5, 28
Jackson, Henry, 89, 95, 107, 139, 145
Jackson, Jesse, 108–21, 125, 158–59, 183; and 1984 campaign, 109–10; and 1988 campaign, 110–11; and black churches, 110, 116; and caucuses, 110–16, 125–27, 146, 158, 172; and civil rights movement, 109–11; and fundraising, 110, 116–17, 122, 127, 147, 178; and open primaries, 121–22, 125; and primaries, 110–16, 121; and proportional representation, 110–11, 114–16, 120, 126, 149, 159; and rainbow coalition, 109, 111, 122. See also rainbow coalition
Jackson, Robert H., 130
Johnson, Hiram, 50–51
Johnson, Lyndon B. (LBJ), 9, 61, 65, 81–83, 101, 104, 136

Jordan, Hamilton, 143

Kefauver, Estes, 23, 129, 132–35, 140–41, 144, 147–49, 152, 170 179; and Democratic Party, 132–34; and media, 132, 149; and nonproportional primaries (delegate, plurality), 134, 149; and open primaries, 135, 174; and plebiscitary ethos, 134, 149; and popular standing, 133–35, 177; and primaries and caucuses, 133–35, 144, 146, 148; and strategy, 134, 176
Kemp, Jack, 118–19
Kennedy, John F. (JFK), 56, 59–61, 73
Kennedy, Robert F. (RFK), 9, 81, 83–85, 102, 176; and fundraising, 103; and Eugene McCarthy, 84; and primaries and caucuses, 84; and supporters, 85–87
Keyes, Alan, 123
King, Mel, 109
Knights of Labor, 31–32

labor, organized, 81, 105, 111, 114, 138, 145–46, 158. See also AFL-CIO; Knights of Labor; National Labor Reform Party; Union Labor Party
La Follette, Robert, 7, 45–48, 50–52
LaGuardia, Fiorella, 51
Lamm, Richard, 167
Lindsay, John, 88–89, 103
Lodge, Henry Cabot, 62–63, 69
Lowenstein, Allard, 83, 86
Luce, Henry, 131

Maloney, J. P., Jr., 97
Mandel, Marvin, 145
Mason, George, 3
McCarthy, Eugene: and 1968 campaign, 81–85, 100, 105, 120, 127, 134, 176; and 1976 campaign, 155; and caucuses, 84, 97–98, 172; and delegate primaries, 85, 92, 176; and fundraising, 102–04; and open primaries, 92, 174; and popular standing, 85; and primaries, 83–85, 87, 92, 99; and reforms, 9–10, 20, 82, 85, 90, 120; and supporters, 86–87. See also new politics movement
McGovern, George, 9, 12, 17, 76, 80–82, 111–12, 115, 129, 134, 141; and 1968 campaign, 84–85; and 1972 campaign, 86–107, 127, 144; and caucuses, 89–91, 94–100, 105–06, 114, 137–39, 172; and fundraising, 87, 98, 102–05; and Miami convention, 89, 107; and mixed system strategy, 93, 98, 105–06, 176; and nonproportional primaries, 89–92, 105, 115, 148, 176; and open pri-

maries, 92, 98, 174; and popular standing, 81, 87, 100, 177, 180; and primaries: 87–100; and reforms, 81–82, 90–92, 96–97, 100–01, 105–07, 127, 183; and volunteers, 87–89, 99. See also McGovern-Fraser Commission; new politics movement
McGovern-Fraser Commission (1969–70), 9–12, 14, 81–82, 85–87, 91, 169, 172; regional hearings of, 10, 86; report and guidelines of (Mandate for Reform), 10–11, 89, 92, 100, 180
McKinley, William, 36–37
media: and William Randolph Hearst, 130, 149; and Estes Kefauver, 132, 149; and political parties, 17–18, 26, 150; and primaries and caucuses, 112–13, 171, 182; and reforms, 16, 182; and unconnected outsiders, 25, 130–31, 144, 149–50, 155, 167, 170, 173, 181–83; and George Wallace, 136, 138, 148–50; and Wendell Willkie, 130–32, 149
Mikulski, Barbara, 11. See also Mikulski Commission
Mikulski Commission (1972–73), 11, 92
Mills, Wilbur, 95
mixed system of presidential nominating, 7–9, 27–28, 47–54, 67–68, 105, 170, 179, 186; arguments for, 8–9; biases of, 73–76; candidate drafts in, 70–71, 134; caucuses in, 8, 78, 84; and conservative movement, 66–76; and convention nominating system, 79–80, 101; criticisms of, 9–11, 80; development of, 7, 47; movements in, 27, 48–52, 66–80, 90, 97–99, 123, 179–80; openness in, 11, 27, 52–54, 67–70, 73–80, 98–99, 123, 179, 183; organization in, 67, 99–100, 105, 114, 116, 179–80, 183; plebiscitary element of, 7–8, 54, 69, 134–35, 148, 179; political parties in, 8–9, 49, 52–53, 69–70, 73–75, 79–80, 84, 99, 132–34, 147–48, 180; primaries in, 7–8, 50, 54, 68, 179; and reform nominating system, 116; and stability in, 52, 77–80, 179; and unconnected outsiders, 27, 129, 132–33, 135, 147, 179
Mondale, Walter, 110, 114, 116, 145–47, 176
Moral Majority. See Christian right movement
Morris, Gouverneur, 3
Mott, Stewart, 103–04
movements, political, 2, 19–23, 170–71; and caucuses, 27, 67–68, 75, 77, 95, 105, 114–15, 118, 128, 171–74; in convention nominating system, 27–52, 178–79; and Federal Election Campaign Act Amendments of 1974, 103–05, 127–28, 177–78; and ideology, 20–22, 80, 170, 182; and institutionalized groups, 21, 67,

Mott, Stewart *(Cont.)*
74; in majority vs. minority party, 29, 39, 49, 52, 67, 75–78, 101–02, 106, 121, 125, 174, 179–80; in mixed nominating system, 27, 48–52, 66–80, 90, 97–99, 123, 179–80; and nominating system, effect on, 20; and openness, 19–20, 98, 114–15, 123, 185; and organization, 20, 23, 41, 70, 75, 79, 99–100, 106, 170, 173–74, 180; and personalism, 21, 171; and plebiscitary ethos, 101, 177; and political parties, 19, 21, 26, 40, 49, 67–70, 73–77, 99–100, 131, 170, 183–84, 186; and primaries, 50, 52, 68–69, 77, 79, 118, 171–74, 176; and proportional representation, 115, 174, 176; in reform nominating system, 27, 82, 90, 95, 98, 100–01, 105–08, 120, 123, 125–28, 151, 167, 180–81, 183–85; stronger vs. weaker, 22, 27, 41, 70–71, 82, 104, 106–08, 111–16, 120–22, 124, 126–28, 170, 172, 174, 177–78, 180–81, 183–86; and third parties, 21, 29. *See also specific movements*
Muskie, Edmund, 81, 87–89

National Education Association, 114
National Independent Party. *See* Greenback Party
National Labor Reform Party, 31
National Party. *See* Greenback-Labor Party
national party conventions, 4–5; delegate discretion in, 8, 13, 15–16, 18, 69, 116, 177. *See also* Democratic National Convention; Populist Party; Republican National Convention
National Review, 55, 61
National Student Association, 83
New Delegate Selection Commission. *See* Mikulski Commission
new politics movement, 22–23, 81–107, 144, 146, 151, 171, 177; and caucuses, 84, 94, 98, 127, 144; and Democratic Party, 82–88, 92, 95, 102, 107; and "Dump Johnson" movement, 83, 86; and fundraising, 102–04; and Robert F. Kennedy, 83–85; and Eugene McCarthy, 83–85; and George McGovern, 86–107; and National Conference of Concerned Democrats, 83; and New Democratic Coalition (NDC), 86, 89; and new left, 82–83; and openness, 105–07; and plebiscitary ethos, 100–01; and reform clubs, 86, 89, 102; and reforms, 82, 85, 90, 101; and stability, 106–07
New York Review of Books, 102
Nixon, Richard M., 54–57, 62, 66, 69, 76
Nonpartisan League, 47–52
Norris, George, 7

O'Donnell, Peter, 59
openness in the presidential nominating system, 1–3, 26–27, 48, 183; axes of, 171; in convention nominating system, 5, 7, 27–29, 40–44, 52, 78–79, 178–79; dimensions of, 19, 26–27, 78–79, 106–07, 169, 183; as goal of nominating system, 2–3, 5, 7, 8–9, 10–11, 44, 82; in mixed nominating system, 11, 27, 52–54, 67–70, 73–80, 98–99, 123, 179, 183; and movements, 19–20, 98, 114–15, 123, 185; and new politics movement, 105–07; primaries and, 48–52, 68, 77–78, 95, 98, 105, 126, 147–48, 160, 166, 171–74, 179; and third-party option, 155; in reform nominating system, 11, 17, 27, 54, 82, 98, 102, 106–07, 114–15, 123, 125–28, 147–51, 179–81, 183–85; and stability, 1–3, 16–19, 168–69, 186
outsiders, 2, 17–19, 22–23, 26–27, 52, 152–53, 167–71; change as central goal of, 2, 19–20, 23, 47–49, 82, 168, 183; and FECA, 104; and third-party option, 182; and nonsystemic factors, 181–83. *See also* movements, political; unconnected outsiders

Parker, Alton, 130
Patrons of Husbandry. *See* Grange
peace groups, 111, 158
People's Party. *See* Populist Party
Perot, H. Ross, 23, 130, 150, 153–54, 163, 166, 170–71, 182; and 1992 campaign, 153–55, 164, 166, 176; and 1996 campaign, 154, 166–67; and Patrick Buchanan, 167; and media, 150; and primaries, 154, 166; and proportional representation, 176
Phillips, Kevin, 66
Pierce, Franklin, 17
Pinckney, Charles, 3
Pingree, Hazel, 45
plebiscitary ethos in nominating system, 11, 47, 176–77, 179–80; and Estes Kefauver, 134, 149; in mixed nominating system, 7–8, 54, 69, 134–35, 148, 179; and new politics movement, 100–01; and political parties, 177; in reform nominating system, 100–01, 106; and Pat Robertson, 119–20; and unconnected outsiders, 177; and George Wallace, 140, 149
political movements. *See* movements, political
political parties, 2–4 73, 186; and caucuses, 50, 67, 114, 116, 119, 127, 144, 164, 172, 181, 186; in convention nominating system, 5–6, 28–29, 34, 38, 40–44, 49, 79, 101, 179; decline of, 17–18, 26, 79–80, 114, 136, 149,

political parties *(Cont.)*
155, 167, 181–82; and favorite son candidacies, 8, 80; and media, 17–18, 26, 150; in
mixed nominating system, 8–9, 49, 52–53,
69–70, 73–75, 79–80, 84, 99, 132–34,
147–48, 180; and movements, 19, 21, 26, 40,
49, 67, 69–70, 73–77, 99–100, 131, 170,
183–84, 186; and patronage, 5, 49, 73,
79–80, 87; and plebiscitary ethos, 177; and
primaries, 49–50, 52, 174, 176; and reform
nominating system, 11–13, 16–18, 82, 93, 95,
97, 106, 116, 183–86; resurgence of in 1964,
70; state regulation of, 6–7; and unconnected
outsiders, 131, 147, 170, 181, 184. See also
third parties; *specific political parties*
populist movement, 22, 28–44, 50; culture of, 30,
32; and Democratic Party, 36, 39, 42; and
Grange, 30–32; and Nationalist Clubs, 31;
and progressives, 38, 44; and prohibitionists,
43; and Republican Party, 39–40
Populist Party (also People's Party), 30, 32–42;
and fusion with Democratic party, 37, 39–40;
midroad faction in, 40; and national convention of 1892, 34; and national convention of
1896, 36; and press, 34; and fusion with
Republican Party, 35, 37–39; and silver issue,
35–37, 39
presidential nominating system: components of,
14, 18, 171–78; importance of, 26, 183; and
movements, 20; possible future reforms of,
185–86. See also *specific nominating systems*
primaries (also direct primaries): adoption of, 6–7,
19–20, 28–29, 45, 48; bonus, 15, 114, 147;
closed, 14, 16; cost of, 51, 67–68, 70, 98,
104–05; criticisms of, 16–17; defense of, 17;
delegates of, 11, 174, 176; Democratic vs.
Republican, 14, 120–21; frontloading of, 149;
increase in number of, post-1968, 12, 14, 15,
18, 90, 95, 106, 179; and loophole, 15,
114–15, 176, 147, 149; and media, 112–13,
171, 182; in mixed nominating system, 7–8,
50, 54, 68, 179; and movements, 50, 52,
68–69, 77, 79, 118, 171–74, 176; national, 47,
50, 54, 134, 140; open, 12, 14, 16, 90, 167,
174; and openness, 48–52, 68, 77–78, 95, 98,
105, 126, 147–48, 160, 166, 171–74, 179;
plurality, 10, 12, 15, 115, 179; and political
parties, 49–50, 52, 174, 176; in reform nominating system, 11–14, 16–17, 90, 111, 126–27,
179; and stability, 160–61, 171–74; and
unconnected outsiders, 147–48, 154, 160,
171–74; voter turnout in, 173. See also *specific
candidates and movements*

progressive movement, 22–23, 28, 44–52, 78;
and caucuses, 50–51, 67; and convention
nominating system, 6–7, 28–29, 44–52; and
Democratic Federation, 46; and National Progressive Republican League, 46; and National
Social and Political Conference, 45; and open
primaries, 14; and populists, 38, 44; and primaries, 19–20, 45–46, 49–52, 67–68, 93, 96;
and reform system, 13, 176; and Social Christianity, 45; in Wisconsin, 51
Progressive Party (also Bull Moose Party), 7,
46–50, 52, 54; and Committee of Forty-Eight,
48; and Conference for Progressive Political
Action, 48. See also La Follette, Robert; Roosevelt, Theodore
prohibition movement, 22–23, 28, 42–44; and
Anti-Saloon League, 43; and Democratic
Party, 43; and Republican Party, 42–43; and
Women's Christian Temperance Union, 43
Prohibition Party, 42–44
proportional representation, 11–15, 18, 186; and
movements, 115, 174, 176; and movement
strength/weakness, 106, 108, 126, 128, 174,
179–80; and plebiscitary ethos, 100, 177; and
unconnected outsiders, 148, 176, 179–80. See
also *specific candidates*
Pryor, Samuel, 131
PUSH (People United to Save Humanity), 109

racial minorities, 81, 86, 109–11, 113–14, 143
railroad regulation, 30–33, 36, 39–40, 42
railroad strikes, 31, 35
rainbow coalition, 22–23, 108–17, 122, 128, 171;
and Jerry Brown, 122, 157–58, 166; and
Democratic Party, 108–11, 122–23, 126; and
fundraising, 178; and Jesse Jackson, 109, 111,
122; and organization, 111. See also Jackson,
Jesse
Ramparts, 102
Reagan, Ronald, 54, 65–66, 108–09, 117,
123–25; and caucuses, 124–25, 172; and
fundraising, 125, 127, 178; and open primaries, 124–25, 174; and primaries, 124–25;
and proportional representation, 124–26, 176
Reed, Ralph, 123
reform system of presidential nomination, 13–18,
27, 53–54; arguments for, 17; candidate drafts
in, 70; and Jimmy Carter, 143–44; caucuses
in, 11–15, 18, 94, 96–97, 100–01, 105–06,
108, 115, 126–27, 172, 179–80; criticisms of,
16–17; and Democratic Party, 14–16, 82, 93,
151; effects of, 97, 102, 105, 108, 114–16, 121,
126–30, 147–51, 165–67, 172, 179–81,

reform system of presidential nomination *(Cont.)*
183–86; and Gary Hart, 147; and Eugene
McCarthy, 9–10, 20, 82, 85, 90, 120; and
George McGovern, 81–82, 90–92, 96–97,
100–01, 105–07, 127, 183; and media, 16, 82;
and mixed nominating system, 116; movements in, 27, 82, 90, 95, 98, 100–01,
105–08, 120, 123, 125–28, 151, 167,
180–85; and new politics movement, 82, 85,
90, 101; openness in, 11, 17, 27, 54, 82, 98,
102, 106–07, 114–15, 123, 125–28, 147–51,
179–81, 183–85; and organization, 106, 114,
120, 126–28, 180, 183; plebiscitary character
of, 11–13, 100–01, 106; political parties in,
11–13, 16–18, 82, 93, 95, 97, 106, 116,
183–86; primaries in, 11–14, 16–17, 90, 111,
126–27, 179; and progressives, 13, 176; and
Republican Party, 14–16, 120; reforms, post-
1968, 9–13, 80–82, 85, 89, 96–97, 100; stability in, 16–17, 106, 111, 150–51, 160–61,
173, 180–81; unconnected outsiders in, 27,
129–30, 147–51, 165–67, 180, 183–85. *See
also* Fairness Commission; Hunt Commission; McGovern-Fraser Commission; Mikulski Commission
Reform Party (1870s), 30
Reform Party (1990s), 154, 167. *See also* Perot,
H. Ross
Republican National Convention: of 1896, 36; of
1912, 46; of 1916, 47; of 1940, 131; of 1948,
54; of 1952, 54; of 1960, 55; of 1964, 58, 62,
64, 75; of 1968, 66, 102; of 1976, 124–25; of
1984, 66; of 1988, 120; of 1992, 122, 161
Republican Party (Jeffersonian), 4
Republican Party (Lincolnian): 1912–1964,
54–55; and Pat Buchanan, 160; and Christian
right movement, 117, 120–23, 127; and conservative movement, 55–59, 64–66, 71–76,
107; decentralization of, 71–72, 78; delegate
apportionment of, 16, 71–72, 78, 125; and
direct mail fundraising, 75; and David Duke,
159; and election of 1894, 35; and Farmers'
Alliance, 34; and five state rule, 15, 120, 126,
161; and liberal Republicans, 53–54, 56,
63–66, 68, 71–73, 75, 131; in Midwest
(1964), 60; and "Modern Republicans," 54,
56; and mugwumps, 44–45; New England
primaries and, 186; and National Federation
of Republican Women, 56, 66, 71; and
National Progressive Republican League, 46;
and New York Republican Party, 55; and
Nonpartisan League, 47–49; and populists,
32, 35, 37–40, 45; and progressives, 45–47,

49, 54; and prohibitionists, 42–43; and
reforms, post-1968, 14–16, 120; and Republican Governors Conference, 56–57, 64, 66,
72–73, 76; and Republican National Committee (RNC), 16, 60, 65, 71–72; and Ripon
Society, 56; and silver issue, 36–37, 40; in
South (1964), 60, 75–76; and Wendell
Willkie, 131; and Young Republicans (YRs),
56–58, 60, 63, 66, 71
Reynolds, John, 136
Rhodes, James, 62
Robertson, Marion G. (Pat), 108, 117–22,
125–27, 183; and caucuses, 118–21, 125,
172–73; and fundraising, 118, 121–22, 127,
178; and open primaries, 121, 125, 174; and
plebiscitary ethos, 119–20; and plurality pri-
maries, 120, 126; and primaries, 118–21. *See
also* Christian right movement
Rockefeller, Margaretta "Happy" (née Murphy),
59, 63
Rockefeller, Nelson A., 55, 59, 62–64, 68–69
Romney, George, 64
Roosevelt, Franklin D. (FDR), 131–32
Roosevelt, Theodore, 46–47, 49–50, 54, 79. *See
also* progressive movement; Progressive Party
Rusher, William, 57–58, 61, 65
Russell, Richard, 133

Scranton, William, 64, 69
Sears, John, 124–25
Sherman Silver Purchase Act, 35
Shrum, Bob, 141
silver issue (1890s), 31, 33, 35–40, 42–43, 45
Smith, Margaret Chase, 62
Snider, Charles, 137
Socialist Party, 34, 48
Southern Christian Leadership Conference, 109
stability in the presidential nominating system,
1–3; in convention nominating system,
28–29, 41, 43–44, 79, 178–79; dimensions
of, 27, 169, 183; as goal of nominating system, 2–3, 5, 8–9; in mixed nominating system, 52, 77–80, 179; and new politics movement, 106–07; and openness, 1–3, 16–19,
168–69, 186; and peer review, 2, 4, 8, 16–17,
106; and primaries and caucuses, 160–61,
171–74; in reform nominating system, 16–17,
106, 111, 150–51, 160–61, 173, 180–81; and
third-party option, 155
Stavis, Ben, 84, 99
Stearns, Rick, 89, 96–99, 106
Stevenson, Adlai, 100, 133–35
Stewart, William, 39

Student Nonviolent Coordinating Committee, 102
Students for a Democratic Society, 83
Suite 3505 Committee, 57–59, 67, 70, 101, 109. *See also* Draft Goldwater Committee
superdelegates, 16, 110–11, 114–16, 146–47, 186
Super Tuesday, 111–12, 119, 165
Supreme Court. *See* United States Supreme Court

Taft, Robert, 66, 131
Taft, William Howard, 46, 49–50, 54
third parties, 2, 21, 132; and ballot access restrictions, 41, 48, 52, 79, 150, 155, 182; in convention nominating system, 27, 29, 38, 40–41, 44, 52, 79, 155, 179, 182; and finance law, 155; and fusion with major parties, 29, 30, 41–42, 44, 49, 52; in mixed nominating system, 52, 77, 79, 182; and movements, 21, 29; and openness, 155; and outsiders, 182; in reform nominating system, 150, 155, 182; and stability, 155. *See also specific third parties*
Thompson, Tommy, 121
Thurmond, Strom, 66, 123
Tillman, Ben, 33, 50
Tower, John, 66, 123
Truman, Harry S, 132–33
Tsongas, Paul, 23, 129, 153, 155–56, 166, 170–71; and Democratic Party, 155; and fundraising, 164; and open primaries, 156, 174; and primaries and caucuses, 156, 164

Udall, Morris, 145
unconnected outsiders, 22–26, 128–67, 170–71, 186; and alienation, 25, 141–43, 148–50, 154, 157, 159, 166–67, 170, 173, 182; antecedents to, 130–32; and caucuses, 27, 171–74; and convention nominating system, 28, 129; and demagoguery, 170–71, 185; and fundraising, 149, 167, 178; and media, 25, 130–31, 144, 149–50, 155, 167, 170, 173, 181–83; and mixed nominating system, 27, 129, 132–33, 135, 147, 179; and organization, lack of, 22–23, 129, 148, 170, 178, 182; and personalism, 22–23, 170; and plebiscitary ethos, 177; and political parties, 131, 147, 170, 181, 184; and primaries, 147–48, 154, 160, 171–74; and proportional representation,

148, 176, 179–80; and reform nominating system, 27, 129–30, 147–51, 165–67, 180, 183–85. *See also* Brown, Edmund G.; Buchanan, Patrick; Carter, Jimmy; Duke, David; Forbes, Malcolm S.; Hart, Gary; Hearst, William Randolph; Kefauver, Estes; Perot, H. Ross; Tsongas, Paul; Wallace, George; Willkie, Wendell
Union Labor party, 31
union movement, 28–31
United States Supreme Court, 36, 117

Van Buren, Martin, 5, 185

Wallace, George, 23, 129, 135–51, 154–55, 159, 170–71, 179; and 1964 campaign, 135–36; and 1968 campaign, 136–37; and 1972 campaign, 88, 91–92, 95–96, 100, 137–41; and 1974 Democratic midterm convention, 140; and 1976 campaign, 141–43; and Jimmy Carter, 135, 141–45; and caucuses, 95–96, 135, 139–42, 146–48, 172–73; and Democratic Party, 136–37, 140–41; and fundraising, 137, 142–43, 145, 178; and George McGovern, 137–40; and media, 136, 138, 148–50; and open primaries, 92, 136–37, 140, 174; and plebiscitary ethos, 140, 149; and primaries, 95–96, 135–40, 142, 144, 146–48; and proportional representation, 91, 138, 140–42, 145, 147–49, 176; and reforms, post-1968, 138, 140, 143, 183
Walters, Ronald, 111
Washington, Harold, 109
Watson, Tom, 37–38
Weaver, James, 34, 40
Welsh, Matthew, 136
White, F. Clifton (Clif), 57–58, 61, 63–64, 67, 75, 123
Williams, Luke, 59
Willkie, Wendell, 130–32, 149
Wilson, James, 3
Wilson, Woodrow, 7, 46–47, 50

Yerger, Wirt, 60
Young Americans for Freedom (YAF). *See* conservative movement
Young Republicans (YRs). *See* Republican Party